WILLIE, WAYLON, AND THE BOYS

Also by Brian Fairbanks

Wizards: David Duke, America's Wildest Election, and the Rise of the Far Right

WILLIE, WAYLON, AND THE BOYS

HOW NASHVILLE OUTSIDERS CHANGED COUNTRY MUSIC FOREVER

BRIAN FAIRBANKS

NEW YORK

Jacket design by Richard Ljoenes
Jacket photographs: Johnny Cash, circa early 1960s © Everett Collection Inc/Alamy; Chris Stapleton © John Shearer/ACMA2019/Getty Images; Waylon Jennings RCA cropped © Archive PL/Alamy; Brandi Carlile © Gary Miller/Getty Images; Willie Nelson © SuperStock / Alamy

Hachette Books
Hachette Book Group
1290 Avenue of the Americas
New York, NY 10104
HachetteBooks.com
Twitter.com/HachetteBooks
Instagram.com/HachetteBooks

First Edition: June 2024

Published by Hachette Books, an imprint of Hachette Book Group, Inc. The Hachette Books name and logo is a trademark of the Hachette Book Group.

Print book interior design by Bart Dawson.

Library of Congress Control Number: 2024931072

ISBNs: 9780306831089 (hardcover); 9780306831102 (ebook)

Printed in the United States of America

LSC-C

Printing 1, 2024

Journalist: You're gonna get in trouble if I write this.

Waylon Jennings: I don't care. You write what I tell ya.

CONTENTS

INTRODUCTION

"Country music," writes musician Jesse Dayton, "is not really a genre but an actual place."

Although that may make sense, it leaves us with the question of *where* that location might be. If Nashville, which, like Hollywood, is both an idea and a geographic location, then which area of Nashville? Is it the city's Music Row, with its boardrooms and algorithms and meetings with radio programmers, country music television networks, hairstylists on the payroll, award shows, and the Grand Ole Opry and twangy FM truck songs? Or is country music in East Nashville, the rapidly gentrifying neighborhood "alt-country" pays rent in, with its niche XM radio channels, self-released records with self-penned songs about murder and drugs, the ubiquitous acoustic guitars, and busking for spare change?

Even were one to figure out "where" Nashville is, one might not be able to get in. With conservative artists banning Bud Light from concert riders over an LGBTQ+-friendly beer can and women of color—or women, *period*—struggling to get played on the radio, the offices of Music Row are welcoming only to straight white men. This is the way it's been for the nearly eighty years country artists have made records in Music City: "It has already been suggested that country artists with r&b-styled material, or r&b-styled delivery, be excluded from the best-selling country charts," *Billboard* noted in the 1950s. There is a chink in the "Row's" armor, however: it is a hive of power amidst a surprisingly progressive city; Nashville has never elected a Republican mayor, for instance. In the 1950s and '60s, before the end of the Jim Crow South, it was not uncommon to see Black men and white men walking together. Nashville launched the first-ever African American medical school in the South, and has a large Indian community, a prominent Hindu temple, and a Bible company that boasts of having produced "millions" of books. However, during the Civil War, it was a Confederate supply depot, and Native Americans were originally banned from taking up permanent residence on land there. Well into the modern era, Nashville record labels were and are generally run by conservative white men who pushed the most saccharine, the most pop-radio friendly, the most regressive songs. In 1998, a country producer, who moved to Los Angeles, told a journalist: "There's a machine in every kind of music and there's one in Nashville, too. They make records for radio instead of letting someone make a record and then being there as the promotional entity." Songwriter Gretchen Peters said she was livid at Nashville's inability to tackle big themes or break free of country's cliches. "Because Garth [Brooks] got so big, we all had to go out and find another Garth," she said. "We're always making copies of something instead of looking for the real thing." The irony is, the poppier country gets, the more die-hard country fans buy it and the general public disdains it.

"I can't stand modern country" goes the typical lament from a casual fan of the genre. "What happened to the old school style?"

The old style is seen most famously in the work of the Highwaymen, the first country supergroup, consisting of Waylon Jennings, Johnny Cash, Willie Nelson, and Kris Kristofferson. The four were once described as the barbarians "at the gates of the Opry," and battled the establishment every year of their careers. "Groups like the

Highwaymen weren't following any style of country music," says musician Eddie Bayers. "They were their own."

The four had mainstream success in their own right before the group formed in 1985, and their peak-period solo albums are mostly timeless, often more ragged than the classic rock of the '60s, and generally free of the Music Row polish that has doomed nearly everyone before or since to the dollar bin. Collectively, they saved country from becoming "commercialized folk music," as one historian had warned. Their acolytes today, ranging from Uncle Tupelo to Old Crow Medicine Show in the alt-country genre to Brandi Carlile, Adia Victoria, Chris Stapleton, Sturgill Simpson, and others named in the press as possible members of "The New Highwaymen," are rarely heard on country FM radio, but that hasn't stopped each of them from building major followings through word of mouth, ecstatic reviews, and late-show appearances. When the Highwaymen ruled country music, however, they shared the airwaves with the sellouts and retreads; now, country has split into two genres: one with the radio hits and music videos, the other with neither. Country may be a single place, but there are two populations living one atop the other, with each claiming the real estate.

The Grand Ole Opry *is* still an actual place one can buy tickets to most nights of the week, but it's no longer the holy site. "The Opry is full of shit," says the youngest member of one of country's storied families, "and they treated a hundred people horribly. Music City isn't Music City if it's just about bachelorettes and hot chicken." Although he expects the city "to get better," the current Nashville is "an abortion," he said.

He, like many current Nashville residents, is staying on for the ideological battle. These "alt-country" players are half furious about the Music Row decision-makers, half relishing the fight to be heard over the din. "Ain't this shit fun?" Cody Jinks asked rhetorically in

2018. "See, this is shit you used to see back in the '70s when all those motherfuckers were out there singing and playing together, playing and singing and recording each other's songs. We're bringing that back! We said 'Fuck Nashville, we'll start our own goddamn club.'"

This is the story of how that club came to be.

PROLOGUE

FEBRUARY 3, 1959

In the end, all of us are just angels flying too close to the ground.

—Willie Nelson

They were originally going to call me Wayland: "land by the highway." It's no wonder I've spent my life on the road.

—Waylon Jennings

On the day the music died and the rebirth of country music began, a single-engine plane idled quietly on a runway in Mason City, Iowa. The owner of the Surf Ballroom in nearby Clear Lake had booked the three-seat, V-tailed, silver and white Beechcraft Bonanza for a one-way flight. He had promised some clients speedy transportation to their performance in Moorhead, Minnesota, near the Fargo, North Dakota, airport.

The Beechcraft would crush together three passengers from a touring rock and roll revue that included J. P. "The Big Bopper" Richardson, teenage Chicano rock phenom Ritchie Valens, Bronx-born Italian doo-wop singer Dion DiMucci, and headlining guitar rocker Buddy Holly and his new, ragtag assemblage backing each act: guitarist Tommy Allsup, drummer Carl Bunch, and Holly's twenty-one-year-old protégé Waylon Jennings on bass. A lone, rickety, yellow, church-owned school bus shepherded this horde between two dozen Midwestern cities in as many days. One passenger remembered zigzagging through the Upper Midwest with the wind so strong he could hear tree branches cracking in his sleep. "The Big Bopper," normally the tour's loud, jocular, and massive beer-drinking cheerleader, had flulike symptoms, possibly due to the bus's subzero conditions. Now, with a misery trifecta of Bunch hospitalized due to frostbite on his toes, the bus's heat on the fritz, and snow expected along the 365-mile route to Moorhead, the musicians were talking mutiny.

During Frankie Sardo's opening set at the Surf, Holly decided he couldn't stand another bus ride. Surf Ballroom owner Carroll Anderson called Dwyer Flying Service on the spot. "I've chartered a plane," Holly told Allsup and Jennings. Greatly relieved, and following the other acts, Buddy Holly and his reconstituted Crickets took the stage to the shrieks of teenagers, all of whom paid $1.25 plus ten cents for coat check. They opened with their rockabilly version of folk standard "Gotta Travel On," fast becoming the theme for the tour: "I've laid around and played around this old town too long / Summer's almost gone, yes winter's coming on."

"I saw him only but once," said Bob Dylan, who would later close his shows with "Gotta Travel On." "I had to travel a hundred miles to get to see him play, and I wasn't disappointed. He was powerful and electrifying and had a commanding presence. I was only six feet away. I watched his face, his hands, the way he tapped his foot, his big black glasses, the eyes behind the glasses, the way he held his guitar, the way he stood, his neat suit. Everything about him. He looked older than twenty-two. Something about him seemed permanent, and he filled me with conviction. Then, out of the blue, the uncanniest thing happened. He looked me right straight dead in the eye, and he transmitted something. Something I didn't know what. And it gave me the chills."

After running through each Holly-penned hit, the Crickets left the stage at eleven thirty. What happened next has been debated ever since.

In one telling, Holly offered the two remaining seats to his fellow headliners. "We're the guys making the money," he explained to DiMucci, Valens, and The Big Bopper. Instead of fighting for his spot in a literal game of musical chairs, DiMucci claimed the $36 ticket was out of his price range. But there's another version of events backed by several eyewitnesses. In Tommy Allsup's version, the guitarist claimed he and Waylon Jennings were always meant to be on the plane with Holly. As Allsup brought the Crickets' guitars to the bus, someone tapped him on the shoulder. Valens was standing beside the vehicle, signing autographs. "Come on, guy," said the seventeen-year-old. "Let me fly."

Allsup dipped into his pocket for the largest coin he could find, coming up with a silver dollar. "Call it," he said.

Valens called heads and won the toss. A dumbfounded Valens said: "That's the first time I've ever won anything in my life."

Anderson drove the three passengers to the runway at Mason City Municipal Airport in twenty-five-mile-per-hour winds and light flurries. H. Jerry Dwyer joined them to inspect his charter company's plane, and to ensure proper procedures were followed before takeoff. Nothing to worry about after takeoff, as pilot Roger Peterson, twenty-one, had logged hundreds of hours of flying time, as well as several dozen in instrument lessons—the aviation, not the musical kind. Not until months later did the details of Peterson's training emerge, which (if fully known to his boss, Holly, and others) might have led to the postponement of the flight.

Instead, at nearly one in the morning, the Beechcraft, with the trio of musicians aboard, lifted off into low-lying clouds. Disc jockey Bob Hale, who had been broadcasting from the Surf Ballroom, turned back toward home at about the same time the Beechcraft launched. Snow whipped hard against Hale's car windshield. "Look at that, it's incredible," Hale, shifting uncomfortably in the driver's seat, told his wife. "I hope the guys got off the ground before this storm came into town." Back at the airport, Dwyer watched the Beechcraft ascend to roughly eight hundred feet, whereupon he lost sight of it temporarily in the clouds. A moment later, he noticed its taillight, still low, before it disappeared into the churning dimness. Approximately four minutes had passed since takeoff. Without ground crew or ground lights, Dwyer himself placed a distress call from the street level to the radio tower, requesting they make immediate contact and confirm the aircraft had righted itself. But despite several attempts, the radio operator could not contact pilot Roger Peterson.

As a child, Waylon Jennings's seminal memory was seeing cowboy movie star Lash LaRue do a patented whip trick in person, which resulted in permanent damage to the only movie screen in Littlefield, Texas. Waylon happened to step out into the lobby when the cinema's proprietor confronted LaRue about it.

"I told you that stage was too small when I went out there," LaRue shouted. "You should have had insurance to cover it."

"Well, you're gonna have to pay for it," the owner said.

"I got a gun and a whip that says I won't."

Waylon had been sucked into the world of show business early. In Littlefield, every weekend evening meant a farmyard hoedown or town-wide, booze-soaked party with a guitar passed around for sing-alongs. On weekday afternoons, despite an injury that stunted the growth in his left leg and a subsequent odd and distinctive lean on that foot, he pulled cotton alongside a diverse collective of child and adult coworkers, and on Sundays, he went, dragging his dress shoes, to the Church of Christ, which didn't allow women to speak and prohibited music at services. He was rewarded on Saturdays when his father rigged jumper cables to his truck's battery and radio to pick up the Grand Ole Opry broadcast from Nashville. At thirteen, Waylon started bringing his guitar to class on Fridays, with his music teacher's permission, and played hillbilly songs for the kids. He won the school talent show by singing "Hey Joe," later a hit for Jimi Hendrix. In tenth grade, Waylon yanked the paddle out of the principal's hands before he could hit Waylon with it. At sixteen, he was asked to quit or leave high school—several of his fellow dropouts from that year later ended up in prison. At seventeen, he lost his job driving a cement truck after crashing it on a hairpin turn, and later got booted from a country disc jockey job after being told not to play a record by "black devil music" singer Little Richard and then spinning it again, immediately. (Richard was not "one of our boys," the station owner said, meaning he wasn't white.) Around the same time, he experienced his formative musical moment: hearing tinny speakers blare "Cry, Cry, Cry," the first single from Johnny Cash. However, Cash, who was considered too "rockabilly" for the country program, was rarely featured on the Grand Ole Opry, and soon Waylon, who incorporated Johnny's guitar licks and bass-baritone in talent show auditions, was fiending for more outsider art.

While listening with his father to "I'll Never Get Out of This World Alive," ironically the final single of Hank Williams's lifetime, Waylon mused aloud an idea of melding the white country of Hank and Johnny to the Black rhythm and blues of Chuck Berry. "I don't believe anybody can really sing country as well as the old boy who's lived it," he later explained. "Country music comes from the Black Man's Blues and it's the same man singing the same song about the same good times and bad times and a woman he can't hang on to. I think people are reaching for that because it's real. I think they're reachin' back and finding simplicity." When Elvis came along a year later, Jennings cursed him under his breath: *He beat me to it.*

He didn't push beyond the boundaries of hillbilly country and western swing, not yet. After occasionally hustling up country, rockabilly, and pop singing and guitar-picking gigs at a town dive, he spotted superstar rock and roller* Buddy Holly's thick, black, horn-rimmed glasses, then the hottest fashion accessory in the country, on their standard-bearer in a local restaurant.

Holly had tried Nashville in 1956, had been told he was too rockabilly for country radio and the "biggest no-talent" by a Decca executive, and realized, "I don't know how to succeed, but I know how to fail: try to please everybody," and ended up back in his hometown of nearby Lubbock. He drove up to recording sessions in New Mexico in 1957, one of which was for his self-penned "Peggy Sue," which made him among the earliest rock stars to compose his own hits.

Jennings, with typical Texas smarminess, bet Holly—born Charles Hardin Holley—he couldn't write a song on the spot; the hitmaker dashed off "You're the One" on a napkin and won the bet.

"He taught me that you can take country songs and put different rhythms to 'em. He taught me calypso-type things, and 'straight-A' things like 'Peggy Sue'...taking a waltz and doin' it in 6/8 time instead of the usual 3/4."

When word reached the star that DJ Waylon Jennings had put Buddy Holly and the Crickets' "western and bop" 45s on heavy

* He and Holly had started out playing country music because "there wasn't anything else, really," Jennings said. Holly's music was now "country—with a beat," he added.

rotation at KDAV, the area's first all-country station, Holly dropped in on-air to give the show a ratings boost. While there, the two cracked jokes and carried out pranks, including one in which Jennings switched the label on a gospel record so a pious coworker would accidentally play Jerry Lee Lewis. As DJ, Jennings would read commercials himself and play guitar and sing live between 45s. "I have a wide range, even though I don't have a falsetto," he later said of his singing. His voice and playing style, which incorporated country and rock and roll flourishes, impressed Holly to the point that he offered to produce Waylon's first single, "Jole Blon," the so-called Cajun national anthem, and put a Jennings original on the B-side. With that in the can, Holly got the producing bug. He told everyone in his orbit that he wanted to start a record company and open a studio in Lubbock. Going indie didn't sit well with Holly's own producer, Norman Petty, who owned most of the star's songs. When Holly tried to pull out of his deal with Petty, the producer blocked him from his own bank account. By 1958, despite a worldwide number one with "That'll Be the Day,"* Buddy Holly had no income stream. The Crickets refused to be some wannabe producer's secondary consideration and refused to come to New York to record more singles. The band's breakup also meant Holly couldn't go on a moneymaking tour to make up the lost income. After turning down one tour offer, he caved at the next, which involved twenty-five shows in as many days in the Midwest and in the dead of winter, but came with a $2,500 advance. He would have to assemble some band, somehow.

Holly enlisted Tommy Allsup, guitarist on "Jole Blon," and drummer Carl Bunch to replace most of the Crickets. Then, Holly begged Waylon Jennings to play bass. Jennings begged off. First of all, said the young DJ, he didn't even know how to *play* bass.

---

* Originally recorded at and rejected by Decca.

“I’ve never even held a four-string electric,” he claimed. “Hell, I have as much star quality as an old shoe.”

“There’s no doubt you’re going to be a star,” Holly said. “I know. The way you sing, there’s no limit. You can sing pop, you can sing rock, you can sing country.”

There were, however, ominous signs. At the Dallas airport for Waylon’s first-ever flight, he overheard a radio bulletin about a plane crash in Shreveport. Once on tour, Waylon learned that Holly packed a pistol in order to deter tour receipt thieves, and Freddy Milano of the Belmonts often twirled a handgun like a drunken cowboy.

Waylon, Buddy, and Dion sang Hank Williams, battled for spare blankets, and slept on luggage racks made out of sheet metal. Now, unable to stand any of it, flu-stricken J. P. “The Big Bopper” Richardson cornered Jennings in the hallway of the Surf Ballroom. He couldn’t keep warm, he said, even in a nearly floor-length leopard-skin coat, and besides, he weighed 250 pounds and the bus seats were meant for children. Would Waylon mind another road trip so Richardson could rest up in the Minnesota hotel?

Jennings hesitated. He considered himself lucky to be included and had kept his mouth shut about the miserable bus and was conscious of hurting Holly’s feelings by dropping out. But Richardson was a fellow Texas DJ and Waylon may have related to him more. Finally, Jennings told him: “If it’s okay with Buddy, it’s okay with me.”

Instead of informing him of the change in plans, however, Waylon let Buddy hear it from others. They played their nearly hourlong set without discussing it, although Holly yelled at his bassist to turn the bass amp down when Jennings, now cocky after so many shows, cranked it up to get attention from the girls. “That just crushed me,” Jennings later said of the scolding.

After midnight, Waylon passed Buddy in the hallway with a pair of hot dogs. Holly hung up on his screaming producer and did a 180.

"Ah, you're not going with me tonight, huh?" he said, smirking. "Did you chicken out?"

Waylon explained the situation with The Big Bopper and denied being afraid.

"Well," said Holly, "I hope your damned bus freezes up again."

"*Well*," Jennings shot back, "I hope your ol' plane crashes."

More than eight hours had passed since takeoff, and Jerry Dwyer had yet to hear a report on the plane he'd rented. The storm that powdered the streets of Mason City had long passed. In the light of the gray February morning, Jerry Dwyer staggered back to the airport, got in another plane, and hightailed it to the spot on the horizon where he had last seen red taillights. Some seven miles distant, at nine thirty, he found what he was looking for. Peterson's craft had shattered near a cornfield on W. D. Hurd's farm. Peterson's mangled corpse sat close to the remains of the cockpit. Only the aft stairs remained intact, resting in the snow as if having been gently set down in it. Ejected from the craft and face down on the scene were Holly, twenty-two, and Valens, just seventeen. Richardson, twenty-four, was initially missing, leading to speculation he might have survived and crawled away. Instead, his body was discovered over a fence and in the neighboring property; he, too, had been ejected and died on impact. His lifeless form somersaulted into the thicket of the cornfield. At the scene, and before positive identifications were made of the victims, police discovered Tommy Allsup's home address on an envelope and Waylon Jennings's business card from KLLL radio and, with those items in mind, began making calls.

The plane had an older outdated Sperry F3 attitude gyroscope. Without a flight recorder, investigators could only speculate, but when they learned that a wing dusted snow off the roof of a house and a thin layer of scraped-up grass turned up at the foot of the crash site, they guessed Peterson misread his gyroscope and plunged the aircraft into a near nosedive, while the misread indicators suggested they were aimed skyward. One wing clipped the ground at the scraped-up, grassy spot and, considering the hard, deep freeze in progress and the estimated 170-mile-per-hour momentum of the aircraft, the plane corkscrewed, rolling like a hay bale across the plain. The fact that Peterson was in his seventeenth hour of flying in a twenty-four-hour span did not emerge then, either.

The wire story ran on the front page of the *Bulletin*, above a story about the Soviet deputy minister admitting the U.S.S.R. possessed long-range nuclear warheads. As the UPI report spread, Holly's pregnant wife received a call for comment from a reporter about her husband's death. She immediately suffered a miscarriage. (This inspired an American press blackout prior to authorities notifying families of a deceased person.) Shortly after noon, Surf Ballroom owner Carroll Anderson arrived and made correct, positive identification of the bodies. He slunk off to make a collect call to Moorhead, where the bus was soon due to pull up at the band's hotel.

At noon, Tommy Allsup disembarked first and headed to reception. Jennings tried to rouse himself after another bitterly cold night. He peered through the window. No one was around, and he assumed it meant the headliners were asleep in their rooms. Inside, Allsup immediately stopped at the sight of Richardson on a TV in the lounge. Within seconds, Allsup raced back to the bus to deliver the news. "They're gone," Allsup stammered. "They're all gone."

Unbeknownst to the musicians, the wire service had the story wrong and had been broadcasting misinformation for hours. Waylon got lucky that his mother didn't fully believe the news she heard—"Buddy Holly and his band have been killed"—on KLLL.

I hope your damned bus freezes up again, Jennings recalled immediately. *Well, I hope your ol' plane crashes.*

"I was just a kid, barely twenty-one," Waylon said. "I was about halfway superstitious, like all Southern people, scared of the devil and scared of God equally. I was afraid somebody was going to find out I said that, and blame me. I knew I said that. I remember Buddy laughing and then heading out for the airport after the show. I was certain I caused it."

Minutes after the news hit the bus, another hammer blow came down. Jennings, Dion, and the rest of the survivors were contractually obligated to continue the tour. Jennings found himself playing bass in a defunct band that had itself replaced a defunct band. Increasingly addled, he reasoned that since he had no experience playing bass and should have never been offered the job, he had no right to be on the tour, no right to the seat, no right to give it up for someone else to die in his place, and certainly no right to continue in his dead friend's place. But without another rockabilly singer, the tour manager inevitably turned to Waylon, especially since Holly believed in him as a vocalist. Waylon initially refused but then learned that, should he walk, the whole tour would be canceled. They had three shows in Iowa back-to-back-to-back, and a further nine throughout the Midwest over the next twelve nights. Besides, he didn't have the money to get to the funeral anyway. The band played Moorhead as planned, but when Frankie Sardo covered Valens's hit "Donna" to open the show, the concert turned into a wake. Most of the audience was in tears by the time the Crickets appeared, and so Waylon was nearly knocked back by the screams of ecstasy that greeted his deep, arresting vocal, "Rave On." His first star moment.

Less than two weeks after the crash, en route to Texas, Jennings added a stop in New York to return Buddy's guitar to his widow, living on 5th Avenue. On the train ride there with the original Crickets, he noticed drummer Jerry Allison popping tablets to stay awake. "Those pills will kill ya," Jennings muttered. He soon found himself pacing relentlessly and monologuing into the wee hours. Drenched in sweat and claiming to be on the verge of a nervous breakdown, Jennings grabbed his bandmates by their lapels, asking them to get him to a doctor. Another passenger set him partly at ease by admitting that he had seen Allison dose Jennings's vodka with Benzedrine.

The hits kept on coming: On the drive from Manhattan to Littlefield, the men witnessed a hotel burn to the ground. Their car, borrowed in New York, sputtered under the strain of high speeds and cold weather, and, with pills he got from a trucker, Waylon drove home through the night. "Things going up in smoke," he muttered all the way. "My whole world was destroyed," he later said.

When they made it back to town, Waylon Jennings had all of $90 to his name.

In the years following his death, Buddy Holly's legend only grew. The Beatles based their name and their music on the Crickets formula, and the Rolling Stones' first US single, already a Top 3 hit in the UK, was Holly's "Not Fade Away." "American Pie," Don McLean's 1972 song about the crash, which coined the phrase "the day the music died," was named one of the five most significant songs of the twentieth century. However, Maria Elena, Holly's widow, said she thought that if Buddy had lived, he might've become a country hitmaker in the Ray Charles vein. In 1979, Tommy Allsup, who lost his seat to Richie Valens in the coin toss, capitalized on all the notoriety to open a country music club in Fort Worth, Texas, with the rather tasteless name Tommy's Heads Up Saloon.

Jennings, who grew up an hour from Holly, did not last long back in Texas. Once gone, he would never reside there again. He landed in Arizona and accepted another job spinning records. He lost his enthusiasm for music and declined to work up a demo recording. Just over a year after the crash, his wife gave birth to a son, Buddy Dean, named for Holly and actor James Dean.

"God Almighty, for years I thought I caused it," he later told a documentary crew. "I was just trying to figure out what to do with myself... a completely changed person. I quit for a while—I wouldn't even play a guitar; I wouldn't pick it up.

"J.P. Richardson is dead," he said. "And because he's dead, I'm alive." He struggled with his next thought: "It took the best people, the best people," he said finally. "Kind, good-hearted people... To this day, it doesn't seem fair."

In the decade following the crash, Waylon Jennings became a hearty country music balladeer, "the Telecaster Cowboy," belting out saccharine melodies and impersonal lyrics, until the fateful day he went to war with RCA Records and Music Row. That decision would lead to the birth of a new country music, one still played today and in high regard, even from those who claim to hate the genre. Along with Johnny Cash, Willie Nelson, and Kris Kristofferson, Jennings would take what he learned from Buddy Holly and barnstorm Nashville for the next four decades. He clammed up, however, until the last years of a crammed, electrifying lifetime whenever interviewers mentioned "the day the music died." Only in 1994, thirty-five years after the deaths of Holly, Richardson, and Valens, did Jennings finally speak about them at length. That year, he received a call from a promoter at the Surf Ballroom, who wanted to know if he was finally ready to literally face the music.

PART I

THE OUTLAWS

CHAPTER ONE

THE RECORD MAN

I tried to fit in by looking the way they wanted me to look, and I just didn't look like me. I also tried to sound the way they wanted me to sound, and I didn't sound like me either.

—Willie Nelson

Interviewer: Do music or lyrics come first for you?

Willie Nelson: Yes.

Willie Nelson had a new song and he was willing to let it go for fifty bucks. "Come on," he said. "You can have it and I'll bet you it makes you a killing."

"Then why don't you keep it, Willie?" his target said, moving down the bar.

Willie Nelson, married father of three, pursued Larry Butler, local hitmaker, through the Esquire Ballroom, a dive for country artists along Houston's Hempstead Highway. In 1959, both men played Texas Shuffle there, alongside musicians both Black and white. Nelson had been writing songs and performing in Texas under his own name, a rarity for songwriters, who typically joined bands of "pickers" and sang other people's material or didn't perform at all, preferring to live like Van Gogh, hoping to offload sheets of lyrics and melodies, but he had been fired repeatedly for refusing to play "dance songs."

"Hell, let me play it for you," he said.

Without waiting for a response, Nelson sat with his guitar and ran through "Mr. Record Man," a breakup song like so many he'd dashed off over the previous year, including "Crazy," "Night Life," "The Party's Over," "Funny How Time Slips Away," and "I Gotta Get Drunk." He played them all back-to-back that night for local mainstay Larry Butler as the bandleader tried to go over his own material for the evening. Butler, a dark-haired bushy-eyebrowed man in his late twenties, didn't have time to waste on this redheaded stranger, even if they were the same age and working for the same patrons.

"Mr. Nelson," he said, "what you want for them?"

"I figure about ten bucks apiece," said Willie with a one-shoulder shrug.

The prospective buyer frowned. "Mr. Nelson, I'm not gonna buy your songs," he said.

Willie had expected this. He'd been rejected up and down Houston's saloon scene, a.k.a. "Murder City, USA," all week, often without an audition. Butler had graciously allowed him that, at least.

"What's the matter?" said Nelson, rising with his acoustic guitar and angling for the case. "No good?"

"I think they're great," Butler said, almost in awe. "Very goddamn great. In fact, they're too good to buy off of you. You'd better hang on to your copyright, Mr. Nelson."

Nelson smiled sheepishly and waved him away. The clean-shaven redhead with the goofy grin had already sold one song for rent money, "Family Bible," a tender, nostalgic ode to family values, which had jolted "Heartbreak Hotel" hitmaker Mae Axton, whom he'd met when she swung by his radio show. "If I could write half as well as you," she told him, "I would be the happiest woman in the world. Either come to Nashville or go home."

Instead, he sold "Family Bible" to a songwriter he knew, who slapped his own name on it and turned it into a Top 10 for another musician, but Nelson didn't complain. He had more ideas for great songs, which he judged by the standards of Harlan Howard, the man who coined the unofficial country music motto "Three chords and the truth." In Howard's view, it had to have a memorable title and lyrics that distilled a person's history down to the length of a 45 single. Willie, though, leaned more toward another famous saying by Howard: "A lot of the songs you write are just exercise—pencil sharpeners." These weren't going to be the compositions he would be known for, he assumed, and thus he suffered no pangs of guilt by giving them away for rent money.

"You're insane to give them up, fool," Butler went on. "Those are hit songs and you're sitting on a pile of cash with 'em. I'd be ripping you off."

"But I'm broke and I need money right now, and pssh, I can always write some more songs."

Butler followed him to the doorway, where Nelson pointed to his jalopy containing three bored, sleepy youngsters. The bandleader shook his head pityingly.

Willie Hugh Nelson, born in Abbott, Texas, in 1933, smack-dab in the middle of the Depression, was no stranger to hard times. "Our motto down there was 'all we know how to do is fight, fuck, and throw rocks,'" he joked. To avoid punishment, he had to respect his elders, particularly women, even the boxcar transients moving through the community. As toddlers, their poverty-stricken parents handed Willie and sister Bobbie over to their paternal grandparents, living next door, and then, a year later, split up and left Abbott. (The departure of his parents, he later wrote, was worse than any death he experienced because they went on living their lives, unconcerned with his.) Despite their fractured relationship, Willie inherited a genetic disposition toward sparse livin', drinkin', and, in particular, fiddlin' from his dad, Ira, who had a gig playing in saloons over the county line and left three days after his son's birth to play one. Abbott was in a dry county, post-Prohibition—yet at age six, his son had his first beer near there. In one memoir, Willie recalled smoking "corn silks, cedar bark, coffee grounds, and grapevines," anything that approached the buzz of tobacco, minus the cost. Lung cancer would kill several family members, including his parents.

Willie and Bobbie, his elder by two years but forever referred to as "little Bobbie," ended up crammed together in the back room of "Mama and Daddy" Nelson's one-story home on what the kids called Booger Road. There, his grandparents took music lessons through the mail, and Daddy Nelson taught Willie how to play three chords on a mail-order Stella guitar—"D, A, and G... the building blocks of country music."

"I grew up across the street from... the Villarias, which was a great Mexican family," he said. So, day and night, I listened to Mexican music... my guitar playing, singing, writing, whatever, has a lot of Mexican flavor there, but it comes natural."

Bobbie called Willie "a born explorer"—his minders often leashed him to keep him in the yard; "yet for all his wanderings," she marveled, he "had the patience to sit down and write beautiful poems." By age ten, Willie had so many tunes that he could cobble together his own songbook. In adulthood, he clearly had "the fire burning inside him," but he would spend many years teaching guitar, selling books door-to-door, and even leading Sunday school—gratis, of course—while developing his songwriting and musicianship.* He then languished as a Texas DJ, sometimes picking up a guitar and belting out Arthur "Guitar Boogie" Smith's "Red Headed Stranger," an Old West tale of shootings and horse thievery, as a bizarre choice to lull young listeners to sleep. When Ira was around, he and his two teenagers would play with Bud Fletcher and the Texans, whose audience grew incrementally each night.

In a town with signs reading NO DOGS OR MEXICANS, the Nelsons had a post-atomic, pre-hippie devotion to peace and were "developing love for all humanity," as his mother claimed. It all boiled down, Willie quipped, to two rules: "Don't be an asshole [and] don't be an asshole." When he began playing professionally at age nine, jamming on "Stardust" and other American songbook classics with Bobbie and her future husband, Willie noticed with discomfort that whites would pack the local jazz and blues clubs to hear Black musicians, but Black residents couldn't get into country and western venues. Neither were the Nelsons normal for standing outside Black churches to listen to the singing inside, or for questioning segregation.

Despite his laid-back nature, Nelson learned to play in front of shootings and brawls, and stuck up for the ostracized with his fists and wouldn't hesitate to throw sucker punches should anyone make fun of his red hair. "People didn't start calling me an outlaw till I was forty years old, [but] in Abbott, I was an outlaw in training."

"I tease him a lot, but Willie is truly a good person," said Waylon Jennings. "Some people say he's the most irresponsible person on Earth, but I believe he's truly the only true free spirit...we're both

---

* After getting a job as a tree cutter, he immediately fell and nearly broke his back—"Zeke," he told the friend who got him the gig, "I don't believe trees is my line of work."

right. Lotta people call him 'laid-back,'" he joked, "but we just call him 'lazy.'"

"He's a hard man to know," said Johnny Cash. "He keeps his inner thoughts for himself and his songs. He just doesn't talk much at all, in fact. When he does, what he says is usually very perceptive and precise. . . . He has a beautiful sense of irony and a true appreciation for the absurd." Willie, though, thinks he's still the same kid from Abbott, "smoking, drinking, and cussing" in the face of authoritarian opposition.

"I believe my brother's happy-go-lucky personality stayed happy-go-lucky because he wasn't traumatized by the shock of our parents' departure," said Bobbie. The experience, however, turned his sister into an introvert. At the Abbott United Methodist Church, she took up piano and Willie the guitar, "picking" on bouncy, handclap-ready spirituals such as "Will the Circle Be Unbroken" and "Uncloudy Day" from a dusty hymnal. The siblings wouldn't break between songs, not even in front of a barroom crowd; one would simply shout out a four count and launch into the next number. Nelson's voice had bluesy elements to it but he sang in off-beat phrases. "I picked cotton up until I was ten or twelve years old," said Willie, "so to be able to make some money playing music in a beer joint—I felt pretty lucky. And the funny part of it was the people that I was singing to on Saturday nights—I was also singing to a lot of them on Sunday morning, at church."* It may be difficult to imagine *the* Willie Nelson, author of "Bloody Mary Morning" and singer of "Beer for My Horses," as a goofy-grinning gospel player, but Nelson has always been more of a saloon singer crossed with a bluegrass or jazz musician than

* After several parishioners reported seeing their Sunday school teacher playing in the local saloon, Willie Nelson was forced out of his volunteer job at the Baptist church.

the typical country artist. That may be due to a childhood worship of Bob Wills, the western swing legend who stormed off the Grand Ole Opry after being told he couldn't use a drummer on-air—and, worse, that he had to put out his cigar. When Nelson saw Wills, he experienced his idol's standard four-hour, no-break-between-songs hootenanny. A seed was planted.

"Let's do this," said Larry Butler, a songwriter himself, sizing up Nelson, who—in Nelson's own view—looked like a stuffed shirt of an insurance agent. "I'll loan you fifty bucks. You can pay me back by playing in my band. Meanwhile, hold onto those songs."

Nelson, touched by the gesture, accepted both offers. Over the next five decades, Butler would tell and retell the story of how Willie Nelson, one of the great American songwriters, almost sold him "Crazy," among the all-time bestselling country singles, and four other classic A-sides for all of fifty dollars.

Nelson went on to cut "Night Life" at his first session at Houston's Gold Star Studio, where The Big Bopper had knocked out "Chantilly Lace," the hit that landed him a spot on the Winter Dance Party tour. Willie almost didn't show, however, such was his stubbornness about being a songwriter and *only* a songwriter. He didn't believe he had a country radio–ready voice. Willie's friend Paul Buskirk persuaded him to record and release the track under a semi-anonymous credit—"Paul Buskirk and the Little Men featuring Hugh Nelson"—but after the record company heard the cut, they said: "That ain't no country song. It's a blues song, something for Lightnin' Hopkins. No country station is ever gonna play it." Over his daughter Lana's cries, Nelson sold it to Buskirk for $50. Claude Gray immediately recorded "Night Life" and took it to the national country Top 10.

Nelson was apoplectic: not only had he sold a winning lottery ticket for chump change, he had been right all along about the song's commercial prospects.

Mae Axton and other friends thought Willie could've negotiated a better record deal and put "Night Life" out himself, but the only place that *hadn't* turned him down for a contract was country's Mecca. Short on cash but buoyed by Butler, Axton, and Buskirk's faith and his family's gypsy spirit, Nelson took the plunge and moved to Nashville in 1961. Along the way, he dropped off his wife, Martha, and their three youngins at his in-laws. He tried to ignore the parallels between his upbringing and the one his children were embarking on, but he'd be lucky if the family's 1946 Buick, four payments behind, made it to Nashville anyway.* And then there was the matter of how he would have provided for the fivesome in Music City on songs sold for ten dollars a pop. But, said bandmate Johnny Bush, he was "fearless," believing everything would work out.

"Nashville liked to bill itself as Music City," Nelson would later say. "I just saw it as the Store." The Store, meaning the place where the songwriter, tilling the creative fields like a farmer, had to go to beg and plead for producers to "stock my merchandise." Nashville didn't know what to make of the short, grinning ginger with the Texas twang and a family tree with Cherokees, one of whom died on the Trail of Tears, and who obsessed over New Age meditation practices and psychic Edgar Cayce. Sure, Nashville honchos liked the songs they'd heard, but he'd already sold most of those. *What have you done for me lately?* they'd say. Besides, Nashvillians still wore ties in the summer and Nelson didn't even own one. The few executives who knew Nelson those

* It ultimately survived until Nelson turned the corner onto 16th Avenue South, Music Row, Nashville's publishing Main Street, whereupon it promptly sputtered to a permanent stop.

years might have known him only for his unauthorized "appearances" at songwriting awards dinners, where he, Roger Miller, and Harlan Howard would rush the stage and accept each trophy no matter who won, even if the winner was seated in the front row. They were up against the post–World War II "Music Row" kick-started by Decca producer/arranger Owen Bradley, after he opened the first major label branch in Nashville. Bradley was credited with several recording innovations, including magnetic tape and isolated vocal booths to cushion sound. He had come from humble beginnings, too, building a Quonset hut on 16th Avenue South, amid boarded-up retailers and behind the one-story house he shared with his brother.

In the late '50s, as rockabilly evolved into rock and roll, *Billboard* noted that record labels were "pushing out an increasing number of disks which are cut by country artists, but which have a definite r.&b. [*sic*] quality about them." As these new melded styles took over the pop and country charts, country-and-western producers gawked as their singles struggled to climb the lower depths of the country rankings, threatening everyone's job security. Initially, the Nashville Sound, which is what emerged from the change in direction, ran counter to the entrenched business model of Music Row. Executives, however, realized the new wave was "rock and roll for grownups," and it eventually became the dominant style. Bradley, as well as Chet Atkins at RCA/Victor, Don Law at Columbia, and freelance producer Anita Kerr, decided the strategy would be to bring a pop sensibility to country. Bradley set about radically altering the popular, ramshackle, and hillbilly style, giving his artists' songs a glossy finish to appeal to metropolitan crowds and other winners of the Eisenhower boom years. With piano and violins added for classiness, rhinestone suits swapped out for tuxes, and a ruthless focus on profit margins above all else, Bradley banged out three songs in one three-hour session each day using the same musicians for every track, every time. "Producers steered clear of the traditional honky-tonk sound in order to appeal to America's large middle class," the Country Music Project noted. Country had what became known as "crossovers," thanks to more polished backing tracks and more universal and less slice-of-rural-life lyrics. "At first, this style was criticized for not being country, but with time it became clear that it was necessary to save country music."

Seeing Bradley's success, the *New York Times* noted, "Nashville producers began to smother these rhythm instruments under sticky-sweet orchestral arrangements and mooing vocal choruses." Bradley boasted of ditching fiddle and steel guitars, and suggested that adding choruses would keep the music competitive with rock and roll.

While country fans were irritated by the change in direction, the invigorated arrangements helped convince DJs to spin Nashville singles. New York noticed, with executives convincing teen idol Tony Bennett to cover "country as corn likker" Hank Williams's "Cold, Cold Heart," which went to the top of the pop charts. Bradley, though, wasn't a kingmaker, whiffing with more artists than he clicked with—Buddy Holly was but one artist his hardline vision drove from Music City.

The "allure for a songwriter is that one needs to be here—on the streets, in the bars and on the stages—to be a part of its story-making machine," wrote Elizabeth Elkins. "It's a voyeuristic creative life. . . ."

"You stop and think now, if you're an A&R man and he came in to sing—'cause you know the man was not a great singer—he might have a hard time getting a deal [today]," said Waylon Jennings. Willie Nelson—who saw those "old" Hank songs as having been crafted by a "song-singer," a craftsman working vocally to find his way through the lines, and skipping the typewriter—wholeheartedly loved fiddle music, but kept this to himself. "The first thing you learn playing music on the stage is you have to sell yourself," he said, "before you can sell the song to the audience." His early efforts to market himself, however, were disastrous: A critic called him a weirdo. When a DJ refused to air something Nelson recorded, Nelson curled up into a ball on the floor.

"I can't tell you how much these guys scared Nashville," said songwriter Dave Rickey. Nelson never fit in there, on account of his oddball nature. Few were willing to call him into their inner offices to hear what he had to play—after all, there were long lines of other so-called songsmiths in the lobbies along Music Row, and those guys wore neckties. Even Harold Bradley, Owen's brother and later producer of Nelson's first album, admitted he wasn't sure how to wrangle Willie's idiosyncratic vocals onto tape.

But Nelson caught a break on his first full day in town. He bumped into Billy Walker, a fellow performer from Texas. After two years in Nashville, Walker had earned a coveted spot on the national Grand Ole Opry radio program, which aired country music every weekend. Walker, who made the successful push to include Elvis Presley on the *Louisiana Hayride* radio show in the 1950s that launched Presley as a phenomenon, prided himself on his ability to connect likeminded players. He immediately offered Nelson a spare bedroom for the length of either his stay or until Willie managed to sell a few songs.

By the time Martha and the kids arrived three months later, Willie had already reached a make-or-break point. Nothing had sold. Chipper Willie, grating on Billy Walker and the missus, moved out to a creaky trailer park, later both denigrated and immortalized in the classic Roger Miller song "King of the Road." The Nelsons quickly became personae non gratae in the trailer park, not an entry-level achievement among so many madmen, alcoholics, criminals, and low-lifes. Martha was far from blameless. Willie called his wife a "full-blooded Cherokee maiden, and every night at our house was like Custer's last stand." One evening, while waitressing at the Wagon Wheel on Broadway, Martha became enraged over a wisecrack from Willie. Without warning, she launched an ashtray at his head, missed, and instead hit songwriter Hank Cochran in the face. In one of their fights over his infidelities, Martha tied Willie up with bedsheets so he couldn't leave, then beat him senseless. During another, she bit off so much of Nelson's left index finger that he worried he would never properly play guitar again. He later admitted to packing a gun during a night he searched the streets for Martha's boyfriend, and lying down on Nashville's sleepy Broadway, in sight of the Opry, in the hope a car would run him over. He thought of bluesman Lightnin' Hopkins's song about laying one's head on a train track to take care of his "troubled mind." Instead, bored, he got up and wandered into Tootsie's, where he tested out songs at an open mic night known as a guitar pull, or "red light party."* The club, along with the only slightly peeved Cochran, would keep Nelson in beer, whiskey, and unpaid performance slots for months to come.

Garland Perry "Hank" Cochran, fellow player at Tootsie's pulling sessions, had only just arrived, as well, in this case from Mississippi. The difference was that he promptly composed hits for Burl Ives and Patsy Cline, including her fall 1960 number one, "I Fall to Pieces," and landed a gig writing songs for a weekly salary. After hearing him play at Tootsie's, Cochran brought Nelson aboard the Pamper Music publishing company, not telling the whippersnapper—actually two years older than Cochran—that Willie's salary would be coming out of his own. Nelson said it was the moment that he finally thought he might just make it as a songwriter.**

* Listeners were instructed to treat the start of someone's song as they would seeing the light come over a recording studio door—shut up or leave.

** Nelson would repay Cochran two decades later by featuring him on the *Honeysuckle Rose* soundtrack album, a chart-topper.

By 1961, country music, too, had hit a rut. Some of the biggest hits of the day were "Are You Lonesome Tonight?" and "He'll Have to Go," two sleepy breakup ballads popularized by crooners, and "North to Alaska," a peppy duet about the nineteenth-century Gold Rush. The industry had been invaded and infected by rock and rollers, but radio had yet to incorporate that new guard. Jerry Lee Lewis pounded his way through the Ray Charles R&B rave-up "What'd I Say," and the tune started up both the US and UK pop charts, but with a caveat. "I saw that many of the stations which had banned the tune started playing it when it was covered by white artists," Charles said. "That seemed strange to me, as though white sex was cleaner than black sex. But once they began playing the white version, they lifted the ban and also played the original." Ultimately, it would be another decade before Music Row unlocked the gates to Black artists or wild party songs. Meanwhile, Willie Nelson, though as hard partying as Jerry Lee, would have to self-censor if he wanted to break in.

Willie tried to interest Patsy Cline's manager in a song, "Night Life," to no avail. Hank Cochran, hearing that Nelson was still coming up empty, told him he was taking lunch and would turn on the light above the porch that signified "writers at work." He playfully demanded Nelson come up with something, anything, before he returned. Left to his own devices, and partly as a gag, Nelson responded by muttering: "Hello, walls." It struck him as an amusing opening line, albeit one that *surely* wouldn't work in a full song. Almost without noticing, he soon had a first verse, a tongue-in-cheek ode to writer's block caused by heartbreak. Heartbreak, real or imagined, led to most great country and western tunes of the era. When Cochran returned, he jokingly demanded to hear what Nelson had created, not imagining he would have actually mustered something. Willie told him he had, and although it was pretty ludicrous, it might be "worth a listen."

"It's worth a fuckin' *fortune*," said Cochran upon hearing the words. "Willie, my friend, you just wrote a hit."

Faron Young, who heard Nelson play the song at Tootsie's, made the same prediction. The hit singer of five consecutive Top 10 singles in the mid-'50s, including the near-scandalous "Live Fast, Love Hard, Die Young," gave "Hello Walls" a unique spin, "having a subdued, one-way conversation" with plaster, as one critic interpreted it. What seemed strange on paper fit perfectly in a year dominated by "Are You Lonesome Tonight?" with Elvis whispering and occasionally abruptly shifting to a near-monotone. With a steady delivery, Faron's "Hello Walls" captivated radio audiences, breaking Faron Young into the pop Top 40 and reaching number one on the country charts.

Willie Nelson was as surprised as anyone. Before his first check arrived, he offered to sell the copyright to Faron for $500. The reply: "You're crazy! That song has already sold more than that. Here's the five hundred. Pay me back when you have it." When the initial royalty payout finally arrived, Nelson suddenly found himself with tens of thousands of dollars to his name. (He would've had even more if not for laws regarding parodies—several satirical songs, including "Hello Fool," hit the charts in the ensuing months, but Nelson wouldn't get royalties or songwriting credit for the melodies they lifted.) After cashing a $3,000 check—worth ten times that today—en route to a reported $30,000 in earnings from the song over the next several years, Nelson, truly in high cotton, showed up to pulling night at Tootsie's waving hundred-dollar bills around, trying to kiss Faron on the mouth, and, most of all, to pay off his own bar tab. In the audience that evening was Charlie Dick, who managed his wife, Patsy Cline.

"One of the greatest singers in the history of country music... helped blaze a trail for female singers to assert themselves as an integral part of the Nashville-dominated country music industry," one historian wrote of Cline. It was certainly male-dominated when Virginia

Patterson "Patsy" Cline, née Hensley, started. The rare women allowed onstage were often the butt of jokes centered on their escape from the kitchen. The dress code was, unsurprisingly, equally restrictive. Cline refused to learn mandolin or another "cute" instrument, and wore a sheath dress more often than a fringed cowgirl leather top. "She never attempted to tone down her sexuality," marveled Nashvillian Minnie Pearl. When Cline showed up for a Grand Ole Opry broadcast, a producer told her she couldn't wear the pantsuit she had on—a Nudie—even though the Opry was a radio broadcast.

The Grand Ole Opry is, "even today, the first thing people think about when they think of country music," as singer Vince Gill put it, and for performers, that meant they had to abide by its rules or risk their careers. Even Hank Williams had been too cavalier and smart-mouthed, and been banned for drunkenness and missing a single performance. TV *and* radio producers demanded Cline trash her cowgirl clothes and wear a Music Row–worthy evening gown like a good little housewife, and they weren't the only ones bossing her around. She had also been held to a restrictive recording contract that required her to use only material developed by her own publishing company; because of this clause, following her breakthrough Top 20 pop hit "Walkin' After Midnight," Cline suffered a four-year chart drought. When the phone company cut her off over unpaid bills, she asked her agent to forward her messages to the Opry. "I'm gonna be something one of these days," she grumbled.

"Today, Patsy Cline could not get a record deal. She was too overweight, too homely, and too outspoken," said Gail Davies, a country producer, in 2002. In an era when the norm was a "monotonous high-pitched nasal twang," Cline's voice, too, baffled tastemakers. Her vocal delivery had a strange, deep affect to it, the result of a teenage rheumatic fever that left her hospitalized and permanently damaged her throat.

Hooking up with producer and "Music Row" coiner Owen Bradley in late 1960, Cline picked out a composition by Cochran and co-writer Harlan Howard to put a torch song spin on. The sheet music for "I Fall to Pieces" had been turned down for recording by singers all across Music City, but Cline instantly recognized a way to finally break out of her rut. Howard claimed that while he and Cochran came up with the tune, "I have to believe that Patsy Cline, her treatment of the song, made it better than I thought it was." Everyone thought her breathy single would make a run up the charts—everyone except Patsy, suddenly crippled by self-doubt. But the Opry didn't back its singer, and key southern DJs decided not to enter it into rotation, leaving Cline to schedule a promotional tour for a song she didn't believe in. Before she could leave for it, however, she was involved in a car accident.

Sam Hensley Jr. was driving his sibling home from Nashville on June 14, 1961, when their car was hit head-on. Patsy wasn't wearing her seat belt—the three-point version had only recently been introduced—and she was catapulted into the windshield. When the press somehow got wind of who lay in one of the automobiles, they broadcast the news, and friend and fellow singer Dottie West raced to the scene, where she found Patsy bleeding from the forehead, suffering a dislocated hip and a broken wrist. She waved away the ambulance crew; the three people in the other vehicle were in far worse shape, she suggested. Two died before reaching the hospital.* Cline claimed she "was gone twice during the sewing up" and received multiple pints of blood to stem the losses, but the damage may have been less serious than it may have appeared.

Cline can be seen in archival photos with a bandaged, heavily made-up face, and one concert attendee claimed to have witnessed her

---

* West herself would tragically die in a crash almost exactly thirty years later, en route to the Grand Ole Opry.

in a wig and with scarring along her forehead. Most music industry insiders, seeing the extent of her facial injuries, expected her to retire, and Cline considered resting on her laurels after "I Fall to Pieces" topped the country charts two months later. She was a mother and a wife, after all—not necessarily in that order—in the eyes of the establishment. Her monthlong hospital stay, too, had some questioning whether she was up to the demands of an ascendant recording career.

Instead, she told Charlie Dick, her husband, that she had a vision of Jesus Christ in her hospital room and that He told her: "No, not now. I have other things for you to do." Cline reflected: "I suppose I could have sat back and pitied myself. For a time I wondered if I'd ever be able to go on to a stage and perform again. After a couple of weeks, I thought to myself: 'Pity never did anybody any good. Go on, Patsy, show 'em what you can do.'"

After "Hello Walls" went to number one, Faron Young and other artists wanted Willie Nelson to tell them *first* when he had another tune, but Nelson was working on redirecting all the attention to his own record. Yet despite getting a convincing, powerful sound from his early demos, Nelson says, "the record companies overproduced it. They'd have had a real good record if they'd just released the demos." While Willie's recording career continued to flatline, his songwriting career started to falter with Billy Walker's take on "Funny How," which stalled in the Top 30. Now, here stood Charlie Dick in front of Nelson at Tootsie's, representing the hottest act in country radio.

"Would you consider a song called 'Crazy'?" Nelson ventured.

"Hell, I'd consider anything," said Cline's husband, "long as it's a hit."

Nelson didn't have much confidence in the song, which he'd been trying to unload for at least the better part of a year; for starters, Billy Walker had already turned down the song, originally known as

"Stupid," in a less commercial permutation. (It was based on the old Abbott, Texas, saying "If you ain't crazy, there's something wrong with you.") This time, however, the disinterested party offered a key piece of advice: "Pitch it to a girl," Walker suggested. Ironically, Mr. Patsy Cline loved the tune, while most recollections have it that Patsy herself was less than enthusiastic.

"I don't care what you say," Cline reportedly snapped at her husband, perhaps due to the lateness of the hour. "I don't like it and I ain't gonna record it. And that's that."

Dick suggested his wife had balked due to Nelson's eccentric vocal delivery on the demo. "She just didn't even want to hear Willie Nelson's name mentioned" after listening to Dick play the 45 repeatedly. Cline was certainly struck dumb by the tune, particularly Nelson's odd phrasing, which included surprise leaps ahead of the beat or deliberate slacking on the tempo. (No one mentioned the obvious—Nelson had lifted the first stanza from a Floyd Tillman song. "Hell, Willie," Tillman would say years later, "I probably stole those same notes from someone else.") Hank Cochran, eager to help Nelson make a sale, drove to Cline's house with Nelson in shotgun and, worried that Patsy had a personal dislike of his friend, left "that little sonofabitch" (in Patsy's words) in the car to go make his case. Cochran's version of events ended with Cline stomping out to the car and dragging Nelson's "ass in and had him sing it to her."

Cline was never an easy sell on the breakup songs that made her a legend. "She was a very powerful singer and very versatile, capable of growling or purring, vaulting octaves with ease," noted historian Paul Kingsbury. "But beyond just the raw technique, Patsy was able to give you a window into her soul. You feel that you're hearing exactly how Patsy feels, almost as if she were a neighbor coming over for a cup of coffee and spilling her heart out to you." For Cline to do it justice, she needed to believe the song could have emanated from her own experience.

Her producer, Owen Bradley, however, flipped for "Crazy" and scheduled a recording date of August 17, 1961. It had been a month since her car wreck—*only* a month—but she had a number one single out, needed a follow-up to stay visible, and, well, had stacks of duds in the vault. What was one more stinker? Bradley brought in Nashville's "A Team," seven of the dozen or so musicians responsible for most of the uncluttered backing tracks on any country single. Now, Cline only had to figure out how the hell to *do* it.* Her bruised ribs didn't help with the vocals. Neither did Nelson's original phrasing or the four or five chord changes, far more than the three in a typical Nashville song. "Look, hoss, there ain't no way I could sing it like that guy's a-singing it," she told Bradley.

"Screw Willie Nelson and his screwy sense of meter," Bradley said. "You sing it your way."

She did, in one take.

"No one should try to follow my phrasing," Nelson said. "I'll lay back on the beat or jump ahead. . . . I believe in taking my time. She understood the lyrics on the deepest possible level. She sang it with delicacy, soul and perfect diction." Later, he explained: "That's a pop song. There's nothing country about it—unless Patsy Cline sings it."

With a version of the song in the can, Bradley contrasted his words with his actions, hiring the Jordanaires, Elvis Presley's background singers, to lay down another track in a session all their own, virtually unheard of in Nashville at the time. (Singles, B-sides, and potential alternate singles were usually recorded in a single day.)

* She also had a maximum of two takes, which was generally the rule at Nashville labels.

With a piano tinkling away, and a "tick-tack" bass and "chink" guitar backbeat, Bradley's finishing touches were all hallmarks of the Nashville Sound.

Despite not being released until October, "Crazy" led the country sales rankings for 1961, became Cline's first pop Top 10, and made her one of the only women with multiple country smashes. "Crazy" remained so popular it made the overall Top 10 for the year at the end of 1962, as well. It's now considered the song "that changed the sound of country music," and the most-played jukebox 45 of all time, next to "Hound Dog."

Nelson now had a pair of the year's most lucrative songwriting credits. Coupled with the Ray Price cover of "Night Life," the copyright to which Nelson had unfortunately sold, and Roy Orbison's version of "Pretty Paper," Willie Nelson was suddenly the hottest songwriter in Nashville. "Give a man a little luck and shit will do for brains" was his motto. "I have had more dumb luck than anybody I know. There must be a covey of guardian angels working twenty-four hours a day looking after me." He landed a regular gig with the Grand Ole Opry, at which he was accidentally introduced as "Woody" Nelson; he quit after a year of wearing ties, performing each song exactly as rehearsed, and not being able to use his touring band. By August 1961, he would have a recording date under his own name with small but enthusiastic Liberty Records, and an advance single, a duet with Shirley Collie, who was the only person who seemed to be able to keep up with Nelson's eccentric phrasing, and all produced by Tommy Allsup,* the guitar player who lost a plane ticket to Ritchie Valens. Collie turned down a recurring role on *The Beverly Hillbillies* to become Willie

* Allsup explained: "He sang behind the beat, but he was always in meter… the way jazz singers sing."

Nelson's touring bassist, divorced her singing partner, and got engaged to Nelson. After Willie's own divorce and remarriage, the newlyweds snapped up farm country an hour from Nashville and raised hens and hogs, signing the deal on the morning of November 22, 1963.*

But after Willie recorded his own versions of the hits he'd written, Nashville Sound pioneer Chet Atkins "smothered" Nelson's vocals. And although these generated a few popular singles, some of which he recorded and *rerecorded* at Atkins's insistence, he lacked a breakout hit of his own to move even five thousand full-length albums, the industry's new business model in the wake of the British Invasion. Atkins positioned Nelson as "the Voice of Texas," and he soon packed Panther Hall in Fort Worth and Randy's Rodeo in San Antonio, but the producer wouldn't let Nelson use his touring band in the studio.

"My demos were always better," Nelson said, "than the records that came out. After all the voices and the strings had been put onto the record, it wasn't anything that I could reproduce live." His singing put the public off, irritating sold-out crowds by singing far behind the beat, making it impossible to tell if he was doing it on purpose—he was—or just had trouble remembering the next line. On album covers, he was depicted as "clean-shaven, smiling, and looking straight as your local insurance salesman," but these manipulative images glossed over the fact that Nelson had abandoned the slick Nashville for the country beatnik life, and had formed a band called, appropriately enough, the Offenders. They became sensations everywhere they appeared, except in Music City. Indeed, his 1965 LP *Country Willie: His Own Songs*

---

* Ray Price stopped speaking to Willie after the songwriter shotgunned Price's prized rooster for killing Shirley's hens. He had already pissed off Price earlier by taking a job as his touring bass player, which he was secretly wholly unqualified for. Nelson: "I bet you didn't know I'd never played the bass before." Price: "I knew the first night."

tanked everywhere outside Texas cities, where buyers could appreciate his swingin' singin'. Even those who admired Nelson were wary.* In Nashville, he was known "as a loser singer," he said. Executives did little to dissuade people in the business from this assumption.**

It seemed neither Music City nor the buying public that occasionally bucked it were ready for the real Willie Nelson.

Patsy Cline never recorded another Willie Nelson tune. In 1962, she told June Carter and several others that she had a foreboding feeling, and that she wouldn't be around much longer.

In March 1963, following a Kansas City benefit for a fellow country artist who had been killed in a car accident, she chartered a flight with fellow singing stars Cowboy Copas and Hawkshaw Hawkins to get back to her children quickly. (Billy Walker was originally scheduled to join them, but Hawkins switched tickets with him.) After the flight was initially grounded due to heavy fog, friend and fellow singer Dottie West encouraged her to stick to the road. "Don't worry about me, hoss," responded Cline. "When it's my time to go, it's my time to go."

On March 5, after two refueling and rest stops, their third flight of the day crashed in a forest in Camden, Tennessee, ninety miles west of Nashville. Superstar singer Roger Miller, learning of the crash, threw on his jean jacket and drove out early in the morning to walk the

---

* "One of the reasons Kris [Kristofferson] and I didn't meet for so long was because we are a lot alike," he said.

** Nelson, who loved to fire off a joke in a sticky situation, would often bring levity to the proceedings with remarks like: "What's the difference between a record executive and a single sperm? They both have a one-in-a-million chance at becoming a human being."

woods. He soon crested a hill and discovered a guitar strap stamped with the name "Hawkshaw Hawkins." Nearby, he found a littering of suitcases and the relatively intact plane. The bodies inside were recognizable but battered and bloody. "It was ghastly," he recalled. "The plane had crashed nose-down." Cline was identified first by her watch, stopped at 6:20 p.m., the time of impact. It became the Day Country Music Died. Coupled with the death of singer Jack Anglin, killed in a crash en route to Cline's funeral, as well as the assassination of President Kennedy that November, it was a key development in the schism between sentimental, ballad-driven heartbreak numbers and darker, even cynical, introspective singer-songwriter material.

Meanwhile, Willie Nelson was literally knee-deep in hog shit.

CHAPTER TWO

JUST THE OTHER SIDE OF NOWHERE

It's like a ghost writing a song like that. It gives you the song and it goes away. You don't know what it means. Except that the ghost picked me to write the song.

—Bob Dylan

In the Quonset Hut Studio, where Patsy Cline recorded "Crazy," Bob Dylan sat hunched over the piano, scribbling on a yellow legal pad. He, head down in dark sunglasses despite being in a windowless room in the middle of the night, had a vacant face on. A closed copy of the Bible rested on a music stand close at hand. His pen shuttled unbroken across the page as if scribbling in cursive. Perhaps he *is* transcribing, thought the janitor watching him from the control booth.

Everyone else was gone. The janitor, a baby-faced, shaggy-haired, blue-eyed twenty-nine-year-old in faded jeans and black T-shirt couldn't bring himself to clear out with them. He had stumbled into the silent control room with his mop and bucket, assuming that at the ungodly hour (even for him) of four a.m., Dylan, his producer, and his band would have long since crashed. Standing there, nearly face-to-face with the star himself, however, the janitor, a nobody named Kris Kristofferson, could not bring himself to back out of the room and into the dank hallway. But if he moved, the songwriter might see him. Although technically allowed to be in Dylan's presence, Kristofferson was practically the only man in Nashville so designated.

Dylan continued to scribble away for a few moments. Suddenly, he reached for the unfurled clump of paper, rolled it back over his current pages, and slapped the legal pad down. At the same time Dylan glanced up, Kristofferson turned his head and reached over to pick up a coffee cup from the console. He could feel Dylan's penetrating stare but said nothing. "I wouldn't have dared talk to him," the janitor recalled. "I'd have been fired."

Dylan's arrival in Nashville had made the front pages of music magazines worldwide. For the first five years of his career, he, one of America's biggest rock stars, had recorded exclusively in New York. But during one session with new producer Bob Johnston, a Texan, Johnston said, "You know, this would sound way better in Nashville." Dylan demurred, but in the spring of 1966, he assented to moving recording operations to Columbia Studios in Music City. Said musician Charlie Daniels: "There was skepticism about Bob [Johnston] coming to Nashville because he was taking the place of a legendary producer, Don Law, who was an institution in town."

At the first session, Johnston had sneered at the baffles, structures that created small rooms within the studio for each musician to play without "bleeding" into nearby microphones. But Dylan wanted to see the other players and for them to see and feed off him. "The sound would be shit [with the baffles]," Johnston said. "I got a saw. We stripped it, took everything outside and had the fire department burn it and put the drums against the middle of the wall, and put everybody else around there, so they could walk around and see each other."

Dylan took up a position behind the glass so his vocals couldn't leak to other microphones, and, just as important, so everyone could spot his unpredictable chord changes. Despairing over the destruction, colleagues at the Columbia Nashville office ratted Johnston out to their boss, who responded by promoting him.

At four a.m., Dylan ducked out a side door and into the hallway. Kristofferson took a deep breath and held it, waiting for the New York superstar to pop in and harangue the country bumpkin staring at the side of his head. Instead, Dylan disappeared, returning several minutes later with bassist Charlie McCoy, drummer Kenny Buttrey, and guitarists Wayne Moss and Joe South shuffling behind. McCoy had appeared on Dylan's previous record, as well as dozens of country recordings in the past year, all on a strict nine-to-five schedule; *Now?* his face seemed to say. *You want to record now?*

Kristofferson could've argued that, as an "engineer's assistant" tasked with cleaning up the studio between takes, he had a need to be in the control booth, even when producer Bob Johnston went out to Columbia's sloped parking lot to guzzle beer and let the bottle roll into the gutter. But in the wee hours of February 16, 1966, Kristofferson wasn't feeling buddy-buddy with Nashville or Columbia.

After traveling to London on a Rhodes Scholarship to study English, Kristofferson fell back on the army to please his father, a major general in the air force. It almost killed him, literally. Stationed at Fort Benning and on his final parachute jump before Airborne/Ranger School graduation, the Ranger that leapt with him did not clear and Kristofferson became tangled in his chute. Kristofferson's own chute collapsed and, while he fought with it and the second Ranger's, the second Ranger pulled his reserve chute, sending Kristofferson spinning out of control. His chute activated seconds before it would've been too late. "Everybody thought we were dead, but we both landed without getting injured. It was blind luck because I didn't do one damn thing to save myself," he said.

As an ROTC platoon commander, Kris struggled to enforce discipline, never handing out demerits, even for serious infractions. By 1965, the airborne Ranger captain hesitated over a job teaching literature at West Point Military Academy. He leaned toward trying songwriting. Kristofferson confided in a general he knew, and expected a tongue lashing. Instead, his superior quickly responded: "Follow your heart." Kristofferson decided to take his two-week leave to check out Nashville. His only contact there was Marijohn Wilkin, a songwriter on Music Row.

"He had flown helicopters with her second cousin in Germany," says Marijohn's son, John "Bucky" Wilkin. Bucky, writer of then current radio favorite "GTO," picked Kristofferson up at the airport in a 1965 Alfa Romeo Giulia Spider and shepherded the skinny, clean-shaven, and giddy twenty-nine-year-old around. Marijohn even brought the uniformed Kristofferson backstage at the Ryman, where a wiry, rail-thin Johnny Cash, with hollowed-out cheeks, stood smoking in the wings. "The exhilarating electricity of a handshake backstage at the Grand Ole Opry," Kristofferson says, "put the final nail in the coffin of my military career."

Marijohn and Bucky both assumed Kristofferson would enjoy the fortnight and head up to New York for the West Point job, never to be seen again. Instead, just days into the trip, Kristofferson informed the Wilkins that he had turned down the gig and resigned from the military. A year then went by without head nods at any of Nashville's fifteen studios and two hundred music publishers, and he became conscious of the fact that, as one observer put it, his songs were "too esoteric. More to the point, his hair was too long." Kristofferson joked: "I have a great future behind me." He seriously considered volunteering to be shipped off to Vietnam before friends convinced him that would be crazier than sticking with Nashville.

He took to walking around muttering a stanza by the Romantic poet William Blake that advised readers to embrace one's God-given talent or be pursued through eternity by the shame of what-might-have-been. "I felt, from a time as early as I can remember, that that's what I was supposed to do, is to write songs," Kristofferson said. Meanwhile, looming over him in 1965 was the knowledge that his idol, Hank Williams, the father of modern country music, had died at the same age, twenty-nine. Kristofferson was "ten years older than my peers," he said, and earning $200 per month pushing a mop around a studio where emerging and established stars knocked out hit after hit. His main strategy was to "misplace" his written compositions between lyric sheets or in jacket pockets. His tactic didn't lead to any calls.

When Kristofferson quit the military to become a grunt on Music Row, his mother and father howled. "I was told, 'Don't visit any of our relatives. You're a disgrace to us.... We thought it was cute when you were little and you liked country music.... Nobody over the age of fifteen listens to that trash.... Please don't write or come home....'" (The same went for Kris's wife, Fran, and four-year-old daughter, Tracy.) Their reactions were surprising, given that they were relatively liberal; when Kris was eleven, his parents had brought him to a ticker tape parade in Brownsville for Jose Lopez, a Mexican American World War II veteran—they were the only white people in sight—and his mother, Mary, paid the college tuition of each of their minority housekeepers' offspring. Decades later, Kristofferson defended them: "My father was a great spirit," he said. "Any shackles I had I put on *me* and my expectations on *me*. When I finally decided I was going to be a songwriter for the rest of my life, it was almost like a religious conversion." Nonetheless, upon learning that their son's one and only produced composition, "Vietnam Blues," an *anti* anti-war story song ("Course he looked at me like I was kinda crazy / Just another warmonger") released by Ralph Emery, had failed to dent the charts, the Kristoffersons doubled down, giving him the silent treatment. But the news of Bob Dylan's arrival in sleepy, square Nashville electrified Kristofferson, and he began to view the janitorial job and break from his parents as prognostic.

Kristofferson had discovered Dylan's breakthrough album *Bringing It All Back Home* soon after its release in March 1965, finding, as singers like Joni Mitchell did, that it now meant pop songs *could* be literature. Flipping over that LP, Kristofferson discovered that Dylan had written: "If someone thinks norman mailer is more important than hank williams that's fine." That, along with Dylan referring to Williams's songs as mathematical perfection, Kristofferson decided, was the most agreeable thing he'd read from a contemporary about country music and his heroes Hank, Johnny Cash, and Jimmie Rodgers. Little did he know that Dylan's own musical awakening had come at a Buddy Holly concert in January 1959.

Decades later, Kristofferson clearly recalled their first encounter. "I saw Dylan sitting out in the studio at the piano, writing all night long by himself. Dark glasses on. All the musicians played cards or Ping-Pong while he was out there writing. I was the only songwriter allowed in the building. They had police around the studio, they had so many people trying to get in."

Since he couldn't risk his job to corner Dylan and perhaps ask him for advice or slip him some pages he'd been working on, Kristofferson turned to others to develop professional relationships. He charmed Dylan's towering manager, Albert Grossman, a mover and shaker in New York, who spent sessions throwing quarters at the ceiling to see if they would stick. Unable to learn much from Dylan's bizarre work ethic, Kristofferson tried to make himself useful on the other end of the soundproof glass. While the star knocked out "Absolutely Sweet Marie," Kristofferson noticed that the singer was rooting around in a bag for harmonicas, which he needed for multiple breaks, including the middle 8, and needed to work in the key of D and when the song shifted to a high G. But Dylan hadn't brought the correct ones to Nashville. Kristofferson immediately volunteered to round up a couple of harps around town, beelining straight for his friend Chris Gantry's house.

At ten p.m. on a weeknight, Gantry, also an aspiring songwriter, was roused to his front door by a banging. He blinked incredulously as Kristofferson materialized beneath the porch light, yammering away about needing "all your harps, for Dylan." Gantry didn't quite believe him but assented anyway, because Dylan was Bob *Dylan*. "He took all of my harmonicas and gave them to Bob to use on the session—I had a slew of them. I never got them back, but that was cool."

The wee-hour sessions continued until the night Dylan dragged his players back into Studio A at four in the morning. He had just completed a manuscript, an epic, Chaucerian ode to his wife, Sara. He called it "Sad Eyed Lady of the Lowlands," but other than the title, he offered no hints for the musicians to prepare. He began to blow softly on the harmonica while McCoy and the organ player, Al Kooper, who had given life to Dylan's breakthrough, "Like a Rolling Stone," fell in behind.* Dylan started reciting what felt to some of the players like a slow dirge, an even softer, gentler, and more haunted "Visions of Johanna"—nailed in its first complete take at the previous day's session—slowed to a near collapse on take one. Somehow, the musicians, used to two-minute, up-tempo boppers or mournful

* Kooper, a wild-haired New Yorker, had earlier been chased out of a record shop by hoodlums over his mere appearance.

waltzes meant for country radio, couldn't believe they were supposed to slog through a churning, swelling epic at this ungodly hour.

"It's impossible to tell," wrote one Dylan biographer, "whether the Lady is a creature of dream or nightmare; but she's beyond good and evil as the cant phrase has it, only in the sense that the simple, hypnotic, even corny waltz tune contains... both fulfillment and regret. Mysteriously, the song even erases Time. Though chronologically it lasts nearly 20 minutes,* it enters a mythological once-upon-a-time where the clock doesn't tick."

It certainly ticked for all present, including the musician *not* allowed to play on the song or participate other than retrieve the harmonicas for it, Kris Kristofferson. He could only gape as Dylan ran through a rehearsal—yes, *following* the initial take—to make sure the assembled knew what they were getting into. "This is going to be like a couple of verses and a chorus and an instrumental," Dylan casually offered. "Then I'll come back in and we'll do another couple of verses, another instrumental, and then we'll see how it goes." Not a potential single, but not an unwieldy beast, either. Buttrey and the others expected a standard album cut, maybe a bit longer than a real bit of folk storytelling like "El Paso" by Marty Robbins or Red Sovine's "Teddy Bear," both four-minute country chart-toppers.

After ten minutes, the musicians were in hysterics, having brought the melody to a crescendo at each of five choruses across fourteen verses. They kept thinking, "Man, this is it.... This is gonna be the last chorus and we've gotta put everything into it we can." Instead, Dylan went on and on, to well over eleven minutes. With the completion of each chorus, the musicians would nearly lose the beat and Dylan would have an abrupt, almost a capella half measure before taking it up and Buttrey and Joe South, the bass player, fell back in.

* Actually, just over eleven.

In doing so, Buttrey noted, "the dynamics had to drop back down to a verse kind of feel." The musicians glanced at each other clandestinely, all sharing the same thought: "I mean, we peaked five minutes ago. Where do we go from here?"

Despite Dylan freezing them out on the plan, his half-dozen accompanists made it through another take. They were exhausted but enraptured by the hypnotic, indecipherable lyrics, ostensibly a paean to Dylan's wife, Sara, and disguised as a Bible passage. Haunted by the two versions, Dylan's zombie band drifted flawlessly through another complete take, and then bolted for the exits. It was by now five thirty in the morning and the "janitor," too, could slink off down the near-freezing concrete to get a few hours' rest before the daytime session. Too tired to sleep, bassist Henry Strzelecki asked his Ouija board if *Blonde on Blonde* would "either be the biggest album in the world or it ain't gonna do nothin'."

Working on *Blonde*, even tangentially, changed Kris Kristofferson as a songwriter and an individual. He had written one single, a defense of a military life that increasingly did not agree with him, but after hearing Dylan do "Sad Eyed Lady," "Absolutely Sweet Marie," and especially "Rainy Day Women #12 & 35," a transparent ode to drinking and drugging disguised, once more, as a biblical lecture ("Everybody must get stoned"), with the band acting soused, alcohol started to appear in Kristofferson's lyrics and a rambunctiousness infiltrated his melodies. Singer-songwriter Tom Waits suggested "Sad Eyed Lady" was capable of inspiring you to "leave home, work on the railroad, or marry a gypsy. I think of a drifter around a fire with a tin cup under a bridge remembering a woman's hair. The song," he said, "is a dream, a riddle and a prayer."

"I just figured that thanks to people like Dylan that I could do my own stuff," said Kristofferson, "because a voice that doesn't fit into a groove can be accepted doing original material." Kristofferson began dropping in at the songwriter's hangout Kountry Korner to guzzle beer and pass his material around the picnic tables out back. Rarely did he attempt to sing a demonstrative version, or "demo," of these songs. In kindergarten, he had sung with his back to the audience but still couldn't escape his mother's critique: "It was horrible," she'd say. Billy Sherrill had produced Kristofferson's first demo as a solo singer-songwriter and, listening back, Marijohn agreed with Mrs. Kristofferson's sentiments.

He tried slipping demos to Johnny Cash, the god of country music experiencing a career peak with a number two pop hit, but Cash was handed demos as often as pens and autograph books. Then, one day, Kristofferson's supervisor at Columbia, unaware of what the janitor was doing, put him in charge of preventing people, employees and gate-crashers alike, from giving Cash material. That didn't stop the flow, and he was demoted to labeling tapes in the basement. After two days, the Man in Black came down to shoot the shit, flustering Kristofferson, who revealed that he had been punished. From then on, Cash said he wouldn't start recording until "the kid comes up." He soon began giving Kristofferson advice on the music business. After finding out that Mary-Ann Kristofferson had fired off a missive calling on her son to return to California and labeling Cash a drug fiend, the Man in Black smirked. "It's always nice to get a letter from home," he quipped.

Kristofferson took a second job making biweekly helicopter runs for oil workers employed by rigs in the Gulf of Mexico. When one of the musicians in Cash's band passed away unexpectedly, the star called the helipad to tell Kristofferson. His coworkers suddenly wanted to know everything about Kris Kristofferson's life. Eventually, Cash's sister-in-law, Anita Carter, cut one of the demos Kristofferson spread around with an up-and-coming singer named Waylon Jennings, but it was related to the B-side of an unsuccessful single. Kristofferson still needed his big break.

Although she gasped when Kristofferson said he wanted to stay in Nashville instead of taking the West Point gig, Marijohn Wilkin came around to the young songwriter. *Your songs are too long*, she told him, adding affectionately, *you're a rascal*. She related to his struggles, having also turned down a teaching job to try Nashville over her family's objections. With reservations, she signed Kristofferson to her publishing company.

Meanwhile, the legend of *Blonde on Blonde* enraptured Nashville and the music industry. The album, rock's first double LP, peaked in the *Billboard* Top 10 thanks to surprise smash single "Rainy Day Women." With it, the "anarchist" hipster Dylan rose in Music City's esteem. Despite being warned Nashville "don't take well to outsiders," Dylan found he had been greeted with perfect professional courtesy. He, in turn, spread the word in interviews about the Nashville scene, as well as the musical accompaniment that gelled behind drummer Kenny Buttrey's brilliant, on-the-fly arrangements. He told *Playboy* his hired musicians brought him "the closest I ever got to the sound I hear in my mind... that thin, that wild mercury sound. It's metallic and bright and gold." Budding singer-songwriters, especially folkies like Loudon Wainwright, stayed up for days, resetting the needles on their record players to hear the new style. "I just have an image of my friend George and I hunched over some speakers," recalled Wainwright, "under the influence of *some* substance, and trying to figure out what Bob was saying, particularly one sentence: 'The country music station plays... soft,' or is it Sartre?"

Record labels previously deleted liner notes that mentioned that a pop record had been cut in Nashville, but once word got out about Dylan's sessions, several top singer-songwriters, including Leonard Cohen and Neil Young, suddenly considered Nashville as the center of the music world. Kristofferson himself would later say: "Our generation owes him our artistic lives because he opened all the doors in

Nashville when he did *Blonde on Blonde* and *Nashville Skyline*. The country scene was so conservative until he arrived. He brought in a whole new audience. He changed the way people thought about it—even the Grand Ole Opry was never the same again." Guitarist Charlie McCoy pinpointed the release of *Blonde on Blonde* and later *Nashville Skyline* as "when the floodgates opened." Recording sessions began to loosen on Music Row; after the seventy-hour *Blonde* session, the eight-hour Nashville Sound day to knock out an entire record seemed pre-Enlightenment.

While everyone involved in *Blonde* parlayed that gig into more high-profile ones in Nashville, Kristofferson couldn't. Shortly before becoming a private pilot, he made an appearance at the *Nashville Skyline* sessions after learning through Bob Johnston that Dylan wanted to try out duets with Johnny Cash.* After getting roped in to play cowbell on "Lay Lady Lay," Kristofferson encountered Cash in a hallway and tried to get him to listen to a Dylan-inspired new song, "Help Me Make It Through the Night." Cash never recorded it.

In the three years since *Blonde* wrapped, Kristofferson had been employed by Petroleum Helicopters International of Lafayette, Louisiana, to fly workers to and from offshore oil rigs in the Gulf of Mexico. He had been writing the whole time, but no one wanted to record his songs, not even Dottie West, a singer he crashed with after separating from his wife. "I would work a week down here for PHI, sitting on an oil platform and flying helicopters. Then I'd go back to Nashville... and spend a week up there trying to pitch the songs,

* According to Kristofferson, Dylan and Cash met at the 1964 Newport Folk Festival and "Dylan just looked at him like a big tree. The friendship they formed had a profound effect on country music and it led directly to what's happening in country music today." In Nashville, the duo ran through several country blues numbers, including "Big River," Cash's tribute to Mississippi bluesmen, before falling back on a folkie Dylan original to cover.

then come back down and write songs for another week." Without wine, women, *or* song, Kristofferson had little else to do but write, and then write some more. He finished "Help Me Make It Through the Night" and "Me and Bobby McGee" perched atop an oil rig. After seven days, he would return to his $50-a-month Nashville apartment, where "the holes in the wall were bigger'n I was." Once, he came home to learn that someone broke in and stole his military uniform and street clothes. "They wrecked it," the responding officer said of the apartment; in reality, nothing had changed.

His ex took their two children back to California, where the youngest, who had issues swallowing, could get specialized care. Kristofferson became another Skid Row bum, getting bailed out of the drunk tank by Bucky Wilkin, his first friend in town. Bucky let Kris crash at his place, a one-nighter that turned into squatting after Kristofferson was fired from the offshore gig. (Depending on which version one believes, it was due either to falling asleep in the pilot's seat with the copter blades still whirring violently overhead, for being hungover once too often, or for seducing his boss's girlfriend. Regardless, Kristofferson abandoned his beat-up car at the Lafayette airport and flew back to Nashville, moving in with Bucky.) Kristofferson's brother traveled to Nashville to confront him, pleading, "When are you going to do something you can *do*?"

After seeing Johnny Cash walking "around the stage like a wild animal" at the Ryman, he tried writing specifically for the gruff-voiced, hard-livin', underdog champion, but still, the Man in Black resisted. Kristofferson later said: "There are points in your life, especially if you have creative ambitions, where selfishness is necessary." On a day off, possibly drunk, mostly just out of other ideas, Kristofferson decided to borrow a helicopter, without permission. He wouldn't need coordinates to find Johnny Cash's house on the lake.

In later years, Kristofferson claimed he wanted to offer Cash "Help Me Make It" again, which ended up in a stack of dusty demos. Most assume that Kristofferson first offered "Sunday Mornin' Comin' Down," an anthemic drinking song about "losing my family" and a stronger match for the recovering addict. Cash's son John Carter believed it actually was another, inferior tune destined for the dustbin. Regardless, in most reports, the story went that one day, Kris got in a Tennessee National Guard chopper—they had hired him for weekend work—and hightailed it to the sprawling Cash property fifteen miles east of Nashville. After avoiding eighty acres of Cash's forested land, the budding songwriter nearly dropped onto the roof. Instead, he set the deafening machine down in the yard to general panic from the groundskeepers.

The thick, carved front door opened and out stepped Johnny Cash, squinting from the swirling dust kicked up by the rotor blade. Kristofferson couldn't see far into the home, with its "sumptuous foyer, its heavy brocades, its gilded Tennessean Louis XIV furniture, its massively framed photographs" of the family and not the usual "plated horrors and wild beast horns to be seen in other Country stars' homes," as one biographer put it. Kris grinned sheepishly and averted his eyes.

Cash recalled: "As I approached, out stepped Kris Kristofferson, with a beer in one hand and a tape in the other. I stopped, dumbfounded. He grabbed my hand, put the tape in it, grinned and got back into the helicopter and was gone, a bit wobbly, but almost straight up, then out high above the lake where all his songs lay on the bottom."

"I think he told the story that I got out the helicopter with a beer in one hand and a tape in the other," the interloper said. However, Cash was more likely hiding from "a raid" in a closet the whole time.

As for June Carter Cash, "she wasn't there either. But, you know what, I never was going to contradict either one of them."

Bucky Wilkin claimed that Kris occasionally landed a chopper at Marijohn's house in Brentwood—"that was just his way of saying hi," he insists.

One Cash fan recalls being picked up hitchhiking by the Man in Black and taken into his residence for a hearty meal, whereupon an unknown scruffy fellow dropped in on his lunch break. Kris Kristofferson begged off the meal, opting instead for a beer and to play a new song. After sitting in silence for two or three minutes, Cash said: "It's not bad, but I don't know if it's for me." He did, however, take to carrying around a Kristofferson lyric in his wallet. "For me, that was as good as having a gold record or something," the lyricist said.

Regardless of the true circumstances, Cash definitely received "Help Me Make It Through the Night" this time. June claimed that Cash's reaction was concise: "That man's a poet," he said, rising to his feet. "Pity he can't sing." But word of "Make It" spread like the rep of a *Blonde on Blonde* session player. Everyone, it seemed, wanted to listen to it, but once they had, no one had the guts to record it. Dottie West let her houseguest down easy over "Help Me Make It Through the Night" due to the sexually frank lyrics. ("Shadows on the wall," "come on, lay down by my side," "let the devil take tomorrow, 'cause tonight I need a friend," etc. Loretta Lynn's "The Pill," with lyrics explicitly mentioning—and supporting—birth control, would be subject to the 1975 equivalent of a shadow ban by country radio, even though she was a major star—dozens of radio stations announced they wouldn't play her single. "The Pill," which producer Owen Bradley and Lynn's label shelved for three years, racked up tens of thousands in sales each week on word of mouth, especially after religious figures lambasted it from the pulpit. Meanwhile, a song from a man's perspective about having sex on a hot day made it to the country Top 3 that year.) "Rock and roll meant fuckin', originally," said Waylon Jennings, "which I don't think is a bad idea. Let's bring it back again." But Bobby Bare reflected what conservatives and executives felt: "In country music, we want wet eyes, not wet crotches," he said. Nonetheless, Bare tried to break "Help Me Make It Through the Night" on country radio because "I always felt that [the song was] in the tradition. Country music was more real than pop music at the time. The songs spoke about cheating and getting drunk and maybe they didn't talk about sex quite as directly as that." Radio stations refused to spin "For the Good Times," a Kristofferson song covered by Billy Nash and Elvis Presley, over the line "lay your warm and tender body close to mine." Jennings tried to get his producer to accept "Help Me," saying Kristofferson "kind of dresses like a bum, but God, what a songwriter"—not to mention he'd changed the way Waylon thought about western swing—but RCA thought the song was "too suggestive." Much later, Sammi Smith, recognizing the tenderness of "Help Me," cut it. Her record company refused to distribute the single until an LA disc jockey spun it for yuks. The station instantly became inundated with requests to hear it again.

Writing conservative, pro-military music had gotten him nowhere with white collar Music Row; now that his characters were heroic hippies and lonely alcoholics having nervous breakdowns and praying to Christ they could get wasted, square singers ironically welcomed him. Some even wanted to record him. Ray Price, Roy Drusky, and Ray Stevens were on the straighter, more establishment end of the spectrum, but Jerry Lee Lewis, Bobby Bare, and Faron Young had the hard-living personas that Kristofferson seemed to have written for—after all, he lived it. All would soon try his material.

By the end of the sixties, the country music establishment had finally built their business into a legitimate one. The industry had been at its nadir at the beginning of the decade—the Grand Ole Opry, around since 1925, had been dropped by NBC Radio, which meant only a few die-hard programmers in the South kept it on the air. Record sales declined almost every year until, suddenly, in about 1968, they ticked up again, thanks to crossover blockbusters "Stand by Your Man" and "Harper Valley P.T.A.," as well as the redemption story of former ex-con and superstar country artist Merle Haggard, and the enduring influence of Dylan and *Blonde on Blonde.* Simultaneously, the Country Music Association's self-congratulatory award show landed a live, primetime spot on national television and received more than six thousand RSVPs for the ceremony. In 1969, the year Kris Kristofferson finally landed a record deal, there were three TV shows focused on country performers: *The Johnny Cash Show*, *Hee-Haw*, and *The Glen Campbell Goodtime Hour*. Suddenly, there were hundreds of new country radio stations. With interest in "Music City, U.S.A." building nationally, Nashvillians pushed back. Publicly, they criticized hippie musicians who came to town and the sudden rock music tilt they saw in those imitating Dylan, Tammy Wynette, or Jeannie C. Riley. They sneered at the sight of a snare drum, previously an anomaly in Nashville studios, as a sign of the harder-edged sound the interlopers had introduced.

But a growly, off-putting singer like Kris Kristofferson struggled to sell himself to major labels as a solo artist. After years of waffling between being a singer-songwriter or sticking to writing, he embraced the former. After his demo got to publisher Combine Music, company president Fred Foster called him in. Kristofferson arrived in a faded and cracked brown leather suit and tried to hide the peeling flap from one of his boots. Foster always required a four-song audition to make sure his artists weren't just playing their handful of passable compositions, but he couldn't have imagined wanting to hear *more* from the shaking hobo who wandered in. "I thought, honestly, before he finished those four songs, that I was hallucinating," said Foster. "They were sophisticated, and yet 'rootsy' and country. Not a wasted word." Kristofferson also signed to Foster's recording label, Monument Records, known for Roy Orbison and not much else, though Orbison had been plenty. Foster helped craft Roy's groundbreaking, operatic vocal technique* and 1961's "Only the Lonely," which led to a blurring of lines between pop and country. Foster and Orbison shocked the rented musicians by coming to the studio with the "Pretty Woman" guitar riff already intact, which caused the players to mistake the producer for a clock watcher, racing to cut down his studio time. "But," Foster said, "we still took as long as I thought we needed to and I listened to any suggestions the musicians had." Once everyone was plugged in, Foster let them know they might only do one or two songs in a day rather than several different cuts in the hope one might jump out as an obvious hit. "The old guard down here was trying to do four songs in a three-hour session," said Foster. "I looked at Motown, where they had a house band which went into the studio and stayed there all day until they came up with something everyone was happy with. I wondered how the hell we were supposed to compete with Motown." He started out with two songs, an A-side single and a B-side—the latter usually an afterthought—and then finally just tried finishing the A-side in a day's work. Neither the musicians who did endless takes of a single song nor Music Row execs appreciated this methodology or the Orbison style; in fact, Foster claimed multiple people told him to his face that he "was ruining Nashville." His philosophy, though, was: "If it pleases *you*, it's good."

---

* Johnny Cash had told newcomer Orbison to change his name and drop his voice a few octaves, advice Cash cringed to recall.

Meanwhile, Kristofferson's deal with Combine matched what most songwriters in Nashville received at the time: the company got 100 percent of his publishing earnings, he got 100 percent of his *writing* earnings. As a newbie, he couldn't ask for half of the publishing profits Combine got for merely printing up sheet music and getting his songs cut around town. Eventually, if he had a hit that sold fifty thousand copies, his 2-cent royalty rate would earn him a mere grand.

Foster did give Kris quite a break, however: the idea to write a song about his receptionist, whose name was Bobbie McKee. "You know, somebody would give you a title and then bet you couldn't write a song to fit it," Kristofferson said. "Since [Foster] owned the publishing company that I was writing for, I felt obliged to try and write it. I have never written a song on assignment before or since. But it worked, after about three months of hiding from him."

Kristofferson hashed out the immortal opening verse while driving based on a daydream he had of ditching his job and car in Baton Rouge and hitchhiking with good-looking hippie Bobby McGee ("I couldn't write a song about Bobby *McKee*"). "I can remember when the last line came to me," Kristofferson told *American Songwriter* on the song's fiftieth anniversary. "I was driving to the airport in New Orleans, and the windshield wipers were going 'windshield wipers slapping time and Bobby clapping hands…' and it finished the song for me." The refrain "freedom's just another word for 'nothing left to lose'" touched a generation emerging from the sixties. Southern whites, while not necessarily part of the Civil Rights and anti-war movements, decided their government wasn't interested in rescuing them and dropped out of society, too. Songwriter Marshall Chapman wrote that "Bobby McGee" drew a line in the sand among Americans: "You're either sensitive to the world or you're not," she said. Although often assumed to be a hippie bozo philosopher, Kristofferson claimed he could not actually relate. "Unless you've lost everything—and I certainly haven't—you're not free. If you've got a family, you're not as free as if you're alone. I don't want to get free of my family, my home, and people I love."

In 1969, at Foster's insistence, his salaried songwriter cut an album of his own tunes. *Kristofferson*, that debut album, included "Me and Bobby McGee," "Sunday Mornin' Comin' Down," "Help Me Make It Through the Night," and nine other tunes written in the prior few years, including "Blame It on the Stones," cowritten with Bucky Wilkin, and "The Law Is for Protection of the People," also a sarcastic title* and pro-hippie, pro-longhair, anti-cop song in a season dominated by "Okie from Muskogee," the anti-hippie anthem from Merle Haggard. The players on Kristofferson's album weren't sure what to make of Kristofferson's progressive, even abrasive tunes, including one, a boisterous, satirical take on the "Mr. Marvin Middle Class" types and their propensity to blame society's ills on rock and roll. "If it sounds country," Kristofferson tells the players at the start of "Bobby McGee," "that's what it is. It's a country song." He was recalling *Blonde on Blonde*, too, remembering how fellow night owl Bob Dylan had labored relentlessly over his lyrics until he was ready to commit them to posterity, Music Row's 9-to-5 schedule be damned. Jack Clement, Johnny Cash's former producer, heard Kristofferson play "Me and Bobby McGee" in a hotel room and said: "That's a hit." Kristofferson's confidence soared. Now that he was ready, really, really ready, he cornered Norbert Putnam.

The bass player was told the first record he played on in Nashville was "too R&B, too rock and soul." But by the late '60s, Putnam was

---

* It's also a vague reference to the 1933 Reichstag fire, which was blown out of proportion by the Nazis and led to their "Decree of the Reich President for the Protection of People and the Reich."

one of the top session musicians in town, and playing at Columbia when the janitor invited him out for a beer at Ireland's Pub. As one of Nashville's in-demand backing musicians, Putnam's schedule was booked solid, even on the weekends. Still, he suspected that Kristofferson needed a loan, so he bought him lunch and asked how much he wanted.

"I appreciate that," Kristofferson said, unfazed. "But I need a bigger favor, potentially. I showed Scotty Moore some of my songs and he's letting me have some studio time for a demo. Can you play bass on it?"

Putnam doubted the session was real. Just looking at Kristofferson's clothes, he imagined he couldn't even get Moore, Elvis's guitarist, to listen to the songs, let alone agree to record them. Putnam forgot about the request until a few weeks later, when he personally received a call from Moore—*it's happening*. The musicians were tuning up when Kristofferson arrived, plunked down his guitar case, and took out his instrument and a bottle of Southern Comfort. "Hey, bud, ya wanna have some?"

"It reminded me of the cough syrup my mother made me take," Putnam recalls. "No," he told the songwriter. "It's ten o'clock in the morning."

"Well, I'm just gonna have a little sip to steady my nerves. I'm not really a good singer."

"He took down half of it," says Putnam. "He knows how to *drink*."

The musicians lacked the necessary headphones, so they stood close to Kristofferson to follow his guitar lead. "Kris starts playing the first song, and he was beating the guitar so loud, we couldn't hear his voice. He's kinda mumbling. Being studio guys, we had legal pads, so we kinda sketched out the chord progressions, notating the chorus and verses. . . . " After a run-through of the song at the standard 100 decibels, Moore called from the control booth: "Well, let's play one."

"Perfection is *boring*," an exec had told Putnam earlier in his career. "Just play with as much feeling and emotion as possible."

The musicians counted off, still unable to detect the vocals, and made it through a take of "Help Me Make It Through the Night" without even knowing what the song was. The musicians assembled around Moore while Kristofferson sat, nursing his bottle. When Moore hit playback, Kristofferson's voice came booming back at them.

"This sonofabitch is worse than Dylan," said another musician to cackling laughter.

Another verse passed. Putnam and Briggs, who owned a publishing company, started exchanging startled glances. *You hearing this?*

"Damn!" said Briggs. "Pretty good lyric."

They, like most Nashville kingmakers, had missed the boat on Kris Kristofferson the songwriter, but at least they caught up in time to play on his first two albums.

Once the publisher's demo hit Music Row, Charley Pride recorded "Bobby McGee"; later, Willie Nelson, Gordon Lightfoot, Dolly Parton, and Johnny Cash recorded it, each adhering closer to its original country incarnation. But the first demo, with Billy Swan on vocals, ended up at Liberty Records, where Bucky Wilkin left it to be circulated to their recording artists. Due to the apparent ineptitude of the executives there, no one listened to it. Meanwhile, Roger Miller, the Nashville renegade who won a record for total Grammy wins just a few years earlier,* seized on "Me and Bobby McGee." Although not a smash by Miller's usual standards, his version, at long last, broke its songwriter onto the country charts.

Kristofferson told "more of a story in one line than most of us can in five," said hitmaker Tom T. Hall. Story songs like "Bobby McGee"

* His record of eleven Grammys from 1964 to 1965 and six in one night would stand until Michael Jackson took home eight for *Thriller* in 1984.

helped move country "closer to its roots," as historian Bill C. Malone put it, "with the story songs and nostalgic but often bittersweet evocations of rural and small-town life." However, he noted, "their recollections were sometimes disquieting." At the time of the early "Bobby McGee" demos, country wasn't ready for upsetting message songs. The Grand Ole Opry had Roy Acuff, Dottie West, and Bill Monroe as regulars, older artists known for their "picking" or humorous yet inoffensive love songs. Each was superficially beloved with the core demographic of conservative geriatrics in the South, but with almost zero mainstream or pop interest, and their records weren't exactly bolstered by the program. Acuff had last had a country hit a *decade* earlier; he may have blanched when he heard "freedom's just another word for nothing left to lose" and "holding Bobby's body next to mine."

Kristofferson, released in the summer of 1970, sold thirty thousand copies in its initial print run, solid for a country album, but not enough to dent the national charts. It connected with the type of breakout country singer looking for more material to cover—and no one else. *Rolling Stone* later praised "the unspooling melancholy of his melodies [which were] every bit as key as his philosophizing" and called his take of "Sunday Mornin' Comin' Down" "perfectly imperfect, a little down-on-the-ground masterpiece." Contemporary reviews, however, were as indifferent as the public. His early performances were tentative. One was preceded by a fawning introduction from Johnny Cash at the Newport Folk Festival, but still he muttered: "I can't play the guitar, I can't carry a tune," and wouldn't go out. June Carter heard him and literally kicked his ass. When he finally went on, she recalled, he went over so well, his picture made the front page of the *New York Times*. At one Georgia show, a fan recalls, he was ejected from his own gig for cursing out of nervousness and frustration. Kristofferson didn't care. Everyone was recording his music; he didn't need to fly helicopters anymore, not even to get on Johnny Cash's radar. He meanwhile began seeing or, more accurately, sleeping with Janis Joplin. The UT Austin dropout* struck gold as the blues-belting frontwoman for Big Brother and the Holding Company, and, despite diminishing success as a solo act, recently co-headlined Woodstock.

Joplin's road manager Bobby Neuwirth, the only man who could drink Kristofferson under the table, introduced her to the song "Me and Bobby McGee" at the Chelsea Hotel, and then connected the two singer-songwriters in person. "[Bobby] introduced me to half the people in the world that I know," Kristofferson says. Joplin and Kristofferson immediately hit it off. "I spent about a month up there in her house," the latter says. "She was quite different from anything I'd experienced before."

Janis lulled Kris into sticking around her Sausalito, California, cottage for no-strings-attached fun and to complain about the material she had for her next record. "I dug her, but I had itchy feet," he said. "I'd get up intending to get out, and in she comes with the early morning drinks and pretty soon you're wasted enough and you don't care about leaving." She complained incessantly about being *hounded* incessantly by groupies, record company execs, and up-and-coming singers, all of whom wanted a piece. At first intending to suggest "Bobby McGee" to the pop star, Kris eventually decided to say nothing about his own material. Unbeknownst to him, however, Joplin's producer, Paul Rothchild, had heard *Kristofferson* and slotted a day for Janis to record "Bobby McGee" in her own raggedy but triumphant style. When Janis arrived at the studio, she already had it down pat, catching everyone unaware.

It was meant to be a surprise. Joplin didn't mention it during their final calls. She threatened to take up heroin again, which had had her

---

* After protesting racial discrimination, she had been named "Ugliest Man on Campus," which devastated her.

in its thrall throughout 1969 and 1970. "Man, you got everything going for you," Kristofferson told her. "You got a man you love; you got a producer you love. Chicks, artists, never have either one. Why blow it?"

"What's it all worth?" Joplin shot back.

"Unfortunately, the first time I heard Janis's recording of 'Bobby McGee' was when I had just gone down because she had died," Kristofferson recalled. "I remember the producer, he asked me to come by his office the next day. He had something he wanted to play me. I didn't even know she cut it. He played it for me and I had to leave the room. It was impossibly hard to hear. So much love and emotion going into the song and knowing that she wasn't there to enjoy that." Privately, though, he cringed at the alterations she made to the lyrics to fit her vocals—and gender—he knew the public would consider hers the "true" version.

Joplin didn't live to see the song's success; she died a few weeks before its release in 1971. "Bobby McGee" became her signature song, the second-ever posthumous Billboard chart-topper. Foster reissued *Kristofferson* under a new title—*Me and Bobby McGee*—and with a close-up, well-lit photo of the shaggy-haired and bearded songwriter on the cover, it went on to sell half a million copies.

By then, everyone in country music had joined the Kris Kristofferson train. In the '70s, Joe Simon, Gladys Knight, and John Holt had hits with "Help Me Make It Through the Night" on the Hot Soul Singles, Hot 100 pop, and British pop charts, respectively. Royalties from the countless covers enabled Marijohn Wilkin, who had been Kristofferson's publisher at the time of "Make It"'s writing, to buy a boat with her earnings. Sammi Smith's career peaked with "Make It." She said her attempts to equal it were "like trying to follow a Rembrandt with a kindergarten sketch." Her version, however, was named the greatest country music single ever in 2006.

"When I first heard 'Bobby McGee,' I thought, 'why didn't I write that?'" said Willie Nelson. "It has all the ingredients I like to see or hear in a song . . . all about the freedom and traveling, even down to the 'red bandana' [I wore], so naturally I related to the song a lot." Ironically, as Nelson suggested, the hippie anthem "gave us a deeper look into the human being, and that added respectability to country music."

Said Waylon Jennings: "He had a lot to do with showing that country music wasn't some Hee-Haw backwoods character with a bottle of sourmash likker and a corncob pipe, and that roots don't have to trap you in the ground."

Bob Dylan claimed that Nashville split into two camps, "pre-Kris and post-Kris," and that Kristofferson's songs broke the monopoly Music Row songwriters had on hitmaking. To top it all off, in the 1980s, when asked who the greatest songwriters were, Dylan said simply: "Gordon Lightfoot and Kris Kristofferson. Those are the guys."

At Columbia Records, executives were just learning what Kristofferson did before recording his debut. One Monday a.m. meeting resulted in this possibly apocryphal exchange:

"Why did we let our own talented employee sign with another label?" one executive demanded.

"But, sir," said a junior exec, "he wasn't a very good janitor."

It was Johnny Cash, however, who truly came through and broke Kris Kristofferson. Cash later claimed that the moment he heard "Sunday Mornin' Comin' Down," he decided to do it live on TV and release that version rather than wait until he had studio time again. "The lines of the song started running through my head," said the Man in Black, "and I realized I could identify with every one of them."

The week of the Country Music Association Awards—an event thrown by Music Row for Music Row—Cash's version of "Sunday Mornin'" topped the country charts. Without a tie or a haircut, Kris

Kristofferson attended in a black coat and hid beneath his shaggy mane, saying he was there to support Cash for Entertainer of the Year. He still lived in the same fleabag downtown apartment he'd rented before his first record had been released, only now his wife was officially divorcing him. For the award he qualified for, Song of the Year (the Songwriter's Award) for "Sunday Mornin' Comin' Down," he faced Marty Robbins and Conway Twitty, well-established, popular singers, and Merle Haggard, nominated for two songs, including "Okie from Muskogee." Knowing that the CMAs were seating him in the back in keeping with their estimation of his chances, Kristofferson prepared nothing in the way of a speech and dozed through the ceremony.

When his name was called, Kristofferson's head careened so hard against the back wall, he nearly knocked himself unconscious. C&W legend Marty Robbins elbowed Kristofferson until he rose to his feet, whereupon he glanced around helplessly, then, grinning sheepishly, bounded to the stage. He turned his back to the camera for several seconds, collecting his award and his thoughts. But they didn't come. He stammered something in the ballpark of gratitude, and expressed thanks that another, superior Haggard song had been overlooked by the nominators. He remained stunned a year later, after several nominations, when he won the Best Country Song Grammy at the 1972 ceremony for "Make It," beating two of his other songs.

While Kristofferson had dominated on the 1971 CMA ballots—Sammi Smith won an award for "Help Me Make It Through the Night" and Ray Price took home Album of the Year honors thanks to his chart-topping cover of Kristofferson's "For the Good Times"—another man ended up emerging as the night's breakout act. Charley

Pride, the rare Black country music singer—and an even rarer star—not only made history by winning the Male Vocalist trophy but took home the top honor, CMA Entertainer of the Year. Pride, who named "Sunday Mornin' Comin' Down" as the song he wished he'd written, broke Nashville's so-called color barrier, first performing at the Grand Ole Opry in 1967. "I ran into him one night," said Johnny Cash. When Pride told the superstar white singer that he felt country music in his bones, Cash stopped him. "I told him, if that was what he really wanted—if he really felt it... that's all there is to country music. If people know it comes from the heart, no matter how prejudiced they are, they'll invite you home to a chicken dinner." Then he booked Pride on season two of his TV series.

Before his appearance at the 1970 CMAs, where he was nominated for an award, Pride had been a copper smelter and lived mainly off royalties and did not tour as much as other acts. His record company issued his first three singles to radio stations without a publicity photo. His entrance at his first major concert, in Detroit, was initially greeted with stunned silence. "Friends," he told the crowd, "I realize it's a little unique, me coming out here—with a permanent suntan—to sing country and western to you. But that's the way it is." After his face flashed on fans' screens during the CMAs, Pride reflected, they started calling him the "'first Negro country singer;' then 'first Black country singer'... [then] the 'first African-American country singer.' That's about the only thing that's changed. This country is so race-conscious, so ate-up with colors and pigments. I call it 'skin hangups'—it's a disease." (Waylon wrote that Black musicians had to fight twice as hard as he had to just to get noticed at all. Ray Charles had gone gold and hit number one on the national album charts with the "countrypolitan" *Modern Sounds in Country and Western Music* in 1962, but he had artistic control, which allowed him to release country-R&B despite his record company warning he would lose Black fans. Ironically, despite its success, Charles was still seen as a soul singer by most country listeners. "The words to country songs are very earthy like the blues," he explained. Country lyrics, he pointed out, might say "I miss you, darlin', so I went out and I got drunk," while a pop song might go: "I missed you... so I went to this restaurant... and had dinner for one.")

Regardless, Pride's biggest triumphs came following the broadcast, when "Kiss an Angel Good Mornin'" not only topped the country charts but broke into the pop Top 20, and led to him topping the country LPs chart for thirty-two consecutive weeks. But in the wake of Pride's success, he was discouraged to see not only few Black musicians try their hand at country singing or picking but even fewer to line up record deals, as he had done with RCA.

"The new writers were probably more important for what they said, rather than how they said it," noted historian Bill C. Malone. "They opened up new realms of expression for country singers...." One singer observed: "Nashville was really getting shaken up by these guys." It was about to get shaken up a lot more. The hurricane-force winds of change, represented first by Kris Kristofferson, were about to strike in new forms.

CHAPTER THREE

THE ONE ON THE RIGHT IS ON THE LEFT

> People call me wild. Not really though, I'm not. I guess I've never been normal, not what you call Establishment. I'm country.
>
> —Johnny Cash

Johnny Cash had experience as a troublemaker.

In his 1971 singles "Man in Black" and "Singin' in Vietnam Talkin' Blues," the country legend protested everything from poverty to American involvement in foreign wars to the treatment of America's youth. When executives, producers, and advertisers told him his bleeding heart lyrics and appearance were off-putting, Cash chuckled and said nothing. His preponderance for black clothing and accessories could have been convenience—he once claimed it was the only color he and each of his band members all owned, or it could've been due to his obsession with black shoe polish, dating to his days in the air force. "I wore black because I liked it," he said. "I still do, and wearing it still means something to me. It's still my symbol of rebellion—against a stagnant status quo, against our hypocritical houses of God, against people whose minds are closed to others' ideas."

Hearing that, one might suspect that J. R.—his birth name—was an atheist or at least a born subversive. "There's a lot of things blamed on me that never happened," Cash said, "but then, there's a lot of things that I did that I never got caught at." His family brought him up on spirituals, singing along to their battery-powered Silvertone radio to keep sane through cotton-picking season, a staple of "Colonization Project No. 1," the Arkansas community created through Roosevelt's New Deal, and where Cash's father had built a shotgun shack. As he slogged through puberty, J. R. developed a deep bass baritone.

"God's got his hand on you," his mother said after hearing it once. "You're going to carry the message for Jesus Christ."

She vowed to somehow pay for J. R.'s singing lessons to fulfill her prophecy, but when an unimpressed instructor asked him to try a tune he felt passionate about, J. R. belted out not a hymn but "Long Gone Lonesome Blues" by Hank Williams. *Don't ever come back*, the teacher told him, *I can only ruin your gift*. Then Jack, J. R.'s ministry student brother, sliced himself open while working on a fence post. A week later, surrounded by family and telling them he could hear the angels singing, Jack Cash died. At dawn the next day, J. R. rose, unasked, to help the gravediggers shovel dirt. Within hours, twelve-year-old J. R. and his parents were back in the field, pulling out cotton from its blackened soil, singing gospel hymns through their tears. Jack's death prompted J. R.'s own true "birth," he would say. From then on, when J. R. wondered, "WWJD?," he was referring to Jack, not Jesus.*

One of his first memories was watching through a window as Eleanor Roosevelt cut ribbon for the Dyess, Arkansas, public

* Although Cash often claimed his father said: "It should've been you, J. R.," it is unlikely, or at least an exaggeration.

library, where he borrowed *The Last of the Mohicans* and the works of Edgar Allan Poe, kicking off a lifelong obsession with the written word. Cash simultaneously developed an interest in bouncy, joyous country-bluegrass and, despite his father's racism and his uncle's Klan connections, the gospel of Sister Rosetta Tharpe. He decided he could sing *and* still serve Christ, as Jack had planned for himself, but as a gospel singer.

In the air force, he was assigned to decipher Morse code from intercepted Russian communications, and claimed he reported Stalin's death to the outside world. He got to hear WSM Radio and the Grand Ole Opry while stationed in Germany, and began writing both Christian and secular songs, including a radio hit he plagiarized, added snippets from Jimmie Rodgers, and retitled "Folsom Prison Blues."* But air force life drove him and several of the elite unit's radiomen to breakdowns. One repeatedly pounded his head into a wall, complaining that "the door" wasn't opening. One night, without explanation, Cash tossed a typewriter through a window and broke out in sobs. He snapped in random violent moments, including by taunting a Black airman on a date with a white woman, and as soon as his three years were up, he looked at his life and realized he didn't recognize himself. He needed that southern soil.

Once out of the military—he later joked he'd spent "20 years" in it—Cash hightailed it the forty miles from Dyess to Memphis, Tennessee, languished in odd jobs, and played rudimentary guitar. At one point, he worked as a door-to-door salesman, offering appliances to bored housewives who probably didn't find his stony face trustworthy, or his lanky, Depression-era frame and ears that stuck out particularly attractive. He practiced Hank Williams's "Lovesick Blues" and

* His cowritten "I Got Stripes" is a near line-for-line copy of Lead Belly's "On a Monday."

listened faithfully to the Grand Ole Opry, but he felt the pull from his mother to stick to the gospel plan. When his bandmate Marshall Grant started slapping an *E* back and forth on a standup bass, Cash doubled over in hysterics. *There's no way that sound would work*, he thought.

Then, in 1954, he learned that a local studio, Sun, had been behind Elvis Presley's recent ascension on the national charts. He called them about an audition and, when dismissed, camped out outside its Memphis studio, where he hoped to head off owner and producer Sam Phillips. "Mr. Sam" would take in just about anybody for a two-song audition, hoping for another miracle. Cash, though, tried to sell himself as a gospel singer, commercial poison in Phillips's view. After being turned away on the first go-round, Cash reworked a poem called "Hey, Porter" into a piece of secular music, and brought his band, later dubbed the Tennessee Two, to back him at the second audition.

But Phillips didn't think "Hey, Porter" worked as an A-side, so Cash went home and doodled once more. He soon heard a Memphis DJ shout "stay tuned, we're gonna bawl, squall, and run up the wall!" The rhyme inspired "Cry, Cry, Cry," originally "Bawl, Bawl, Bawl." Still, Phillips seemed noncommittal. "There's something squirrelly about you guys," he admitted, believing they had developed an intriguing "boom chicka boom" shuffle style that he thought might appeal to fans of fast-paced Elvis records. Besides, Cash had an astonishing bass-baritone voice, Phillips decided, not that it was to everyone's taste. "Sam Phillips saw something new in what I was doing," Cash recalled. "In his mind he saw this as a way to break tradition maybe and reach more people in country music." "Mr. Sam" told Cash he didn't see the whole "fiddle and steel guitar" Music City model lasting, and that Nashville would have to evolve or fizzle out. He decided that Cash's "Folsom Prison Blues," initially a dirgelike slog, needed that same "boom chicka boom" churn and that the explosive lyrics should be delivered not mournfully or amorally but as a "cry against confinement," as one writer described it. When former country artist Bill Haley's "Rock Around the Clock" came out and blew out minds and eardrums only months later, Sun Records' investment in Cash as a member of the newly emerging rockabilly (combining "rock and roll" and "hillbilly") movement seemed fortuitous. A cabal of competitors pooled money to campaign for the banning of Sun's output, especially "Folsom," with its infamous lines "I shot a man in Reno / just to watch him die." They couldn't stop that single or any other Sun release, however.

"Newly married"—as he put it—to Vivian Liberto, Cash wrote his first number one, "I Walk the Line," in her honor. (Cash had tried it up-tempo multiple times, before Sam Phillips tricked him into a single slow take, which the producer then released without Cash's consent. "Now your country music can no longer be locked into any one category," marveled Phillips. "That's what music is all about. It should be universal.") Although the Cashes finally had income, Vivian had to contend with screaming fans, letters pouring into her house, and her husband's career taking over everything. She was "incredibly ill-equipped" to deal with the pressures of fame and any challenge to domestic bliss, as her future documentarian put it. Her husband, rather than try to stay humble by living with his parents, as Elvis had done, began to drink, take amphetamines, and hang around with fellow Sun star Carl Perkins, an alcoholic. Together, they commiserated tearfully about their lost brothers. Cash's bandmates, guitarist Luther Perkins (no relation) and bassist Marshall Grant, either actively encouraged this behavior or were unable to stop it. Luther cackled as Cash took an ax to a hotel wall separating their rooms and even started kicking over equipment in a rage, just as Johnny might do. Unaware of these antics, the stodgy Grand Ole Opry invited Cash aboard, first as a special guest, and later as a permanent member. It was in Nashville, after making his Opry debut, that backstage, Johnny Cash met June Carter, the middle daughter of the "First Family of Country Music," and flirting outrageously, got down on one knee to "propose" for a photo op.

The Grand Ole Opry, dedicated to "inoffensive and inexpensive" broadcasts, prohibited "drinking, smoking, [or] cussing," rules blindly accepted by most country singers. The Opry's 50,000-watt broadcasts made stars of its regulars, who had to appear at least twenty-six weekends per year. Cash favorite Hank Williams had been the Opry's problem child and was eventually suspended for drunkenness. The Opry snubbed Cash's other heroes hailing from the thematically darker, postwar, Texas honky-tonks, with their songs about "despair, adultery, and the rigors of the city." Moreover, the Opry forced Cash to sit through an interview (read: an interrogation) for the gig while, in the wings, several members grumbled that rockabilly was *not* country music. Despite this reception, the Opry's poor pay, and the broadcast's diminished influence among teenagers, Cash eagerly accepted a role on the show and, in his first program, was called back for encore after encore, inadvertently preempting several performers.

In the 1960s, with Cash's songs performing well on the pop charts, Columbia Records lured him away from Sun with the promise of a gospel LP and a mountain of advance money. Sam Phillips raged that his artists were getting diva treatment with him and would be lost in the shuffle at a corporation, but he also refused to increase Cash's royalty percentage. Cash signed the Columbia deal in secret and then lied about it to "Mr. Sam" for weeks.

Later that year, Cash carried on an affair with Hank Williams's widow, Billie Jean, who was married to Cash's best friend—and the year's country singing sensation—Johnny Horton. Cash began to ignore Horton's calls, perhaps imagining his friend had learned about the relationship, and decided to cancel a gig at the Skyline in Austin, Texas, the site of Hank Williams's last show, citing a chill that had come over him. On November 4, 1960, Horton played there and then took to the road to Shreveport, where he was killed in a head-on collision. In the months after, Cash retreated to the desert in his camper van, alternately proposing to Horton's widow and visiting with his own wife, who was pregnant again.

Throughout his life, Cash struggled with a Dr. Jekyll and Mr. Hyde personality. "Sometimes I am two people," he said. "Johnny is the nice one. Cash causes all the trouble. They fight." Johnny Cash collectively caused a mountain of trouble. When his singles began crossing over to the pop charts, Cash dipped into energy-enhancing prescription drugs to handle performing up to four times per day. Despite ticket sales, he racked up a mountain of debt, alienated his wife, and disappointed his kids, who often went three or four tours without seeing him. "You had to have something to come down off the pills," Rosanne Cash noted as an adult. "He was locked in a terrible, terrible cycle." The cycle continued—Cash needed the pills to keep him awake and chipper for concert after concert so he could make money to keep his family, having moved to California, fed and under a $75,000 roof. "I was evil," he admitted in 1971. "I really was."

"When I was six years old, it was like my daddy always came home," daughter Rosanne said. "But when I was eight, somebody else came home. . . . The drugs were at work. He'd stay up all night. He and my mom would fight. It was so sad. He would always be having accidents. He turned the tractor over one day and almost killed himself, and we had to call the fire department after he set fire to the hillside." Rosanne, age nine, had to call them herself and ended up wishing she hadn't.

"He took me on his lap and put his arms around me and said, 'I'm glad to be alive,' because the tractor could have rolled over on him. He held me so tightly. I felt so close to him. I wished it could always be like that. But then he'd be gone again." When her father would go on tour, she believed, it became Rosanne versus the unfamiliar world, and when Johnny returned, "the chaos, self-destruction and addiction" deepened.

In the sixties, he spent four hours in a Nashville jail and escaped a public drunkenness charge in Georgia after a fan intervened with her husband, the judge. ("You want to kill yourself, I'm going to give you your God-given right to go ahead and do that," His Honor shouted. "Take your pills and go.") Cash once tried to strip down in public and was dragged into the Carson City, Nevada, drunk tank, whereupon waking hungover, he begged forgiveness from his brother's ghost and sang a doleful "Folsom Prison Blues." (Said his cellmate: "Me and you are a couple of drunks, but you sure sound like Johnny Cash.") Once, chased by California Highway Patrol for six miles and caught without a license, he was merely cited. His drug habit deepened; he often borrowed friends' vehicles, only to lose them in a blackout. On June 27, 1965, with the first American offensive underway in Vietnam, Cash was puttering along in Big Sur, California, with his nephew Damon, who tried to bail when he found a half-finished bottle of whiskey and a fruit jar packed with amphetamines. Along a less-traveled road in the national forest, Damon stormed away, and Cash, nodding off, accidentally set the camper ablaze. His nephew returned with only seconds to spare, and had to hit his uncle over the head with a tree branch to rouse him. After being hauled before a judge over the fire, Cash blamed his camper but quipped that it was "dead, so you can't question it."

His 1958 Caddy blew up just days later. Driving it with an unsecured propane tank, Cash took a turn too hard. The passenger side of the vehicle instantly went up in flames, and Cash crawled out quickly, escaping with only minor facial burns. On tour a month earlier in Mississippi, he'd been arrested for public drunkenness, and, soon after the forest fire and car crash, he was busted again for taking a taxi to Juarez for what police assumed was heroin, but was in actuality more than one thousand uppers (discovered in his luggage), enough to refill his fruit jar several times over. Cash spent a night behind bars in El Paso before making bail, but faced major felony charges.

Although he ultimately received a thirty-day suspended sentence for it, the El Paso incident permanently wrecked his marriage and deeply strained his relationship with his four daughters. White supremacists, apparently upset that Cash sang even then of Native Americans and refused to paint the white man as the hero in his songs, spread a rumor that Mrs. Vivian Cash was dark-skinned and that their children were mongrels.* With all these charges and scandals hanging over his head, and with the Country Music Association's more conservative members calling for him to resign from the group, one would think Cash would have immediately announced he was going to spend more time with his family. The problem was, he simply didn't want to. He was in love with someone else.

The problem began coincidentally about the time drug use started to become part of his lifestyle. Singer Rose Maddox, fed up with canceled or delayed shows because of Cash's daily regimen of twenty amphetamines (to get going) and booze and barbiturates (to calm down), quit in a huff. On February 11, 1962, after finagling and finessing and tweaking his tour schedule so she could join, his tour manager enlisted June Carter in *The Johnny Cash Show* at Johnny's request.** At

---

* Vivian Cash thought of herself as having Italian heritage, but a 2021 DNA test showed not only that she had Sicilian heritage but that her great-grandmother was a woman of color, born into slavery.

** As a protégé of both Chet Atkins and film director Elia Kazan, she had more than enough charisma to keep up with Cash.

an early stop in Des Moines, Iowa, for a star-studded bill headlined by Patsy Cline,* and with minutes to go until showtime, June demanded Johnny let her press his shirt. That was all it took. "She was a tonic," he realized immediately.

After the tour, he brought everyone, including Carter, out to Southern California to surprise his family, which enraged Vivian. After Patsy Cline confronted Carter about the adulterous relationship she had sniffed out, Carter skipped the "after party." She spent the next three years on tour with Cash, almost constantly gritting her teeth in anticipation of the day either the press would out her affair with Cash or that the pills would end it for good. She was "a Florence Nightingale type," one friend observed, and later, Carter would say: "I'd watched Hank Williams die.... I thought, 'I can't fall in love with this man but it's just like a ring of fire.'"

Cash left Vivian and their daughters and set up shop in Nashville with up-and-comer Waylon Jennings as his roommate. There, hounded by death threats over his "Black" wife, Cash began carrying a shotgun, pistol, and teargas canister, sleeping three days on, three days off, and would wake up coughing to the point that friends would sprint toward him and shovel water into his mouth.

"One of my worst times came early," he recalled of a show at Carnegie Hall in New York, the first time he performed alongside June's family. Before the show, he had a heart-to-heart with June, in which they both admitted they were falling in love but vowed to keep things professional on tour. Onstage, Cash had visibly lost so much weight from stress and amphetamine use that, coupled with his costume choice of yodeling hero Jimmie Rodgers's blue and white railroad

* When Cash knocked on Cline's door one night, she instantly yelled: "Get away from my door, Cash!" He hadn't announced himself. When Cline left to headline her own tour, Cash took it hard. After her death, he called her "a great road buddy," and said she had "the biggest laugh in the world."

uniform, the audience didn't recognize him.* Doubling the audience's bafflement, Cash could barely croak out the words to Rodgers's country standards or his own "Give My Love to Rose." Over grumbling from the crowd, he apologized for his "laryngitis." A fellow musician, however, confronted him backstage, bluntly asking: "It's called Dexedrine, isn't it?" The man recognized a fellow traveler and the side effects of his newly cemented pill dependency. Cash, however, waved away the man's health guidance.

After the disastrous Carnegie Hall show, Cash claimed to have been deeply depressed—but only for a few hours. He caught Columbia artist Peter La Farge that night in Greenwich Village, and flipped for "The Ballad of Ira Hayes," a lament for the Native American WWII hero used as a prop by the government and then abandoned when his usefulness dissipated. Cash went on to record five of La Farge's songs, including "Ira Hayes," the re-release of which became one of Cash's defining moments.

The single was at first ignored by *Billboard*, so DJs were mostly unaware of it; the stations that knew about it refrained from spinning it, lest it alienate social conservatives. Cash's concert audiences, who seemed unfamiliar with Hayes or were indifferent to the plight of Indigenous people, greeted it with lukewarm applause, but Cash wouldn't accept defeat. After complaining that "nobody else seemed to speak up with any volume or voice" about Indigenous issues, how could he let the song vanish into obscurity? When a journalist asked him if he would resign from the Country Music Association in protest, he reacted swiftly. He took out a full-page ad in *Billboard*.

"D.J.s—station managers—owners, etc., where are your <u>guts</u>?" his screed read. "You're right! Teenage girls and Beatle record buyers don't

* "He was skinny as a snake," said Kris Kristofferson, recalling his introduction to Cash at the Opry a few years hence, "and just as impossible to predict. Everybody was afraid of him."

want to hear this sad story of Ira Hayes—but who cries more easily, and who always go to sad movies to cry??? Teenage girls."

Surprisingly, the ploy worked. "Ira Hayes" began getting airplay and inched up the charts, eventually reaching the country Top 3.

It was a rare bright spot in those years. At one show, a Canadian TV producer reported seeing Johnny slap at "bugs" he felt on his face. His downward spiral became more apparent when he ended a single-song appearance on the Grand Ole Opry by wielding his microphone stand like a spear and harpooning the footlights, all fifty-two of them. "Get him out of here and don't bring him back!" a manager yelled at bassist Marshall Grant. Still cranked up on pills and steamed over the firing, he crashed June's new Cadillac into a utility pole, breaking his nose and crushing his front teeth against his upper gums. Miraculously, even though June's husband, a cop, investigated the accident, Cash walked away without charge.* The bottom came rushing up at him in October 1967, when he weighed 125 pounds and had to cancel a tour and recording sessions due to drug-related throat damage. In a continuous black mood over his family situation, and pressuring himself to keep his long-desired relationship with June churning along, Johnny promised to get clean if June married him. She at first refused, a rejection Cash used as fuel to triple his pill intake. Mother Maybelle Carter, who had been close with Hank Williams, staged an intervention. John's mother attended and had a heart attack on her return home, but even that didn't serve as a wakeup call for her son. Although he and June Carter did marry in 1968, it would take the birth of their son two years later for Johnny to finally get clean, and he would keep his pill intake under control for the next seven years.

---

* Around this time, in one incident kept secret for years, Cash nearly had a mental breakdown, believing that there were wood splinters under his shirt, which he tried to tear off.

Energized by his engagement to June in a spontaneous onstage moment, Cash tried to put his career back on track. While he had hits throughout the late fifties and sixties, they were often jukebox bait, cloying pop songs DJs spun with their ears plugged. After his nominally loyal, chummy producer insisted he record more teen-friendly tracks, Cash snuck into the building in the middle of the night, according to Kris Kristofferson, then still sweeping floors, to cut more pop trash for jukeboxes. When Cash did show up during "working hours," he got into shouting matches with producers who shot down his realer, bouncier Memphis rockabilly style. In those years, he recalled "doing my own thing, staying away from politics and Music Row, making albums my way."* It paid off when he asked for a mariachi band on "Ring of Fire," resulting in a groundbreaking arrangement Cash could hear in his head but couldn't write out.** Instead, he hummed the parts for each musician; the song was in the can in thirty minutes. To many, it seemed anathema to add trumpets to a country song, especially one by Johnny Cash, but he was simply fulfilling a dream he had had in which Anita Carter, June's sister, laid horns over her version, which seemed to blend perfectly. Without permission, he called in an unaffiliated producer who had worked with him at Sun Studios.

"Cowboy" Jack Clement didn't get a credit for his work on "Ring of Fire" due to contractual agreements—Clement, for his part, didn't care about credit: "Fuck the world, we're here to create," he said—but Cash's firm decision to violate the rules of the Row by bringing in an out-of-state arranger marked a turning point in the struggle for

* "His politics," one biographer insisted, "were defined by empathy, nothing else."

** Sturgill Simpson and Jason Isbell have done similar things with horn sections.

independence in Nashville. "Ring of Fire" immediately became his first gold seller, and Cash gave his next single, Dylan's "It Ain't Me, Babe," the same horn section treatment. The latter, like other duets Johnny and June recorded between 1964 and 1968,* including the ironic "How Did You Get Away from Me," were at least minor country hits, rarely more. "Jackson," which won the couple a Grammy, was overshadowed commercially by the Lee Hazlewood–Nancy Sinatra version.

As he drifted along in narcotic-drenched squalor, rarely showing for studio dates and canceling $40,000 worth of gigs in a year due to "laryngitis," Cash heard out his new producer, *Blonde on Blonde* helmsman Bob Johnston. Johnston encouraged him to make a bold move to resuscitate his career. He decided to fight for his dream album: live, from maximum security.

It wasn't as crazy as it might've sounded to outsiders. His mentor, Sam Phillips, had bussed in Tennessee state prisoners with great voices as background vocalists going back to 1953, and Cash had recently recorded several solid "prison" songs. *At Folsom Prison* would simply commit to wax the concerts Cash had played at correctional facilities going back to the late '50s, when he performed every prisoner's favorite, "Folsom Prison Blues," for Huntsville, Texas, inmates and they greeted him with a rule-breaking surge toward the stage. In the near-decade since, he had been inspired to continue entertaining the incarcerated after reading reports of deplorable conditions for prisoners in Arkansas. "By 1968," noted the *Socialist Worker*, "a growing prison reform movement had developed in the U.S.—inspired by the strength of other political and social movements, and spurred on by several high-profile prison scandals, including at the Tucker Prison Farm . . . where investigations revealed a lack of food, 14-hour workdays, systematic rape

* June joked that their duet spotlight was "the sex part" of *The Johnny Cash Show*.

and the torture of inmates by both guards and inmate 'trustees.'" At a time when recidivism rates were 70 percent and Folsom was raking in upward of a quarter-million bucks annually, Cash received nothing for playing there.

Merle Haggard, confined to San Quentin State Prison in 1959, watched Cash perform there only reluctantly. "He lost his voice that day. It was just a whisper.... When he didn't have a voice and he was able to bring the people around, I understood the power of Johnny Cash.... He had the right attitude. He chewed gum, looked arrogant and flipped the bird to the guards—he did everything the prisoners wanted to do. He was a mean mother from the South who was there because he loved us. When he walked away, everyone in that place had become a Johnny Cash fan." He did later couch his statement: "Johnny Cash understands what it's like in prison, [but] he doesn't *know*!" Out of prison months later and inspired by his new idol, Haggard began a country music career that, by the end of the sixties, included "Sing Me Back Home," "Mama Tried," and more number ones. "The first time I ever saw you perform, it was at San Quentin," he would say on *The Johnny Cash Show*. After Cash set him up by saying he didn't remember seeing Haggard on the bill, Merle responded: "I was in the *audience*, Johnny."

Having canceled the first prison recording due to Cash's unreliability, Columbia now demanded Bob Johnston vouch for Cash—apparently, they were unaware that Johnston considered record companies enemies of creativity. The natural choice should have been California's Folsom all along, as his breakthrough hit had been inspired by it, but it was only after no one answered his call to another prison that Johnston phoned the warden there. They booked two shows in Dining Room #2 for January 13, 1968, each for roughly half of the prison population in good standing, but Cash's fairly new, first-ever drummer grumbled that the unpaid gig wouldn't even be worth hauling their gear for.* Although Cash rarely showed up for rehearsals, he practiced with June and the Tennessee Three until midnight. "I knew this was it," he said, waiting in the wings on twenty pills, "my chance to make up for all the times I had messed up." Cash took the stage shortly before ten a.m. after some fanfare involving MC Hugh Cherry, who told the prisoners to react loudly to anything they appreciated, and opening numbers from faded rockabilly star Carl Perkins and the newly minted Mrs. Cash. With his back to the audience, Cash was met by silence. When he whirled, took the mic, and intoned: "Hello, I'm Johnny Cash," the audience roared.

Each of the nineteen songs he played seemed carefully chosen for the prison audience. From the literal gallows humor of "25 Minutes to Go," with Cash's ragged voice starting to "go" in tandem with the character's life, to the devastating "Long Black Veil," Cash focused mainly on prison songs, and the inmates mostly cheered in all the right places. He skipped "I Walk the Line" for the first time since 1956; instead, he pulled out "Busted," written by Harlan Howard for a Cash LP meant to show the average Black person's experience under white supremacy, and a cover of a Ray Charles song** to break up the all-prison-tune monotony.***

Johnston added canned cheers to underscore the gleefully insane "Cocaine Blues" and a few hoots after the line in "Folsom Prison Blues" about murdering a man in Reno—that part would be sliced from 45s after Robert Kennedy's assassination. Between songs, Cash tried his hand at standup comedy, spitting out the tap water a guard handed him, referring to his set list as his "idiot sheet," and saying, "Come

* An undetermined number of men, serving out punishments for infractions within the system, were confined to their cells and listened over the PA system.

** Both would be excised from the *At Folsom Prison* album.

*** In the second set, Cash tried to re-create the magic, but only two superior versions made the record.

on, you don't mean that," when inmates booed the associate warden. "This show is being recorded for release on Columbia Records," Cash deadpanned, "so you can't say 'hell' or 'shit' or anything like that." He shook hands with the front row, took requests, and teased producer Bob Johnston. The prisoners "related to him as being one of them more than anything else," said drummer "Fluke" Holland. "He realized how it could have been if the stories [about his past were] true. He could've been out there, looking at somebody doing a show."

"Let me know if there's ever anything I can do for you all.... I'll do it," he told previous prison audiences, and he tried his damnedest to believe it. "How ya doin', Sherley," Cash said, stunning thirty-two-year-old Glen Sherley, an inmate in the front row. Unbeknownst to the prisoner, a chaplain had passed along Sherley's composition "Greystone Chapel," an ode to God for saving him, and Cash's debut of it would close the live record.

Backed by a publicity mill that heralded a Cash returning to his roots—as in, that he was an ex-felon—as well as praise for its "soul music of a rare kind—country soul from the concerned and sensitive"—*Folsom* reinvigorated Cash's career. After turning down an initial date at Madison Square Garden for one at a South Dakota reservation, he became the first country act to sell out the famed Manhattan arena. He used his platform not to challenge his audience to rise up in protest or to blindly support the American government in Vietnam, but rather to call himself a "dove with claws." While baffling to critics at the time, Cash made his position clear: *I believe in people, not causes.* The titles of subsequent singles speak to this: "What Is Truth," "Flesh and Blood," "Man in Black," and "Singin' in Vietnam Talkin' Blues."

Mere months after *Folsom*, he released an inferior, somewhat forced quasi-sequel, *At San Quentin*, which became Cash's top seller thanks to a one-off, impromptu reading of "A Boy Named Sue," a comedy piece by Shel Silverstein.* ("San Quentin," which Cash wrote for the prisoners, became the B-side, serving as an almost literal fuck-you to Columbia for releasing a novelty song as the single. When he performed it, one of the African American prisoners stood to give him the Black Power salute.) *San Quentin* topped the *Billboard* 200 charts in 1969, a rare feat for a country artist or live record in any genre. Cash then pushed his luck. He released two more prison concert albums, both of which vanished without a trace. One, recorded in Nashville in 1974, featured ex–Folsom inmate Glen Sherley, performing his own material on the bill with Cash. Criticism spread that Cash had used the captives and their plight to "buoy his own rep," as writer Amanda Petrusich put it. It didn't help that Cash moved on to other charitable pursuits in the '80s after inmates at Vacaville, a minimum-security prison in California, allegedly spit on him and threatened to rape his wife. Afterward, Cash downplayed his efforts for prisoners or any other cause. "I've pretty well stayed out of the whole issue of prison reform, actually," he claimed. "I've just sung my songs. I've gone to the prisons because, you know, I was concerned. . . ."**

Cash knew his newfound success and riches came with an unspoken demand from the American public: *no selling out. Folsom Prison* led to a two-season contract with ABC to do a music-related TV series, making him *the* preeminent ambassador for country music and even the South.*** He had become the most popular man in America, and a janitor had his attention; on February 25, 1970, *The Johnny Cash Show*

---

* Buddy Holly's drummer Tommy Allsup of Winter Dance Party produced "In the Year 2525," the song that kept "Sue" from the number one spot on the pop charts.

** He added: "Prisons just make 'em worse."

*** As a nod to the men of Folsom who had helped him ascend to national prominence, Cash dedicated "The Wall" to them on the first *Johnny Cash Show* in 1969.

aired live on national television from the two-thousand-seat Ryman Auditorium, and, during a rehearsal, Cash stepped to the mic to lay it all on the line for him.

Cash began strumming and, seemingly offhand, mentioned that the new number they were about to hear was written by "a friend of mine, his name's Kris Kristofferson."

After watching the rehearsal, network executives told director Bill Carruthers that Cash would need to alter the line "wishing, Lord, that I was stoned" in the chorus of "Sunday Mornin' Comin' Down," as it was listed. No one asked Cash directly, however. Perhaps they recalled previous battles he'd won, including the right to include folkie Pete Seeger, a partly blacklisted communist "sympathizer," on one program. Another exec approached Kristofferson and asked if he would be amenable to a slight but painful rewrite. "I remember being advised that I could change it to 'Wishing Lord that I was home,' which was not the same thing." He told Cash to do it if he thought it would be essential for protecting his relationship with ABC. "John didn't tell me one way or the other which one he was going to do. I would have lived with whatever he did because I idolized Johnny Cash: anything he did was okay with me." Cash had had his battles with the network and had promised to stop being a thorn in its side.* In the show's premiere episode, Cash brought on Ervin Rouse, forgotten songwriter of "Orange Blossom Special," then living on a Native American reservation, but because the show ran long, Rouse was cut without anyone informing either him or Cash. The host was furious but helpless against the faceless, all-powerful corporation. "I was determined from then on that I wouldn't stick my neck out, that if I was going to do TV—I didn't own the networks, so I'd [just] have to do it their way."

---

* He also said: "It's good to know who hates you and it is good to be hated by the right people."

Nonetheless, in 1969, he had African American folksinger Odetta perform her song "Black Woman," with part of the audience incorporated into a set labeled "Confederate Gallery."

Shortly before the show, Kristofferson took a seat away from the cameras in the Ryman's distant balcony, head down. The glaring white lights rose on Cash and a chorus line of eight singers and five players behind him.

> *You know, not everyone who has been on "the bum" wanted it that way. The Great Depression of the '30s set the feet of thousands of people—farmers, city workers—it set 'em to ridin' the rails. My daddy was one of those who hopped a freight train a couple of times to go and look for work. He wasn't a bum. He was a hobo but he wasn't a bum. I suppose we've all—all of us been at one time or another "drifter at heart," and today, like yesterday, there's many that are on that road headin' out. Not searchin' maybe for work, as much as for self-fulfillment, or understanding of their life... trying to find a meaning for their life. And they're not hoppin' freights much anymore. Instead, they're thumbin' cars and diesel trucks along the highways from Maine to Mexico. And many who have drifted—including myself—have found themselves no closer to peace of mind than a dingy backroom, on some lonely Sunday morning, with it comin' down all around you.*

He originally spoke for much longer, but the ABC–Screen Gems network producing and airing the program cut it, either for time or because of its pro-hippie message. Then, a spotlight came up on Cash, guitar slung over his shoulders once more.

"Here's a song written by Kris Kristofferson," he said, launching into "Sunday Mornin'." "Don't forget that name."

Kristofferson held his breath for the first two verses. Cash's eyes wandered up to the balcony, finding Kris's baby blues sparkling in the dark. He paused, let a beat go by. "When he got to that line, he looked up at me and sang, 'Wishing Lord that I was stoned.' It offended a lot of people, but it saved the song for me. The song wouldn't have been nearly as strong without it."

Lisa Kristofferson, Kris's future wife, said: "They were up against everything together and they knew it, sink or swim." Asked about the moment later, Cash simply said: "There's nothing wrong with singing the truth."

CHAPTER FOUR

PHASES AND STAGES, CIRCLES AND CYCLES

He played guitar like Segovia and phrased absolutely unlike anybody, like a jazz singer.... He was a hero of all the serious people.

—Kris Kristofferson

We're going to keep doing it wrong until we like it that way.

—Willie Nelson

While Kris Kristofferson's career was taking off, Willie Nelson's was hovering somewhere between has-been and never-was. Patsy Cline's "Crazy" had been released ten years earlier and not been remotely duplicated, certainly not by its songwriter. While Nelson recorded folk-country covers and was lucky to make the country Top 30, new running partners like Kristofferson had hit the pop charts and made it to the marquees of LA and, in December of 1972, New York City.

At the storied Philharmonic Hall, part of Lincoln Center for the Performing Arts, Kris brought Blakeian country music to 2,700 metropolitan folks, who paid between four and six dollars. Intended to become an album release the following year but shelved in favor of more original studio product, *Live at the Philharmonic* was a wild experience. Kristofferson rushed through most of the songs—some were halted before the two-minute mark, with the original instrumental breaks or even entire verses skipped over. The New Yorkers greeted the recent songs with polite applause.

Kristofferson was under incredible contractual and executive pressure to produce original songs, not live versions of familiar hits his publisher had already sold to a dozen other artists. Several songs on the *Kristofferson* LP were more than five years old; the tracks on his second effort, *The Silver Tongued Devil and I*, between one and five; by his third and fourth albums, *Border Lord* and *Jesus Was a Capricorn*, released just months apart in 1972, virtually all the music had been copyrighted circa their recording dates. "The old saying in the music business is that you get a lifetime to write your first record," says songwriter Dan Daley, "and six months to write the second." With Nashville record budgets so tight and thus studio time limited, rushing was only natural—only twenty months separated *Border Lord* and *Kristofferson*. A retrospective review suggested: "New or old, the songs on *Border Lord* often seemed like retreads of already familiar Kristofferson themes. No doubt Kristofferson and Monument would have been better advised to have waited until he had a collection of songs to match his early hits." *Capricorn*, meanwhile, led off with the title track, a humorous yet too-pat political song that suggested, should Christ return in the 1970s, "they'd just nail him up again" for being a Commie. "I was trying to point out that He would have as hard a time today with conservative people as He had in His own hard time,"

Kristofferson told an interviewer. "Everybody has to have somebody to look down on. The whites hate the blacks, who hate the Klan and so on. Jesus was eating organic food, which was a typical image of the long-haired hippie. Everybody in Nashville was down on them." *Capricorn*, recorded with members of Dylan's *Blonde on Blonde* band, featured another songwriter's composition for the first time; the addition of upstart Larry Gatlin's "Help Me" barely pushed the record over the thirty-minute mark; the inclusion garnered more attention for Gatlin than perhaps even the album received. *Capricorn*'s initial singles all failed to make impressions on radio airplay lists, but Kristofferson didn't seem to care. He was paying it forward. Instead of releasing it as a single, Kristofferson gave pop singer Brenda Lee the cut "Nobody Wins," the most commercial tune he'd written in years. (Its memorable couplet—"The lovin' was easy / it's the livin' that's hard"—was quintessential Kristofferson.) Lee, whose adult contemporary career had faded after fifteen years of hits, rebranded herself as a country singer with "Nobody Wins," nearly taking the single to number one. She would subsequently rack up nine more Top 10 country hits.

He blew it as a producer that year, as well: Joan Baez offered him a job helming her next record, but he got blitzed to the point of passing out. Bassist Norbert Putnam, who had played on Kristofferson's demos and first two albums, swiftly arrived. "All you got to do," Putnam said, "is go sit in that control room and me and this rhythm section will give Joan Baez a hit record." But after Baez's pleading, Putnam took the helm and gave her that smash, and thus launched a lucrative career for himself as producer.

Next, Kristofferson invited fellow ex-janitor Gatlin to the Philharmonic and featured him in a solo spotlight on his religious-minded tune, "Help Me," which Kristofferson said "really shook me up. I'm kneeling there, and I carry a big load of guilt around, and I was just out of control, crying. It was a release." Next, he ran his band through a song written by "Funky" Donnie Fritts, his pianist. These were not the typical concerns of a "best living songwriter in Nashville," but he wasn't finished shining on other artists. His fiancée, Rita Coolidge, performed a set midway through her "better half's," after which he would join her to duet on and close the show with "Help Me Make It Through the Night" and "Me and Bobby McGee." *Capricorn* launched several careers, and the Philharmonic show, despite going unremarked upon for two decades, was instrumental in launching two future stars, and that's what he focused on.

The first was Coolidge. The Cherokee woman had been born outside Nashville twenty-eight years earlier and grew up with her father, mother, and both grandmothers singing "Amazing Grace," known as the "Cherokee national anthem," and other favorites as a "natural part of our lives, just like sleeping and eating," she said. In college, Rita smoked weed and fell under the spell of Bob Dylan and Delta blues singer Muddy Waters. A friend introduced her to Tina Turner, whom she admired, but what stuck in her mind wasn't Turner's stage presence but a backstage warning. Turner took off her wig to show Coolidge a tremendous scar jutting across one side of her skull. *My musician husband gave this to me*, she said.

Coolidge's epiphany about music and her destiny came in her early twenties when she heard Aretha Franklin's soul-stirring cover of the Sam Cooke civil rights anthem "A Change Is Gonna Come" on her car radio, during which she pulled over and bawled. She developed a breathy singing voice, of which she said: "I've always felt singing is about the spaces left, the spaces not taken up, about breathing space."* Her voice earned her offers to sing radio jingles, but she refused to record anything she didn't believe in. "I was always in control of the

* All that excellent breathing contrasted her with Kristofferson's oft-criticized growl, "raw and expressive" though his may have been.

songs that I sing," she recalled. That control and determination were rare in the music business, certainly among unknowns and especially among up-and-coming women solo artists, and her voice captured the commercial interest of industry insiders who heard it. She became a muse for Leon Russell, inspiring both "Delta Lady" and "A Song for You." After "Delta Lady" became Joe Cocker's most requested song, the British blues singer invited Russell and the single's namesake out on the road.

The tour, which resulted in the blockbuster live album *Mad Dogs & Englishmen*, was for Coolidge "rock 'n' roll university. I had only been out of college for a year and had, kind of, a sheltered life. My father was a preacher and my mother was a schoolteacher. When we left the A&M [Records] lot to go to the airport to get on the plane, there were 55 men, women, children, dogs—and I think the plane only held 45. So, there were people sleeping in the aisles on the plane. It was crazy. And that was just the beginning."

Inevitably perhaps, Coolidge and Russell soon split, leaving Rita to date and inspire songs from Stephen Stills or David Crosby, and just as inevitably, when Coolidge left Stills to shack up with Graham Nash, the supergroup CSN descended into jealous sniping and collapsed. She wondered what she was doing wrong. Her parents' marriage was a fairy tale—they would be married for seventy-four years. She was close with her sister, Priscilla, with whom she'd form a band dedicated to popularizing the music of the Cherokee people. At the time of her first encounter with Kristofferson, on a plane returning to Nashville from California and the end of the grueling "Mad Dogs" tour, she was still recovering from another breakup, the worst yet. She had dated touring drummer Jim Gordon, but out of nowhere, he'd given her a black eye in a hotel hallway. He also stole the melody from "Time," an in-progress song Coolidge had developed, and let Eric Clapton use it as the instrumental coda to "Layla." Her flight home was November

9, 1971, as Joplin's "Bobby McGee" crested at number one on the pop charts. (Although "Layla" limped from #53 to #52 on the Cashbox charts, it stung Coolidge to hear it on the radio.) Kristofferson had recently split with Samantha Eggar, an Oscar nominee and convent graduate. He, reported Coolidge, didn't want to meet anyone, especially a woman. Nevertheless, in her memoir, she recalled him patting the empty spot by the window and saying: "I've got a seat for you."

Kris, whose major general father had died suddenly in California on New Year's Day, and thus missed much of his son's success, had flailed throughout 1971, rush-releasing his second album and tentatively reaching out to his family again in his grief. But things were still tense—if, as Kristofferson told Coolidge, his "mother could have been a general, she would have been the first female five-star general." He didn't turn on the charm for her; he was "no eyes," Mama Cass's nickname for him, referring to his inability to hold another person's gaze. Coolidge sized him up as "a big kid and kind of clumsy. You could never call him a polished man—you had to bribe him to get him to put on a suit or tux."

He told Rita he was following her career, which greatly surprised her considering that even music industry insiders had never heard of her. She wrote, "He has a mighty ego but his self-effacement and interest in others, no matter who they are or what they do, is genuine." It didn't hurt that he still had the beard from the new cover of his reissued debut album, which made him "devastating" looking. "On top of which, he absolutely radiated outlaw," she said. "Kris would go out and sing these songs that moved people's hearts and pulled them closer together. And the audience seemed to melt into one. You could feel the sweet energy in the room. I felt it and it was overwhelming."

They were inseparable for the next year, during which Coolidge worked on her third solo album. Her first two had fizzled, but this time, the hottest young country act in the biz, Kris Kristofferson, was helping arrange or suggest material. (Although he ultimately contributed only one original composition, "The Lady's Not for Sale," the tender, overlooked love song became the title track.) "When you've got a great song and you've got a great team and I happen to be the singer, I don't know where the magic comes in," said Coolidge. "There's no formula. We're all just trying to do it right." Released in November 1972, the same month *Jesus Was a Capricorn* hit shelves, *The Lady's Not for Sale* peaked just outside the *Billboard* Top 40, at the time a more successful effort than either of Kristofferson's recent albums. A few days after its release, the couple appeared at the New York Philharmonic, part of Kristofferson's eighteen-month tour, a brutal run by anyone's standards. (Kristofferson hadn't even wanted to tour as a headliner. Approaching Merle Haggard's manager about being Merle's opening act, he was rebuffed—unless he was willing to shave.) Although critics scoffed that the two spent entire shows lost in each other's gaze, it was clear that he and Rita Coolidge were on their way. Now, if only Kris could be supportive offstage, too.

Recalling the Durango, Mexico, shoot for Sam Peckinpah's *Pat Garrett and Billy the Kid*, in which her boyfriend played Billy, Coolidge wrote that she simply wanted him to "talk to me or reach out to me—which was so strange because I knew he loved me as deeply as I loved him." Kristofferson, though, had his hands full—literally, in the case of Peckinpah and a gun, which he separated the drunk director from after Peckinpah fired into the ceiling. They experienced lighter moments, too. While Bob Dylan made his screen debut as "Alias," Coolidge bonded with Dylan's wife, Sara, and learned from her, almost by osmosis, how to handle the ego of a beloved public figure. When the Dylans were reintroduced to the former studio janitor from *Blonde on Blonde*, Sara told a story about living in Woodstock, New York, the year after that album's release. An unhinged fan broke into their modest, discreet village home and nearly collided with the mistress of the house. "Oh man," said the stoned fan, "are you, like, the 'Sad Eyed Lady'?" They all laughed at Sara's response: "No, I'm the woman who just called the cops. Get the fuck out." They bonded to the point that when Dylan went into the studio to cut the film's score, Kristofferson and Coolidge were invited to contribute the "oohs" and other background vocals to "Knockin' on Heaven's Door."

Kristofferson had been hanging around the Professional Club, a rowdier, more violent dive than his usual songwriter haunts. There, up-and-coming musicians took black beauties and yellow pills. Waylon Jennings claimed to have stayed awake there for nine consecutive days. Overdoing it landed Kristofferson in the hospital with a four-month bout of walking pneumonia, during which he grew a beard. The music press covered the beard as if it were a new LP, and unanimously panned it. Women swarmed him to caress it, though, much to the newly married man's consternation. Although Coolidge said her husband's philandering and drinking led to their eventual split, there were other major issues, including Kristofferson's touring schedule and film commitments, which kept him away from his family for months at a time. Regardless, the friction isn't audible on their seductive, well-balanced duo LPs. Kris's subdued yet gruff, higher-register readings of his more obscure songs and Rita's soothing, gentle, and dreamlike voice gave them the feel of a romance cover come to life—"a musical mismatch of beauty and the beast," as one biographer suggested. Another reason for the first LP's success, according to Kristofferson: they recorded it on the West Coast. "Sunset Sound in L.A.—different city, different producer," he said. Regarding collaborating with his wife, he added: "We worked well together at first, and it hadn't gotten to where we were fighting—yet."

With Coolidge pregnant and Kristofferson quipping that one "can't bring up children in motel rooms," the clan decamped for nearby

Malibu, where Casey was born in 1974, and which partly prompted Kristofferson's quarter-million-dollar tax bill that year. *A small price to pay for freedom*, Kristofferson admitted. Escaping Nashville allowed Kristofferson more creative control, and he wielded it, ironically, to make his most conservative album, his first with Rita and with cover songs, and his sweetest, most polished pop record yet. "From the Bottle to the Bottom," a duet on a 1969 Kristofferson demo, earned the now-married couple a Grammy win en route to nominations three years in a row. Kris Kristofferson was now a firmly established Nashville superstar, albeit with numerous compromises. One of these included the release of "Why Me,"* with its unlikely sing-along chorus of "Lord, help me, Jesus, I've wasted it / So, help me, Jesus, I know what I am," as another single from *Capricorn*. Despite his objections—he worried, quite correctly, as it turned out, that listeners would assume it was sacrilegious—"Why Me" made it to number sixteen on the pop charts and went gold. To earn full acceptance in Nashville, however, he still had to clean up his image and record with his charming, straight-edged wife. Would they keep a place for him if he left town for Hollywood?

At the Philharmonic, Kristofferson drove the hard-hitting backing band** through "Lovin' Her Was Easier," with its lines of twelve to sixteen syllables, more than double the standard country length, but a Top 30 pop hit, and new material like "Jesse Younger," a retread of "The Law Is for Protection of the People." Finally, the headliner took

* Titled "Why Me" on most labels, with "Why Me Lord" in parentheses.

** When Barbra Streisand later criticized their playing, Kristofferson said: "They ain't sidemen, that's my band."

a breath. "It'd have been a gas if I could've brought all my friends," he told the Manhattan crowd. One more *had* to be included, though. "There's a cat backstage," Kristofferson said. "He's one of the true heavies who sucked me into going to Nashville. Down there, they regard him as kind of a guru. He's probably one of the heaviest cats I've ever met and I've asked him to do a couple of numbers. His name's Willie Nelson."

Kris later said: "Willie was the idol of all the undiscovered songwriters who were serious about songwriting in Nashville, but by the time I met him, he had become disenchanted with Nashville, where they didn't really understand the kind of songs he had written."

From the polite applause for the opening line of "Funny How Time Slips Away"—"Well, hello there!"—to the explosive cheer that greeted the first chorus, Nelson galvanized the audience. It didn't hurt that he was playing his hits, which the New York crowd had probably never heard performed, at least not from the source. He had a beard, inspired by Kristofferson, and a sheepish grin, but otherwise, Nelson's superior singing capabilities and guitar picking drew stark contrasts to his host. But there was more to it. Though virtually unknown outside Texas, where his audiences stood dumbstruck instead of dancing, he came off like a national star, seamlessly transitioning between classics in a medley, plucking hard-charging, bluesy solos on "Trigger," his Scotch-taped guitar, bouncing melodies back and forth with drummer and sole accompanist Paul English, charming the audience with between-song banter and generally acting as if this *wasn't* a "big break." The 2,700 New Yorkers in the house yelped and hollered, spontaneously applauded at choice lyrics and tasty guitar solos, and clapped to the beat, at last acting like a Southern honky-tonk crowd they secretly wished to be. By the final drumroll in "Mountain Dew," with the audience on their feet, Willie had taken Manhattan.

"They didn't have a clue," says Kristofferson of the audience that night. "But it went over great."*

"Look at me, Ma!" Kris marveled as he retook the stage—*his* stage, supposedly. "Willie's playin' on my show."**

"When I came to Nashville," Kristofferson later recalled, "the people I hung out with were serious songwriters, none of whom were successful. Willie was the hero of the soulful set—the people who were in the business because they loved the soul of country music." Of Kristofferson's songs, Nelson said: "They are words to live by and that's about as much praise as you can say about any writer." Between the late sixties and early seventies, Nelson covered everyone from Kristofferson to Joni Mitchell without a hit under *anyone's* name. Career-wise, he was influenced by Ray Charles and Bob Dylan, both of whom, he later wrote, "had a strong sense of where they wanted to go artistically. Their inner confidence was greater than the outside influence of record moguls or best-selling producers." Disc jockeys loved the folkie Willie. Kris Kristofferson recalls hearing Nelson's music in the early '60s while hitchhiking in Europe, thanks to a DJ who hated the countrypolitan Nashville hits and often slipped in deep cuts.

"You have to understand the way Nashville worked," said songwriter Dave Hickey. "The 'talent' were basically slaves of the record company. They'd come off the road once every three months, go into

* Attendee Anita R. Lay remembers: "It was colder than blazes when we left Philharmonic Hall (in NYC the wind whips down those canyonlike streets and pierces to the bone), and we were so bowled over by the music and the ambiance.... Kris was incredibly generous with singing other people's songs."

** He then dedicated "The Pilgrim" to Nelson, improvised some advice to the guru at the end of its lyric, brought on his "better half, Rita Coolidge," and closed with a raucous "Bobby McGee." As Coolidge's honeyed voice soared above the clamor, Kristofferson, listening to the New Yorkers singing softly along, wanted to remind them: "There *is* a freedom to it but it's a two-edged sword."

the studio, get handed lyric sheets, sing to prerecorded songs, and then go back on the road." Now in his late thirties, Nelson no longer had the whippersnapper energy to battle that mentality and push for his self-penned originals. Then tragedy struck.

On December 22, 1969, he cowrote a song with Hank Cochran called "What Can You Do to Me Now?" The following evening, as he got bombed at a Christmas party, his Ridgetop farmhouse burned to the ground. When he learned of the blaze, he asked his nephew to put the car in neutral and push it into the garage for insurance reasons. Once on the scene, Nelson vaulted over fire hoses to rescue "Trigger," his Martin guitar, newly acquired, as well as a garbage bag stuffed with two bricks of "Colombian tea." "I wasn't being brave running in there to get my dope," Nelson admitted. "I was trying to keep the firemen from finding it and turning me over to the police." He called saving Trigger the smartest decision he ever made, especially after it developed a curious hole in the body that gave the instrument a vibrating twang. He had recently acquired it in Nashville after smashing his electric guitar, and his desperation to save it baffled his family.

After sifting through the rubble and finding only his 1961 Nashville demos, he didn't know if he wanted to rebuild or even stay in Tennessee. "The pigs had a great time," he said of his farm years, "but I didn't make any money at all." He took the opportunity to temporarily move the family to Bandera, a Texas town about two hours from Austin. By the time Willie and Shirley Nelson's dream home had been rebuilt, the man of the house had soured on living, commuting to, or even working in Nashville. Music Row didn't consider him an insider, one of their own, a true country artist. He would go where at least the offstage Willie Nelson persona seemed normal.

He announced his retirement from recording and left town, leaving the negotiating table just as RCA offered him a new deal, albeit on the same terms as before: no say-so in creative decisions. (Only someone of Ray Charles's stature and genius, it seemed, earned that power.) The offer, to Nelson, therefore held little appeal.

Something, too, was drawing him to humid, remote Bandera, where less than five thousand people resided. "Bandera had its own kind of beauty," Nelson says. "There were hills and creeks and rivulets and best of all, a golf course that called to me."* Besides, he wanted to retire not only from record making but from touring—with the Texas nightclubs packed in past fire code maximums to see him, why travel? Even better, moving from Tennessee made it easier to give up drinking. "Whiskey and Chesterfields were flat doing me in," Nelson admitted. "Pot slowed me down and made me more reflective. What could be better?"

Shirley, though, didn't have the same moment of clarity and couldn't understand Texas at all, let alone Bandera. *Why*, she wondered, *should they move there instead of at least Austin proper, city of a quarter-million and an almost halfway exciting culture? Maybe*, she thought, *Thomas Wolfe was right in saying "you can't go home again" and Willie just needed to find out that truism the hard way*. But then the *actual* truth came out: Nelson had a good reason to move to Texas, specifically.

Months after a trip to Houston for what Willie originally claimed was a minor procedure, young Lana Nelson opened a letter from the hospital and murmured. It was an invoice, but not for her father's stay. Shirley snatched up the paper and read that her husband owed money for "Paula Carlene," daughter of a "Mrs. Connie Nelson." Willie admitted the affair immediately, but that didn't seem to help. Shirley threw his things into the front yard, and then, when he tried to collect them, cornered him with a gun. With that, his marriage became irrevocably severed.

---

* Referring to Texans, Jessi Colter cracked: "They think the rest of the world is overseas."

Willie and Connie (soon to become the third Mrs. Nelson)* decamped to stay with sister Bobbie Nelson in Austin. Willie brushed off the crisis. With his cowboy mentality, he marveled that, in his new city, he could "stand downtown and look west across the river to the limestone cliffs that rise abruptly on the other shore . . . where the West literally begins." More importantly, Austin wasn't Nashville but "a scene where art and originality triumphed over corporate concerns." Rednecks, suits, young people who didn't know what they wanted—all hung out together at the same country venues. Nelson was dumbstruck by the sight of a long-haired cowboy in a nearby town, which he had never seen anywhere. Only a few American cities promoted "progressive country" on their radio stations. Austin was one.

Willie, though, alienated some of his Texas fanbase with a stunt involving Charley Pride. In the sixties, he had invited the sultry-voiced Pride to open for him on a statewide tour, but ran into issues immediately. Country Music Nights were restricted to white adults in Dallas, with the exception of Nigger Night, which was held on Tuesdays, which were usually dead. Nelson forced the two crowds together by bringing Pride to Dallas on a whites-only night. As Pride took the stage, Willie clambered up, too, and kissed him full on the mouth. The audience chortled. "If you think that people whose skin color is a different color from yours are beneath you, then you are particularly not my friend," he said. At Panther Hall in Fort Worth, the crowd seethed about Pride's presence until they heard him belt out "Crazy Arms." Then they, indeed, went crazy.

"At that point, you wouldn't have bet on Willie," said Texas singer-songwriter Kinky Friedman. Indeed, despite the New York

* They had met after a show, following the possibly apocryphal exchange between Nelson and steel guitarist Jimmy Day: "Anything I can get for you, boss?" "That tall blond over there."

triumph, Willie Nelson, approaching his fortieth birthday, felt he had nowhere to go but up. The Austin press gave him a sliver of hope. When word spread that the writer of "Crazy" and "The Party's Over" had arrived, reporters ignored signs of Nelson's downward slide and went nuts over him.

"This time, it seems, the prodigal son brought the fatted calf home with him," wrote *Texas Monthly*. "Willie Nelson has thus become a symbolic figure, the one man whose approach to life and music makes sense out of Austin's curious mix of freaks and rednecks, trepidation and ambition, naïveté and striving professionalism.... Where symbolic heroes move, cults often follow." The cult of Willie began in March 1972.

That month, twenty-four miles outside the state capital and more than seven miles from the main highway in the Hill Country, a gang of music aficionados and capitalistic neophytes staged a weekend-long music festival in the style of Woodstock, which it intended to mimic "for your short-hair, conservative types." (For a few more months, Willie Nelson would have neat hair and a clean shave.) The bill was stacked with bluegrass legends Bill Monroe and Earl Scruggs, and country superstars Dottie West, Roger Miller, Loretta Lynn, Waylon Jennings, Kris Kristofferson, and Nelson, who was involved in the planning. After his daughters Lana and Susie returned raving about the 1969 Atlanta Pop Festival, headlined by Janis Joplin and Joe Cocker, Willie mulled the idea of a country knockoff. His obscurity, though, was such that he wasn't listed on the program cover. The cover was about the only marketing the four promoters planned, instead plunging thousands of dollars into electrification, adding running water from a well, and building out private Hurlbut Ranch into a closed-off concert venue with no tree canopy but a sturdy stage. The overhead led to staggering cost overruns, while the nonexistent marketing budget kept turnout under a thousand on the first day. Promoters expected to earn back their $250,000 overall stake on sixty thousand magically generated tickets—per *day*. Instead, upon learning Hays was a dry county, most people got drunk and stayed in Austin. Those who showed were college kids for whom even a case of unwanted Lone Star beer cost too much in comparison with a shared joint. Pot smoking and streaking were rampant, and the dozens of off-duty police officers hired as security arrested lawbreakers by lassoing them from horses. A contractor, witnessing one such scene, quipped: "They probably didn't have that at Woodstock."

"The audience was as twisted as we were," said Jennings, "all day and all night drinking hot beer."

Tensions developed, too, between the Nashville Old Guard and the local hippie acts like Nelson, who were inclined to smoke a joint and strip down themselves. Up at the main house, beer and barbecue served as peace pipes, with Willie trying to unite "the so-called rednecks and the blacks" over two sacred Texas traditions. Meanwhile, onstage, Tex Ritter seized the microphone and grumbled: "Maybe if some of these stagehands would get haircuts, they could see the equipment and move it better." But it was too late for that. Nelson had inspired "hippies and rednecks to realize they weren't all that different from each other," said Kinky Friedman. "The next thing we knew, the rednecks had grown their hair out, the hippies were wearing boots, and you couldn't tell them apart anymore." Kris Kristofferson's keyboardist, Donnie Fritts, gazing into the horizon, saw only the Woodstock of progressive country. "You'd look out there and it'd be hillbillies, cowboy guys, and then you have the hippies, all having fun together.... It was one of the most important gatherings of the seventies...and it happened through Willie Nelson."

Despite "high praise" for the performances from attendees, who numbered seventeen thousand over the following days, plans to repeat the Dripping Springs Reunion annually were scrapped. After the festival, Jessi, Waylon, and Willie broke down on the side of the road. Locals waved but no one stopped to offer them a lift, which Waylon assumed meant they didn't want stinky hippies in their cars, a metaphor for their feelings on the festival. Nelson was unfazed. Over the next year, as he tiptoed back into live performance, Willie remembered the warm reception he received. Why not put another picnic together in '73, this time as a showcase for himself? When Nelson was approached about a second festival, he responded: "You mean if the same people was runnin' it, or somebody else was?"

"The Reunion helped spark the rise of progressive country music and recognition of Austin as a music hub," said Nelson biographer Joe Nick Patoski. "Without it, Willie might have gone back to Nashville... and the great migration of musical talent from around the state, nation and world to Austin would have never happened."

George Jones said that most music fans considered Music Row artists hopelessly lowbrow, with their "three-chord songs that were played on tiny AM stations scattered mostly across the rural South," but where else did country listeners have to go? While Castle Creek and budding venue Armadillo World Headquarters regularly hosted hot country singer-songwriters, those were uniquely Austin and most artists lived elsewhere. Willie Nelson not only called the city home in the early seventies, he brought with him an even more electrifying sound—and not just because he had a band of electric players. With them came a change in his appearance. After the Dripping Springs Reunion, Willie grew out his hair. "I never did like putting on stage costumes, never did like trim haircuts, never did like worrying about whether I was satisfying the requirements of a showman," he said. "It felt good to let my hair grow. Felt good to get on stage in the same jeans I'd been wearing all damn day."

In the Armadillo, the high school clichés of football players in slacks and arty kids in ratty T-shirts played out in the real world, "with the war in Vietnam drawing a line that felt like a moat," one reporter noted. It helped that 1972's number one pop album and its chart-topping lead single were country records made in Nashville by hippie Neil Young. However, Willie struggled to connect with "what was happening"—pop music purchased by millions of youngins.

"I can't get the youth market to listen to my old country music because they think it's what their mothers and fathers are doing. They want to discover their own deal, something rebellious, personal." He had grown up in saloons and now would headline them, he decided. In the early Austin days, Nelson played a car dealership sales event on Sixth Street; then, on August 12, 1972, the day the last American troops were evacuated from Vietnam, he headlined a gig at the hippest place in Texas. Two DJs, one in Fort Worth and the other the first woman to spin country records in Pennsylvania, were superfans, helping spread the gospel of Willie to anyone with a high-powered radio; and in Austin, a legendary football coach told everyone he could find that their attendance was expected at his friend's 'Dillo debut. Willie took the stage that night thinking of the record execs he'd flipped off on his way out. "In Nashville, I was taking advice from the experts—they were telling me what to do," he said without bitterness. "It wasn't that they were wrong, it's just that it was wrong for me. Someone said one time that a leader is a guy who sees a lot of people going in one direction and then jumps out in front of them."

The Armadillo World Headquarters was tucked behind the Skating Palace in a brick building that formerly held the National Guard armory. It had been refashioned into a cavernous concert hall and beer garden, with a half-carpeted, half-concrete floor serving as the bulk of the fifteen hundred "seats," and which had been stained with cigarette and marijuana smoke from the moment the club opened almost two years to the day earlier. The air was worsened by the absence of A/C or any air circulation in the Texas summer—as Arlo Guthrie put it: "Awful acoustics but great place to play!" The neighborhood wasn't ready for the 'Dillo, either. One music obsessive began leaving early to make the last bus to the countryside because of skull-cracking rednecks patrolling the area, while two musicians playing western swing were arrested and had their heads forcibly shaved by police. Despite the hostility and thanks to decent advance sales, the concert became a financial success, and Willie would have been invited back regardless of his reception. Nonetheless, he "went to that audience, to get the energy from those young people," country fans who in turn found the "edge" they long craved.

"The guys who made the records in Nashville were people like Owen Bradley," recalled an assistant vice president who knew him, and Bradley spent his time "mostly telling people what to play," as Waylon put it. He was an astonishing pianist who would pull aside his players and whisper: "Norbert, on bar seventeen, the third beat, you play the fifth beat there, but I need you to stay on the time in the first and third beat. It'll work better for the melody" for the female vocalist. Norbert Putnam recalls that Bradley "had an orchestra that played high school proms on the weekend, but during the week they played on Webb Pierce and Brenda Lee records. They had a round sound, no edge. In Texas you'd hear people like Billy Joe Shaver. They had an edge."

Not everyone was convinced of Nelson's edginess, though. In a review of the R. Crumb–inspired Armadillo show bill, one *Austin American-Statesman* critic wrote: "Ole down-home, country boy Willie Nelson on a psychedelic poster? Sure 'nuff!"

Nelson played his greatest hits—for others—including "Funny How Time Slips Away," which Elvis had been doing on tour, and "Hello Walls." To make sure they were properly received, he introduced a medley: "Here's one my friend Faron recorded. Kept my alimony paid for a few months." The liquor guzzlers—shots of booze were available in Texas for the first time that year—pot smokers, and wigged-out acid droppers alike were astonished to find that many of their favorite tunes of the past decade had all been crafted by one man, a local, to boot. They marveled at the hillbilly band playing these sophisticated songs, too, including twenty-year-old harmonica player Michael "Mickey" Raphael, who had honed his technique after studying at the feet of Waylon's mouth harpist. But even the eager, still-evolving Raphael, who has played with Nelson almost every night ever since, took a while to adjust to this radical "country" picker and his oddball tunes.

"He's kind of a benevolent dictator," Raphael noted. "He doesn't really tell anybody what to do, but he gives you enough rope to hang yourself. And that's a lot of rope. His idea is just to have people he's comfortable with around him and to make music. We're just winging it. . . . He doesn't play the songs the same every night." Nelson's "phrasing could lead a band up a creek and drown you," moaned bassist Bee Spears.* "He goes where he goes," said Raphael. "Our task is to follow him." The band also included sister Bobbie on piano; drummer/treasurer Paul English, a former collections agent, burglar, and proud member of Fort Worth's "10 Most Unwanted List"; guitarist Jody Payne; and steel guitarist Jimmy Day. Most of them started taking cocaine around this time and the tempo accelerated

---

* Spears, who brought a jazz style to country bass playing when he joined at age eighteen, often flung himself around stages in a Peter Pan harness. When learning Raphael wasn't charging them for these gigs, Nelson told English to "double his salary!"

accordingly. That made even Willie grouse about the beat, which was saying something.

Throughout, Nelson plucked guitar strings with ragtime jazz fervor and sung as if each line was a spaceless word and the band was contractually obligated to fit twenty songs into as many minutes. The radical, often up-tempo reworkings and blended medleys of Nelson's most recognizable material kept the players at full throttle and the audience hooting and hollering with excitement. Even Bobbie Nelson, who had been playing with her brother practically since birth, struggled to hear herself well enough to keep up, and started "hitting those keys with greater force [to let] those guys know I was here and had something to say. When I did so, Willie looked back at me and smiled." To her delight, Willie began to work in swing and jazz chords, having held them back at the insistence of producers. "We were just playing the same music we'd played since forever," Bobbie said. "It was just a different audience." Whoever they were, they were hooked. "He looked out in that crowd—most of them were hippies," one reporter wrote, "and you could see the realization in his eyes: This is my new audience."

The Armadillo show kicked off a new era in Austin's musical story, and for Nelson's. He developed a following "that didn't look like or care about any Nashville ideal," said *Texas Monthly*, and, in fact, preferred their musicians to look like drinking buddies. As one booker told the crowd: "I don't know how long this can last, but I'm with you as long as it does."

Now with a bigger platform, Nelson took over the Hurlbut picnic tradition and moved it to Independence Day weekend. Backed by a proclamation from the governor declaring the anniversary of the United States "Willie Nelson Day," and despite drawing tens of thousands in each of the next three years, the July 4th events were largely considered disasters. In 1973, Leon Russell promised Nelson that if "you bring the rednecks... I'll bring the hippies," which led to rumors that Russell, Dylan, and other national stars would perform surprise sets, and an attendant sales bump; however, a lack of toilets and the long walk from parking sites in blinding sunlight turned the area into an "open sewer" and sunstroke hellscape. Early on, Willie's mother grabbed a microphone and grumbled: "Willie, you need a haircut," and, as if responding to her directly, the sheriff allegedly ordered all the hippies to leave and tried to get passersby to sign an agreement that if they trespassed off venue property, they could be shot. Fights onstage between "long hairs and goat ropers," or local hippies and experienced, bussed-in stage personnel, led one columnist to lament "the industry's major pollutant: carpetbaggers," and following a lighting failure that plunged the area into blackness as Kris Kristofferson hit the stage, organizers expressed firm opposition to hosting a third picnic. The 1974 event, booked at the Texas World Speedway to accommodate crowds, led to an investigation over "moral pollution" caused by public nudity, sex, urination, and defecation on adjacent private property. Paul English got married onstage in a reddish-pink satin-lined black Dracula cape and cowboy hat. Only one person lost money: Willie Nelson. In 1975, with the Pointer Sisters and Rita Coolidge opening, the festival started only ten minutes late; as Willie arrived under police escort and took the stage in a Rolling Stones T-shirt, he was jumped by a naked hippie girl cheered on by ninety-five thousand souls. That turnout got Nelson fined for violating the state's Mass Gatherings Act meant to stop festivals. "It may not be everybody in the world," joked the local paper, "but it sure looks like it if you're trying to find a place to park."

Motivated rather than deterred, Nelson scheduled a Fourth of July Picnic for America's bicentennial. That year, attendance spiraled out of control, topping out near the 150,000 mark, although the event was cut short due to equipment damage from a rainstorm. When cleanup concluded, the body of a drowned worker was discovered. As Willie raced to catch a plane for Hawaii, the police announced 140 arrests, including four attempted kidnappings, three knifings, and three sexual assaults. The 1977 and 1978 fests would both be held out of state entirely.

Nonetheless, several musicians were reborn at the events. "I remember it quite clearly," says singer-songwriter John Sebastian of the '75 extravaganza. "I hadn't had Willie's weed. That was sort of my intro to finding out, holy shit, this is a whole musical *community*. Everybody knows every song, people can sing background harmonies at the drop of a hat, and it would be better than anything you'd hear on the east coast."

"Willie was our Beatles and our Stones," one player marveled. At the picnics, "the hippies and rednecks finally found a way to come together and tolerate one another long enough to create one big festival-attending supertribe, and Willie Nelson was the chief, alpha and omega who started it all."

"We hot, ain't we?" Willie asked Waylon Jennings rhetorically, gazing out on the crowd. Now, with a flock of his own, the preacher man inside Willie Nelson turned his powerful sights on a new town to conquer: Nashville, Tennessee.

Nelson changed his mind about touring after the 'Dillo show, and hooked up with Miles Davis's manager Neil Reshen.* Reshen told Willie he would handle everything with RCA, but Willie didn't want to go back to his longtime label or, really, any label. He stubbornly

* Nelson and the jazz trumpeter became so friendly that, in 1970, Davis made six attempts at a meditative instrumental named after the country musician. Davis "appreciated [Willie's] genius," said manager Mark Rothbaum.

stuck to his position for a few months, and then Jerry Wexler came across his path.

The legendary indie record producer, who launched Ray Charles and Aretha Franklin, visited Music City during the 1972 CMAs, and swung by a Christmas party at songwriter Harlan Howard's place. Wexler, a Jewish New Yawka who cleaned windows and grew up worshiping Harlem jazz vocalists during the Depression, did not seem like the obvious savior of country music. But he was personally responsible for country's mainstream ascent, having brought Hank Williams's "Cold, Cold Heart" to Tony Bennett. He was a self-described "cosmic fuck-up" with the right attitude—as one professor told his mother, "something in him rebels"—and smoking a joint had changed his life. He thus seemed ideal from Nelson's perspective. Plus, the gray-bearded senior citizen had coined the term *rhythm and blues* and helped Black artists break the pop radio color barrier—"they could segregate everything else," he famously said, "but they couldn't segregate the radio dial." If he could revolutionize R&B, why not Nashville?

After Wexler and his pair of business partners sold Atlantic Records to Warner Brothers, they became record company employees. As an executive and producer but with someone else ultimately in charge, Wexler slid. In the early seventies, he had only one gold-seller, *Donny Hathaway Live*, and a slew of critical and commercial stinkers. Crucially, though, he retained the power to sign artists of his choosing.

At Harlan Howard's, the label-less, semiretired Nelson realized an Atlantic producer and VP sat in the living room, but he started a guitar pull mainly to show his fellow songwriters he still had the fire. He didn't play radio-friendly, glossy-pop material for the congregation; he launched into "Bloody Mary Morning"—originally a 1970 A-side castigating himself for neglecting the children he already had before creating more—now recalibrated to match his other selection, "Phases and Stages," which cast blame on both sides for a marriage cracking. The latter mostly consisted of a three-line verse that repeated itself as a kind of theme for several other songs to use as their refrain, including laments from both the wife and husband characters. "He got on the stool late at night when the party had thinned out," recalled Wexler, "and he sang like a total album with a gut string and a stool."

"I've been looking for you a long time," Wexler said breathlessly, his hand out as Nelson put down his guitar.

Nelson practically sniffed at him. "You're not worried that it's not commercial?" he asked.

"Fuck commerce," said Wexler. "You're going for art. You're going for truth. When the art is truthful, sales will follow."

Howard said: "I witnessed what I would later recognize as Wexler teaching Willie that he could control his own musical destiny."

Nelson had been hoping for such an exchange with a music bigwig his whole career. He had mainly dealt with "the kind of music executives who make creative decisions for artists they're paying to make their own creative decisions." He thought he had been a profitable signing for his previous labels, only to end up humiliated after repeat dismissals. The only problem: no one wanted a "concept album," least of all Willie Nelson, who knew nothing like it had succeeded in Nashville, unless one counted the Johnny Cash prison albums. Nonetheless, the producer-executive intrigued Nelson. "I'd never heard a record man talk that way," he would write. "On the spot, I decided that Wexler was my man.

"While Nashville saw my phrasing as offbeat, Jerry saw it as being right on. He compared me to Sinatra, who was, in fact the singer who taught me that you can play with the beat. You can adjust your phrasing any way that suits your style. You can bring the song to you rather than strain to make it sound 'correct.'"

At the time, Willie Nelson was, according to one Austinite, "a geeky-looking guy without much of a chin and with a bad haircut, profoundly ill-at-ease with being photographed from the looks of things."

"I bought jeans and a cowboy hat, while he grew out his hair," said Bobbie Nelson.*

He had been wearing a Nehru jacket or turtleneck in most publicity photos, but under Kristofferson's and Wexler's hip eyes, Nelson grew a creamsicle-colored beard, had wife Connie pierce his ear, and took to wearing dark sunglasses indoors.

After Wexler offered him greater input in song selection, record titles, promotion, and, crucially, it would turn out, band selection—but not the final say—he agreed to sign with Atlantic. Jerry had broken ground by letting Ray Charles use his own band, and Willie, still queasy at the thought of returning to Nashville, came to an unusual agreement: they would bring Nelson's band to New York for a concept album.

His previous attempt at such a record—a cohesive suite spinning a narrative across both sides of an LP—had resulted in 1971's *Yesterday's Wine*, and its commercial misfortunes were among the main reasons he temporarily quit record making. The opening track alluded to Jesus Christ as the perfect "Man," who "rejected the establishment completely," setting the tone for the spiritual, philosophical life story of a religious man. Critics and listeners mistakenly assumed Nelson was comparing himself to Jesus, but he explained: "I was put here to show how imperfect a guy could be."

"Who's going to play this?" one exec asked him.

Nelson answered that he imagined AM radio would just spin the whole thing to let listeners hear the complete story.

---

* When a drunk acquaintance insisted on playing the famed Martin guitar and wouldn't gently hand it over, Nelson threw him against the wall. So much for his new hippie attitude.

Another RCA executive grumbled: "This is some far-out hippie shit."

"It's my most honest album to date," said Willie.

"It's your worst fucking *album* to date."

It didn't help that the songs were subtle, slow, and quiet, their melodies somewhat buried, and the tracks seemingly strung together at random, and ultimately it felt conceptually thin.* Willie blamed the record industry for not knowing how to promote it: "Nashville and I had been trying damn hard but we hadn't really seen eye to eye for most of the sixties," he suggested. "I'd given the Music City establishment a fair chance. After *Yesterday's Wine*, I cut other albums for RCA, but the story was always the same. The sales were slow and the producers lukewarm about my output."

RCA didn't fight Nelson's departure. "We couldn't record him as a hit artist here in Nashville," said Harold Bradley. Manager Neil Reshen, after repaying RCA $1,400 to resolve debts the label claimed Nelson owed, approved the Atlantic contract, making his client one of the first two artists on the company's country roster. As with previous "big breaks," Nelson immediately gambled on a total change in direction: this time, it would be toward gospel music.

Nelson recalled Larry Gatlin's guest spot from the show three months earlier at the nearby Philharmonic and brought him in for his supplemental acoustic guitar. He also added guitarist Doug Sahm, already under the jurisdiction of Jerry Wexler, Waylon Jennings, and more guitarists and fiddlers, and Sammi Smith showed up in jeans stamped with a CAUTION: BUDWEISER-POWERED! patch to anchor the "choir." *The Troublemaker* band reached a robust Sunday church

* "It was depressing as hell," said one West Coast reviewer of an early '70s effort, "but the unusual melodies cushioning his equally strange chord progressions were haunting, as were the doom-laden lyrics."

fever. Willie Nelson & the Family, as they came to be known, featured "Paul's light touch, Bee Spears's mystical bass lines that followed a rhythm pattern only he and Willie could decipher, and Mickey Raphael's distinctive harmonica wail," as one listener rhapsodized. Nelson sounded like he had a "sawmill stuck in the back of his throat," said *Creem*, but with locked-in musicians, carefully chosen, less preachy gospel sing-alongs like "Will the Circle Be Unbroken," and the passion and excitement that come from knocking out a dozen songs in two back-to-back sessions, Atlantic stood at the ready to launch its country division into the stratosphere.

Then they shelved *The Troublemaker*.

The reasons were myriad. A gospel album . . . from a nobody? Old, traditional spirituals instead of one chockablock with radio-ready love or drinking songs (or both)? The modern-day Jesus parable title track (in a way, the original "Jesus Was a Capricorn") or a tune from 1879 as the only possible singles? Atlantic remained mum on its rationale, even after the album emerged three years later on another label.

Nelson, used to constant disappointments and setbacks in Nashville, grinned sheepishly. He still had three days scheduled in New York, and "I damn sure better cut a hit," he muttered. To better position him for commercial success, the music shifted toward a Wexler-worthy funk that had never been heard on a country release. It didn't hurt that the studio permitted marijuana smoking and the trucking in of dozens of cases of Heineken. (Nelson wasn't partaking in the latter, ironically having quit drinking about the time he recorded "Whiskey River," soon to become his set opener and signature tune.) Riled up, the band cut "Devil in a Sleeping Bag," which references the Philharmonic show with Kris and Rita, and includes an expletive: "Travelin' on the road is a fuckin' drag!" However, Arif Mardin, the album's credited producer, later suggested overdubbing a revised lyric—"such a drag"—and Nelson complied.

He'd learned "A Song for You" from its composer, Leon Russell, at a guitar pull, and was reminded of it by Wexler and Mardin, who had propelled the song onto the charts with Donny Hathaway's version. Its powerful lyrics were Russell's way of paying tribute to his muse, Rita Coolidge, while also confessing that, although he was a voracious live performer, it was just an act and obscured his true, romantic, introverted self. Nelson's sparse, spine-tingling version, with only Trigger on accompaniment, closed *Shotgun Willie*, foreshadowing his next phase, and sealed the record as his strongest yet.

Closing with a solo acoustic number didn't hurt *Shotgun*, as Wexler and company had generally fostered a lively session, including Bobbie Nelson taking her first flight to play piano, as well as several tracks with a horn section and backing vocalists. Perhaps doubting his abilities to get this new (or any) style of country music down cold, Wexler smartly deferred to Mardin and coproducer David Briggs, a gruff and at times even caustic bully, available only because he was on the outs with Neil Young, who recorded his blockbuster *Harvest* with someone else at Norbert Putnam's studio.* Despite their diverse backgrounds and tastes, all three producers recognized the quality of the self-penned material right off the bat, particularly when Willie brought in a tune that might've put off listeners if they'd known its true meaning.

On day three, Nelson had pulled out a Holiday Inn envelope and started plucking out "Shotgun Willie," a nickname he received following a disturbing incident involving his daughter Lana. She had recently married an older man, Steve Warren, and it was not going well. When little sister Susie told their father she'd seen Lana with two black eyes and facial bruises, Willie hopped in his pickup truck and sped to the other side of town. He burst in through Lana and Steve's

* Briggs had been in charge during Young's sublime rendition of country artist Don Gibson's "Oh, Lonesome Me," and Wexler may have had it in mind for *Shotgun Willie.*

door, and there he found his own wife cooking with Steve's mom. As the two women whisked Willie's grandson out of the fray and back to Ridgetop, Willie slapped his son-in-law senseless and threatened to drown him. "Don't hit me, Willie," Steve pleaded. "I got anxiety."

Soon after returning home, however, Nelson was putting his truck in the barn when he heard a vehicle rumbling up the road. Almost immediately, .22-caliber rifle shots rang out. A bullet thumped into the barn roof inches above his head. He reached into the truck and grabbed his M-1, whirled, and returned volleys with the rifle chest-high. Steve peeled off, but it didn't end there.* "I drove straight back to Lana and Steve's," Nelson claimed. "Steve had come home and... left again. He told Lana he was going to get rid of me as his top priority."

Nelson returned once more to his farm, this time grabbing a shotgun to supplement the M-1 or make it appear as though two guns were going and Steve was outnumbered. He parked in the garage, raised the door, and tucked down in the bed of the pickup so he wouldn't be visible from the street. When Steve's truck puttered by again, Nelson leapt from his vehicle and raced down the driveway. Seeing Willie, his son-in-law gunned it and left without firing a shot—but Nelson didn't hold back. He chased the truck, firing shotgun blasts. One burst blew out a tire. Luckily, no one was injured, and the police declined to press charges. Interrogated about the tire, Nelson deadpanned: "He must've run over the bullet."

Although the song vaguely detailing the incident became a bunch of "mind farts," as Kristofferson termed it, Nelson realized it helped him make an overdue directional shift. "I thought of it

---

* Martha Nelson, panicked by the shots, escaped from the family home with Steve's mother and hightailed it *back* to Steve and Lana's, but after angrily shouting "fuck Steve" en route, the two women got into a fistfight inside the vehicle.

more as clearing my throat," he said. If nothing else, Willie got a nickname that stuck and, after Wexler chose it, an album title. After Donny Hathaway added strings, Nelson and Wexler eagerly spun the acetate of *Shotgun Willie* for Atlantic Nashville GM Rick Sanjek. After a year of operations, the country division finally had its first LP. Sanjek hopped out of his chair, breathlessly intoning that he hadn't heard anything like it since Elvis. "These songs were *real*, by God!" he exclaimed.

The reviews were generally ecstatic. *Texas Monthly* noticed Nelson "switched his arrangements from Ray Price to Ray Charles—the result: a revitalized music. He's the same old Willie, but veteran producer Jerry Wexler finally captured on wax the energy Nelson projects in person." Way out in Arizona, the *Republic* rejoiced: "It's time to put the kibosh on the nasal twang affection-recoil and... lend old *Shotgun* an ear and find out what C&W music sounds like when it's not sung through the nose—or hat." *Rolling Stone* referred to the album as "flawless" and expected Nelson to finally hit the big time. It was part of the "changing of the guard" in country, as a local DJ would marvel.* Record buyers saw these plaudits and were intrigued enough to help *Shotgun* outsell all Nelson's Nashville LPs combined, which didn't mean much to the bookkeepers.

With the—slight—improvement in sales, Nelson reminded Wexler of the *Phases and Stages* idea. Side one would tell the story of "the woman," a stand-in for ex-wife Shirley, while side two contained the answer songs from a male narrator, a.k.a. the songwriter himself. After sending everyone, including Bobbie, back to Texas, Wexler and Nelson decamped for, of all places, Sheffield, Alabama—"I'd always thought the meat in the sandwich in America is between the

* The more critical remarks, including from one Nelson biographer, noted that the "slips and flubs... stayed in."

two coasts," Wexler wrote—to get that New York sheen off their skin. Atlantic tried to stop them.

"Muscle Shoals is too R&B for Willie," grumbled one of the company's execs.

Jerry Wexler shot back: "Willie is too R&B for Nashville."

"How does it feel to have broken the Atlantic Studio's record for number of cuts finished in a week?" Mardin asked at the end of the *Shotgun-Troublemaker* session. It felt pretty good, Nelson admitted, but he would be more contented in Muscle Shoals. "I was able to sharpen the edges" of those sloppy songs, he said. "Wexler was right. That studio brought out the blues in me, big time."*

But the Atlantic executive was also right. The Muscle Shoals Rhythm Section, which expanded to include twelve-string, pedal steel, fiddle, and dobro players, may have had an anti-corporate mentality that allowed artists to get outside their comfort zones, but they were furious at Nelson's freestyle vocals. One even got up to scold Nelson to his face for going off the beat.

Wexler later defended Nelson's vocals. "The three masters of rubato [phrasing] in our age are Frank Sinatra, Ray Charles and Willie Nelson," he said. "The art of gliding over the meter and extending it until you think they're going to miss the next actual musical demarcation—but they always arrive there, at bar one. It's some kind of musical miracle." Yet Wexler caved, booking rerecording sessions in Tennessee, this time with the Family. Ironically, Atlantic chose the original takes for release. They were more refined, while the Nashville

* Wexler hadn't told Nelson & the Family that the Shoals was a dry county, but luckily, the State Line Gang ran beer from the nearest liquor store.

version was full of warmth and otherworldly intimacy, said Marshall Chapman, who sang backup on the latter.

Despite having completed three concept albums, counting *Troublemaker*, Nelson still had the bug. He claimed that after the success of the Beatles' *Sgt. Pepper* he and everyone else in the biz started to think about whether they were talented enough to pull off such records. The concept (of concept albums) appealed to him as an artist long pressured by Nashville to produce singles, but who needed a different challenge to remain inspired after several decades. He rose to the occasion, producing stunningly evocative, deep lyrics. Quite simply, *Phases and Stages*, released in 1974, helped birth a new form of country music. Conceptual, mature, unconcerned with commercial success, and capitalizing on the popularity of introspective pop albums, especially records by Joni Mitchell, Cat Stevens, Marvin Gaye, and James Taylor. Younger music fans, open to twangy vocals and battered acoustic guitars after the overkill of the psychedelic sixties, became obsessed, too, with deciphering lyrics: "Is that the same guy who had short hair and a suit on my grandparents' records?" wondered one future musician, baffled by the red-bearded hippie on the newer album covers. While most assumed each and every song had an autobiographical component, even the "wife's" songs, "the overall theme was not a reflection of my own life," Nelson said. "I was simply making up a story. Sure, I'd gone through breakups and heartaches of my own. What human soul hasn't?"

Rolling Stone marveled at Nelson's ambition presumably so late in his career. "Ordinarily, concept albums strike me as pretentious bores (someone will call this one 'the *Sgt. Pepper* of C&W,' 'the shitkicker's *Tommy*'), but I find *Phases and Stages* extraordinarily convincing. The oft-married Nelson has obviously seen his share of redeyed [*sic*] dawns." It was a "Bloody Mary Morning" indeed. "'I Still Can't Believe You're Gone' (which must be the single from the album) is without doubt the saddest, most compelling C&W song I've ever heard. The sadness of the lyrics is echoed in Nelson's voice, which is as bare and desolate as the monochromatic West Texas plains."* Asked why he had written countless sad songs and waltzes, Nelson replied: "I guess you might say I'd had thirty negative years."

The critics and fans were especially captivated by side one, with a fully realized, clearly rendered wife character and her memorable first-person perspective: "Sister's comin' home / Momma's gonna let her sleep the whole day long / Mirror's gonna tell her / Just how long she's been gone." AllMusic called "Pretend I Never Happened" icy enough with its title alone, "perhaps the coldest ending to a relationship ever written."

Despite the occasionally depressing lyrics, there were up-tempo numbers, and the public noticed those first and foremost. "Bloody Mary Morning" rose to number 17 on the country charts. The album, however, only made it to the thirty-fourth spot. Nelson didn't care. He went to Wexler with plans for the follow-up, an even sparser concept album with no commercial material at all. But Atlantic stunned them both. They called Jerry Wexler into a meeting with his old partners, Ahmet and Nesuhi Ertegun, now also executive-level employees, and delivered the news that the country division was being eliminated.

"You're shutting it down?" exclaimed Wexler. "We've barely put anything out!"

"Yeah, and it's done barely anything, sales-wise, either," an executive pointed out.

"But we have Willie Nelson!"

"Willie who?" one said. "Shut it down."

---

* Nelson had written it in tribute to drummer Paul English's wife, who had committed suicide in 1972. In despair, English lost dozens of pounds and had to be temporarily supplemented by a second drummer while he regained his focus.

Nelson didn't take it as hard as Wexler expected. "If you forgive your enemies, it messes up their heads," he wrote. "I never met a pig or a record executive worth holding a grudge over anyway." Moreover, he wasn't surprised, or all that disappointed. He'd already turned away from western swing and into a new zone: neither hillbilly nor countrypolitan hipster, now somewhere between hippie rocker and bluegrass cowboy. And with his next album, *Red Headed Stranger*, he wouldn't put his music in any discernible category, either. Now, if only he could get someone to listen to it. But for that, he would need a peer more successful than he, an artist with street cred, a record deal, and chart hits. For some crazy reason, his first call was to Waylon Jennings.

CHAPTER FIVE

ARE YOU SURE HANK DONE IT THIS WAY?

You lose all identity when you put a bunch of labels on something.

It's a great compliment when they drop the labels off of you.

—Waylon Jennings

Honky-tonk patron: "Who the hell do you think you are? You're just a kid. You don't know nothin'."
Waylon: "Sir, I may be younger than you, but I've been awake a long, long time."

They're not doing enough for Waylon. They just don't know what to do with him!

—A fan

The headliner at the Native American reservation bar couldn't get up onstage. He sat hunched over near the stairs, head hung and dampened hair dangling over his forehead, angrily waving off the chanting.

"He resembled a biker chieftain," wrote journalist Chet Flippo, "shiny black leather pants and vest, black needle-toed boots; beard, mustache and long dusty brown hair slicked straight back over his ears and flowing across the collar of his yellow shirt. His face—all angles—looked hard but his eyes were almost vulnerably gentle. They were always moving, questioning, evaluating, measuring." Other critics were not as impressed: "The long, greasy hair could use a shampoo," one wrote. But most fans cared only about his voice, all "honey and molasses on a biscuit, topped off with a pack of Marlboro Reds."

The crowd alternated between aggressively cheering or heckling the singer for being a "bum," saying they had paid their four dollars and they'd damn well better get it. But Waylon Jennings, thirty-five, didn't believe in canceling shows. THIS IS NO DRESS REHEARSAL read a sticker he slapped on his road case. WE ARE PROFESSIONALS, AND THIS IS THE BIG TIME. Nonetheless, "the Chief" told the Waylors, his band, he was "sick and battered," and they, not knowing what else to do, snickered nervously.

Jessi Colter, his wife and fourth within a single decade, met him stage right and, peering up into his face to kiss him, found it had developed a yellowish hue. She hesitated, then laughed at herself, thinking it was just a trick of the light hitting the golden fabrics of Waylon's button-down. But Jennings couldn't stand up straight, almost as if he'd thrown his back out playing honky-tonk songs on guitar. Something else was bothering him. Along Route 491 in Colorado that afternoon, he stopped near the New Mexico state line to meet the priest who booked him on the Southern Ute Reservation. The priest warned him of a hepatitis outbreak on the rez, so Waylon stuck to what he thought were safe bets: milk and pie.

After "ten years on the road / making one-night stands / speeding my young life away," as a song would later put it, his illness could have been brought on by any number of things. Jessi suspected botched dental surgery was to blame. It might have been the narcotics he'd been gobbling, or perhaps his touring regimen of three hundred shows per year for so little money; he often returned with less cash than he'd started with, and debts. Oh, the debts. The Waylors would have to be paid first, although he was doing them a favor at this point, using them as his touring band when Nashville wouldn't even allow him to record with them. His choice would've been to flip the bird at Music City and use them in the studio, too, but RCA executives were emphatic. Like all Nashville label heads, they required seasoned studio pros to handle the delicate business of cranking out easily digestible singles, considering live bands too loose and untrained. It was another reason Waylon was thinking of getting out of the music business when his contract expired at the end of 1972. "How many years can I keep bangin' around the honky-tonks?" Jennings asked rhetorically.

"Baby, you look real yellow," said Jessi, touching his arm soothingly.

"Nah," he said tersely. "It's the reflection of this shirt."

Jessi insisted he return to the hotel, and Waylon was on the verge of arguing—"Bullshit, I ain't going"—when his six-foot frame toppled over. The nasty fall was cushioned by his wife, standing five foot four.

From the day the music died to that night near Gallup, New Mexico, Waylon Jennings had been living three or four lives at once. The hardest of these was the one that had taken over in the mid-sixties, when he was only twenty-six. Jennings moved to Nashville and into the $150-a-month Madison Apartments, a bug-ridden hotel ten miles from Music City already inhabited by methamphetamine addict Johnny Cash. Together, they turned the place into a full-time drug den.

Later, both men would marvel that they managed to last even a month in such conditions. There they were, blowing up balls of black gunpowder with sticks of dynamite for amusement, kicking down the door when one of them, home alone, latched it shut and passed out, and using amphetamine, an upper producing an effect equivalent to a half-dozen cups of coffee, all while trying to write songs and get some money in the bank. They alternately complained about their respective loves and claimed a reunion was just around the corner, with Cash later admitting: "The only woman who would talk to me is Betty Ford." Their lovers—Barbara, Jennings's third wife, and June Carter, Cash's girlfriend—moved into separate apartments downstairs and tried to keep the men's place tidy. They were essential. "Man, you're the worst housekeeper I ever saw," Jennings had told Cash on move-in day. "What have you been doing in the kitchen, fighting?"

"I cooked biscuits and gravy."

"Do me a favor," said Jennings, "and don't ever cook me any."

Carter would show up periodically to do the dusting and mopping the place needed practically at the top of every hour. Mysteriously, Cash's amphetamines always managed to spill into the toilet. Once, while enjoying a visit from Bob Dylan, Cash hid in a closet when June came to the door. But Johnny would neither return to his estranged wife nor give up on June Carter, who repeatedly declined to marry him, even once breaking things off for five minutes, just long enough to discover he had stolen her clothes and hidden them in his hotel room to keep her from leaving. Within weeks, Waylon's drug intake skyrocketed. "Twenty amphetamines a day was normal, and thirty wasn't unusual. I'd hit the ground running; I never had a hangover because I never gave myself a chance." At true low points, John, down from 200 to 140 pounds, would become "Cash," a Mr. Hyde to Johnny's Dr. Jekyll, as when the Man in Black cut all the legs off the furniture for no reason or tore apart his roommate's car looking for his hidden stash, and then lied about it. One time, Cash hallucinated he "was an Indian flyin' through the woods," only snapping out of it when he discovered he was barefoot in a murky puddle.

"That Waylon," said the Man in Black, deflecting. "He'll take a doorknob down if he thought it would taste good."

"Too much was never enough," Jennings admitted of the Desoxyn, Alka-Seltzer, white cross, and coffee regimen that kept him upright. He wouldn't ever eat, either, which made getting obliterated easy. Jennings's drummer frequently arrived to find him comatose and would rush to check his pulse. On the other side of the living room, guitarist Luther Perkins might be pawing Cash for a heartbeat—"he'll sleep twenty-four hours," Perkins said. "If he awakes, he's alive. If he doesn't, he's dead."

But despite their seemingly parallel paths of self-destruction, the roommates didn't discuss it. "While they knew that the other one was indulging," recalled Waylon's future wife, "they never shared their stash." Later, they would regale fans with stories about those days, as if they had been just some goofy potheads.

"Hey, John, remember that time the cops pulled me over in Bucksnort, Tennessee, for writing a check for cocaine?"

"Yeah, and they didn't even arrest you," Cash said, "just took your stash and said, 'Waylon, don't write checks for that stuff,' and sent you back to Nashville! Did you write 'drugs' on the memo line of the check?"

"Imagine being so strung out that they get me of all people to talk to John. Hell, I was doing as much speed or more than he was!"

"I had a few good hiding places in that old apartment that you never knew about," said Cash, laughing, "but I always found your stash!"

As roommates, though, they were dead serious about their intake. Conversation consisted of debates regarding the effectiveness of the "overandunder," slang for a combo of amphetamine pills and tranquilizer dose, which Jennings assured Cash would balance them out, whatever that meant. It never did. "With the pills, I was always chasing the high amphetamines gave me during the first six months. I lost it somewhere along the way, that feeling."

Jennings blamed the mythic story of "Hank's road to ruin," which spurred his acolytes to burn out before they could live long enough to fade away, for leading him off the path set for him by Buddy Holly. "It was ironic," said Jennings. "Rather than give me strength, the drugs made me vulnerable."

As he began to cobble together cult fanbases in rural Maine and Ohio and on New Mexico reservations, Jennings blew through his increased earnings at an increased rate. He admitted to forking over cash to anyone who asked and picking up every check. "I would joke about being a junkie and crazy," he said. "All I was doing was saying, I'm not really crazy. I'm wrong."

After a tour in which Jennings opened for Cash, Waylon politely suggested Johnny find his own house "so your kids can visit." He was crushed when June Carter, as a condition of her marrying Cash, insisted Johnny cut Waylon and other "bad influences" out of his life. Other than June, though, Nashville didn't seem to know about Jennings's dependency or tumultuous personal life. In the spring of 1966, Music City welcomed him to town with overblown press releases trumpeting the hot new singer of "Stop the World (and Let Me Off)" and "Anita, You're Dreaming." But he wasn't thrilled to be there. "Buddy Holly loved music better than anybody I ever saw," Waylon said. "In his last few months, he talked to me about never compromising and staying away from Nashville." Instead, Jennings cultivated what he called "Waylon's music," which melded his teenage rockabilly sound and the forlorn style of Roy Acuff's "Wreck on the Highway," which his mother had played at full volume until she burst into tears. RCA kept pushing him as the leading artist of their invented "Folk-Country" movement, and Waylon, intimidated by his producer and personal god, Carter Family guitarist Chet Atkins, kept mum about his ambitions.*

Atkins "handled" Jennings with an iron fist, requiring Jennings to adhere to the Nashville Sound. That meant singing compositions with hooky pop choruses, on which Atkins overlaid strings, a "sugar sweet" style, as Waylon's wife called it.** (Jennings and others "felt that there was too much clutter—strings, backing vocalists, and extra instruments—between their music and the public," one Nashville historian wrote. Musicians stared at their charts while playing instead of watching Waylon's hands for changes, infuriating the singer.) At the time of Jennings's arrival in town a few years later, "countrypolitan" songs from Atkins and other Music Row overlords "were generally easy listening with a vocal twang and conservative lyrical bent," critics lamented. Atkins and others indulged in Beatles spoofs and saccharine, string-drenched "weepers" in the sixties, which bordered on self-parody. TV networks approved content that met its definition of "LOP," Least Offensive Programming, to please sponsors rather than audiences, and Music Row followed suit in country music. "You couldn't even cut a song Chet didn't like," said one songwriter, "and it produced a war of cultures. In Nashville everybody acquiesced to the class. They'd think, 'We may be poor, but we don't want to be destitute, so we won't make waves.'" Jennings, as "an introvert in an extroverted business," rarely mustered the courage to push Atkins harder on broadening the material.

"They don't want to analyze lyrics," Atkins explained. "Just hit 'em in the face with it."

---

* In 1967, RCA did put out a Skeeter Davis album of Buddy Holly covers with Jennings as its guitarist.

** Atkins later claimed, however, that he just wanted "to keep my damn job and sell records."

"But," said Jennings, "what if we didn't hit 'em there?"

"Program directors say, 'Well, that song's too *deep* for our audience.'"

"Bullshit!" said Jennings.

Chet and his studio team insisted on selecting the material for recording and instruments to be used, "often eliminating fiddles and steel [guitars] in favor of backup vocal groups" and coaching local musicians through a maximum of two takes. That meant the Waylors, earning $1,500 a week in Scottsdale, were barred. Left alone with unfamiliar musicians, including Charlie McCoy, the *Blonde on Blonde* guitarist, Jennings made an immediate faux pas, trying to play a twelve-string guitar, a folkie's instrument, and, worse, sing at the same time, which was frowned upon on Music Row. At least, as he later learned, Buddy Holly had made the same mistake.

At the end of the sixties, Chet Atkins received a promotion to vice president and delegated his oversight of Waylon Jennings to producer Danny Davis, a Tijuana brass trumpeter. The contrast couldn't have been more dramatic. Jennings, "Singer of Sad Songs," faced off against a classically trained A&R staffer whose music industry cred was originally borne of homogenized Latin jazz performed for the white upper-class sect. Everyone, including Davis, followed the model of Billy Sherrill, a producer at Epic, who turned everything into Southern-accented, commercial-minded pop. With the much older Owen Bradley, Patsy Cline's producer and coiner of the term *Music Row,* Sherrill established the Nashville Sound—an often "full-throated wail [with an] orchestrated crescendo, while all the time [the singer held] onto that deep well of sadness." Sherrill, a racist and a sexist, was nauseated by curse words, eye contact avoidant, and stubborn—he refused to let George Jones use the melody from "Help Me Make It Through the Night," not due to plagiarism concerns but because he insisted it was garbage. Even after Tammy Wynette had a pop smash with "Stand by Your Man," a tune they wrote together, Sherrill still wouldn't let her have much say in the material. He told the Baptist and fellow small-town-Alabama-raised divorcee he couldn't permit her to release songs about infidelity because "that isn't what the public expects [from] me."

After the Sherrill-penned "Almost Persuaded" topped the charts for a record-breaking nine weeks in 1966, Music City began copying everything he did, right down to the studio, background singers, and even the engineer. In Nashville, wrote Andrew Grant Jackson, singers "stuck to moon-and-June lyrics and didn't" get much say in which of those songs they got to record, then had to sit back as "producers laid orchestra strings and a choir" over your precious track; singers were contractually obligated to keep mum about it.* Jennings, despite being billed as "The Rebel" in press kits, was not immune. Davis set upon Waylon's material with a red pen and warned Jennings that his booming voice needed to be more measured. His work with Atkins and Davis "were good, smooth records," Waylon said publicly, "and there I was rougher than a goddamned cob. All the damn sand I swallowed is in my singing."

Truthfully, Jennings and his producer clashed from the get-go. After their initial session, Jennings returned to listen to mixes, only to discover someone had waylaid his tape—surely, *this* wasn't what he recorded the other day. He claimed he didn't recognize Danny Davis's work, a criticism not without some validity. "He'd overdub arrangements without asking me, and turn songs down without even playing them for me." Jennings had been approached to record Dick Holley's "Abraham, Martin and John" and agreed to do it; Davis went behind his back and told Holley to take his tune elsewhere. The topical yet

---

* One's contract also called for one to avoid personal appearances in jeans and to avoid being photographed without a tie.

uncontroversial lament to assassinated American icons became a million-seller in the hands of Dion, a fellow Winter Dance Party "survivor." Aggravating Waylon further, one executive asked: "When are you going to cut a country record?"

"You don't know what that is," the singer deadpanned.

Worse, Davis's recording philosophy couldn't have been more antiquated. He used a patented system devised as a big band member in the '50s that began with asking artists to have each part written out for the musicians ahead of time. Jennings crafted melodies on the fly, with players expected to wing it for a looser, more lively sound. Davis would make wisecracks, roll his eyes in boredom, or even leave the studio if Jennings didn't start the first take immediately. During an overdub session, with Jennings laying a second guitar line on the original track, Davis, thinking he was alone in the booth, muttered under his breath about Waylon's professionalism just as Jessi entered.

"If I told him what you said," she seethed, "he'd kill you."

Jennings returned for the next session armed with a .22 handgun on loan from felonious country phenom Merle Haggard. When Davis tried to get the musicians to carefully follow their charts, Jennings warned them: "Anybody still looking at his chart after the third take, your ass is dead." He whirled toward the control room and glared through the glass. "And, Danny," he said, "I don't want to hear any shit out of you."

Atkins finally admitted he had made a mistake in pairing an anti-authoritarian "rebel" and a studio hardliner. When Atkins told Waylon he would be changing producers, Jennings was ready. *Why*, he asked, *don't you let* me *produce my records?* He had, after all, landed a few Top 10 country hits. "MacArthur Park" won him a Grammy, but that was the recording Atkins had panicked over, leading him to bring in Davis to wrangle it into a proper, clean, Music Row–ready tune. Recalled Waylon: "I knew exactly what I wanted the strings to do; I had to hum the parts. He probably had his own ideas." When asked why he opposed Waylon's independence, Atkins claimed he feared RCA's top guys would feel underused and defect to rival companies. "I feel sorry for the old men in Nashville," Waylon told a reporter. "They can't see things are changin' and they won't be able to change. They're the same ones who ruined Hank Williams."

By the end of the sixties, country songs made up the majority of RCA's 45s. Music Row, raking in $100,000,000 annually, gave unprecedented power to producers, just as pop labels had ceded authority to them in the '50s. Jennings, like the hippies, called it "the System," but while Music Row vocally supported Richard Nixon, Atkins endorsed Democratic presidential candidate Hubert H. Humphrey in 1968 and may have been more liberal about record making than he let on. Later, Atkins would say that he admired Jennings *because* he never backed down on his musical principles.

On his way out, Davis took one last potshot at Waylon: "This guy could be the biggest star in the world," he said, "but he's his own worst enemy." Atkins ignored the alarm bells and brought in Ronny Light, another in-house producer.

Jennings complained he felt that his great purpose in life had been unmet, and that Nashville had penned him in. The public didn't seem all that aware of him, and the Country Music Association responded accordingly. Jennings had prepared "Only Daddy That'll Walk the Line" for their 1971 awards, but at the last moment, a producer raced across the stage to tell him the show was running long and Waylon's song would be cut off by a commercial break after a verse and chorus.

"Why don't I just dance across the stage and grin? Maybe do one line. That'll give you a lot of time," he cracked.

"Don't get wise," the flunky said. The shortened option was the only option. "We don't need you," he told Waylon, and stomped off.

"They wouldn't let you do anything," Jennings recalled. "You had to dress a certain way, you had to do everything a certain way.... You start messing with my music, I get mean."

Lonesome, On'ry, and Mean, in fact, the title of a 1973 Jennings record. Shortly before it came the albums *The Taker/Tulsa*, which featured Cricket Sonny Curtis and contained a hit cover of a Kris Kristofferson–Shel Silverstein collaboration,* and *Ladies Love Outlaws*, featuring Jennings on the cover in nineteenth-century western cowboy wear and brandishing a six shooter.** Forgetting the melody for a song, he improvised a new one, a technique that became his studio style. The resultant records, as well as *Good Hearted Woman*, contained immortal, robust, and Waylon-ified title tracks, were at least coproduced or produced solely by Light, and were semi-successful on the country LP charts, although none made the *Billboard* 200.

Although Jennings didn't trust him, Ronny Light understood Waylon better than his previous overseers. He was "younger and less doctrinaire," as well as looser in his studio methodologies, allowing Waylon to record a few Kris Kristofferson songs in Hollywood with the steel guitar player of his choice. Jennings said: "I couldn't accept the phrase 'musically, that's wrong,' because if I mixed a horn, a dobro, and a harmonica playing in unison and it worked, then that was like a whole orchestra in three pieces for me." Drummer Richie Albright had reminded his boss that "there's another way of doing things, and that's

---

* Impressed with Jennings's version of "The Taker," Kristofferson told everyone who'd listen to pay close attention to check Waylon out.

** Both easily outperformed his next-most recent record, which had been coproduced by Danny Davis and initially shelved. RCA didn't like his having recorded an authorized song at an unaffiliated studio in LA and, even when execs relented, the company's advertising department ignored it.

rock 'n roll," and Waylon, remembering how he started in the Phoenix clubs, was starting to wonder if Richie might be right.

It was Jessi Colter who ultimately gave Jennings the confidence to break with the Nashville method. "I been married four times, the first time when I was 17," he said. "When I met Jessi, I was pretty well at my lowest point... bent on self-destruction. Wallerin' in self-pity... depressed all the time and stoned." Colter, then known by her married name of Mirriam Eddy, had signed to RCA, where Chet Atkins decided to change her name* and introduce her to the public through a duet with Waylon Jennings. "Ain't no bigger than a nickel," Jennings said of Colter, who had to stand on a box at their shared microphone and sing her original "I Ain't the One." He joked: "The poor little ugly thing... can barely sing." After, deep in conversation with her, he neglected to mention that he'd been divorced multiple times, preferring to discuss his kids.

The two should never have matched. Mirriam/Jessi, married at the time and raised in the Pentecostal church, where she belted out spirituals to a rapturous reception, tried to stay far away from her toxic labelmate. When they went on a couple of dates, Jennings kept returning home in a rage, frustrated at how she needled him. Only later did he realize her ribbing was playacting, prodding him until he ignited, which quietly thrilled the twenty-five-year-old. In addition to the death of his father, Jennings was still grieving the loss of his bass player; he endured news stories honoring the tenth anniversary of his best friend Buddy Holly's tragic demise, as well as departures from the Waylors, all in 1969. Nonetheless, he felt emboldened to propose to Mirriam in an offhand remark.

"You want to run away with me?"

---

* Although Colter was rumored to have a familial connection to "Jesse Colter," a pal of outlaw Jesse James, historical documents contradict that.

"Just like that?"

"Just like that," he said. *Do you have concerns?* he wanted to know.

"You know I do," she fired back, almost giggling. She claimed to have laughed nervously about the marriage from that moment and through their wedding day, October 26, 1969, in Las Vegas. "It felt more like an elopement than a thought-out marriage," she said decades later. Waylon had three children, ages ten to thirteen, from his previous marriages, and when Colter arrived, Jennings started to become more conscious of his pill intake. But his running around, sleeping with every of-age creature in motel rooms and tour buses, "inability to completely reform and tendency to disappear unaccountably for days" didn't stop, and caused her extreme "anguish." Their marriage was a series of "tornados," she wrote. Colter turned to spiritual pursuits and channeled her heartbreak into plaintive love songs. Her second album featured a Top 5 pop single, which led to an onslaught of questions about whether her success affected her marriage. "People used to ask me... 'How does it feel when she has a big pop hit right out of the shoot and you don't have one?'" Jennings said. He told them it felt *fucking great.*

While her own career took off, Jessi had to butt into Waylon's professional life, since his management took a substantial cut of his earnings and seemed to relish starving him. Jennings used longtime friend W. E. "Lucky" Moeller as his manager *and* show booker, which seemed unethical even without the disturbing fine print: as manager, Lucky took 10 percent of what Waylon made per show, but instead of hearing offers to perform and taking the highest, Lucky would propose shows to clubs at a low rate to make a booking more likely. Promoters and club owners stole from Jennings, then pulled pistols when he asked for his pay. When Jennings returned home broke after one nine-month tour, Colter snapped: "What does he pay you?"

"Hoss, how is it that I come to owe you thirty thousand dollars?" Jennings asked.

"Look, son," said Moeller, laughing, "I've always kept you working and I always will."

That was the problem, though. The regimen of hundreds of shows per year didn't cover the alimony and child support, legal fees, evictions or moves across town to avoid it, amphetamines, or health problems. He had a half-million dollars in debts, and the only company that wanted to give him any cash was his record label. "The more I worked, [the more] Nashville was fencing me in," he moaned.

Waylon's transportation didn't improve after the Winter Dance Party tour, either. He sometimes traveled six hundred miles by sputtering bus for the following night's gig. When strange noises rang out, including the sound of a bottle of gin rolling around, the band would chalk it up to the ghost of Hank Williams, who rode with Jennings at all times, and the Lubbock "ghost," Buddy Holly, of course, that threw a hunk of wood at the head of drummer Richie Albright. Driving from Nashville to Phoenix, gigging at J.D.'s bar from nightfall to breakfast over the weekend, originally for only twenty patrons at $35 per night plus tips when he'd lived in Arizona, now in the hundreds per show, served as a cash lifeline. He first used his platform at J.D.'s to develop a style to suit his booming baritone, trying a Dylan song he'd repeatedly recorded without getting quite right, as well as Holly's "It's So Easy" and "Rave On," and an original, "The Stage, (Stars in Heaven)," his hokey tribute to the three crash victims. (He claimed to have destroyed the master of "The Stage," but a tape resurfaced in record company archives. After a while, he told anyone who asked about Holly's death: "It's none of your business. Don't bring it up again.") Mostly, though, he covered country artists who were palatable to mass audiences, especially Roy Orbison—Waylon's version of "Crying" could stop a chattering barfly mid-syllable. *L.A. Times* critic Robert Hilburn marveled at the "ragged strength in Jennings' voice and an amazingly delicate sensitivity." As demand for appearances in Phoenix increased, he struggled to find a drummer who could re-create the style of Johnny Cash's band, so Richie Albright ended up inventing a newer, hard-hitting one.* The Waylors would get so locked in that Jennings didn't need a set list. He started each song on guitar and, by the third note, the band would recognize the tune and join in. Eventually, thousands would turn out to see him at J.D.'s, and not to dance—it got too cramped—or coldcock someone, he joked. After each Phoenix return engagement, he'd collect roughly $2,500 per night and escape ahead of the sheriff waving liens for nonpayment of alimony. His third ex called his business philosophy "a five-year-old at a candy store," especially after Waylon turned down a $50,000 offer from her father to retire from touring, but at least she didn't want anything after their breakup. Turning down the loot was a gut-wrenching decision. RCA's royalty advances were so small his manager called recording for the company "servitude," and Jennings's booker still had him doing a slew of shows at low rates instead of scattershot dates for increased fees.

Jennings enjoyed tours—while doing one. "On the road, we thought we were bullet-proof," he wrote. "We loved the music, but music was secondary to what we were doing. All we did was party." Without any real pay, his main motivation seemed to be making the scene. "We were teetering and toppling ever closer to the precipice," he said. "You can only break the law of gravity for so long."

But America's small towns were growing increasingly volatile. In Salisbury, Maryland, he entered a club and immediately ducked to avoid a thrown cueball. Seconds later, someone punched him in the

* Country drumming was unapologetically polite and unobtrusive until the early seventies, whereupon it and the music generally developed a swagger.

gut, and another person threatened to fight him, all before he reached the stage. Soon after, at a gig in Kentucky, the bouncer jokingly offered to give Waylon his girlfriend in exchange for a cigarette lighter. When Waylon declined, a random patron volunteered to take the woman home, and the bouncer punched him in the face. As Waylon scampered away, the patron pulled a gun and shot the bouncer.

After his third marriage collapsed, he started firing his handgun at road signs from his limo, until his secretary-driver, going wildly around a curve, caused a car accident that they were lucky to walk away from. Sadly, that didn't make the Waylors cautious enough to avoid a series of tragedies that occurred near the tenth anniversary of "the day the music died."

One occurred on supposedly safe turf at J.D.'s. After a show, one man suffered a psychotic break and threatened to shoot Waylon; catching the star unaware outside, the gunman forced him face-first onto the pavement. When cops arrived, the man turned the barrel toward them and was blown back by gunfire. Another tragedy played out in Georgia just a few days after the assassination of native son Martin Luther King. Waylon, six foot but down to 138 pounds, attended a birthday party accompanied by the Waylors, where, on little food or sleep, they quickly got trashed. One guest began throwing knives for amusement, nearly hitting the band. Paul Nelson Gray, the bass player, screamed at the assailant, and shots rang out. In an instant, Gray lay dead. Then, in the winter of 1969, the Waylon Jennings tour split into a two-car caravan with the headliner following in his personal Cadillac. While approaching a bridge near the Canadian border, the lead car skidded on black ice and ejected sleeping bassist Chuck Conway into the icy, shallow depths below. Conway, who had replaced Gray only eleven days earlier, was killed. A keyboard player, severely injured in the crash, had to be replaced. Although police officers recognized Waylon and took pity on him by throwing away the marijuana they found, Jennings was slapped with a multimillion-dollar lawsuit. The nightmare didn't end there. Hours later, Merle Haggard and his manager cleaned Waylon out of the tour proceeds, almost $5,000, at poker, and a brawl with a bar patron who had called out "Baby, do you want to dance?" led to the arrest of every member of the tour except Jennings. After getting those involved out of the local jail, the Waylors attempted to recross the American border. Instead, two of them were busted for marijuana possession.

When the two musicians were again bailed out, Jennings fired them, but told one: "I wish I could go with you." Something had to give, and his career in Music City might go first. "I don't need Nashville to make it," he claimed. "If I have to move, then I move." He considered going back to being a DJ or accepting a residency at J.D.'s, but drummer Richie Albright persuaded him to give it one more year.

"It takes a lot of strain and guts to fight the system," Jennings told a journalist. "If I win, they feel like they've lost." He added: "It's always hard, going up against the tradition . . . to me, it's worth it. For the bottom line on everything is that the artistic urge had to be handled as carefully as sex."

A dozen RCA LPs between 1966 and 1970 didn't catapult him to stardom. TV appearances weren't launching him. He was a "darkly handsome young man with deep brown eyes and a beautifully crooked grin," said publicist-songwriter Mae Axton, but he would arrive "like a cyclone" and affect an indifferent attitude. Once, he was kept in *The Joey Bishop Show* green room until one a.m. and told his host he didn't appreciate playing "fuck the cowboy singer." The Grand Ole Opry had him on for what one attendee recalled as "probably the most rockin' country performance up to that time at the Opry. Waylon blew the roof off the joint. He was not well received by the old boy conservative country crowd. I was one of the few . . . that gave him a standing ovation."

But with even chart-topping country albums petering out at thirty thousand in sales, he had to build a following outside traditional radio stations and venues and try to break through to the pop buyers. "I couldn't go pop with a mouthful of firecrackers," he confessed. Whenever he would hear a producer "saying scornfully, 'Man, that sounds like a pop hit... ' I'd remember Buddy talking to me, telling me they thought he was crazy" on Music Row. Jennings started pushing back. He reportedly told one producer: "I want to cut this song today." When the company man told him they'd already recorded a master take the day before, Waylon clapped back: "We did—*your* way! Today we're gonna do it my way."

When RCA shrugged off his original song "Love of the Common People" and relegated it to a flip side, Jennings seethed. But a New Mexico DJ hated RCA's choice for the A-side and turned it over. Within seconds, the phone lines were full. Indigenous teens rang from hundreds of miles away at a whopping ninety cents per call to learn the song's title and request it. The DJ played "Common People" six consecutive times, after which the lines lit up once more. *When you gonna play that Waylon song again*, they wanted to know.

That's how Jennings ended up back in New Mexico during the hepatitis outbreak. Kids would hitch "a hundred miles through the snow" for his gigs there, and he might play "Common People" five times per show. "That song," said the promoter at one high school gymnasium show, "has become the Navajo national anthem. They respect him. He sings it *to* them, not down to them."

Thus there was no backing out of the New Mexico gig, ill as he felt. The venue fit four hundred, but the bouffant and orange-jumpsuit-sporting proprietress had sold six hundred tickets, including the table for the band, and canceling might trigger a riot. Once he collapsed near the stage, though, he was involuntarily hospitalized. Sammi Smith swooped in to finish the tour without him.

When he woke up in the hospital, he learned he did indeed have hepatitis. "After ten years of banging around the honkytonk circuit... my health was shot." His deceased father came to him in a dream and asked him to not "do this to yourself." The "this" was implied: the lack of sleep, the three hundred shows in nearly as many days, the philandering, the drugs, and, hardest of all to stand, wasting his career doing saccharine crap for Music Row idiots. Waylon considered telling Jessi to haul him a few hundred miles west to Phoenix and calling it a career. Instead, he asked RCA for $25,000 to help get him through his time off. They said they'd think about it. That actually helped in the long run, as their indifference would make him immovable at their upcoming contract negotiations.

Following his recovery, Jennings took things down a notch. That went for more than the musical tempo. He quit drinking for a year, and soon quit shaving on the advice of a bearded Willie Nelson in order to appear more dangerous and like the "outlaw" ladies loved. Jennings explained: "Our vision of country music didn't have any shackles attached to it. We never said that we couldn't do something because it would sound like a pop record, or it would be too rock and roll. We weren't worried that country music would lose its identity, because we have faith in its future and character."

"In the mid-60s, Waylon was a handsome, swarthy leading man," one critic later wrote. "He wore suits. His hair was medium length and combed back into a pompadour. By 1972... he emerged shaggy and bearded. He had one foot out of Nashville and both feet in blue jeans." Jennings blamed executives for casting too wide a net to appeal to Top 40 radio with "sweetened" tracks and believed "country music had gotten safe and conservative" because of it.* "Awash in strings, crooning

* His cover of Holly's "Rave On" was similarly ruined, in this case by Tijuana brass.

and mooning and juneing," as a critic described it. The problem was that country's blue collar roots were coming up against the corporate strategy of positioning the genre for middle- and upper-class Americans by smoothing out country music's rougher, rawer elements, even if that meant smothering creativity. "When country moved into the pop market," historian LeRoy Ashby noted, "some performers and fans fretted that the music was losing its way, falling victim to the Nashville establishment's preference for disposable songs and prettified, cloned performers." Executives, though, were more concerned that the music wasn't catchy or poppy enough to *become* disposable—after a long run on the charts, of course.

As he reworked his style and fought for his artistic vision, he was increasingly told that, as an outlier, he was tough to market. Jennings's followers were on the attack on the other side, inundating *Country Music Magazine* with letters complaining about Waylon's new look, while Dan McPhail, a previously supportive DJ, ranted on-air about Jennings's hair running past his shoulders, his fashion choices, and his way of living.

"What does Nashville think about your hippie band?" another DJ asked.

"I don't care *what* those motherfuckers think."

"You can't say *that* on the air!"

"Well, hoss," said Waylon, "I just did."

It didn't help that he sounded so dissimilar to other singers, even in the budding outlaw movement. Johnny Cash pointed out that because Waylon didn't sound like anyone else, he needn't worry about getting shunted aside when tastes changed. Cash's daughter Rosanne said, "That voice, you couldn't ignore it. If it was on the radio, you had to stop." But if the record companies didn't get him on AM stations and the fans didn't like the new direction, none of that mattered. Luckily, after agreeing to Willie's suggestion of playing the Armadillo and Dripping Springs for Austin ruffians and Bohemians, he started to feel like he wasn't alone.

Waylon and Willie first met at the Adams Hotel in Phoenix half a dozen years earlier. Jennings had a show at J.D.'s, Nelson played a touring gig at the Riverside Ballroom. (Willie insisted on the Riverside; at J.D.'s, he'd had his head cracked open by a tire jack wielding assailant after the man's wife leered at Willie.) When he learned his new friend was considering a move to Music City, Nelson shook his head: "Nashville ain't ready for you, Waylon," he said. Then, in 1972, after his own triumph at the Armadillo, Nelson browbeat Waylon into playing there. Although Jennings had lived a few blocks away on 6th Street growing up, the unfamiliar rock venue made him so trepidatious, he almost didn't go onstage. What he didn't know, though, was that thanks to *Shotgun Willie*, the line between hippie outcast and redneck country fan had begun to blur. Looking through the backstage curtain at long-haired rednecks guzzling Lone Star, Waylon exclaimed: "Oh Lord, Willie's playing another practical joke on us. Somebody find that redheaded bastard and get him in here!"*

The tremendous roar that greeted his emergence at the Armadillo made Jennings realize there was no going back to "Music Row" and all that bullshit. "Suddenly, we didn't need Nashville. They needed us," he said. He locked onto the idea of capturing his live sound on wax. "I never did feel at home [on Music Row]," he told an interviewer, totally unleashed. "I was being told over and over, 'You just don't do this . . .' 'there's a certain way we do things in Nashville.'" His manager, chummy with executives and other gatekeepers, wouldn't have

* He also wanted Willie onstage with him in case anything happened, but Nelson had been banished after the venue owner and Nelson's manager got into a screaming match over the presence of armed muscle, holdovers from Willie's hand-to-mouth Chitlin' Circuit days, where acts might do two sets and find out the bar owner "didn't make enough profit to pay" what he'd promised.

dared yank clients from a label or allow them to record outside Nashville, so Waylon fired him, and lo and behold, Neil Reshen, soon to be Willie Nelson's manager, as well, came calling.

"You're not going to like or trust this guy," said Waylors drummer Richie Albright, "but hire him. It'll be the best thing you ever did."*

Jennings took the advice, but with understandable reluctance. Reshen, a self-described "Jew with a black wife" and grating "New Yawk" accent, immediately set to work with his trademark intensity. His first strike was to demand RCA give Jennings a better royalty rate, pronto, as other record companies—he erroneously claimed**—were circling. Before RCA could recover from that, he hit them with the insinuation that he smelled something "cooking" in the company's books. He claimed that Music Row used creative accounting or even outright stole money from performers by withholding royalties owed under contract, daring artists to spend thousands to take the matter to court.

While Reshen battled the label, Jennings went after the rock audiences who could catapult albums onto the *Billboard* 200, like the ones who patronized Max's Kansas City, a New York club frequented by Andy Warhol, or a San Francisco stadium before sets from the Grateful Dead.*** "The long-haired kids—they like country music too; they just don't feel welcome in some of these redneck joints," said Waylon. *Rolling Stone* described a California show days later: "Jennings'

* "Things got better for a while," Nelson said of the Reshen years. "But then they got worse."

** Only one, CBS/Columbia, even acknowledged the problem of Nashville complacency.

*** Still, though, he suffered. Country venues would have a closet with a single hanging bulb set aside for the headliners, not some backstage green room with assorted M&Ms. Returning to these hellholes after the Grateful Dead experience, even for three straight sold-out Bay Area gigs, plunged him into a depression.

tightly reined, rock-based country music kept the audience of booted, mackinaw-clad drinkers at a ragged edge, and his leather-cowboy-stud stage presence and command invariably brought out the fightin' side in the drunks." Waylon, for his part, loved the higher incidence of personality clashes in his audience, guffawing when a reporter brought it up the next morning.

Although one San Francisco critic hinted that he was "a perfect candidate for a crossover to a rock audience," he still needed that crossover *song*. A DJ and supposed longtime fan explained that he loved that Jennings's music didn't hook the listener or seem too catchy on first pass but that one grew to love them eventually all the same.*

"Yeah," Waylon responded, "I've never had a smash." Nonetheless, he said, he believed country music was having its moment, "although they've hollered it for 15 years, every time a country singer'd have a pop hit."

Waylon soon forgot about the Dripping Springs Reunion and a performance he heard backstage by a young man named Billy Joe Shaver. Shaver, neither a redneck nor a hippie nor anything anyone could put their finger on, performed "Black Rose," a twangy, unapologetically autobiographical story song about having sex at age twelve with an African American hooker. The hippies could only blink silently at him. Equally astonishing, this time to the hillbillies, was that Shaver's offstage persona seemed to match his rough, authentic lyrics. "Billy Joe

* Jennings was reintroduced to Nelson at a 1960s breakfast gig at RCA Studios, when the two were asked to play—"for free," Jennings emphasized—for visiting DJs scoping out up-and-comers. They did that gig well into the '70s, which endeared them to country stations.

talked the way a modern cowboy would speak, if he stepped out of the West and lived today," Jennings said.

Cornering Shaver, Waylon leaned in close and asked, "Hey, you got any more of them ol' cowboy songs?"

Shaver most certainly did, including a song called "Willy, the Wandering Gypsy and Me," and Jennings promised to cut one or more of them for his next record. In the six months that followed, however, Jennings snubbed him, as if their meeting and the promise had been lost in a narcotic haze, which it might have been. Shaver, too, wished to forget Dripping Springs. Soon after his arrival, he was bit by a brown recluse spider and developed a high fever. Jennings's tour manager shoved him into a cold shower to save his life, but it didn't seem to stave off the poison. Shaver broke free from the bathroom, sprinted across a field, screamed that he was the reincarnation of Christ, and tried to "heal" the sick. He told passersby he was going off "to the desert"—not reachable on foot—to die. Instead, when Sammi Smith launched into "Help Me Make It," her angelic voice drew him back to the present. He returned backstage and discovered Jennings, watching an orgy while high on cocaine.

Shaver was not about to let Waylon forget him, however. Before his move to Music City, he'd been a poetry-obsessed high school dropout, navy man, and lumber worker; as the latter, he'd, like Willie Nelson, lost pieces of his fingertips and decided songwriting, rather than guitar-playing and performing, might be his bag. (In Music City, he told people he was from outer space. "No," someone corrected him, "you can say, 'just Texas.'") There, Kris Kristofferson covered a song he'd cowritten and produced his first album, *Old Five and Dimers*, for RCA, which went nowhere—his voice was almost as hard a sell as his producer's. Still, Shaver's songs were undeniably worthy of Waylon Jennings records.

Inspired by Waylon's promise, Shaver often paced and sneered incessantly outside RCA. Inside, Waylon's thirsty dog of a manager negotiated their new deal. Jennings unleashed Neil Reshen on RCA, a strange gambit from a guy who owed his record company six figures for studio time and unmet advances. But Reshen knew that Atlantic Records—which still had a country division at the time—hoped to add Waylon to their roster alongside Willie, a powerful one-two punch that might lead to a crossover Top 40 pop duet. Waylon, with emotional support from Jessi, knew, too, that if one company wanted him, he could risk punting RCA out of negotiations by demanding an obscene asking price. (Although Jessi encouraged Waylon to "be more independent in putting [a record] together, so it's truly a result of who you are," she knew that, on Music Row, "there was an 'old guard.' It was kind of like a large conglomerate making refrigerators . . . they took a thoroughbred and treated him like a mule.")

Meanwhile, Jennings didn't have any songs written. None. If he was about to leave RCA, he needed to have his "rebound" hit ready to go. He needed to write a single that would hit the pop charts, and he didn't even have a chorus. The logical thing to do would be to cover someone or even ask Willie or Kris for a song—not that they had had any hits lately, either. Another obvious, dismissed idea would be to step outside Studio A and see what that angry kid Billy Joe had in his notebook. Instead, Waylon sent out a $100 bill as a payoff: *Hoss, I appreciate what it means to be a starving artist, but I'm busy.*

After a couple of hours, Waylon stepped outside. He was surrounded by a gang of bikers, "some pretty tough looking customers—and I'd had enough," Shaver recalled. He shouted: "Hey, Waylon!"

The singer whirled. Spotting a scruffy young cowboy in the dark, he squinted hard but said nothing.

"I got these songs that you claimed you was gonna listen to, and if you don't listen to 'em I'm gonna whip your ass right here in front of everybody."

Everyone froze. The bikers wordlessly shuffled together and then crept en masse toward Shaver, as in a motorcycle movie. Waylon waved them off, almost laughing. "Hoss, you don't know how close you come to gettin' killed," he said.

"Well, I've had enough of this. You done told me you was gonna do this. Now I'm full of songs and I want you to listen to 'em."

In fairness to Waylon, he'd already recorded "Low Down Freedom" and "Black Rose," but the latter had been blocked from release by RCA for its interracial sex saga. Nonetheless, he sighed and waved Shaver into Hillbilly Central. Once alone with his stalker, however, Waylon snapped.

"I'm going to listen to one song, and if it ain't no good, I'm telling you goodbye. We ain't never gonna talk again."

Reading Waylon loud and clear, Billy Joe Shaver pulled out his guitar, skipped "Willy the Wandering Gypsy and Me," which he had played for him in Texas ("Hey, man, I've got to have that song"), and strummed "Ain't No God in Mexico." Without commenting on the song, Waylon encouraged him to do another one. After a trio of original songs, Jennings couldn't contain his excitement. He paced, loudly proclaiming that he would do an entire album of Shaver's music. To show he meant it, he insisted on having Shaver with him in the studio, which turned out to be best for everyone. "Waylon kept messing up my melodies," Billy Joe wrote, "so I'd have to play the songs for him over and over again until he could get the phrasing down."

When the band, including Willie's bassist Bee Spears, rehearsed "Honky Tonk Heroes," Jennings told them: "*This* is the way we're going to do it."

Billy Joe, seated in the back of the control room, leapt up. "What are you doing? You're fucking up my song. That ain't the way it goes!"

The two launched into a screaming match, but Jennings wouldn't change his mind. With the band, he ran through the tune in segments, and then called for a take, which they nailed right off. Everyone turned to Shaver.

"Yeah, that's good," he said. "That's the way it goes."

Despite this hiccup, the two became drinking buddies and had a bar installed in the studio to get the famous cover photo of them with their pals, boozing it up and guffawing so hard their (missing) teeth showed. Shaver signed with Monument Records, Kris Kristofferson's label, and went on to have a career that remained firmly in cult terrain.

With the acetate of Shaver's songs in hand, Jennings, in jeans and leather jacket, returned to face RCA's cavalcade of rhinestone suits. He walked into an environment that prided itself on running "counter to the counter-culture" and stewed in silence as Reshen, the "Outlaw Lawyer," as Willie Nelson called him, shared an item from *The Hollywood Reporter* announcing that Atlantic was signing Nelson; Waylon, he told the assembled, would be Atlantic's next signing. ("You blew it with him, hoss," Jennings said in a previous meeting, pointing above an executive's head to a publicity photo of Willie Nelson. "Don't blow it with me.") Before they could open their mouths in protest, Reshen shouted at Chet Atkins and the rest of the board over RCA's treatment of his client—one marketer had grumbled in earshot of Jennings: "I didn't like his last album; he had some songs on there that sounded like rock and roll to me." Reshen was particularly incensed about an offer to give his client a $1,000 stipend each of the next five years, but with the stipulation that he wouldn't use the Waylors and would stop locking RCA's engineers out. At $5,000 for the next half decade, Reshen reasoned, why wouldn't Waylon go back to J.D.'s in Phoenix and make that in a week?

Except for snarling at an exec who called him "pal," Jennings stewed in silence. His seething anger unnerved Atkins, who couldn't maintain eye contact. Much later, Atkins would observe: "With a record company you can have a whole room full of people who all put their heads together and grind away at a problem and still come up with the wrong answer." That seemed to be what was happening to RCA Nashville, which seemed to be on the verge of dropping its hottest act.

Amidst a discussion about the rights to his earlier recordings, Jennings suddenly exploded. "You sons of bitches," he shouted. "If you keep messing with me, I'll get in the vault and burn the goddamn tapes."* They didn't cave, and so he threatened to start his own label. "I told you he was crazy," one exec shouted.

As the talks resumed directly with Reshen, Jennings slumped in his chair. "Chet," he said, reaching toward Atkins. He paused while everyone gaped, waiting on the next word. "Where'd you get these peanuts?"

"Shut up, Waylon," Reshen growled.

Jennings rose a bit too abruptly, jolting Atkins and his assistant. Before anyone could ask him what he was up to, Jennings stormed out.

"Waylon's mad, I'm sure," said one exec.

"He's crazy," another agreed. "He's liable to do anything."

"Will he be back?" asked the first one.

"I guess he's gone," Reshen said with a shrug, suppressing a smirk, "so we may as well call this to a close. . . ."

Waylon returned ten minutes later to find Reshen alone. Jennings felt the color drain from his face—the words of Willie Nelson ate at

---

* The tape battle would continue for years until Jennings learned that RCA had taken him seriously and moved his master recordings to an Indiana facility. Jennings: "What a bunch of assholes. I wasn't going to burn my tapes. I might burn Elvis's tapes, but I certainly wasn't going to burn mine."

him: "Waylon is not the greatest politician in Nashville. He shot himself in every foot he has, plus a couple of fingers." It seemed that the Tao of Willie had proven correct again.

Reshen burst into laughter when he saw Jennings, blanched, in the office doorway.

"You're a fuckin' genius, walking out like that!" Reshen said. "That sewed it up. Where'd you go?"

"I had to take a piss."

"Well, that was a $25,000 piss," said his manager.

Reshen had discovered that Waylon didn't owe RCA two hundred grand, they owed it to *him*. He also persuaded RCA to increase Waylon's royalty rate by 2 percent, breaking Chet Atkins's rule of holding all artists to a paltry 5. Hell, Jennings now had a better rate than Atkins himself, plus $150,000 in cash to settle "bookkeeping mistakes" and front the purchase of a new Silver Eagle tour bus.* More important than the advance or royalties, the deal gave Jennings unprecedented power.

When news of the contract broke, musicians and music moguls alike were stunned. For the first time, a Nashville artist could record whatever he wanted, whenever and wherever he chose, with his touring band, uncensored. Better yet, it all fell under the umbrella of Waylon's new company—WGJ, for Waylon Goddamn Jennings Productions—giving him a greater understanding and control of his finances. On top of that, a New York agency soon took over most of his concert bookings, getting him out from under his debts to "Lucky" Moeller.

* RCA reneged, giving Jennings only $75,000, which he caved on. To his and Reshen's delight, the computer accidentally produced two $75,000 checks for them, and Jennings cashed both. In 1978, RCA renewed Jennings's deal and gave him the highest royalty rate in country music.

Out from under Music Row's watchful gaze, Jennings started hanging around with cowboy-hat-sporting, bearded-Nebraskan musician Tompall Glaser, who had somewhat scandalized Nashville by not only adding Black members to his own touring band but opening the first independent studio. "When I got to Nashville, everything was sewed up by a few people and I didn't like the idea," said Glaser, who created Glaser Sound Studios. One songwriter, who dropped in to meet the renegade, got a lecture in "the prostituted mess" of Nashville, and a critique of the "rules": "Learn the rules to get your songs recorded. You could talk about black people but only in an avuncular way. Women could not drink in a country song; the man drank—the woman waited at home. . . ." Initially blocked from recording at Glaser's by union rules, Waylon set to work at RCA on breaking that blockade on topics.

He started with Shaver's songs, of which eight made the final mix, including the banned "Black Rose"; another, "You Asked Me To," he cowrote with Shaver and earned himself a Top 10 single. "That no-good Billy Joe," he'd joke when covering those songs in concert. "I can call him that because I can whip 'im."

Although this would technically be the company's first release without an in-house producer, RCA still sent its engineers around and they ratted him out for prescription drug abuse. Once, they complained he asked them to "turn the bass drum up" while they held it to Nashville Sound standards. In response to these reports, RCA head Joe Galante dropped by to check on his investment. Galante, who had a background in marketing, not production, had only been living in Nashville for a year and was trying to figure out what the fuss was all about with country music. After meeting Waylon and listening to playback on the stringless *Honky Tonk Heroes*, he decided *this* was the heart of country. What struck him and critics in particular was the title track, which re-created the band's live sound and acknowledged not just much-maligned honky-tonks but the idea of cutting music down to its rawest core. It reminded Galante of the pure joy and ballsy brilliance of early rock and roll. "He had conviction, and it was the honesty in his voice" that began to resonate across demographics, says the exec. He gave Waylon his blessing. "He liked his creative freedom and he had earned it," Galante adds. "It was never about the money. It was always about the music and the fans."

After the album was finished, Jennings pulled Chet aside to make sure everything was copacetic between them. Atkins, still worried that having a self-producing artist might spur workhouse producers to defect, snapped at him: "You're tryin' to ruin everything we've done."

Waylon said measuredly, "I don't want it to ruin *me*."

Glaser, as coproducer, "really encouraged Waylon on the business side to follow his hunches about himself and to take control of the music," he claimed. Although not a Top 10 hit on the country album chart, perhaps due to its singles having been released far in advance, *Heroes* was "the one that started it all," as Jennings put it. The record supercharged the genre. Thanks to its release, Shaver claimed, "clubs were letting people in with their Levi's and long hair" and hillbillies in dust-laden jean jackets were summoned into Music Row boardrooms. "The outlaws surprised nearly everyone in the Nashville music business establishment by producing some of the best work of their careers," one writer noted, adding that "the records sold equally well to the non-country market and the traditional country core audience." *Texas Monthly* reflected: "To say that Nashville eventually got hip to what was happening would be too kind. Rather, the industry identified a chance to make money and came up with the 'outlaw' label. . . . It was coined to describe country songwriters who wouldn't conform to traditional strictures, who insisted on making music that sounded right to them."

Waylon quickly followed with two records completed at Glaser Sound, *This Time* and *Dreaming My Dreams*. The latter, helmed by Johnny Cash producer and Music Row pariah Jack Clement, kicked off with a cracking drum line and an admission that his music was "the same old tune, fiddle and guitar." Originally titled "Music City Blues," the song asked, "Are You Sure Hank Done It This Way?" and, despite the lack of a chorus and its inherent criticism of country radio, topped the charts. "It was brilliant," outlaw singer Ray Benson said. "[The opening] says it all right there. This has got to change." *Dreaming* became Jennings's first to sell 500,000 copies and, after twenty-two LPs, was his first country chart-topper. It and *This Time* launched a dozen indie studios that aimed to mimic Glaser, and quickly made Music City hip.

For his next trick, the night prior to the 1975 CMAs, Jennings gave the keynote address in front of seven hundred attendees at the Nashville Songwriters Association dinner. Songwriters need greater leeway, he said, and without compromise, Music Row would die. He then took the remainder of his goodwill and put the pressure right back on the industry in the form of Willie Nelson—while Waylon could argue he had the hit singles to prove his worthiness for artistic control, Nelson could make no such claims.

Later, Shaver would tell Jennings: "We were all melted into the same comet." Waylon thought the best thing to "do was grab it by the tail and hang on for dear life." The thing about comets, though, was that, if you caught one with your bare hands, you'd find out they were hotter than hell.

PART II

RAMBLIN' MEN

CHAPTER SIX

MY STARDUST MEMORIES

"I hope you all like what we do. But if you don't like it, you better keep your mouth shut, 'cause we will kick your ass."

"And who in the hell are you?"

"Waylon *goddamn* Jennings!"

—As recalled by Jennings on an episode of *Inside Fame,* about an incident at Max's Kansas City, New York, 1973

The best damn country singer around.

—Kris Kristofferson, on Waylon Jennings

Willie plays to them. He's got this low wave of the hand that covers the first fifty rows. . . . Everybody feels like he's waving at *them.* And he really is.

—Bradley "Budrock" Prewitt

"Remember the money": the road manager's creed.

—John Sebastian

No one could control Willie Nelson or Waylon Jennings. The two were often found at 916 Nineteenth Avenue South, among the

409 crumbling Music Row buildings out of 459,* Glaser Sound Studios, better known as "Hillbilly Central." Waylon turned the joint into his personal hangout, with his entourage drinking or drugging on the lawn or in the newly crafted, windowless recording hub into the wee hours. They played pinball for entire days with interruptions only to eat takeout, use an opener on beer cans, and occasionally to wrap their arms around a groupie's waist. Glaser's staff would unlock the building most mornings to discover a half-dozen nonessential personnel passed out at office desks or in the control room. As Jennings later put it, these men needed someone to tell them they weren't wrong but neither were they quite right. Seldom could they be found writing, let alone recording music in the studio crafted for those purposes.

Somehow, with Willie Nelson almost literally pushing Jennings into the studio, sessions for the follow-up to *Honky Tonk Heroes* were finally scheduled for the fall of 1973. (One major motivation: Buddy Holly's original Crickets flew in to re-cut "That'll Be the Day" and "Peggy Sue." The recordings, not necessarily for public consumption, were finally released in 1999.) But in this case, and for the first time ever on a major modern country LP, the record would not be made in a label's studio—or a traditional studio at all—after Waylon discovered that spies had been reporting everything Jennings said at RCA Studios to executives. Instead, he decided to record at Hillbilly Central.

While RCA thought he was just goofing around, Jennings hired fellow cult artist Willie Nelson to coproduce, brought in the Waylors touring band, and across three days in mid-October, together they recorded a trio of songs Nelson planned for *Phases and Stages*, with the writer working the controls. Ultimately, Jennings wrote only one track for the album, but he made it count.

---

* Jennings asked his manager for a grand in walking around cash, but didn't even have a checking account until Tompall Glaser set one up for him.

Waylon claimed "This Time" had been written about an ex—he joked he couldn't remember "which wife it was about"—and that he'd composed and recorded it much earlier but RCA wouldn't release it. Drummer Richie Albright brought it up again and, upon hearing it, Nelson insisted they put it out. Sure enough, by late 1973, Jennings submitted it as the title track from a stylistically cohesive record.

His timing was excellent. The first all-country station had sprung up in New York, Austin had a popular "progressive" genre channel, and although young record buyers were wary of country music, rock-inflected country appealed to the same people who helped the Allman Brothers and Neil Young top the pop charts. Yet RCA, pouting, sat on the album until they saw how the single of "This Time" performed in April 1974. Shocking the company's executives, it quickly outpaced everything Jennings had ever released. Instead of releasing a follow-up from the same album, however, Jennings used his ammunition on *The Ramblin' Man*, another 1974 record, which contained a pair of number ones and a number two single.

The Country Music Association allegedly leaked to Waylon's camp that he would be awarded Male Vocalist of the Year at their awards ceremony, a nudge to get him to appear. They were right to lay it on thick. Jennings still fumed over his previous appearance at the ceremony, cut for time. Plus, he pointed out, "I knew that block voting and mass trading between the big companies—we'll give you two hundred votes for your artist if you give your four hundred votes to our writer—probably had more to do with [my win] than anything else." After being handed the award certificate, he wrote "Fuck You" at the top and autographed it with a flourish. "They only care for the money and they don't really care for the music," he said.

Jennings's triumphs broke the Nashville studio system. Once word got around that RCA hadn't stopped the Hillbilly Central sessions, other defiant musicians booked outside recordings, and RCA stopped mandating the in-house rule. With his cachet, Jennings could boost friends' careers, as Kristofferson had done, especially that of Willie Nelson. The goofy redhead had just signed to yet another record company, CBS/Columbia, and, thanks to Neil Reshen, negotiated artistic control. Nelson wanted to put out a loose concept album, a cinematic narrative that involved an old preacher, his victimized wife, lost love, revenge, and shocking violence in the Old West. As with *Phases and Stages*, the songs would alternate between the wife's and preacher husband's points of view, detailing the night they danced and fell in love, and the songs the preacher might sing to lull his beloved to sleep, including "Blue Eyes Crying in the Rain," an old ballad from Hank Williams associate Fred Rose, a version of which Nelson would record in a tossed-off take, never imagining it would become arguably his defining moment.

But despite having the basic gist of the album, the individual songs wouldn't come. He could "control whatever happened in the studio," he said, but after the signing with Columbia, he panicked, and with the company calling asking about his first session, the pressure and anxiety mounted. On a drive to Denver, Nelson developed the story's outline with his wife, Connie, and daughters, Lana and Susie, beginning with "Red Headed Stranger," an Arthur "Guitar Boogie" Smith song Nelson had played on his radio show in the 1950s. Nelson realized the preacher would know a tune, "Just as I Am," which Willie and Bobbie had learned from their childhood hymn book. He sang Susie "It's Not Supposed to Be That Way," the father-to-daughter song that serves as the heart of *Phases and Stages*, and then started to see how a transitional song like it or a "theme" could anchor *Stranger*, too. "I took my time, all the while staying focused on the preacher's feelings," he said. "'Blue Eyes Crying in the Rain'...another song about lost love whose mantra—'Love is like a dying ember and only memories remain'—expressed the overall theme and tied all the loose ends together." He eventually had fifteen tracks for *Red Headed Stranger*, half a dozen of which he wrote, and beelined to his new label to schedule recording.

In the wake of Waylon's battle with and victory over RCA in the fight over studios, Nelson wanted to take the same challenge to Columbia. The label imagined he would want to use their technologically advanced studios in New York or Nashville with session players in button-downs surrounding him. Instead, he snuck out to suburban Garland, Texas, three hours north of Austin, as remote a location as one could imagine. Harp player Mickey Raphael had told him about Autumn Sound, the state's only twenty-four-track studio. Because executives were unlikely to drop by unannounced, Nelson didn't hesitate to call in his touring band, with Bucky Meadows subbing for Bobbie Nelson on piano. Despite having the Family and two dozen tracks to record onto, Nelson didn't go hog wild. He kept the melodies simple and the playing tight. The Family band grew comfortable enough at Autumn Sound that they spontaneously launched into a Hank Williams tune, and Nelson guided them through a Bach minuet, which surely must have raised eyebrows when the tape arrived at Columbia.

The first night, the band cut all fifteen tracks before 3:30 a.m., when the sun began to creep over the hills. On the second evening, they returned to fix a few flubs with overdubbing. Willie asked his engineers to remove the equalizer that polished his voice, muttering about how Nashville mixes had ruined previous recordings by cleaning him up. They finished mixing the record on the third day. Ultimately, Nelson used a laughable one-fifteenth of the $60,000 recording budget he hustled out of Columbia, putting the rest toward upgrading the Family's touring gear on the off chance that fame, glory, and larger venues awaited them. Willie did not celebrate this coup for long. He knew that, since Columbia had little skin in the record's game, they had less of an incentive to heap marketing dollars on the project, and that counted double for a "final" mix that sounded like a rehearsal.

After weeks went by without a word, Nelson suspected Columbia was preparing to bury, shelve, or sue over it. As the winter of 1974–1975 receded and the label packed the spring record release calendar without slotting *Red Headed Stranger*, Nelson, Jennings, Reshen, and Reshen's assistant flew to New York to meet with Bruce Lundvall, the soon-to-be company president who had recently made the decision to approve Bruce Springsteen's probationary record *Born to Run*. When Billy Sherrill protested Columbia's potential new signing, Willie Nelson, by calling him too "old," Lundvall corrected him: "He's a genius." He seemed poised to celebrate Willie's creative renaissance.

Reshen and company assumed that, as with Springsteen, they would play a key song, Lundvall would find it an interesting new direction for the artist, and the executive would support *Stranger* with a full-fledged marketing budget.

Instead, after queuing up the tape on a reel-to-reel machine, Lundvall let "The Time of the Preacher" play without comment. As track two began to waft out of the speakers, Lundvall hit "stop."

"Why are you turning in a demo?" he asked.

"It's a new kind of country music," said Nelson. He insisted he had completed the record and wouldn't be making any changes to it.

"It's too rough," Lundvall shouted. "It's too raw. It does not sound like a finished record." *From Columbia Records*, he did not add.

The executive claimed that, since it was supposed to be a "concept album," the songs should feel like one flowing story, albeit with conflict and some up-tempo, single-worthy moments to break up the bleakness of the lyrics and sparse nature of the recordings.

"It doesn't sound commercial," said Lundvall. "There's some pretty good things here, but this needs to go down to Nashville and let Sherrill sweeten it. Put some strings on it."

"Sherrill," as in staff producer Billy Sherrill, had been the one to bring Nelson to CBS/Columbia's attention, in fact. But, reached by phone, he backed his boss, although in more subdued language, calling the record "lousy-sounding." And Billy Sherrill calling it that was a death knell.

"We can't put this out," said Lundvall.

"Well, I agree," Sherrill said. "It sounds like a bad demo." Privately, Sherrill apparently asked: "Did he make this in his living room? It's a piece of shit! It sounds like he did this for about two bucks. It's not produced."

While Lundvall was on the phone, Reshen had to be physically restrained. "He was like a mad dog on a leash," Jennings marveled.

Jennings, no longer content to storm out of a room in silence to make a point, screamed at—of all people—Reshen. "Neil... if you don't get that goddamn tape off that machine and get us out of here, then you won't be my manager, and I guarantee you won't be Willie's." Lest anyone think he had turned against *Stranger*, he whirled and jabbed an accusatory finger at Lundvall. He called him a "tone-deaf, tin-eared, sonofabitch know-nothin'," and stormed toward the door. Lundvall, wincing, calmly asked Jennings to explain the album's appeal.

Waylon launched into a loud, breathless monologue about the Dripping Springs Reunion, the "seventy thousand" souls who had driven through the night from the Midwest to see him, Kristofferson, Loretta Lynn, and Nelson, supposedly the *fool* who didn't know a *damn* thing about what sells, play acoustic music. "Billy Sherrill may be great," he said in summation, "but he ain't got a fucking thing to do with Willie Nelson. All he can do is cover him up."

Before Lundvall could reply, Willie raised a hand and drew the executive's eyes across the table.

"The contract couldn't be plainer," said Nelson. "I turn in the music I wanna turn in. Your job is to sell it."

That night, Nelson clammed up about the record, sulking on a couch at the hotel. Jennings plunked down next to him and told him something he never forgot.

"Hoss, first we got to please ourselves. Once we do that, the fans will follow us—not those guys in suits sitting behind their big desks."

Sherrill surprisingly proved to be the deciding vote in *favor* of release. He suggested releasing *Stranger* with minimal marketing to keep Columbia's investment low, and, when interest quickly fizzled, Nelson would understand that these sparse, bleak, tuneless records were hurting him. Columbia Nashville staffers were convinced of this, too—one insider reported they were "underwhelmed and disappointed with the record" and so were Nelson diehards hoping for a rollicking album that captured the Family's live sound. "But the doubters were outnumbered by radio programmers ready to pay back Willie for all the goodwill he had been building since he arrived in Nashville in 1960," wrote the National Recording Registry in 2009. When Nelson hit Music City, there had been eighty-one country stations; now there were over a thousand. Nelson would only need one.

After a DJ at Houston's KIKK heard "Blue Eyes Crying in the Rain," and despite everything he knew about drum-less, slow, sad old cover tunes, he decided to put the song into heavy rotation. By the time of the LP's May release, "Blue Eyes" had caught fire across country radio, and in October, it became Nelson's first pop hit and country number one, and the top-selling single of 1975 in the genre.* At the promotional tour kickoff at LA's hip Roxy nightclub, Nelson walked through the crowd with his arms out "like a sports star," one attendee recalls, getting handshakes and slaps on the back, "glowing" in the California love. Onstage, he pointed out Dylan, Kristofferson, and Roger Miller from the stage, all of whom lent gravitas to *Stranger.* In a year with Dylan's acoustic, introspective comeback, Emmylou Harris's first number one country album, Springsteen's commercial breakthrough, and mellow classics from Joan Baez, Tom Waits, and Fleetwood Mac, Nelson's LP stood out as arguably the best of the lot. The critics flipped, too. "Going back to Texas sure has been good for Willie Nelson," wrote *Country Music.* "You get the impression that when he was living in Nashville he was sending out his songs like a stranded man sends out messages in bottles...all those bottles...floated to shore among friends." *Texas Monthly* couldn't contain itself, suggesting: "The difference between Nelson's *Red Headed Stranger* and any current C&W album...is astounding. What Nelson has done is simply unclassifiable; it is the only record I have heard that strikes me as otherworldly."

Even Columbia's execs came around. One, Rick Blackburn, said, "It didn't follow the formula, the fashionable mix of the day. There were 1,000 reasons that record should not be a hit [but it] became a hit for all the right reasons—because it was Willie's statement." And in a note accompanying the gold record he gave to Waylon marking the 500,000th sale of *Stranger,* Bruce Lundvall wrote: "This is from that tin-eared tone-deaf son-of-a-bitch. You were right."

Previously, Nelson struggled to land gigs. Incidents at shows, which had nothing in the way of security, left promoters wary. When a brawl broke out in front of one venue and a participant drew his knife,

* "Remember Me," another cover from the album, hit number two.

Nelson's bodyguard pulled a gun, fired, and inadvertently hit a label rep in the leg. "Tim," Nelson told the bodyguard, "I want you to negotiate all my contracts with CBS from now on." Before "Blue Eyes," bookings had declined, too, "after he grew his hair long and wore an earring," as one friend explained. "Club owners would say, 'We love Willie, but we can't hire a guy with long hair and tennis shoes.'" In 1976, they couldn't hire him because they couldn't afford him.

As Willie & the Family fever spread, the media spotlight followed. Mickey Raphael hit the tabloids by dating A-list actor Ali MacGraw. A woman claimed she and Nelson had a nine-hour sex session—Nelson quipped that it was "the only true story written about him." (He later joked that it may be accurate, "but you would've thought I'd remember at least the first four or five hours.") Nelson saved Bob Dylan's ass in Houston in 1976, agreeing to co-headline a tour stop that had had poor advance sales. Nelson, unused to entourages, security teams, and a relentless press, hid out from everyone after it and subsequent shows. He'd say: "If you need me, I'll call you." Throughout, Shotgun Willie himself struggled to retain his collectedness. After he was busted in the Bahamas for having weed in his luggage, Nelson went on a (for him) bender, drinking a six-pack, falling over and breaking his foot, and getting banned for life from the islands. At a Los Angeles football stadium show with Merle Haggard, the crew alone drank dozens of cases of beer, which Nelson condoned. "At one point, somebody figured out we were spending $80,000 a year on beer," said driver "Gator" Moore. Nelson embraced marijuana, which turned him into a grinning Fool, not a fool. In Corpus Christi, Texas, after the band ate particularly strong mushrooms before a gig, Raphael muttered: "I can't wait till Willie gets here—there will be some semblance of normalcy"; he realized he hadn't meant it sarcastically. While executives tried to keep his image from spiraling into actual anarchic, hippie lawlessness, the outlaw country movement took hold throughout the country and swept

Willie, Waylon, and, unnoticed by most at the time, Willie's drummer Paul English with it.

English had been a guiding light for years. When Nelson confessed that he was considering quitting Nashville for Nowhere, Texas, English said: "Just fuckin' do it. You know damn well the rest of us are gonna follow you."* English claimed that he had been with Willie at the shootout with Lana Nelson's husband, and he had the violent history to back this up. A self-proclaimed "street hustler," gang member, six-figure-earning pimp, and mediator of disputes between gangsters, burglars, and their ilk in the Fort Worth underworld, nothing got past him. But though he reportedly committed several shootings and possibly homicides, English claimed to follow a strict code and to not have wreaked random mayhem. "There was more honor among thieves in Fort Worth," said an acquaintance. In the "redneck answer to Sunset Boulevard," as one writer put it, "no one was killed without permission and it was usually for things like beating up on prostitutes or getting out of line with the law." After serving time for a robbery he swore he hadn't committed, Paul ended up filling in for his drummer brother on Willie's local radio show. Problem was, he'd never played drums.

"They told me to just keep patting my foot," he recalled. "They kind of counted out every song for me, just one, two, three, and four." At one point, English sped a song up so much, Nelson turned and shouted: "Play as fast as you want, but we still gotta go till 12:30." It was enough to get him through the gig, land him a three-week stint on-air, and get him a tryout for a permanent spot in Nelson's ragtag group, which had a high turnover rate and needed the English boys to pad it. It didn't help that the players made, at most, $100 a week, which English accepted at the expense of his prostitution racket, which

* "I got no plan," Nelson confessed. "Hell, Willie," said English. "You never have."

netted ten times that. "My brother and I picked up a trumpet player who didn't want to go" to a gig, English said. "I told him it wasn't rough anymore—we carry guns. That night, there were two fights and one knifing." At one gig, English carjacked a nonpaying proprietor, returning his vehicle only after the band received the ransom. Another club owner balked at the performance fee, so English one-eighty'd back to the tour bus to get his gun. The club owner locked the door and had police officers on his payroll shoo the band away. Days later, dynamite destroyed the cheating owner's club.

"I'm a peaceful guy, and I don't want any trouble," English claimed, although he added that he would kill anybody who came at Willie. By playing drums, keeping the books, and brandishing a pistol to collect his pay, English eventually earned one-fifth of Nelson's take, a verbal agreement that would pay incalculable dividends after *Stranger*. Nelson would tell shocked accountants that the gun-toting drummer deserved his astronomical salary because Paul had saved Willie's life; truthfully, the closest he came to doing so may have been during a Fourth of July picnic when, during a rainstorm, he noticed a buckling tarp over Willie's electrified equipment and fired a bullet into the tarp, flooding a barren area of the stage. English had also pulled Nelson's nearly comatose ass from cars, taken away his keys, and kept him from killing himself while boozing or hopped up on pills. Nelson only made it to the big time because English gave him money, no strings attached, from the profits of whorehouses and car dealerships he owned. "If you're writing songs about shooting people," said his son Paul Jr., "it's nice to have a guy who's shot people up there onstage with you." In return, Willie gave Paul free rein, even to use dry ice and wear capes onstage, which Paul started doing regularly, or so he claimed, after fifteen girls rushed the stage for his autograph the first time he did. He pulled a gun on Jerry Lee "the Killer" Lewis when the Killer tried to dance atop Bobbie Nelson's piano. He pulled another to shoot steel guitarist Jimmy Day in the leg after Day insulted his dead wife. Three years after *Stranger*, English was still acting as muscle for the established, highly paid group, browbeating HBO representatives into handing over a $70,000 check before a gig at the cable network. When legendary promoter Bill Graham, who helped both Santana and the Grateful Dead launch to stardom, criticized a sound rig at a show, English tackled him and pulled a gun, hissing: "You might could fire us, but I could fire you from the human race." Nelson, perhaps caught up in English's gleefulness, once stepped off the tour bus during an unrelated parking lot shootout and stopped the starstruck participants and police officers with his twin holsters, each stuffed with a silver Colt .45. In an instant, the cops lowered their weapons and the tension evaporated. Then, after an incident in which harmonica player Mickey Raphael was nearly felled by a thrown beer bottle during a show and English beat the offender to a pulp, things seemed to be snowballing in front of thousands of concertgoers.

Nelson and Paul had been together through two debt-saddled decades, but with Willie's unprecedented success, it became clear to management that, although the music and musicians could remain ragged and hippie-esque, the gun-toting menace would have to be caged. Nelson's manager, who referred to English as "the devil," urged Willie to talk to him. After a heart-to-heart between the two (one the dangerous criminal who lived by a code and the other a loose cannon Zen master), Nelson said he would understand if a new, cleaner touring life might cause English to quit the band. Paul, for his part, acknowledged how Willie had saved him: "If I hadn't gone with Willie," he told *Rolling Stone*, "I would be in the penitentiary or dead." After the discussions, English let other people handle the nitty-gritty money stuff. Management set up ironclad contracts with established venues, collecting deposits and involving lawyers whenever payments became an issue. The tour bus was upgraded to the Honeysuckle Rose, a proper motor coach and a far cry from the 1959 limo with three rusted-out doors Willie drove in the sixties. Willie, though, would play prison shows solo—that way, the band wouldn't have to worry about a strip search.

Paul English reacted to fame by running in the other direction. After accidentally discharging a gun into his leg, he hid most of his weapons and rarely flashed them again. Well into his forties, the drummer married a psychiatrist in her early twenties after she threatened to stay home from the next tour if she didn't get an engagement ring. (They were married for forty-one years, until his death.) Their kids recalled "Dad getting home off the bus, and no matter how long he'd been out or how tired he was, going out and throwing the football." Nelson would glance back at English, silent behind his kit except for the sticks, during eighteen-thousand-attendee shows and, without exchanging a word, know the other was reflecting on "when he and I were driving along in this old station wagon, pulling a trailer, and I just remembered that and thought, 'Boy, this is sure a long way from that blow out.'"

He and Waylon were finally mainstream, thanks to a song written for their voices, "Luckenbach, Texas."* "Let's go to Luckenbach, Texas," the chorus went for Nelson's part, "with Willie and Waylon and the boys"; it and the following track on Jennings's *Ol' Waylon* detailed the "successful life" the two men enjoyed, to a point. While "Luckenbach," in Waylon's estimation, "recaptures a world where everyone is welcome and love never dies," the album's next track, "If You See Me Getting Smaller," a partial ode to Nelson, didn't have the same sweetness. "We have spent a million dollars," Jennings lamented, "to find out what we make." Both tracks had varying degrees of dark undertones about infighting, particularly with estranged friend

* The song was written after another songwriter, Jerry Jeff Walker, reported that two business partners had purchased the town, population three, in order to run its dance hall and concert venue without interference from the authorities.

Tompall Glaser, drug abuse, and the likelihood that if they kept up either, they'd be dead.

The Country Music Association nominated Waylon, Willie, and their song in half a dozen categories, including Duo of the Year. Everyone pressured Jennings to get past his grudge and attend the Opryland ceremony. When Jennings didn't appear and Nelson did, in a tuxedo, Tennessee Ernie Ford critiqued Jennings for hurting the show's ratings. Waylon muttered he had no interest in "picking up a goddamn bowling trophy."* He then lost the cover of *Rolling Stone* for demanding editorial oversight of the story, and mocked Nelson for going to the White House, playing that "big beer joint," as Willie called it, and chatting with President Carter about the Cherokee national anthem, "Amazing Grace," on the night of the Iran hostage raid. He didn't mention that he'd been there, too, snorting narcotics in a bathroom. Nelson simply laughed at Jennings's disinclination to participate in an industry circle jerk, saying, "I keep him young by sending him problems." One problem stemmed from a night celebrating their success atop New York's Rockefeller Center, at which Jennings had to be restrained from pitching an irritating record exec out the window and to his death on Sixth Avenue. "I've always been crazy," Jennings explained in song, "it's kept me from going insane."

But Jennings had a point. Here, Music Row was rewarding him for making music they had tried to stop him and his compatriots from releasing. Now, with half the industry copycatting him, Willie,

* Country-rock pioneer Chris Hillman implicitly agreed with Jennings. After scoring several consecutive Top 5 country singles, Hillman's Desert Rose Band received a Vocal Group of the Year nomination at one CMA Awards, but when Mary Chapin Carpenter revealed the winner, she visibly recoiled, realizing it was a virtually unknown act. The other band had a major label deal, Hillman wrote, "and I discovered that record companies traded votes for certain artists." The reasoning, he surmised, had to do with how visibility on the awards broadcast led directly to a certain number of record sales.

and the boys, he rightly felt that they owed him not an award, but an apology—and royalties. Meanwhile, Nashville and New York execs stumbled over themselves trying to please the new celebrity, offering Willie his own label. Nelson's religious album, *The Troublemaker*, finally saw the light of day after *Stranger*, now affixed with a concert shot on the cover instead of any hint of spirituality. It went to number one, as did *The Sound in Your Mind*, the top-selling country record of 1976. The following year, Columbia tried to bury Willie's Lefty Frizzell covers album even after Nelson's first take on Frizzell topped the singles charts. Nelson decided to go one further—not only would his next record be all covers, it would be entirely composed of standards from the American pop songbook: Gershwin, Irving Berlin, Hoagy Carmichael (twice), and, lest anyone suspect Willie Nelson's taste ended with the Depression, the Righteous Brothers' "Unchained Melody." And he didn't want to use a Nashville producer to help. Instead, he went to Memphis, by way of Malibu.

Booker T. Jones, a keyboardist and hitmaker while still in high school, had once been the darling of Stax Records' rhythm and blues recording operation in Memphis, Tennessee. In 1977, he lived in the beach paradise of Malibu, California, with wife Priscilla Coolidge, Rita's sister. Nelson had moved to town and into the same condo building at Kristofferson's encouragement. After bumping into Nelson jogging on the beach, he and Jones got together for a jam session, Booker T. on electric piano, Willie on Trigger. Booker seemed to believe the choices of "Moonlight in Vermont" and "Stardust" were because of their shared affinity for the Great American Songbook. Plus, the men had similar musical backgrounds, "making six dollars a night playing to four a.m.," as Jones put it. Unbeknownst to the musician/producer, however, Willie and Bobbie had already discussed the idea of an album with their Tin Pan Alley faves, including "Stardust" and "Moonlight." He'd also tested out the former at the Austin Opry

House, where it was met, at first, with an eerie silence. "The kids in the crowd thought 'Stardust' was a new song I had written," Nelson said. "The older folks remembered the song well and loved it as much as I did." Booker claimed: "The way he sang it was the way it was supposed to be sung." As it ended, the Austinites roared, solidifying Nelson's suspicion that he was onto something rather than having a mental breakdown.

One day, he and Jones ended up at the home of singer Emmylou Harris, and miraculously, Nelson's entire band was already there to greet the keyboardist. He and Nelson were clearly making an album, Jones decided, although no formal discussions were conducted. Nonetheless, when word of *Stardust* reached Columbia, the label started misdirecting checks for studio time and salaries. When Jones asked Nelson's manager to get a contract from Columbia for him to produce the record, communication ceased.

Nonetheless, Booker persisted. Upon arrival at Harris's home in the Hollywood Hills, where a semi-trailer housed a recording console, he plunged in, setting Mickey Raphael up in a shower stall, the band in the living room, and himself in the truck. As the arranger, he set a mournful yet seductively sweet tone with "Stardust," a Hoagy Carmichael tune, and brought out Raphael's harmonica to gently countrify both it and "Georgia on My Mind." That mournful harmonica gave "Georgia" a "great natural reverb," Nelson said, and rendered it a supremely unusual country single. Nelson, though, didn't hear a huge leap. His idol, Bob Wills, had, after all, perfected western swing, comprised of "jazz riffs inside a country lyric with a 4/4 beat behind it," as Willie put it.

Jones, for his part, was far from hoodwinked or upset about it. He idolized Carmichael and, as a teenager, took a trip to Indiana to literally walk in the songwriter's footsteps. Booker motivated Nelson, too, hustling him from the golf course and into the studio, sometimes even before nightfall. Ten days zipped by and Booker suddenly found himself with an album in the can, one composed, as planned, entirely of standards. Having a devoted producer who had been a successful artist in his own right proved crucial when Jones was asked whether he stood behind Willie's silly little oldies album.

Columbia's reaction was déjà vu all over again: "These sound like demos," one exec grumbled. Rick Blackburn said *Stardust*'s biggest pitfall was that it consisted of songs only the elderly would be familiar with—or likely to appreciate. Nelson argued that this made the songs fresh and interesting to his young audience, especially given the soulful arrangements. He told the bosses, "If a song hits once, it can be a hit again." Bobbie agreed, saying that the reincarnated songs were a great change of pace from the outlaw country her brother had been cranking out at the label's urging.

Although Columbia staffers who flipped for *Stardust* overstepped their bounds by taking their case to Blackburn, the label at least agreed to meet its contractual obligations to the album, which meant releasing it with little fanfare and a five-hundred-copy test run. "The music was too good to go without promotion," Booker later wrote, "cast aside because Willie had forced country music's first black producer on Columbia." But Jones didn't have a compelling counterargument when executives muttered, "Too ugly, too stark." When Columbia stood firm against "Georgia" becoming the single, Nelson backed down. He didn't believe he had any right to do a song "owned" by Ray Charles. "Ray did it his way, and you'll do it yours," Jones argued, and Charles himself said: "These songs don't belong to us, they belong to the world," which convinced Willie, at least initially. However, Jones lost both arguments—for releasing more copies and for "Georgia" going out as a single. Instead, the cheery but melodically stiff "Blue Skies" went first, followed by an equally upbeat take of "All of Me."

Critics alerted their caught-unawares readerships. Willie Nelson, *Rolling Stone* announced, has a new album out—and you wouldn't believe what's on it! The magazine praised the musicianship for "a jump band's verve and a storyteller's love of a good tale." *Texas Monthly* noted that although "the selections are all at least twenty years old, the songs withstand the test of time." *Orange Coast Magazine* called Nelson, who had struggled to get records on the radio thanks to his quirky phrasing, "perhaps the finest male singer in country music" and comparable to "the best jazz singers." Still, the reviewer asked rhetorically "what's the absolute vanguard of redneck rock doing singing tunes like Irving Berlin's 'Blue Skies'?"

The public didn't dwell on such questions for long. They read the reviews and a *Newsweek* cover story on Nelson's life, and snickered at a rumor that Willie Nelson had smoked an "Austin Torpedo" on the roof of Jimmy Carter's White House. They became die-hard fans after his high-energy shows, in which he and the Family might blast through nearly three dozen tunes in two hours. "That man can't sing, but I *like* it," said one new listener. Soon, despite minimal publicity and the unavailability of the full album in shops, both initial singles hit the country Top 3. Then "Georgia" finally came out and went to number one. Nelson won the argument with Columbia. *Stardust* topped the charts for two months and, during a staggering ten-year run on the pop list, sold six million copies. He became a superstar after finally, as one writer put it, winning over "the American middle class, which had little affinity for country music but had fond recollections of the pop songs that had largely disappeared."

"It took me thirty years and fifteen studio albums to become an overnight success," Nelson wrote, "and that was probably a good thing."

Within a few years, and in an era with Kiss, Pink Floyd, and Fleetwood Mac dominating the album charts and selling out stadiums, Willie Nelson & the Family miraculously became America's top-grossing touring act. Willie was the great uniter of the conservative establishment and the younger, liberal buying public. "I didn't give up the big honky-tonk venues... but I did find myself standing on stages with symphony orchestras accompanying me as I sang 'Crazy' and 'Funny How Time Slips Away.'" One crowd might be all "suits and gowns" while the next could be "overalls and Daisy Mae cutoff jeans." After Gino McCoslin took over security, as well as other managerial duties, from Paul English, he immediately implemented plans to make up for lost time and, more specifically, revenues. He purposely oversold a stadium show in Dallas—"hell, the airlines do it all the time," McCoslin said—and once covered up a venue's exit signs with ones reading "Bathroom" to lead people out into the parking lot, where they would be forced to pay again to see Willie.

Meanwhile, Waylon Jennings's only confidants were his manager, his wife, and his drummer. The two hottest acts in country music were both competing for one or two nightly plays on pop radio and the attentions of their shared manager, and working on compilations and duo LPs. When an RCA employee subsequently asked for a "Willie N. Waylon" at Hillbilly Central, not realizing they were two (supposedly) distinct personas, Jennings was livid, then burst into hysterics. It shouldn't have come as such a surprise, then, that Waylon's "Bob Wills Is Still the King" actually contained a dig at Nelson under the guise of praising Wills as still the best in Austin.

Pissed at Nelson, Waylon decided to compose "a letter... in rhyme." The first time Nelson heard the song, he correctly identified this not as a friendly shoutout but either an attempt at putting him in his place or outright mockery. He barked at Jennings for publicly suggesting he would consider himself at or even above Wills's level and, for a time, the two only communicated through their manager. Then Wills died, unfortunately before Waylon's tribute to him came out as a double A-side and went to number one. Most listeners had simply followed the crowd on the recording, which was recorded live in Austin, and cheered at the mention of Nelson, not reading too deeply into it. "Is it true that all you people in Austin think when you die, you go up to Willie's house?" Over their cheers, Jennings grumbled: "Well, you ain't."*

"I think Waylon was jealous of Willie," said Merle Haggard. Jennings claimed it was something else: Nelson's erratic behavior and indecisiveness. "I've had to start my life over several times because of him," he said without elaborating.

Music Row realized they could capitalize on Waylon and Willie's shared image as the great unifiers, hillbillies with an intellectual's soft spot for Americana. Despite his intense hatred for RCA—he would practice using his throwing knives on the company's ads, pinned to an office wall—Jennings agreed to compile *Wanted: The Outlaws!*, a hodgepodge of mostly previously released material starring himself, Nelson, Jessi Colter, and, at Waylon's request, Tompall Glaser. "You couldn't find two guys who are less like outlaws than Waylon Jennings and Willie Nelson," said manager Neil Reshen, veering off script. "It's all horseshit, really. But if the public wants outlaws, we'll give them outlaws." Jennings agreed: "About the closest thing that Willie ever did to bein' an outlaw is that he probably came to town and double-parked on Music Row." The exaggerations were necessary to push units, however. While *Red Headed Stranger* and Colter's "I'm Not Lisa" sold like

* He added, off the cuff, "Talked to Willie today and he told me to tell y'all… 'enh.'"

gangbusters, *Stardust* and "Luckenbach" had yet to be released. "We're sitting over there," said RCA Nashville head Jerry Bradley, "trying to sell two hundred and fifty thousand records, and we're still struggling." Jennings called the executive in charge of *Outlaws!* a nut. "He didn't have a clue about music, though he always tried to get involved in it, usually by remote control." When Bradley asked for changes, Jennings claimed he agreed, then changed absolutely nothing. The "alterations" were always approved.

Side one, track one, on the biggest country album of all time had an unusual route to production. After Bobby Bare's producer called and asked her to write a cowboy song for a concept album, budding singer-songwriter and sometime TV spokeswoman Sharon Vaughn knocked out "My Heroes Have Always Been Cowboys" in hours. Says Vaughn: "I write songs from a film that plays in my head, and basically it's cheating because I only transcribe what I see." She loved Roy Rogers and had pictured "My Heroes" as a song he might have sung, although Waylon Jennings, piecing together the *Outlaws!* compilation across town, would be perfect. She smooth-talked her way past RCA's front desk and wound up alone in a control room with the "outlaw" himself. Jennings, perhaps aroused by the comely woman begging for a favor, agreed to give her tape an honest listen. He started up the demo but, after the second line, hit stop.

"Who wrote this?"

"I did," she said softly.

He squinted at her, a woman he only knew as the Ray Batts spokesmodel from television. Without a word, he hit play again. Two lines later, he practically punched the "stop" button.

"No, who *wrote* this song?"

"*I* did," said Vaughn, more firmly this time. When he started and stopped the track once more, she reached for the tape player. "That's it! I'll just take this," she said.

Jennings ignored her. As the song spun for a fourth time, finally unspooling entirely, he picked up the receiver and dialed a number from memory. "Jack," he said, meaning "Cowboy" Jack Clement, then semiretired in Texas or, rather, ostracized from Music Row. "I want you to fly in tonight. We got us a song to record."

It had been less than twenty-four hours since Vaughn had written "My Heroes." She recalled that it "broke every rule in the book because I didn't know the rules." When one producer told her "My Heroes" was an instant standard, she had to ask him what that meant.

With that in the can, Jennings moved on to side two, sequencing it to open with a spiffed-up live version of one of his early, minor hits, cowritten with Willie.* "Good Hearted Woman," with overdubs replacing Waylon with Willie's voice on one verse and adding a ridiculously overblown applause track to give it a rowdier feel, became one of the defining country songs of the decade. *Wanted: The Outlaws!*, with its cover styled as an Old West wanted poster featuring each of the album's four singers, became the first country record to receive platinum certification for over a million units sold. Most importantly, it made Nashville almost "hip for the first time," as one observer noted. Said BMI employee Del Bryant: "Immediately, the town turned 'outlaw' happy. Everybody that had been walking through the alleys, looking like an outcast, wearing a hat, was immediately signed as an artist." Those who identified with the music soon migrated to Nashville and slowly became the majority, ousting the suits. The newcomers were anarchists "going up against the Nashville establishment," said Jennings, but "we didn't want to dismantle the system—we just wanted our own little patch."

---

* Willie had contributed the "teardrops and laughter" line, which Waylon said was what was "missing."

"'Outlaws' [was] just another way of saying 'new direction,'" said a somewhat left-out Johnny Cash.

"All of a suddenly, we were outlaws," Nelson says. "I thought it was the funniest thing in the world. And I tried not to disappoint them!"

Although "I'm Not Lisa" had been produced by Waylon at Hillbilly Central, and featured Jennings on guitar and Bucky and Marijohn Wilkin on vocals, Glaser suggested Waylon's wife made no sense on an "outlaws" comp. Jennings shot back: *I ain't doin' it without her.* The brotherhood between Jennings and Glaser frayed; Colter later observed that their bond worked only when they shared a common enemy. Soon after the album, they sued and countersued each other over missing royalties.

Jennings and Nelson, though, buried the hatchet for a stadium tour. With Jessi always opening, the headliners alternated who would close the show, with Nelson closing in New York and Jennings as the star in Des Moines. Regardless of who closed, the audience rushed the stage for them. The entourage expanded to four personnel buses, the last of which became known as "Animal House" for its all-night ragers. (On another, Waylon claimed he and a group of hangers-on invented the popular dice game Farkle.) There were too many roadies drinking too much beer, and a handful of narcs, too. The interlopers were easy to spot, since they inevitably shared the running Nashville joke: "Which one is the woman, Waylon or Willie?" Waylon fired the crew member responsible for sticking transmitters in the bus bathroom and bedroom—not on account of his fear of a drug bust, but because, he claimed, he didn't want to know what the band said behind his back.

The origins of the Highwaymen could be traced to this point, as Waylon did duo albums with both Johnny Cash and Willie Nelson instead of an *Outlaws 2.* Miraculously, Jennings managed to convince his and Nelson's competing record companies to first let him attempt to add his vocals to old, unreleased Nelson recordings, including of two Kris Kristofferson songs, and then to let them record the new tracks for a *Waylon & Willie* album on RCA. (Cash joked that these deals were settled between the labels via "duel.") Executive Jerry Bradley shrugged at the tapes Waylon assembled, which initially contained few new duets.

"You don't really like them?" said Jennings.

"Well," Bradley said, "we'll do well with them, but I don't think there's one as good as what we had with the *Outlaws*."

"What about this one?"

Waylon played "Mamas Don't Let Your Babies Grow Up to Be Cowboys," a recent minor chart entry from Ed Bruce, and suddenly, Bradley's demeanor changed. *That's the hit*, he suggested, and this time, he was right. For the rest of his life, whenever his solo shows ended without a guest appearance on "Mamas," fans would ask Waylon: "Where's Willie?"

Before *Outlaws!* and *Waylon & Willie*, publishers looked down on cowriting; in the latter part of the decade, they began to sign and seek out songwriting and performing duos who might replicate that success. Even Combine Music, the scrappy publisher that had struck gold with Roy Orbison and Kris Kristofferson, sought to match up-and-coming writers with established hitmakers. Retrospective reviewers have noted that *Waylon & Willie*, while a smash, became more about showmanship than creating high-quality music, a criticism each man would try to counter in the future, with ever-diminishing plausibility. One reviewer nailed Jennings's problem: "He was better on offense than defense." Jennings's and the album's success, too, were overshadowed even before its release by a much-publicized incident, which eventually led to the collapse of

Waylon's career and the birth of the Highwaymen. Even before it, as Music Row anticipated, outlaw country had peaked. Little did anyone know, including Jerry Bradley, who called the movement "the music of the future," it would take almost four decades for country's "future" to come to Nashville.

CHAPTER SEVEN

THE BIGGER THE FOOL, THE HARDER THEY FALL

I really have the feeling I'm an outsider every place I go.

—Kris Kristofferson

I have become all things to all people so that by all possible means I might save some. I do all this for the sake of the gospel, so that I may share in its blessings.

— 1 Corinthians 9:23

Despite "Bobby McGee" and his reputation as the greatest country songwriter of all time, or at least the 1970s, Kris Kristofferson is now better known as an actor. In just his first few years in the industry, he appeared in well-regarded and profitable Hollywood gems like *Blume in Love*, *Semi-Tough* (with Burt Reynolds and Jill Clayburgh), and as the male lead in Martin Scorsese's *Alice Doesn't Live Here Anymore*, alongside Ellen Burstyn's Oscar-winning performance. "I guess I ain't no cardboard cutout anymore," he joked.*

* After Kristofferson got into film and moved to California, where he cut his first record outside Music City in 1974, his old Nashville friend Bucky Wilkin joked: "Kristofferson Doesn't Live Here Anymore."

"Ray Price came out to talk to me on the road once," he recalled. "He said performing was going to ruin my songwriting like it did Willie." But Kristofferson's Hollywood career came at the expense of his music career *and* made up for a decline in his songwriting fortunes. His record sales declined, even as he became a recognizable A-list star. "Why Me" had been a number one country single and set a record for its half-dozen *reversals* on the pop charts, a term for a song that repeatedly drops and rises in the ranking. But that year, 1973, as *Full Moon*, his first duo LP with Rita Coolidge, topped the country charts, Kristofferson's solo effort, *Spooky Lady's Sideshow*, recorded in Los Angeles, became his first to miss the Top 10. The next missed the Top 20; by the end of the seventies, his albums wouldn't make the charts at all.

With such disheartening news on the musical front, Kristofferson understandably plunged headlong into a lucrative acting career. "I always knew that music was where his heart was," recalled Coolidge, "that he felt like he was kind of getting away with murder doing movies because he was not a trained actor." The two were so busy when Coolidge became pregnant with their firstborn, they didn't get an ultrasound done and, after three doctors misjudged the baby's sex, Casey, named after a song on *Kristofferson*, a girl, was born. (Kristofferson's mother sniffed dismissively at the baby and walked away without a word; apparently, she decided that Coolidge's Cherokee heritage showed in Casey's skin tone.) Hours after her birth, Kris headed out to shoot another film. His relationship with Coolidge quickly soured. She barred her husband from her solo recording sessions; her bands were mainly composed of men, and since they considered Kristofferson a god, he became a distraction for all of them.

Comedians Bob Zmuda and Andy Kaufman were performing as part of a series of political rallies in California when they found themselves playing co–second fiddle to the actor-songwriter. The parking lot at every hotel would be packed with caravans of young women before the tour arrived. When a shirtless Kristofferson waltzed onto his balcony, the women scrambled from their vehicles and posed so he could approve "the goods." (Zmuda likened their awestruck faces to puppy dogs gazing out at the world from behind retail store glass.) Kris reportedly had the women line up outside his production trailer on other shoots and, one by one, slept with each until he collapsed, got a few hours' sleep, and returned to set. "Kris was a ladies' man beyond belief," said singer Ronnie Hawkins. "He didn't hustle them or hit on them. Women made fools of themselves around Kris—he was spoiled."

"It got to the point where he got to town to do a concert and if you could get on the bus, you were cool," says Nashville friend Bucky Wilkin. "He neglected his writing career, and became this sort of Burt Reynolds character, where people knew him and he was pretty successful, but that magic had gone from his writing... but maybe he'd done enough."

Kris often began the day with a "Dirty Sock," a concoction involving grapefruit and vodka mixed by his wife or assistant. It wasn't nearly enough to get him through a day's shooting. "I had a half-gallon of Jose Cuervo in my trailer and they never let it get empty," he said. "They just kept coming back in and filling it up, the same half-gallon. I don't know how much I was drinking, but it was a lot."

On the shoot for 1976's *The Sailor Who Fell from Grace with the Sea*, Coolidge finally received a message she could no longer ignore. One night, Kristofferson returned from a photo shoot with costar Sarah Miles so intoxicated from red wine that he spiraled out of control and struck Coolidge. Mortified to see his wife with a black eye the following morning, he promised to straighten out. However, when the spread from the shoot hit *Playboy*, the reaction was explosive. Miles and Kristofferson were shown in the buff and, in one infamous shot, he appeared to be at least simulating oral sex on her. Mary Ann Kristofferson rubbed salt in her daughter-in-law's wounds by calling and asking what she thought of her husband's activities.

Coolidge claims the relationship ended then, but they were still performing together two years after the film's release. "It was one of the strangest things in the world to be getting up and singing love songs with somebody who wants to blow your brains out," he said. Rita didn't have these problems—she had bigger ones. While Kristofferson had been busy with movies, Coolidge had gone platinum. Her album *Anytime…Anywhere* blew up big in the summer of 1977 thanks to three mainstream hits, all covers. On top of it all, she carried a stillborn baby for weeks until miscarrying days before *Anytime…Anywhere*'s release. As his wife drew crowds who wanted to hear her radio hits, Kristofferson refused to change his set list and stuck to darker material performed with rock arrangements. He sometimes came out and dispensed with his most popular songs right off the bat. During one performance, Kris staggered out at the end of his wife's opening set. "If you didn't like this show, if I'm too fucked up, you can get your money back," he slurred.

"Don't do that, Kris, don't do that!" their manager howled from the wings.

"Well," said Coolidge, stepping back up to the mic, "I'm not offering my half back because I'm very happy that you all are here and glad that we're here with you."

As the audience applauded politely, Coolidge turned to her husband, telling him that if he insisted on refunds, they could all come out of his take.

Something indeed changed between 1976 and 1978. That year, Cameron Crowe interviewed Kristofferson and determined the songwriter had become "a faithful husband." There had been a surprising upside to "that fucking *Playboy* thing," Kris claimed: It helped spur him to quit drinking. The writer of "Sunday Mornin' Comin' Down" claimed, "I drank all the time. I covered pretty well because I had a long time to learn how. I thought my acting, at the time, was right. Maybe I was good; I don't know." Johnny Cash, then sober, promised: "It ain't as much fun, but you feel much better at the end of the day."*

Crowe pointed out that Kristofferson's newer material no longer expressed a "romantic discontent that may have once led him to write his greatest songs," almost stating directly that they were no longer strong.

"People say, 'Now that you're a sex symbol, do you feel that people are taking your lyrics less seriously?' They weren't listening to them at all before," said Kristofferson.

After the breakup, both struggled to match their success as solo artists or even as a duo. Fans either pestered them to reform or picked their favorite and waged a war on the other, flooding magazines with letters to the editor when the dreaded ex was featured in its pages. Kristofferson, for his part, had an unspoken rule to "never . . . say a bad thing about a woman." Coolidge, without a duet partner or co-headliner to sell tickets, struggled to match *Anytime . . . Anywhere*'s blockbuster success. A&M Records and her producers, which included her sister's husband, Booker T. Jones, pushed her to continue recording adult contemporary fare similar to her Top 20 successes, and she was depicted on album covers as an angelic, whitewashed goddess. But when further smashes did not materialize, she slipped out of view. In the eighties, she moved on to Walela, a group she formed with her sister Priscilla and niece Laura Satterfield, helping bring Native American music to public attention.

---

* Coolidge insisted that Kristofferson went cold turkey later, after watching his alcoholic musician character wreck his life in *A Star Is Born*.

Kristofferson peaked as a celebrity with the holiday 1976 release of *A Star Is Born*. A $6 million Warner Brothers production of a story twice told already, it should not have had a prayer. The corporate decision-makers never accepted Kristofferson as Barbra Streisand's love interest, and the poster, featuring both him and Streisand in a naked embrace, was roundly mocked in Nashville: *Kristofferson's doing skin flicks with New Yorkers now?* Critic Roger Ebert pounced: "We can believe Kristofferson (he didn't exactly have to stay up nights preparing for this role). But we can't believe her [Streisand]." The *Times* dismissed the on-screen couple as looking "completely bogus" and said Kris wandered "through the film looking very bored." Indeed, he was not only miserable on set but, at times, livid with director Frank Pierson, who called the production his worst experience since World War II.

Regardless, *A Star Is Born* became the second-highest-grossing film of the year behind *Rocky*, another rags to riches story. Even factoring in the unpredictable and celebrity worship of the voters, it still stunned everyone, Kris included, when the Hollywood Foreign Press named him Best Actor in a Musical or Comedy. He had become a bona fide star at last, albeit by playing the love interest in a glitzy, maudlin, PG-rated skin flick, about as unhip as joining the police, and, ironically, he wrote none of the material for the multiplatinum soundtrack. Willie Nelson took the opportunity to do Kristofferson's music career a favor, recording *Sings Kristofferson*, consisting of nine Kris covers, which sold over one million copies in 1979. Not long after, Kristofferson finally broke into the UK as a songwriter, thanks to "One Day at a Time," the chart-topping Lena Martell single he cowrote five years prior with his former publisher, Marijohn Wilkin. "There is no other feeling like that," he said of writing a great song, "and to think you would never be able to do that... frightens you.... You know, Hemingway obviously did himself in because he recognized that it was all over—he was dry." Ultimately, "One Day at a Time" would be a smash for virtually everyone who recorded it but him.

"I'd much rather they analyze my songs than my britches," Kristofferson said, but lately, the fans wanted him to be seen (read: ogled) and not heard. When his first post-*Star* LP turned out to be his biggest failure as a solo artist, Kristofferson doubled down on Hollywood. Michael Cimino, director of the 1978 award season juggernaut *The Deer Hunter*, wanted to meet with him about the lead role in his next film, *Heaven's Gate.*

The seventies weren't any kinder to Johnny Cash. He had begun the decade at fever pitch fame, with "Boy Named Sue" and "Sunday Mornin'" selling by the truckload. (A 1973 Opry appearance ended after a bomb scare turned out to be a songwriter with a demo tape, an unexpected consequence of Kristofferson's origin story.) "I'm just looking for that freedom again," he said, looking back on his early career. "I've seen that in people like Waylon. Waylon is more free inside, and freer from the business world of the music business, than anybody I know... more freedom from worry and work and the hassle that goes on at the offices and the recording studios...." After "the CBS power structure on Music Row" (as Cash called it) brought in its own players to do a set of treacly, laughable instrumental tracks on one mid-'70s release, Cash vowed never to accede final authority over his music again. "You can't let people delegate to you what you should do, when it's coming from way in here," he said, pointing to his heart. "I wouldn't let anybody influence me into thinking I was doing the wrong thing by singing about death, hell, and drugs." He recorded whenever and wherever he felt like, including at the House of Cash studio he'd built in Hendersonville, outside Nashville. "If I want to go to California and record, I'll do it," he'd threaten. "I'm not saying I will, but I might."

"Pills were starting to take me in 1967," he said, and a painful broken bone caused another relapse, but he mostly stayed straight for seven years in the 1970s. His doctor had told him that the drugs would always be a problem, and he was right. After relapses in 1977 and 1979, Johnny would drift in and out of addiction and battle the demon his family called "Cash" until his death. He no longer sold records, so, in his mind, he had reason to wallow in self-pity, yet he also had everything he supposedly wanted—June, fame, family, and a sense of destiny as a musician and servant of the Lord. *Get it together, John,* he thought, realizing how lucky he was. *How pathetic you are, despairing and neurotic when you're beloved by all!*

The press repeated the narrative that June had rescued him from drugs, which was true to a certain extent. "She cleared his spirit so many times of the dust and darkness, the anger and pain that often engulfed his life," said their son, John Carter. "He knew inside—though at times he obviously forgot—that she was more than he deserved, that she was his only by some grace God had provided him. And when he did forget, it was only temporary, and he would always remember again. And he would write to her."

Even on drugs, he wouldn't compromise, not even for the president of the United States. After accepting an invitation to play at the White House from Richard Nixon, who, in Cash's view, was helping with Native American causes, Cash reeled at a memo instructing him to play not only "A Boy Named Sue" but Merle Haggard's "Okie from Muskogee" and the racially charged novelty hit "Welfare Cadillac." "I don't know those songs," he told the audience in the Blue Room, lying so the president could save face. "But I got a few of my own I can play for you." Those included "Man in Black," with its cutting references to Vietnam ("Each week we lose a hundred fine young men"),

"The Ballad of Ira Hayes," and "What Is Truth," an indirect response to Merle's pro-war "Fightin' Side of Me" and a thinly veiled ode to Muhammad Ali, the pacifist boxer stripped of his title for refusing to serve in the military. "What Is Truth" had been inspired by an ancient Sufi poem Ali had sent Cash, which Cash subsequently reworked as a rousing gospel number after the Rev. Billy Graham suggested he write something that might connect with the younger generation. At the White House, Cash introduced it by saying he wished the president would get the troops home from Vietnam "sooner," and he challenged the president of the United States to reform prisons and to listen uninterruptedly to uncompromising lyrics like those of "What Is Truth" and "Ira Hayes." Yet the press didn't mention these things, and Cash received flak from the left for meeting with and giving outsider cred to a warmonger.

After Nixon resigned amid scandal, Cash released "Ragged Old Flag," a desperately patriotic song verging on painfully trite. He told audiences he hoped it would collectively "reaffirm faith in the country and the goodness of the American people." He didn't mention that he had, until recent years, little faith in much of anything, let alone American government. As a child, he shuddered at Christianity and its messages of hell, damnation, and sin, and, witnessing the frenzy of worshippers screaming as demons were ripped from their souls, had been alienated from organized religion. Not long after, singer Faron Young was in a car accident in which his tongue became attached to his steering wheel and was nearly yanked out, leading to a speech impediment and singing problems. Cash claimed to have been spiritually shaken by the news.

After decades of hayrides and theaters, unprecedented fame meant Cash could now spread the gospel in cavernous stadiums or sprawling fields. The sound might suffer, the songs could get buried amid the rushed closing medley, but these were *sinners*, and they loved him, and thus he might save some of them. He would perform in slashing rain, despite he and June having been electrocuted in thunderstorms and nearly fainting from heatstroke earlier in their careers, which June said contributed to her memory loss. "I'll stay out here with you if you'll stay out here with me," he promised, and they did. In Toronto, with Kris Kristofferson in the wings, Cash suffered a small panic attack when he forgot the lyrics to the first song. He told a reporter: "For a minute I couldn't remember any song I'd recorded. Then I grabbed 'em again. I wouldn't let Kristofferson see me flop."

After confirming his Christianity in an offhand remark to introduce a gospel number on his TV show, ABC approached him about playing down his religious affiliation. Cash surprised himself by snapping: "I don't cram anything down people's throats, but neither do I make any apologies for it, and in a song introduction, I have to tell it like it is. I'm not going to proselytize... and I'm not going to compromise. If you don't like it, you can always edit it." The network didn't, but when they canceled *The Johnny Cash Show* after two semi-successful seasons, Cash grew suspicious. He figured the "God stuff," coupled with his preponderance for asking unknown country acts, as well as Ray Charles, Louis Armstrong, and other outdated and perhaps not coincidentally Black artists, to appear, proved instrumental in ABC's decision. Later, he would claim to have been relieved when the "dehumanizing" network ended the program.

In 1970, he discovered that an old friend had built a church, the Evangel Temple, on Nashville's Dickerson Road. Reverend Jimmie Rodgers Snow kept pushing Cash to come and perform, but he demurred, claiming that his voice wouldn't hold up in such a venue. Walking into the Evangel, though, he noticed that the congregation, far from hysterical, prayed softly, even holding hands with other parishioners, or calmly sang hymns. Throughout, there was ecstasy of the raptured kind, not the unhinged. Parishioners sang of the Holy

Spirit, angelic doves, and a love of Christ. "They weren't concerned with what the person in the next pew was thinking," he wrote. "It was true worship."

Nor did they gush over the Man in Black in their midst. Cash learned he was far from the only sinner in country music who had started to drift back to God—and not even the only one at Evangel that day. "Most of the ones I knew were people who had a problem with drugs or liquor or some hard knocks of one kind or another, and they were all like brand new." Impressive and comforting, too, was Reverend Snow, who could rattle off Bible verses on any modern subject, to Cash an almost superhuman feat.

Nonetheless, he didn't return for at least several months. When his stepdaughter Rosey, who attended regularly, dragged June, Johnny's wife reported back that it was just like "an old-fashioned service back home." High praise, indeed. The couple returned and attended once more. Gradually, Cash found himself in the pew every Sunday. And that's when he, just as Kris Kristofferson and Willie Nelson would, discovered Larry Gatlin.

After sitting in stunned silence along with the congregation at Gatlin's solo version of "Help Me," Cash couldn't believe someone so young had belted the lyrics so passionately, let alone had written the composition itself. "As young as he is, how lucky he is to know that he can't make it on his own," Cash thought. After hearing Gatlin, "I knew I would not look back in regret," he wrote. "Some burned bridges could not be rebuilt. The future was the important thing now."

He set about filling the time he had left with spreading the good word. In 1973, the man who had quit Sun Records after Columbia promised him a gospel album cowrote, financed, and practically self-released a religious biopic entitled *Gospel Road: A Story of Jesus* and its double-LP soundtrack. Coming off the peak of his chart-topping fame, it seemed like a slam dunk that a major studio would produce and release a Johnny Cash film. However, *Gospel Road* is one of the most unusual "star vehicles" in cinematic history. Shot on location in the desert near Israel and featuring Cash's narration of a life of Jesus through song and Bible passages, it's as uncommercial as Christ Himself. Yet when one corporation expressed interest in funding the film for airing on television, potentially on Easter Sunday, Cash announced he would accept no notes or A-list actors.* "This is one film that cannot follow according to network script approval," he said. "This film is going to be... an expression of our faith, told however we feel it when the cameras start to roll." June and her father, Ezra Carter, who had been teaching Cash the Bible, backed him up. "I always knew you had a special purpose in this life, and this is it," said Ezra. "Just let Him guide you."

Cash worried that organized religion had strayed so far from the teachings of healing the sick, forgiving, and sacrificial Christ that Jesus's image had become bastardized. Cash stuck to the traditional view of the Savior, expounding at length on "His virgin birth, His Resurrection, [and] His miracles." To research for the film, he read biographical texts from modern writers, one of whom called a biblical narrative "a traditional legend," which so enraged Cash that he threw the book out a hotel room window. The effect of his studies was profound: "This is the best I had to offer," he said proudly. "This is me. This is what I would like my life to say."

When 20th Century Fox, which ultimately agreed to distribute the film, struggled to create a marketing strategy for it, a recurring theme in the lives of "outlaw" artists, Cash eventually lost much of his half-million-dollar investment. In the end, the Reverend Billy Graham swooped in to the rescue.

---

* June played Mary Magdalene while amateurs and unknowns filled the other lead and supporting roles.

Graham, one of the most admired Americans of the twentieth century, was so impressed with Cash's conservative vision of Christ's life that he bought the rights to show the film, henceforth to be played mostly after worship services. Soon after, at one of Reverend Snow's ministries, Cash rose to greet Snow as he descended from the pulpit. John quietly intoned, "I'm reaffirming my faith. I'll make the stand, and in case I've had any reservations up to now, I pledge that I'm going to try harder to live my life as God wants, and I'd like to ask your prayers and the prayers of these people."

Reflecting on this period, John Carter clung to memories of his father's joy—"I had my dad back," he said. June, however, had reservations. She had been raised in the Methodist faith, and these newfangled Christians and their kumbaya spirituality made her queasy. Besides, she noted, their fans were going to freak out if they found out the Cashes were into religious "hokum" and making one particular religious leaning part of their live shows. Cash pleaded with her that he needed "a spiritual foundation... when I begin to drift." Besides, he would later say, "telling others is part of our faith.... The Gospel of Christ must always be an open door with a welcome sign for all."

Nothing tested this new piousness like the case of Glen Sherley, the convict whose "Greystone Chapel" dramatically closed the *At Folsom Prison* album. Sherley recorded a live album in prison, the first American inmate ever given that privilege, and it sold better than it had any right to.* For a year, Cash and the prison chaplain worked to get Sherley transferred to the less dangerous Vacaville Prison, and Cash kept up a stream of carefully scripted calls and letters—he called Sherley "a man of destiny"—to California governor Ronald Reagan. Cash also promised to put the inmate up at a

* Sherley closed the show by saying: "The next song here was written in an effort to express my respect and appreciation... especially for you, John."

fully paid-for Nashville apartment and get him a job as a publishing house songwriter, following in the footsteps of Kris and Willie. Once paroled in 1971, Sherley met and eventually married a House of Cash employee in a ceremony at the Cash-Carter compound.

There was another side to the man that bassist Marshall Grant called the happiest groupie ever to visit backstage. Thanks to convictions for stealing $28 in an ice cream company heist, a prison escape, and other convictions, Sherley, age thirty-five the year of his release, had just done eleven years and had been in and out of San Quentin, Folsom, and Soledad since his teens. He tried to capitalize on the buzz "Greystone Chapel" had generated, and seemed to be on his way when legendary country star Eddy Arnold recorded and named an album after one of Sherley's newer songs, "Portrait of My Woman."*

But there were reasons for concern. When Sherley left Folsom, Cash was waiting outside the gates; it didn't seem to alarm him that Sherley had no one else seriously backing him on the outside. He had never really held down a job, certainly not as a songwriter or musician. Like Cash, he had developed a dependency on prescription drugs to keep him alert and energetic, then evened things out after shows with a little booze. "The hardest thing for me to admit to myself was the fact that I was in prison because I wanted to be in prison," Sherley said. "You're fed and you're housed and you're clothed and you don't have to worry about where your next meal is coming from." But as he began to face paying audiences of "straights" as the opening act in seventeen-thousand-seat stadiums, the lifestyle change became overpowering.

"To get turned out of the California penal system and to be put into the world of hillbilly show business, there ain't a hell of a lot of

* His daughter said her father wrote "about real stuff—heartbreak, loss...and that to me is country music."

difference in a lot of ways," said Cash guitarist Marty Stuart. "You're just swapping jail houses."

To boost his career, he needed more than Johnny Cash's endorsement. Soon, he had to do personal appearances on his own, such as record company meetings or ribbon cuttings. "Shaking hands and glad-handing deejays and whatever ads you had to buy in *Billboard* magazine, and kissing babies, whatever back then you were required to do," Stuart noted. "Glen wasn't a candidate for that business, so he was an outsider in that star-making system."

Cash's support for Sherley was, as one journalist later noted, "not just an act of kindness but a powerful reflection of his faith." But Cash did not have the patience of Gandhi, or even of June Carter. When Sherley began following him around, practically hiding behind Johnny's long black coat as strangers tried to shake his hand and snap pictures, Cash pawned him off on his bass player and road manager, Marshall Grant. The bassist woke Sherley one morning for a flight, only a couple hours after shoving his staggering, thrashing body into bed. Grant calmly ran down a list of reasons why he, Cash, the fans, the crew, and the other performers needed him to be on time. "Ticket buyers get angry at Johnny over gaps or shortened shows."

"I understand," Sherley said, nodding apologetically.

"All right, good."

Grant tried to help Sherley out of the bed.

"Marshall, let me tell you something," said Sherley, not stirring. "You know I love you like a brother . . . but do you know what I'd really like to do to you?"

"I got no idea."

"I'd like to take a knife and start right now and just cut you all to hell. It's not because I don't love you, because I do. But that's just the type of person I am. I'd rather kill you than talk to you."

Grant managed to recover. After getting Sherley on a bus to the airport, he told Cash the story. The boss immediately fired the ex-con. Sherley had barely made it through a year of straight life before Cash soured on his protégé. Daughter Ronda Sherley, then just a child, later understood that Cash could see what the drugs were "going to do to dad, and the path he was on, and he couldn't stop him.

"I've heard a lot of people say, do you think John should have taken more responsibility?" she continued. "It wasn't his job to take responsibility. It was never John's job to guide my father through life."

"You can't hasten someone else's recovery or enlightenment," said Cash's daughter Rosanne, at the time a wardrobe assistant and budding songwriter on the tour.* "I think my dad had a sense of maybe he could and it didn't turn out well all the time."

While Cash's management chattered nervously over the prospect that Sherley would return to take a shot at Cash, the parolee vanished. When someone went to check on him, they discovered he had abandoned his Nashville apartment. After taking a job on a cattle ranch in California, his drug use spiked, and he sank into heroin addiction and left his family to become a transient.

On May 9, 1978, Sherley reportedly shot a man under unclear circumstances. He abandoned the truck he had been sleeping in and holed up at his brother's house. Two days later, Sherley contacted his seventeen-year-old daughter, telling her this would be their last phone call because, Sherley said, after all he had accomplished and all those he had promised to stay straight, he couldn't go back behind bars. His brother came home on his lunch break to find Glen, dead of a gunshot wound on the porch.

* After a night of heavy drinking, Rosanne got a lecture from John: "You can stay home and do drugs or you can go on the road with me, see the world, and make a lot of money." To Bono, though, he joked: "But I sure miss the drugs."

Despite their estrangement and the near certainty that Sherley wasn't taking care of himself in exile, Cash was stricken with horror by his suicide. He reportedly remained silent for forty-eight hours, breaking his fast only to agree to pay for the funeral. "He searched for truth and found it in the Father," reads the inscription on Sherley's gravestone. Columnists dinged Cash for being so self-centered he thought he could play a one-man parole board and, with the wave of his magic wand, reverse a man's character. One even questioned whether Sherley had been talented enough to craft "Greystone Chapel" himself.

Sherley's death and the public fallout from it shook Cash's newfound religious convictions, and he never again put himself out there for a convict, nor did he ever seem to quite process it. When the Nashville prison show they performed together was reissued on CD in 2003, Sherley's material had been excised. Twenty years after Sherley's death, Cash bizarrely summarized the ex-con's life as being an accomplished one "for many, many years until he had a tragic ending from, well, actually cancer."

"[Cash] became this bigger-than-life creation," said Lloyd Green, a Nashville studio musician, "with his dark clothes and the dark savior thing he had decided to adopt, which was kind of always a little strange to me and a lot of other people in the business. It was that messianic complex thing kicking into high gear."

Reverend Billy Graham, the country's foremost religious figure, grounded Cash. The two discussed Sherley, God's plan, and Cash's calling, and determined it wasn't to be a traveling preacher. Surprisingly, the reverend insisted he not drop "Folsom Prison Blues," despite its amoral tone, or "A Boy Named Sue," which contained cuss words, "and all those other outlaw songs if that's what people wanted to hear and then," Cash explained, "when it came time to do a gospel song, give it everything I had. Put my heart and soul into all my music." He continued to include "Were You There (When They Crucified My

Lord)," a turn-of-the-century hymn, into his set list as a direct call-to-arms for Christians to make their faith a greater part of their lives, as well as "I'll Fly Away" and "Peace in the Valley," both of which he'd sung at his brother Jack's funeral. Rosanne Cash believes he kept at least one religious tune in each night's repertoire to keep his word to his mother that he would become a gospel singer.

Following 1970's "Sunday Mornin' Comin' Down" and "Flesh and Blood" and except for a fluke hit six years later, Cash would never again top the country charts as a solo artist or make the pop Top 40. Nonetheless, at the same time he was backing off on making Christianity the main focal point of his music career, he worked for several years to study for a degree in theology and did technically become a minister. He never preached, but he did marry off his daughter Karen. The deep religious commitment, however, never wavered, particularly in the seventies and eighties and especially in his record releases.* The titles alone tell the story: *The Gospel Road* (his longest LP), *Holy Land, Jesus Sound Explosion, Sings Precious Memories, A Believer Sings the Truth, Sings with the BC Goodpasture Christian School, Believe in Him*. But aside from *Gospel Road*, none of these were commercially successful, a fact Cash ignored. "Stop going to church and go back to prisons," one exec instructed. He did have the odd, fluke, secular hit, but years might pass between them. He tackled "The Gambler," which Kenny Rogers would soon make one of the biggest jukebox singles of all time, but couldn't muster an enthusiastic take. The minor success "Oney" was dedicated "to the working man" toiling to the point of physical exhaustion under the stern eye of profit-minded company men "trying to get more out of him than he really ought to have to put in." Columbia, increasingly grumbling about Cash's contracts, may

* He also released a children's book that focused on his spiritual growth, *I'm Johnny Cash*.

have seen "Oney" as a thinly veiled dig at their production process, although Cash hadn't written it. When he canned a twelve-track gospel record, they were relieved; when he recorded "Amazing Grace," "The Old Rugged Cross," "Have Thine Own Way, Lord," and similar hymns, they murmured about "career suicide." (When the thematic collection *Murder*, comprised of Cash's more violent material, outsold his *God* collection three to one in 2000, their longtime worries about his commercial direction seemed to have been vindicated.) Cash then put out a concept album about driving around with a hitchhiker, which critics found "forced and stilted...an ambitious, overwrought failure that is fascinating for one listen, but nearly impossible to sit through more than once."

On Christmas Day 1982 in Jamaica, at roughly six in the evening, the Cash family and John Carter's eleven-year-old friend Rob had just sidled up to the dinner table when masked gunmen burst into the kitchen. "Somebody's going to die here tonight!" an intruder screamed. As June slipped off her wedding ring and tucked it away, the gunmen announced their demands: one million US dollars in cash. If Johnny didn't pay up, they'd shoot his son—for emphasis, they grabbed Rob, mistaking him for John Carter. When that didn't produce the promised loot, the intruders locked the household, including staffers, in the cellar with a single plate of turkey.* After Cash and Rob's father busted through the cellar door and called the authorities, the lead gunman was surrounded and apparently summarily executed by responding officers. The others were killed soon after as they tried to escape jail using a ladder rumored to have been given to them by guards. Although he publicly claimed to be unaffected emotionally and that he would not abandon Jamaica, Johnny Cash began using sleeping pills and going to bed with a gun.

* One told June Carter, apologetically, "We were hungry."

He couldn't get over it or other tragedies. During benders, Cash and his son-in-law guitarist Marty Stuart would visit Stuart's predecessor Luther Perkins's grave. "We would lie down on the grave, smoke, and talk to Luther," recalled Stuart, "telling him what a lazy son of a bitch he was for lying there while we were out touring, killing ourselves to promote him."* Really, though, the tours were to make up for Cash and Carter's lifestyle, complete with houses in the United States and Jamaica, as well as the staff to maintain them year-round, and because his royalties had dried up. After two number one country albums to start the decade, he slipped off the chart entirely with three mid-'70s records and all but one in the first half of the 1980s. He poured all his energy into a novel, *Man in White*, a religious work, until his longtime manager, Saul Holiff, gave him an ultimatum: *Get back on track with secular music or I quit.*

Soliff had for years been concerned about the evangelical, proselytizing aspect of Cash's performances, especially during a casino performance in Las Vegas. In response, Cash performed a show comprised almost entirely of religious material. The "religious message" of his film and gospel records alienated audiences, according to Soliff. But when Cash wouldn't back down, his manager bailed. On a tear, Cash fired longtime bassist Marshall Grant for insubordination via a cold letter, which he later admitted was regrettable.

Now surrounded entirely by believers, Cash slid further into irrelevance. A "lack of outside criticism, combined with both a sense of exhaustion from the pressures of his career and a desire to prioritize religion and family to create a perfect storm" led to complete commercial collapse, as one biographer suggested. Cash inadvertently

* Before Perkins died in a house fire, he repeatedly asked Cash to hang out. Years later, Cash would say he believed he'd caused Perkins's death by getting him into pills. He believed a piece of him departed with his guitarist.

summarized what came next in a 1984 song: "Battle of Nashville," his "swan song" for the city, as the lyrics themselves termed it.

That year, after recording a song with Ray Charles for a highly anticipated duets album, Cash watched as five other songs from the record were released as 45s and all made the US Country Top 20 while his disappeared without a trace. He rejected Steve Goodman's "City of New Orleans," even after Kristofferson begged him to reconsider. Willie Nelson put out a version instead, which went to number one. Then Cash received word that Columbia might not re-sign him.

It seemed unfathomable, especially in the closed-off world of the House of Cash. The Man in Black had once been the New York company's most popular artist in the South, but now it had mega-stars, including Pink Floyd and Barbra Streisand. Singles were now released solely to drive attention to the LP, not to earn money themselves. Cash's label allegedly paid a group of extortionist promoters roughly a quarter million dollars per track it wanted in heavy rotation on metropolitan stations; no 1980s Johnny Cash track was worth that investment. The music business, especially country, had changed. The Nashville style now incorporated synthesizers, grating, exaggerated drawls, and handsome, young mustachioed men and poufy-haired women with megawatt smiles. The haggard-looking, deep-voiced, rural-minded Cash was decidedly un-hip in the "Me Decade."

On July 15, 1986, Columbia made it official: "This is the hardest decision I've ever had to make in my life," wrote Rick Blackburn, head of the Nashville division. The company had officially dropped Johnny Cash. The press release reverberated throughout the world, to the point that the History Channel featured it as the seminal event to occur on *any* July 15. "It was like somebody dropped an atom bomb in Nashville," said producer Tony Brown, who overheard musicians comparing Blackburn unfavorably to Satan. Cash, Brown said, "was more than an artist; he was a way of life in America." Outlaw singer

Dwight Yoakam, on his way to country radio stardom, took time out of a television interview to harangue Columbia. "The man's been there thirty fuckin' years making them money," Yoakam snapped. "He built the building." Merle Haggard was even harsher. He told Blackburn: "Let it go down in history that you're the dumbest son of a bitch I've ever met."

In later years, Blackburn blamed Cash and Mercury Records for the move, saying he couldn't offer the same generous terms Columbia's rival had. He claimed, bitterly, that it "became a numbers game" for Cash and explained his thinking wasn't "'What have you done for me' but 'What are you going to do for me?'"

The embarrassment of being dropped by Columbia was compounded by the fact that daughter Rosanne remained under contract with the company. She had ventured out into the public eye in 1978 with a recording session in Germany, creating an album no Nashville label wanted. "I didn't want to think that I was using my dad in any way or trading on his fame," she recalled. She weighed a name change, but realized John would've been crushed by it. After Columbia came across her music and signed her for a second album, she got together with her husband, producer Rodney Crowell, and he helped her cultivate an urban, mainstream sound. Initially, the Cashes had had a somewhat unfriendly competition going. "He would ask me about my contract and how many points I was getting," she said. John, however, dropped the line of questioning as his career faded and hers skyrocketed. She most recently topped the country album charts only a few months before her father's dismissal. ("That was back when country acts would get airplay on Top 40," said singer Ashley Cleveland, "so you would hear some of the more Progressive acts.") "I felt kind of guilty that I was having a lot of number-one records and getting a lot of attention at the same time..." Rosanne said. "He put a lot of stock in being Johnny Cash and everything that that meant...and to not have that, he was a little disconcerted and at sea, and depressed." Partly as an attempt to make it up to him, she released "Tennessee Flat Top Box," a Cash classic, as a single, although she claimed she hadn't known it was an original when she recorded it. It reached number one.

After three decades as a household name, Johnny Cash had finally hit bottom. Even before Columbia dropped him, he suspected his only way back up lay in piggybacking on his musical contemporaries, but he would have to humble himself like never before, not even in church, to get what he knew he needed. And while he had collaborated with Waylon and "made" Kristofferson and subsequently peaked with his songs, neither was much better off in the mid-'80s than Johnny. To truly set the music world ablaze, he would need to convince them, as well as a comparative stranger, the biggest star of 'em all, Willie Nelson, to join them.

CHAPTER EIGHT

THIS OUTLAW BIT'S DONE GOT OUT OF HAND

I was killing people around me, people that were friends of mine. And I was losing everything. . . . I can't blame that on Nashville, because I got into pills in Arizona.

—Waylon Jennings

On August 24, 1977, two weeks after *Ol' Waylon* gave him a career high on the *Billboard* 200, Waylon Jennings heard pounding on the studio door.

He had been up for days trying to write. The $1,500 half ounce of cocaine he ingested daily kept him thinking of lines—*song* lines, usually—but it gave him so much energy and a boatload of ideas, he couldn't clear his mind enough to connect them. After previously claiming that "pills were the artificial energy on which Nashville ran around the clock," now he snorted cocaine in both nostrils at once. Nelson claimed his frenemy lived on coke and eight Hershey's Kisses a day. Later, Waylon claimed the drugs weren't meant to inspire new material, but rather the opposite: to flee from his outlaw image and the pressures of success. "Maybe it's not natural for a country boy to have all that money flowing in from every which way," he wrote. "Maybe I felt, down deep inside, I didn't deserve it. Maybe it was the cocaine, which had taken on a life of its own." David Allan Coe had called Jennings, Nelson, and Kristofferson sellouts in his song "Waylon, Willie, & Me," and Waylon's anemic response—he recycled the insult about Willie double-parking on Music Row—suggested he may have secretly agreed. Jennings told singer-songwriter Tony Joe White that he wished he could start all over, "that winning the war wasn't proving to be as much fun as fighting the battles." Although he didn't have anything to fight for, he *had* beaten Nashville, and gloating about it proved irresistible. Even though Elvis had died a week earlier of pill-related issues, Jennings felt invincible. With an unbroken streak of number one studio, compilation, and live records stretching back three years, he imagined the establishment wouldn't want to risk cracking the golden egg. He was dead wrong.

At the sound of the hammering on the front door, drummer Richie Albright sauntered across American Sound Studios to check it out. When he opened up, expecting an annoyed spouse or drunk groupie, he found himself staring at a badge from the Drug Enforcement Administration. Feeling a slight paralysis, he drifted back toward the intercom to let the agents in and deliberately brushed the call button, which broadcast the commotion to the other rooms. "We followed a package that came in here," said a voice over the system. "What happened to the package the girl just delivered?" Waylon, in the recording booth, needed only a second to realize what was going on before he bolted toward a table where a bag of coke lay, only partly opened.

The cocaine likely originated as an ounce sent by way of apology from Neil Reshen. (Waylon's manager had forgotten to book a getaway for a terminally ill fan, which Jennings had promised to pay for.) His secretary retrieved the delivery from the Nashville airport and drove it to the studio, although it's unclear if she or her boss knew what was in it. Minutes later, more than half a dozen DEA agents burst into the lobby, tipped off by the courier company.* After a courier staffer working at the airport flagged the parcel as suspicious, possibly due to a crack in the packaging, the DEA arrived to take a sniff. After some discussion, they decided to remove 22 of 23 grams and send it on. Waylon claimed plausible deniability of the package, addressed "Personal and Confidential—Waylon Jennings Only," but admitted he correctly guessed its contents before peeking.

Albright claimed he buried the package, but, in truth, it was Waylon who whirled 180 degrees and shoved the coke under a baseboard, a maneuver he could never have done successfully without total clarity, adrenaline, and an addict's blind luck. It was not a moment too soon. As agents breached the control room door, Jennings stood calmly before the mic in the main studio room, listening to playback on his overdub of a duet with Hank Williams Jr. As authority figures swirled in the control room, Waylon, on the other side of the glass, casually asked to hear a musical passage he'd listened to a dozen times.

"What do you want?" Richie asked the agents. "We're recording," he said, stalling. "This is a closed session."

The warrant, Jennings and Richie saw, specifically listed Waylon as their target, which sucked all the air out of the singer. But then he noticed something at the top of the first page. The document made it legal for the DEA to search Waylon's property, but American Sound was owned by *Ol' Waylon* producer Chips Moman. The agency couldn't go spelunking without Moman's say-so—and Moman wasn't there.

---

* Jennings and Colter had their theories—he suspected a narc on his staff; she fingered one of Waylon's ex-wives.

Waylon Jennings and Buddy Holly, early 1959, at a photo booth in Grand Central Station in New York City, shortly before embarking on the ill-fated Winter Dance Party tour.

Willie Nelson & the Family, live at Yale Field in New Britain, Connecticut, in 2004. Jody Payne is at left, Mickey Raphael at far right, and a young Lukas Nelson is behind his father at center. *Photo by the author.*

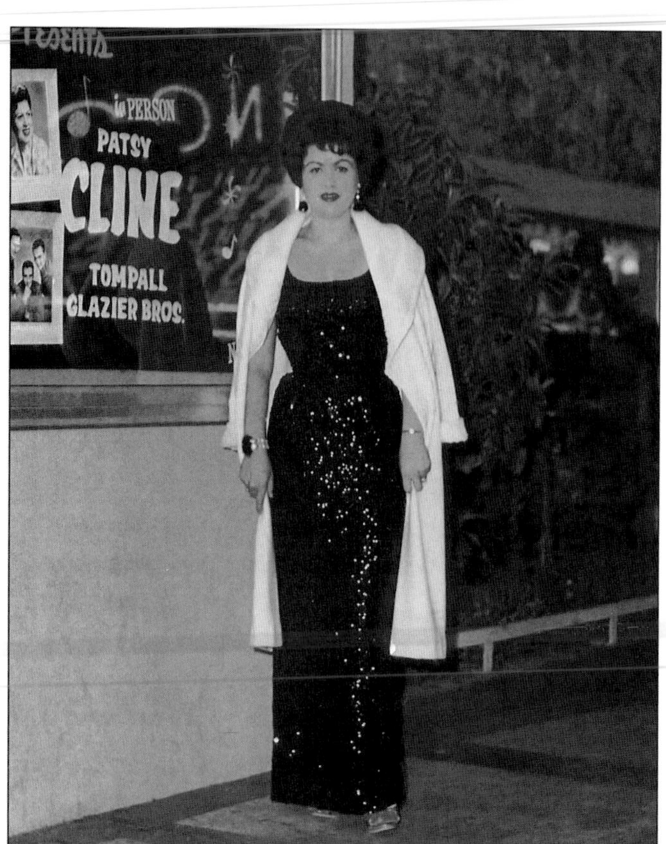

Patsy Cline posing outside a Las Vegas venue in 1962, after her car accident. Note: Tompall Glaser (misspelled on the poster) is the opening act, alongside his brothers. *Photo by Shawn Collins.*

Jack Cash and J. R. "Johnny" Cash in Dyess, Arkansas. *Public domain.*

Columbia Records' Studio A, now leased by producer Dave Cobb, with a Carter Family–branded guitar, on Music Row in Nashville, 2022. *Photo by the author.*

Kris Kristofferson, Willie Nelson, and Waylon Jennings at Dripping Springs. *Public domain.*

Kris Kristofferson and Rita Coolidge at the Dripping Springs Reunion, 1972. *Public domain.*

Glaser Sound Studios, aka "Hillbilly Central," seen in 2022. *Photo by the author.*

Charley Pride in 1981.
U.S. Department of Defense photo/public domain.

Connie Nelson, Neil Reshen, Buddy Jennings, Jessi Colter, Willie Nelson, and President Jimmy Carter. *White House photo.*

Waylon and Jessi with First Lady Rosalynn Carter in 1980. *White House photo.*

Johnny Cash at Sun Records in 1955. *Public domain.*

By the mid-'80s, Johnny Cash had faded from view and was in poor health. *Public domain.*

Wilco, seen here in 2022, and Uncle Tupelo helped launch alt-country in the early 1990s. *Photo by the author.*

Lukas Nelson ripping a solo with Promise of the Real at the New Orleans Jazz & Heritage Festival 2022. *Photo by the author.*

Brandi Carlile, cofounder of the Highwomen. *Photo by John Cowling.*

Carlile, with Allison Russell at City Winery, Nashville, in 2022. *Photo by the author.*

With fellow coproducer Shooter Jennings, Brandi Carlile has helped revitalize the career of Outlaw singer Tanya Tucker. *Photo by the author.*

Alt-country icons the Drive-By Truckers fired Jason Isbell, left, for his heavy drinking. *Photo by Jonathan Lee.*

Today, Jason Isbell is leading a resurgent Outlaw/alt-country movement and is an outspoken progressive. *Photo by the author.*

Chris Stapleton, a breakout country star, could one day lead a new version of the Highwaymen. *White House photo.*

Sturgill Simpson seen here outside the Bridgestone Arena in Nashville, with Outlaw artist Ricky Valido, has taken on Music Row, the awards racket, and country's power structure.
Courtesy of Ricky Valido.

Highwomen cofounder Amanda Shires at Shoals Fest in Sheffield, Alabama, 2022.
Photo by the author.

Shires and Isbell, who were married at the time, playing with Shires's band. *Photo by the author.*

Melissa Carper, an old-timey country singer and member of the industry's growing "out" LGBTQ+ community. *Photo by Lyza Renee.*

Margo Price, carrying the torch for Willie, Kris, and the rest of the Outlaws, in Baton Rouge, Louisiana, in 2022. *Photo by the author.*

Yola, a guest vocalist with the Highwomen and a Grammy-nominated force in Nashville, in 2022. *Photo by the author.*

The Highwomen with Brittney Spencer and Allison Russell, in their first-ever headlining concert at the Gorge in Washington State, June 11, 2023. *Photo by the author.*

The Highwomen with Russell, Spencer, and their backing band, including "the Twins." *Photo by the author.*

Shooter Jennings, producer, solo artist, son of Waylon, Sirius XM's "Outlaw Country" DJ. *Photo by Moofookin.*

Willie Nelson and Waylon Jennings at one of their final performances together, in Arizona, early 2000s. *Photo by Marco Ceglie.*

While discombobulated agents contacted their superiors, Jennings, Albright, and staff scoured whatever areas of the studio the DEA didn't have within its peripheral vision for trashed vials, baggies, and stray uppers or lines of unfinished cocaine. Everything in the studio went down the toilet. Agents, upon their return, tore the place apart—even cutting paintings out of frames—and turned up several vials and baggies in the bathroom. Apologizing to their favorite singer, they booked and fingerprinted Waylon for possession and conspiracy at the Nashville marshal's office. Jennings faced fifteen years' hard time.

Pandemonium ensued. The newspapers that had mocked outlaw country now took it seriously—as a menace. Jennings's publicist pleaded innocent on Waylon's behalf in the press, noting that nobody making $15,000 per appearance would deal drugs. Friends privately reported that, in Jefferson Street bars, the city's Black men cheered the mere mention of his name. When a shutterbug stuck his lens too close to Richie Albright, the drummer thumped him with an unopened Coca-Cola can and got arrested. A friend and former FBI agent checked Waylon's phones and discovered they were all tapped; after removing the taps, the friend returned weeks later to discover they were bugged all over again.

He'd need to add a half-dozen concerts just to offset the legal fees, and he started the next night, appearing as a surprise guest beside Willie in Nashville. "I didn't do it," he told the audience, deadpan. When they played "Pick Up the Tempo," Jennings apparently ad-libbed a line change: "And they say I can't last much longer" became "*I* don't give a damn." His drug intake didn't slow down. "I kept a constant level of drugs inside me," he later admitted. "I'd do a two- or three-inch line every twenty minutes or so. . . . If I got down to a quarter of an ounce, I'd start freaking." He hid vials out of view of hangers-on and band members, and then would lose track and stumble upon pieces of his stash months, sometimes years, later.

Part of the problem *was* that he did write a plethora of new songs on coke. After the raid, he dashed off "Don't You Think This Outlaw Bit's Done Got Out of Hand," which, though a hit, snapped his streak of country number ones. After producing, engineering, and mixing another album for a week without even taking a nap, he began to hallucinate an instrument track that didn't exist. No one in the booth had the guts to tell him. "I was cussing and pulling faders up and down and looking for that [bass], and finally I found it wasn't on there at all." When Jennings and Kristofferson were at an LA restaurant and boxer Muhammad Ali walked in, Waylon begged Kris, Ali's costar in a TV movie, to introduce them. "I was worried because that's when Waylon was really messed up," said Kristofferson. "He looked like death eating a soda cracker—his hair was all greasy, and he'd been up for a month, I think." Reluctantly, Kris brought him over to the champ's table. Jennings heaped praise on the man he most admired, and remained articulate in explaining his appreciation for how Ali "stood his ground" when ordered to serve in Vietnam or forfeit the heavyweight title. The champ later warmed up to Jennings enough to become co-godfather with Johnny Cash of Waylon's youngest son.

After battling the feds and Music Row, he refused to slow down or surrender anything he'd won, even if it killed him. A year earlier, instead of arguing with RCA about where he should record in Nashville, he flew to Los Angeles for a few weeks with Ken Mansfield, who recorded *Are You Ready for the Country*, which included multiple rock and roll covers and first indicated Jennings was short on material.

Around the same time, Hank Williams Jr. gifted Jennings with his father's cowboy boots. That night, lightning took out a pair of trees outside Hillbilly Central, one of which fell on Jennings's El Dorado. Soon after that, while wearing the boots, another lightning storm led to the destruction of the studio's recorder. In another incident, he put his feet up on his office desk to show a visitor Hank's boots; at the mere mention of "Hank," two framed pictures slid from their hooks and crashed to the carpet.

Another ghost continued to haunt his career. On *Ready for the Country*, Jennings penned "Old Friend," a tribute to Buddy Holly, singing forlornly: "It seems like only yesterday / the last time that I saw / you laugh at me and fly away." He joked that Holly was a tyrant, and suggested the deceased singer wouldn't believe "the changes" their music had undergone since 1959. But, he noted, "the funny thing is, lately / it keeps on easing back to you." Once more, Waylon's friends heard his cry for help. Jessi's ex-husband Duane Eddy came in to produce a four-song medley of Holly classics, which Jennings ran through, not with his trademark finely honed, barrel-chested delivery, but a gravel-choked version of the voice that saved the Winter Dance Party tour. It didn't work. (Elsewhere on a 1978 album, he sang "Don't ask me who I gave my seat to on that plane / I think you already know / I told you that a long time ago.") When the original Crickets gifted Jennings with Holly's red motorcycle on his birthday, Jennings had it delivered via elevator to his suite, where he cranked it up at the stroke of midnight.

After Waylon, like Johnny Cash, mislaid several vehicles in a druggie fog, Richie Albright tried a one-man intervention. Unable to persuade Jennings to go cold turkey or ease off, the drummer suggested a few weeks of sobriety so that his next high would be incredible. It actually worked—until those weeks were up, of course, and Waylon plunged back in. Meanwhile, after a DEA agent admitted he'd uncovered no proof Jennings knew about or had even possessed the coke, the judge should have dismissed the case. However, he announced, contradictorily, that although there was not enough evidence to convict Jennings, there was probable cause to charge him. Finally, Reshen's assistant, Mark Rothbaum, pleaded guilty, and the charges against Waylon were dropped.

Jennings, "making no compromises whatsoever," as *Music City News* marveled, started work on another album. However, 1979's *What Goes Around Comes Around* consisted almost entirely of other songwriters' material, with production duties handed over to Albright. A *New York Times* review noted that *What Goes Around* was, surprisingly, "mostly brooding, even wistful, ballads full of vulnerability and self-doubt." Although he still spent time with the other Crickets and incorporated a medley of Buddy Holly's hits in concert, there were no more unreleased Holly covers to pad out side two. "As you get older, you get smarter and that can hinder you because you try to gain control over the creative impulse," said Bob Dylan. "Creativity is not like a freight train going down the tracks. It's something that has to be caressed and treated with a great deal of respect."*

After "I Ain't Living Long Like This," written by Rosanne Cash's husband, Rodney Crowell, hit number one, several red flags appeared, mostly unnoticed at the time. Jennings lost out on the top spot on the album charts to a sanitized, FM-radio-friendly record by Kenny Rogers, *Kenny*, which included hints of disco and bested any position Jennings would ever be in on the *Billboard* 200. Instead, Waylon's *What Goes Around* stalled at number two on the country chart for an aggravating fourteen weeks. At the time, it was seen as an amusing "disappointment"; looking back, it's clear Waylon had peaked.

This outlaw "bit" had gone off the rails.

—★-★-★—

Kris Kristofferson ended the decade looking in horror at financial records, too. His album sales were even worse than Johnny Cash's,

* Jennings's *Greatest Hits* included only one song not yet released as a single: "Amanda," from 1974. Now, it went to number one, helping make the LP one of the top-selling country records of 1979, 1980, and 1981.

even after winning a Golden Globe for *A Star Is Born* and landing the lead role in *Heaven's Gate*, the most anticipated movie of the 1979 awards season. He couldn't even land gigs at Willie Nelson's picnics. "When I was your manager, I was good at being your manager," Mark Rothbaum, now representing Willie Nelson, told him. "Now that I'm not your manager, I'm good at not being your manager." He wrote "Fighter" for *Easter Island*, name-checking Waylon, Willie, and Billy Joe Shaver, as well as the "spider" that turned Shaver "crazy" at one picnic, but it didn't register. After performing with Rita at the Havana Jam, a rare, sanctioned concert of American music hosted by the Cuban government, he headed out to Montana in April 1979 for the *Heaven's Gate* shoot. Either before he left or soon after his arrival, Kristofferson learned his wife had left him, taking their daughter, Casey, and lighting out for parts unknown. Coolidge insists she gave him an ultimatum and they booked counseling sessions, but when Kristofferson said that a cover she had done of his song "butchered" the original melody, she lit into him. She claimed he never made time for their family, seduced women every time she turned her back, and thought he got a kind of marital immunity while on the road, while she explicitly did not. Kristofferson did not deny any of it. As he admitted to Dan Rather around that time, quoting the famous William Blake line: "'The road of excess leads to the palace of wisdom.' By those lights I ought to be the smartest son-of-a-bitch in the entertainment business right now." Said Nelson: "I can out-party Waylon, but Kris, he makes it a religion." Coolidge left him despite his humbling himself, and it stung. He contacted her ceaselessly for months, finally giving up on Christmas Eve, when she served him with divorce papers.

Suddenly, all Kris's fans, especially the women, were paying attention to him again. "The fact that I had done the leaving," lamented Coolidge, "allowed Kris to be portrayed—and to portray himself—as the aggrieved party, and me as the heartless wretch who had abandoned him." In interviews promoting his forthcoming movie, Kristofferson strongly hinted that he had been blindsided by the breakup, which boosted his image ahead of *Heaven's Gate* and *Shake Hands with the Devil*, his 1979 album. But *Shake Hands*, timed for release when Kristofferson was supposed to have wrapped on *Heaven's Gate*, didn't chart. Biographer Stephen Miller blamed the record company, noting that Monument had released nine Kristofferson albums, all produced by the same man; the first thing to change should have been who ran the controls. Instead, despite new Cuban and Latin American influences, critics complained that Kristofferson treated "his recording career [as] an afterthought to his more prominent career in the movies," and Miller critiqued the vocals as "well off-key and with poor phrasing and timing." Worse were the songs themselves, mostly older, forgettable originals, including two Kristofferson had practically given away at the end of the previous decade.

Kristofferson, though increasingly threatening to quit acting, was given top billing, which pushed out A-list actresses who required the same, including Jane Fonda. He accepted United Artists' terms of $850,000 plus 10 percent of the promised mountain of profits. Then *Heaven's Gate* went over budget. And again, and again. Ultimately, costs ballooned from $11 million to over $44 million due to Michael Cimino's methodical directing, including fifty-plus takes of a single moment of action. Cimino giddily told the press about Kristofferson's sullenness, suggesting he had taken a method acting approach to the role. Of course, even casual fans made the connection to the divorce from Coolidge. But Christopher Walken, who had shot to fame thanks to Cimino's previous effort, *The Deer Hunter*, had persuaded Kristofferson to remain in character. Kristofferson said he would just do whatever the "artist" Cimino wanted. "He would go through the different motions, actually act it out: how I would wake up hungover, down to the point of hitting my head, where to do it. I'd never seen anybody do 53 takes I hadn't messed up myself. But I did it without question; to the point sometimes I depressed myself. There's a part of you that's gotta feel, 'Well, I'm just not good enough.'"

When *Heaven's Gate* finally screened for executives as a 325-minute rough cut in June 1980, the film had become a muddled mess, with dialogue so buried in a mix of horses, wind, laughter, and more "authentic" background noise, most reviewers couldn't find the story. Early critics' screenings were so calamitous, with one reviewer dashing from the theater at intermission, that they became news stories in themselves. The movie "fails so completely that you might suspect Mr. Cimino sold his soul to the Devil to obtain the success of 'The Deer Hunter,' and the Devil has just come around to collect," wrote the *New York Times*. "Watching the film is like a forced, four-hour walking tour of one's own living room." The November 1980 New York premiere collapsed when Cimino, standing amid rows of unopened champagne, learned the film's own production team hated the movie. *Heaven's Gate* earned only a few million, United Artists' profits dropped 25 percent, and its parent company's stock price plummeted, nearly resulting in the insolvency of both, and with them into the toilet went Kris Kristofferson's acting career.

"Unfortunately, it was done in," he said of the film in 2016. "And Michael was collateral damage. . . . I think 'Heaven's Gate' is waiting to be rediscovered, just like I think they're eventually going to tell the truth about the Kennedy assassination—but I wouldn't look forward to it being tomorrow."

Unfortunately, *Heaven's Gate* wouldn't be rediscovered until the Criterion Collection reissued the director's cut on DVD more than thirty years later. In the interim, the critics came for Kris Kristofferson, too. He received a Worst Actor nod from the Golden Raspberry Awards for *Heaven's Gate* and *Rollover*, an implausible political thriller costarring Jane Fonda, which opened at number one but soon sank into oblivion due to poor word of mouth. "I went from being right up with the big guys to nobody," he said with a laugh. Except for an uncredited cameo in a horror-comedy, he didn't appear in a theatrical release for three years, and his 1984 films didn't nearly recoup their costs. That year, at the funeral of Sam Peckinpah, his director on *Pat Garrett*, Kristofferson almost quite literally pointed fingers at executives in the audience, suggesting that they had not supported Peckinpah in life.

Jim and Tompall Glaser hit number two in 1981 with their version of Kristofferson's "Lovin' Her Was Easier," and Frank Sinatra recorded "For the Good Times" for the "Present" portion of his *Trilogy: Past Present Future* album, but it seemed like Kristofferson's songwriting glories were safely in the "Past." He was still trying to write a hit single, a fresh one, but all that came out were topical songs about left-wing causes. "It was a bad year," he reflected. "Somoza...got thrown out that summer down in Nicaragua. The shah of Iran got overthrown. And those right-wing revolutionaries were gathering in their offices to assassinate my last real movie, 'Heaven's Gate.'" He claimed that the Reagan administration had asked Hollywood to put the kibosh on movies that reflected poorly on the country.* He didn't give up on his causes, however, performing at a benefit for migrant workers—"Oh shit yeah," he told Joan Baez, who'd invited him, "I'll do it for the Mexicans."

In the studio, he could barely keep his head up. Norbert Putnam, his first Nashville bassist and now the producer of platinum hits, tried

* Yet he agreed to star in ABC's *Amerika*, a dystopian, anti-communist miniseries, after praying that it wouldn't lead to right-wing violence. "I am not one of these people with great correspondence with Jesus," he said. "But I decided to do it and see what damage we could control." Luckily, after an advance review in *TV Guide* savaged *Amerika* as "arguably the most boring miniseries in a decade," audiences mainly ignored it.

to get the singer to show him some material ahead of a recording date. "Naw," said Kristofferson. "Let me just play it for you in the studio. Your best read is your freshest."

Against his better judgment, Putnam agreed. On *To the Bone*, he had to hear Kristofferson's lyrics just before the first take, and then, as they had done on the songwriter's debut, try to build melodies with studio players around rough vocal guides. "I would tell them where to play, not *what* to play," said Putnam. Somehow, they got through the session. But when Putnam played the record for Monument's head of promotion at a Nashville restaurant, the man sadly shook his head.

"Aww, Norbert, we can't sell that."

"Well, why not?"

"It's just too pop," said the promo man. "You know we don't have any money to spend on pop radio."

When he turned to the label's New York parent company for help, they told him: "Norbert, we have all the money up here for pop music and you have all the money for country music. Do you realize if Nashville started having tremendous pop success, they could close us down in New York?"*

The woe-is-me breakup songs, including one from a divorced woman's perspective on her glorious, promiscuous singledom, failed to resonate. With Monument Records verging on bankruptcy, Kris's recording career seemed at an end. Kristofferson called *To the Bone* "probably one of the lowest points of my life. I was recovering from a marriage that had fallen apart. And I was a bachelor father with no experience at raising a kid by myself."

Johnny Cash and Willie Nelson tried to lure him out of seclusion with the chance to collectively save Monument. Nelson, Dolly

---

* In the early '80s, LA labels had six-figure budgets for rock records, while $30,000 was Nashville's max.

Parton, and Brenda Lee brought him in to collaborate on a new album of duets, released as *The Winning Hand* to benefit the company. (Of its twenty tracks, almost half feature Kristofferson, although neither single did.) Cash hosted a TV special promoting *The Winning Hand*, as well as a seven-day tribute to Kristofferson at the annual Country Music Awards.

The highlight, though, and one that set the stage for the breakthrough to come, came when Waylon and Willie joined Cash and Kristofferson to do Kris's new song, "Love Is the Way," with each of the four taking a verse. The Man in Black claimed that the new tune would go down in history as one of the songwriter's best ever, but Kris didn't capitalize on this memorable performance by releasing a recording of it. In an attempt to combine his two (faltering) careers, he agreed to costar with Nelson in the comedy *Songwriter*. The story must have resonated—a country singer (Nelson) ducks calls from his songwriting "coauthor," a gangster who weasels him out of control of his publishing company, and links back up with his grizzled old collaborator (Kristofferson) for one more crack at Nashville. Kristofferson's character, having been stuck on a duo tour with a less talented, more pop-focused woman, helps Nelson hatch a plan to write hits under a pseudonym to bypass the gatekeepers. Willie considered the film snarky revenge on profit-driven music executives, or "asshats."

"The pacing is flash. bang. pop, with nonstop singing, talking, and carrying on, suggesting the manic pace entertainers on the road must endure," one critic noted, but after the film's run ended with a take of one-tenth its budget, Kristofferson found, again, he had few great offers on the table.

"Way back in the day, I was selling records up till, oh about '80, I guess," he reflected. "Then I started selling fewer." His politics weren't helping, not in the Reagan years, with country audiences still stubbornly conservative: "I've had audiences where 300 of 'em wanted their money back," he admitted.

His staunchest supporters remained his fellow Nashville outcasts, including Nelson, Roger Miller, David Allan Coe, and Mickey Newbury. The five, whose visits to Music City overlapped for one night only, broke out their instruments for a guitar pull that could have packed football stadiums. Kristofferson, however, didn't think of it as a breakthrough. "It's been a long time since I stayed up all night playing music," he said, "especially straight, so you remember what you did."

It must've been the best natural high in years. Afterward, Kristofferson would get another call from Cash, and at the same time Jennings and Nelson were trying to figure out how to work together again, and soon the foursome would try out a similar guitar pull. Despite their best judgment, they were going to drive, seat belts unattached, straight toward one another.

PART III

ALWAYS BE AROUND

CHAPTER NINE

ON THE ROAD AGAIN

Art isn't the tools, material, equipment you use. It's in the way you see the world.

—Rick Rubin

It was like Mount Rushmore onstage.

—Mickey Raphael

As the 1980s began, *Urban Cowboy* and *The Electric Horseman*, costarring Willie Nelson in his film debut,* were birthing a cowboy and honky-tonk revolution. The cultural impact of *Cowboy* was less seismic than John Travolta's *Saturday Night Fever*, but it created for country what its predecessor did for disco. Waylon Jennings was supposed to reap the benefits of it. His first mistake, though, was turning down the title role in the film. His second was beyond his control.

The film's music supervisor, former A&R executive Becky Mancuso-Winding, had had the novel idea to package composition and recording artists, including Waylon, and pitch an on-screen performance of the song to a film director. It worked. Two of the soundtrack album's six hit singles—selected by Combine publishing—became

* "He plays Willie Nelson better than anybody," quipped actor Slim Pickens.

country number ones, although there was a catch. The film's producer had insisted that Mancuso-Winding focus on pop-country or country-rock hits by LA artists: "This is not a trailer park, Becky. You can have the trailer park in the film but not on the soundtrack," he said. With no choice, she ditched her plan to use Jennings and instead slotted the Eagles and Boz Scaggs. The film made back five times its production budget at the box office, and sales of western wear skyrocketed, including among women inspired by Debra Winger's button-downs and brown cowboy hats. The record companies used the new income to snap up publishing companies, monopolizing power in Nashville and effectively becoming "their own bankers," as one miffed songwriter noted. In keeping with *Saturday Night Fever* and the death of disco shortly thereafter, however, *Urban Cowboy*'s influence on fashion and record sales quickly evaporated, which, according to songwriter Dan Daley, doused Music Row's "hopes for a long, lucrative run for country music." Johnny Cash wrote that while the outlaw movement had sparked a rebellion among independent-minded creatives, the *Urban Cowboy* craze spurred "a kind of feeding frenzy among their opposites." Artists, especially rock artists, who tried to capitalize on it with country albums of their own, were sorely disappointed. Neil Young was even sued by his record label for releasing country and rockabilly records they were contractually bound to release and that tanked.*

In 1981, country music made up roughly half of all new recordings sold; three years later, it accounted for just 10 percent of album sales. Catalog purchases like *Stardust* or *Folsom* were bigger sellers than the latest releases by anyone. Singer Crystal Gale's mid-'80s "success"

* When Young played chicken, threatening to record nothing *but* country until the matter was dropped, the lawsuit was withdrawn.

told the story: she released two Top 5 singles, yet her total album sales were well under six figures. Rock fans shunned the Nashville Sound and its "lovesick laments, tales of marital strife... the saccharine string arrangements, the note-perfect but utterly bland vocal choruses, the excessive sentimentality." Jerry Bradley, who had shepherded *Outlaws!* to platinum glory, retired. The new music video channels ran material almost exclusively from newer acts. Charley Pride, who started the '80s with thirteen straight Top 10s (and was the only solo Black artist with any), railed against RCA in public for the label's spotlighting of younger artists over himself and Jennings. "Those good times are gone," though, said the *New York Times* in 1985, "and they won't be coming back." Tammy Wynette, one of the genre's biggest stars of the sixties, warned: "The country artists are going to have to band together and try to turn this thing around. If we don't, we're all going to be out of business."

In keeping with the industry at large, Waylon Jennings, Kris Kristofferson, and Johnny Cash suffered career nadirs that year.

Jennings's life had turned into a variation on that of his hero Elvis Presley: Both men had incredible runs, beating others to freshly written songs and getting to have first hits with them, and experienced downfalls when hot songwriters stopped offering them tunes. Between 1980 and 1985, Jennings would hit the country charts, occasionally topping it, mostly with Kenny Rogers tunes, rock hits by the Eagles, and duets with Willie Nelson on Buddy Holly–inspired songs Jennings had written in the sixties. If he hadn't been at such astonishing creative heights only a few years prior, these hit singles might have fallen under the rule "If it ain't broke, don't fix it," but they instead came off as last-ditch, even pathetic attempts at glory. When 1984's *Never Could Toe the Mark* peaked at only the twentieth spot on the country album charts, Waylon's lowest showing since the early seventies, sirens went off at RCA. These are all "bad songs," one exec scoffed.* Jennings himself, though, was too busy trying to pay for drugs. On cocaine, he had shorter highs and thus higher costs to feel the effects, but friends told him he came out of his shell on coke—how could an introvert who had a deep desire to connect with others go straight after hearing that?

Those friends who were once caught in the mesh wire of addiction noticed his problem, but they had their own crises. When Johnny Cash came downstairs for Christmas dinner in 1983, he walked into an intervention. Embarrassed to be confronted by both his family and the Carters, especially on Christmas, of all days, Cash assented to a monthlong stay at the Betty Ford Center, a detox clinic named after the former first lady, for amphetamine abuse. Told of this intervention, Waylon cracked: "Betty Ford didn't get me on it and she can't get me off it." As his health rapidly collapsed, Jennings canceled a brief tour, citing laryngitis. In an early '80s TV appearance with Cash and George Jones, Jennings appeared pale, sweat-soaked, and agitated. It took his son from his first marriage, Terry, now in his twenties and working in the music business, and Shooter, age four, to set him straight. "[Dad] would take a McDonald's straw, cut it, put it in each nostril and [snort] just about every fifteen minutes for three or four days at a time," Shooter recalled. Seeing their only child together sticking a used one up his nose became both the proverbial and literal last straw for Jessi Colter.**

In 1984, Jennings told her: "I'm not going to quit. I'm just going to stop." On April Fool's Day, cocaine-addled Motown genius Marvin

* The public apparently wanted their white singers to turn soul classics into country singles—three R&B gems hit it big that year.

** For years, she had remained mum when Waylon's son Terry booked three rooms for Dad, including two for his mistresses, on tour.

Gaye was shot and killed by his father after punching him during an argument. That morning, Waylon Jennings went cold turkey on coke.

He gave himself a month's ceasefire—no drugs for thirty days, just to see if he could take it. He, Jessi, and their son Waylon "Shooter" Jennings Jr. returned to the cozy Paradise Valley suburb of Phoenix, that scene of early triumphs, to detox. "The cloudless sky was a blanket of blue," Jessi wrote of their walks in the woods. "The air was clean. The jagged rocks, the flowering cacti, the audacious mountains were exciting and calming all at the same time." In a cabin owned by the proprietor of the Bobby McGee restaurant chain, with $30,000 in cocaine tucked away in his tour bus in case of severe withdrawal, he got clarity. His son Terry convinced him he was on a path that meant not seeing Shooter, about to turn five, grow up. Soon after, in a booth at a local restaurant, Shooter put one arm around his father and held him close while, for an hour, he doodled in a coloring book with the other.

Going cold turkey whipped his ass. Despite the diet of taco salads and tuna fish, hold the mayo, he seemed to rapidly put on weight. Although he didn't complain, he suffered from dizzy spells that forced him to give up driving. Nonetheless, he cautiously used the term *quit* instead of *stopped,* which had suggested a stalemate. Colter thought he might mean it when he had her flush all the coke. Johnny and June threw him a sobriety party in Tennessee and played him songs they'd written to congratulate him on getting clean. He choked back a sob. The following year, he told David Letterman: "I'm going on eleven months," and later, he would tell *Spin*: "I wasted a lot of years. I wish a lot of things. I could have been a lot more creative. You know, I spent the last five years that I was on drugs—I withdrew completely from people."

Jessi Colter found out that sobriety didn't mean her husband would become a family man overnight. "To live with Waylon, to be with Waylon, to love Waylon with the kind of love he required meant being on the road.... There was a flow to life on the road that, once I surrendered to its rhythms, provided a certain comfort." Where previously he had "put the tour in entourage," he now lost $200,000 for missing shows and faced astronomical legal fees and the threat of bankruptcy. WGJ Productions cut staff, resolved debts, and added tour dates with the Crickets, packing Red Rocks and Midwestern basketball arenas.

He was on the road so long, he almost gave himself a literal heart attack. In the hospital waiting for an $8,000 pill to take effect and stave off that possibility, he narrowly escaped death on two fronts. Gang members, who had already gone after and hospitalized one of their rivals, entered the wing and began blasting away at their enemy. Jennings, about to enter surgery, was immobile and, as nurses hit the linoleum around him, could only pray the bullets didn't come his way.

On the road to recovery, Jennings began making amends and reached out to fellow addicts. Hearing that comedian Richard Pryor had burned himself after suffering from cocaine-related psychosis, Jennings offered to donate skin for a graft. He volunteered to back up Johnny Cash for five shows in Toronto after Cash's guitar player fell ill, and hung unnoticed behind the drumkit for so long, the Man in Black had to point him out to the audience. Jennings called it the most enjoyable thing he'd done in a decade.

Meanwhile, Chet Atkins had become the whipping boy of the country music scene. "In the wake of the Outlaw movement," Colter observed, "the press had labeled Chet a super-conservative, a company man who'd roped in the renegades trying to break free." Colter and her husband owed the RCA producer their careers. When Jennings got sober, he started to realize the bridges he'd burned and threw Atkins a party to celebrate his work. At it and subsequent recording sessions, Jennings's voice burned up tape. It was newly reinvigorated and passionate, but less commercially appealing now, thanks to his succedaneum of chain-smoking Winstons and drug-related damage to his voice. After narrating the hit show *The Dukes of Hazzard* and matching his highest pop chart showing with the single of its theme song,* Jennings failed to remotely approach its success. After avoiding him for several years, he caved to label pressure and re-teamed with Willie, as well as *Ol' Waylon* producer Chips Moman, for *WWII.* Willie's only new idea, "Write Your Own Songs," was a surprising, full-on assault on Music Row, years after his last major battle with Nashville: "Mr. Purified Country, don't you know what the whole thing's about? / Is your head up your ass so far that you can't pull it out?" It would've landed harder—instead of on deaf ears—if *WWII* hadn't been a commercial disappointment. The two men reunited for a short tour, including a stop in Lubbock, Texas, but the album was overshadowed by Willie's next project, *Pancho & Lefty*, a collaboration with Merle Haggard, which sold a million copies within a year. "We're going to make lemonade out of horseshit," Willie would joke, but it was kind of accurate. Everyone, it seemed, wanted to be seen making lemonade with Willie Nelson.

Everyone except the Man in Black. Johnny Cash called himself "invisible in the '80s." At rock bottom, he played abolitionist John Brown in a TV movie and became the spokesman for a Canadian bank. ("Johnny Cash Money Machines from Canada Trust. 'Cause, friends, life's too short to walk the line.") At one session, John left to get "milk and cookies," crashed the Mercedes he had given June as a gift, and did not return; his young son had noticed that he would occasionally pass out and stop breathing at random, but never told anyone. (*You're still a beautiful woman*, Kristofferson told a fretful

* He claimed he did the song and the show's narration to prove to the haters that country music wasn't "something with kazoos."

June, *you'll do OK out there.*) He busted a kneecap, had eye surgery, and needed twenty-one pints of blood to survive another surgery. He nearly died after an ostrich he owned attacked him and ripped his stomach open. One afternoon in Erie, Pennsylvania, his DC-9 circled the airport in the fog, and in an attempt to land, tilted too far. The left wing hit the pavement and the tip snapped off. As Johnny and June closed their eyes in prayer, the pilot brought the plane down again on a closed runway and miraculously landed upright.

Cash further tested his own principles with a single that reunited him with Billy Sherrill.* Released the year Country Music Television launched, the 45 of "The Chicken in Black" came accompanied by a promotional video featuring Cash wearing a chicken costume behind bars and mugging for the camera. When Jennings saw the "Chicken" video, he said, "You look like a buffoon." The single had been inching up the charts for nearly three months when Cash had Columbia delete it.

After a combined 135 years on the road, Jennings, Kristofferson, Nelson, and Cash finally came together in Nashville. In retrospect, a trial run for the Highwaymen** was held following the October 1983 CMA tribute to Johnny Cash, at a late-night jam at David Allan Coe's house in Music City. "There's nothing on earth I like better than song trading with a friend or a circle of them," Cash later wrote. A year later, Cash invited Jennings, Kristofferson, and Nelson, whom he'd met only a handful of times, to celebrate and perform with him in Switzerland as part of a Christmas concert and TV broadcast. Asked at a press conference why they went all the way to Montreux to tape

* After Columbia dropped him, he played his new songs for another label head and didn't even receive so much as a generic rejection letter.

** Four years earlier, Willie, Johnny, and Waylon had joined host Kris Kristofferson in a TV tribute to Mother Maybelle Carter.

a country music special, Jennings grabbed the microphone and shot back: "Because this is where the baby Jesus was born." Later, he would recall the joke and add: "This funny looking quartet was born, again like the baby Jesus, out of an immaculate conception."

Lisa Kristofferson marveled at how the four voices gelled, calling it "very magical." She and John Carter Cash referred to the camaraderie at an after-show guitar pull as electrifying. But what to do with it? The four men giggled their way through Nelson's "On the Road Again," and one of the men reportedly said: "We should do something else, we shouldn't stop," but the others seemed to miss the significance of it. In one version, the Highwaymen was actually born during a Chips Moman session. While the producer, who had attended the guitar pull, was cutting songs with Johnny and Willie, Waylon and Kris popped in for a quick hello. Regardless, the eventual involvement of Moman, hitmaking producer, proved crucial.

Collaborating with one other artist was complicated enough, but these were *four* stars. Each was signed to a different label with different producers and little commercial momentum at their backs. How would a partnership work, even for one song? Any collaboration ran into a wall they swore they'd never put around their music—that of business interests, contracts, and money. "Kris didn't want to desert his band," wrote Colter. "Johnny had scheduling conflicts. Willie had his picnics to worry about." Colter suggested that only Waylon wanted it, initially. As Ken Burns and Dayton Duncan would later ask of the era, the question became: "Would [the stars] and the music itself lose their way, or would they heed the old saying, 'Don't get above your raisin'?"

Willie Nelson had the most to sacrifice by joining the Highwaymen. Mark Rothbaum, out of jail and now Nelson's and Jennings's manager, didn't need to do much to sell his client. "He's like a train going in one direction," Rothbaum said. "You can either get on or get run over." Nelson, however, suspected his peak had passed; of the eleven studio albums he'd appeared on in the three years since *Always on My Mind* made it to number two pop, only two had made the pop Top 40, and one LP had stalled at number 152 despite a chart-topping country single. He had been coasting on old songs, soundtracks, covers, and gimmicky duets, often a combination of the above; his 1983 album *Tougher Than Leather* was his first album of original material since *Red Headed Stranger* eight years earlier. *Country Music Magazine* ribbed him: since he seemed to have exhausted all his ideas for duet partners, they suggested he phone Margaret Thatcher and Princess Margaret next. Even Tom "No Prostitution of My Ex-Client Elvis Presley Is Too Skeevy" Parker considered him overexposed.

Death stalked him, too. On a flight to Brackettville, Texas, Nelson's single-engine plane started to go down. As his touring crew watched from the runway, the plane hit a sizable crack in the tarmac, flipped over, and thudded to a stop on asphalt. His team raced via Jeep to the wreckage, trailed by the media that had come to welcome him. Stopping beside the overturned jet, which appeared to be crushed, onlookers sobbed, assuming the worst. Then, amazingly, both Nelson and his pilot emerged on two legs, limping but otherwise unaffected. When everyone gasped, Nelson laughed. It was the perfect touchdown, he said, because he could walk away.

"He's accident-prone," said one Nelson employee. "You have to be careful around him at all times...you don't never know when something might fall on him."

In 1980, on a helicopter flight in Hawaii, looking sideways down at a volcanic crater, he and Connie nearly died when the pilot lost control. Later, along a rural road in Canada, a passenger car sideswiped the Honeysuckle Rose. Gator Moore steered the tour bus into a snowbank and its riders survived. Once, when the brakes went out in his camper, he said serenely, quietly, and simply: "Deal the cards." Even without near-death experiences, he had serious health problems, including four bouts of pneumonia in a single year and, before he quit drinking whiskey and smoking cigarettes, a collapsed lung.* "He who lives by the song shall die by the road," said Nelson, quoting Roger Miller.

But it was his mother's December 1983 funeral that finally cracked Willie's happy-go-lucky facade. After missing the service due to a late-arriving flight, he broke down in tears at the gravesite, and then, with his wife and children telling stories, including of the shootout with Lana's husband, and imagining how his mother would have reacted to her hippie family hanging around a graveyard in spotless tuxedos, he cackled. Togetherness, whether in the form of family or friends, mattered deeply, he knew. When Johnny Cash called to feel him out for an album of holiday songs for 1984's Christmas shoppers, he was ready for anything.

Nelson and Cash, the man who had fallen hardest of all four, held out. For years, Kris couldn't get on John's schedule for two days in a row, such was the demand on his talent. Now, Cash tried to sell himself to Nelson: "Hell, Willie, you've recorded with everyone in the world except me," he said. The remark wormed its way into the Texan's conscience. He had booked a few days in a recording studio to do duets with some of his favorite performers, following up on his success with a Julio Iglesias collaboration, but after days of trying out various songs without nailing one, Willie suggested their voices clashed. Marty Stuart watched his boss/father-in-law retreat into his shell. "John and Willie didn't know each other really," Stuart explained. "John and Waylon were close, John and Kris were close, Kris and Willie were close, Waylon and Willie were close." Stuart, undaunted, had an idea for combining all four voices on a

---

* Nelson punched out a windshield in a drunken rage just before he gave up booze, according to daughter Lana.

particular song, one that would allow for each to have exactly the same amount of solo lines.

Glen Campbell, a legend now also suffering from a commercial decline, had recorded Jimmy Webb's "Highwayman" in 1979, but it did not come out as a single; in need of that rare beast with "no harmony required," Marty Stuart suddenly remembered it. He asked the Man in Black to stick around after a session at Moman's Recording Studio in Memphis after everyone else had gone. With a grumble, Cash agreed to at least hear the recording, but he wouldn't wait all night. Stuart called up his cousin, who ran Glen Campbell's publishing arm, and asked if the company still had a copy of "Highwayman" lying around. Stuart drove to Nashville, grabbed a tape of it, and one-eighty'd it back over two hundred miles to the studio where Cash sat, stewing. As Stuart hit play, he went nearly staccato to get the words out quickly: "Listen: four verses, four guys, no harmony required."

"You know, that song's as good as it used to be," Moman said.

Cash said nothing but nodded begrudgingly. Stuart quickly cued up the cassette. When Campbell's three-minute rendition concluded, Cash scratched his chin. "I want the verse about the starship," he said.

"Highwayman" became the fifty-one-year-old Cash's "first glimmer of hope"—and first number one—in almost a decade. It is one of the most startling chart-toppers in the entire country canon, an eerie ghost story with no chorus but a chill-inducing refrain. Yet the single became so popular, Marty Stuart, who had connected the song to the quartet, could go to Columbia and ask them for a contract; Rick Blackburn flipped—in a good way. "Highwayman"* was credited to all four men individually—the deal with a preexisting group called the Highwaymen was not finalized for their first two albums—and each

* Later, the single would rack up nearly twenty million views in just three years on YouTube.

brought in a few songs to cover, including protest/prison song "Welfare Line" and Woody Guthrie's bitter, anti-racist "Deportees (Plane Wreck at Los Gatos)," with Johnny Rodriguez joining to croon the lyrics in Spanish, as well as Cash's "Big River," which, with its missing verse added in, had parts for each vocalist. Suddenly, they had a platinum LP, *Highwayman.* No Kristofferson originals made the cut, but the group did win the Academy of Country Music Single of the Year trophy, and Kristofferson was inducted into the Songwriters Hall of Fame. The men immediately capitalized on the growing public interest in the group by costarring in a remake of *Stagecoach*, which became the highest-rated TV movie of 1986.

"It was really accidental," Kristofferson said of the group's formation and success. In the studio, he said, "I looked up to all of them and felt like I was kind of a kid who had climbed up on Mount Rushmore and stuck his face out there."

"We had so much fun," wrote Cash, "we decided to make a habit out of it."

"I think he had the most fun with the Highwaymen," Terry Jennings said of his father.

The album cover reflected this. The four appeared to be either chiseled into rock or the characters from the title track, ghostly, omnipotent beings watching over their children. Whatever their intentions, whether it was to anchor their legacies, return to commercial glory, or just to have a blast with pals, the chart-topping *Highwayman* album arrived at a pivotal moment. "These successes caught Nashville's music establishment off-guard," Mikal Gilmore wrote. "A more pop-minded sensibility was sweeping country," especially on FM radio, which dismissed rural life in favor of a slicker, more polished Reagan-era style. Rothbaum saw *Highwayman* as arriving just in time. "Country music wanted to usher these guys out," Willie's manager suggested. "They need compliant artists; the Highwaymen were free thinkers."

Rosanne Cash later insisted that the Highwaymen idea arose "out of pure friendship" and that there was "no marketing guy who came and said, 'This will be a good idea,'" but perhaps inevitably, money became a factor in their continuing. They certainly didn't gel right away, finding it difficult to develop a rhythm, figuratively. Their shows were tentative, with none of them taking a guitar solo, lest he be accused of hogging the spotlight. "It looked like four shy rednecks trying to be nice to each other," said Jennings. "It was really bothering me, how different we were onstage than when we were sitting around in the dressing room." He and Cash both wanted out. Nelson addressed the elephant by suggesting they admit to having "egos the size of a bus." They all had complicated or even tumultuous relationships with their fathers, had peaked artistically and commercially, and enjoyed a long history of fighting the system, sometimes in tandem. After they cleared the air, Jennings saw the change within a few shows. They all played guitar and harmonized passionately on one another's songs, often trading verses, and each man got two mini-sets of their own, carefully planned material.

They all brought something to the table, through their vocals, gravelly or otherwise. Wrote *Rolling Stone*: "Jennings sings with a devilish swagger; Kristofferson, never the most pristine of vocalists, commands with steely determination; Nelson delivers his unconventional quaver; and Cash holds it all together with an imposing gravitas." Kristofferson dubbed them thusly: "Willie's the old coyote, Waylon's the riverboat gambler, I'm the radical revolutionary, and Johnny's the father of our country." Cash said: "There's not a one of the four that could be replaced and the program would proceed as usual." Cash wanted Kristofferson, the youngest of the group, for that "fire" he always had in his eyes. Merle Haggard, having just finished his hit duo album with Nelson, had originally been invited to be a fifth member but decided to pass. Adding another voice or swapping one of them out for Charley Pride, David Allan Coe, Hank Williams Jr., or even Tanya Tucker wouldn't have worked, Waylon claimed. The makeup of the group *was* the reason it worked. He may have been hiding his feelings about Haggard, too, which stretched back to the night Waylon's bass player was killed, when Merle and his manager took Jennings for every cent at poker.

Their first concert, the 1985 4th of July Picnic at Willie HQ, was a layup. Despite a heavy rainstorm, virtually every ticket holder turned out. Although playing for ten thousand attendees, they were under no pressure and could have harmonized on obscure spirituals to deafening "yee-has." Critics were unimpressed, however. The Highwaymen were kitschy, and their greatest-hits-style revues with slick production values and carefully programmed set lists were, at best, a Vegas-worthy cash-in. One fan wrote: "It felt like one of those thoroughly inauthentic experiences that concert events sometimes turn out to be. The shows didn't tax them overmuch."

In 1990, they finally had the sense—and good timing—to all be available for a world tour. After flying between continents, the four would travel almost exclusively in the same convoy, with Jack Clement, producer of Cash and Jennings, as musical director. After a brief absence for his mother's funeral, Clement returned to help manage the arrangements and set list. His first night back, at the concert after-party, the one-time dance instructor pranced around with a full wineglass atop his head and inevitably spilled its contents all over Waylon's shirt. Jennings dismissed it as no biggie, but then Clement started complaining to the others about Nelson singing ahead of the beat on "Good Hearted Woman."

Nelson laughed and said: "Fuck you, Jack." As he walked out of the elevator, he turned back. "I've always wanted to say that to someone named Jack," he joked.

When the doors closed, Jennings turned to Clement.

"You shouldn't criticize Willie's singing," said Waylon. "Only I can do it."

Though Nelson remained inscrutable to the others—except to Jennings, who simply found him mildly irritating—he at least recognized the awkwardness and, for levity, pulled harmless pranks on the others at every opportunity. When Kristofferson confessed to the crowd that his voice was going, Nelson cracked: "How can ya tell?"* Jennings responded by singing over Nelson's songs, substituting *stupid* for the word *crazy* in the song of the same name. "I know where he's going even if I can't figure out why," Jennings would say of their duets. Kristofferson and Jennings were still awestruck by Cash every time he sang alongside them, but they gradually relaxed enough to try some gentle ribbing at one another's expense. After singing the line "I don't care what's right or wrong," Kristofferson corrected himself ("Yes, I do") and, after "Best of All Possible Worlds," he'd say: "That was a long time ago. We don't get in trouble like that anymore," and then add: "Willie does."

"I could have never imagined that back in the days when they wouldn't let me sing my own demos, that I was able to sing right along with Johnny Cash, whether he liked it or not," said Kris. Cash, though, distanced himself from Kristofferson as the latter grew more politically outspoken, especially on Reagan-era interference in foreign conflicts. Kris, for his part, while still considering Johnny a hero, often turned down ideas his mentor offered, including performing together at a "religious Woodstock."

Dismissing the rumors of offstage strife, Nelson, who called his reputation "the kind you can't ruin," referred to the Highwaymen as an endless, globetrotting party. It was easy for Nelson, Jennings claimed,

* For his part, Nelson said of Kristofferson: "He shows more soul blowing his nose than the ordinary person does at his honeymoon dance."

because Willie would "learn" a song and then cheat by having his sheet music onstage before thirty thousand spectators.

Despite a five-year wait and a lack of a clear, radio-ready single, their second album spent ten months on the country chart and peaked inside the Top 5. Their third and final album, the aptly titled *The Road Goes on Forever*, was a commercial failure, but Jennings was proud of it regardless. "There were things like 'Wild Ones,'" he said, "where I remembered the times when me, Willie, and Jessi had come to town and how we had shaken Nashville's hierarchy up in our fight to keep the music honest."

"Individually, these gentlemen had their own style, their own thoughts, their own feelings, their own emotion," said John Carter Cash. "But they came together as friends, and that's the unifying power of the Highwaymen."

In the 1980s, the Highwaymen were a major factor in country's comeback.* Other supergroups formed, most notably Trio, which combined the forces of Linda Ronstadt, Dolly Parton, and Emmylou Harris to sell in the several millions. Previously, as Harris noted, the genre had "a tendency to be too constricted or afraid of anything that colors outside the lines." Darius Rucker, who would later break Nashville's color barrier (again), agreed: "All those guys were lone-wolf solo artists, rebels who did what the fuck they wanted to do. They said, 'We're going to be rebels, but we're going to rebel together.'" Rebelling against a Music Row that no longer wanted them seemed almost natural, an unspoken idea that snowballed, and

* The album's other hit was "Desperados Waiting for a Train," a Guy Clark song Kristofferson knew from Rita Coolidge's version.

for the next decade, it would be something for each Highwayman to fall back on—if ever they needed a career boost or just some serotonin, why not book a gig with the other three and hear the stadiums roar again?

It didn't last longer than that decade, however. The press said it was on account of egos, and certainly Nelson's lackadaisical nature had a way of slowing down shows and causing people to fall all over themselves to please him, which Cash stewed about in silence. One night, Cash entered Jennings's dressing room before a show, glanced about, and while Waylon raised an eyebrow, said, "Just wanna make sure they didn't give you anything that they didn't give me." Shooter Jennings recalled Waylon and Johnny having a blowup and giving each other the silent treatment, and later argued bitterly over 1995 tour dates, with Cash unwilling to commit to more than previously agreed. Jessi Colter dismissed the "little-boy rivalries" and said she considered them "four little boys who'd just happened to have grown tall and wore boots." Nelson, too, called "bullshit" on the rumors, while Jennings insisted that their egos blended. Whenever a problem arose and one of the four tried to use veto power, someone would smooth things over with a tightly rolled joint.

Essentially, though, the Highwaymen stopped in 1996 because of their diametrical views. As one fan noted after meeting each individual Highwayman, they split into the four main factions in American politics: libertarian, hard-right conservative, progressive, and centrist. Waylon compared them to four heads of state—had anyone ever seen that many egos get along? He and Kris had at least one fight about the 1992 presidential election and civilians bombed during the Persian Gulf War.* "I didn't say he was all wrong," said Jennings. "Main thing

* Johnny Cash stayed out of it, although he sat at home the night war broke out, drawing "dark, brooding images," according to one biographer.

I was saying was he shouldn't be doing it onstage with three other people who didn't share all of his thoughts."*

Colter explained that Waylon wanted to keep politics out of their shows, while Kris intended it as a focal point of his solo spotlight. After he spotted General Colin Powell in the front row of a concert, Kris lit into the Bush administration for bombing Baghdad. Waylon, who was giddy over Powell's presence, nearly attacked Kristofferson. "You can't say that to our fans!" Mickey Raphael heard him shout. Waylon claimed that although his rage was mainly just venting, "we came pretty close to punching it out."

"Kris was pretty opinionated," observed David "Fergie" Ferguson, Jack Clement's engineer and a fill-in musical director on tour. "He would talk about his political views, and Waylon didn't really like that." Ferguson recalled another tense moment when, unable to get Kristofferson to shut up during a press briefing, Jennings lunged across the table.

"I'm gonna whip your ass," Waylon hissed.

"Well, you better get those flippers working again," said Kris, nodding at Jennings's arms, which had been giving him pain. That got them all cracking up.

Cash, who performed for Nixon but rarely voted for president, spoke out against child homelessness and for prisoners and Indigenous Americans, served as the centrist among the dueling factions. At one concert, after Kris's spotlight, Cash suggested: "You have the right to burn the flag. We have second amendment rights, and if you burn the flag, *I* have the right to shoot you." (A strange speech from the man who recorded "Don't Take Your Guns to Town." Cash later clarified that he supported Kristofferson's right to burn the flag—not that Kris

* Hearing of the spat, Nelson joked: "I'm glad, it's giving me a chance to have some rest. Waylon's usually on my ass about something."

had suggested he might.) Willie Nelson befriended President Carter, backed independent Ross Perot, who used "Crazy" as his presidential campaign theme song, played benefit shows for Democratic Senate candidates, and was stopped and arrested en route to Democratic governor Ann Richards's funeral. Nelson and Cash, having been mere acquaintances before the group formed, stuck to sniping at each other over song selection, running order, and, perhaps inevitably, who got too long a solo spotlight during the shows.

Nelson called Cash "a straight-up patriot," which he said he didn't mean as an insult, and praised Cash's *Bitter Tears: Ballads of the American Indian* and support for Indigenous people. But according to Nelson's memoir, Cash's political awareness "came out of a... conservative tradition [while] I wasn't a card-carrying member of any political party, but I did have my causes." Rather than be an issue, the orneriness of his fellow travelers melted Willie's own icy front. "We grew closer. We laughed louder. Our band got tighter. Our music got better," he insisted. "I thought it was fun watching Kris and Waylon argue about politics." Cash agreed. Asked why he'd done the Highwaymen records when his demanding career had been incomparable, Nelson said, laughing: "Still trying to bring Waylon back."

Kristofferson called the Highwaymen heaven on earth, telling PBS: "I was up there on stage with my heroes—the people that I worshiped. We did nothing we didn't want to do. And we stood up for things we believed in. And it was a beautiful life that way." Like the legendary figures in the Highwaymen hit "Desperados Waiting for a Train," Jennings believed each man saw himself as a desperado and had faced down death for real on numerous occasions—from gun battles to deep depression to drug abuse to health crises—and that helped them survive. "I love them all like brothers," Nelson recalled in a documentary about the group. "We all got along... made a movie together. We toured the world a couple of times. And they're just some of the best times in my life." He later called their concert tours "the most fun I've ever had with my clothes on." Said John Carter Cash: "This is something that 200 years from now, it'll have a greater import than even it does right now. It'll be more clear, wherefore our tree came from. We're looking back over the history of our modern recorded music."

"The thing that surprised me was that the Highwaymen ever got together in the first place," said Bucky Wilkin, early Kristofferson confidant. "I know there was some mutual admiration but they had a bond like the Beatles. It was a band of brethren with respect and camaraderie."

CHAPTER TEN

AN ALTERNATIVE COUNTRY

Cash: "What's going on over there at Warner Brothers?"
Exec: "Oh, well, you know how it is. We're just looking for the new Randy Travis."
Cash: "What's wrong with the one you've got?"

It's why he doesn't spend time in Nashville. There are simply too many people telling you what you should do.

—Norman Hamlet, on Merle Haggard

Great to be back in Music City. It's still Music City, right?

—Bob Dylan, to a Nashville audience in 2022

There's a little thing in our industry that's been forgotten. It's called mystique. Don't ever wear out your welcome, don't ever forget where you came from, and always be humble, always be kind to people, but always keep a little something back that you don't show everybody.

—Johnny Cash, to Travis Tritt

Between 1985, the year Waylon decided not to re-sign with RCA and the Highwaymen formed, and the mid-2010s breakthrough of alt-country to the mainstream, the outlaw movement lay dormant.

In 1988, though, he anticipated alt-country, Americana, and the outlaw comeback in an interview.

"I've always noticed that through history, ever since the fifties, when pop and rock 'n' roll music, when it self-destructs, they come back to country for the basics," he mused. "Nashville is right on the verge of that again. They're kinda searchin' for what to do, and that happens all the time. They have a little taste of the cross-over and then they try to cut pop records . . . but if you look back through history, the things that have crossed over have been the most grassroots country things . . ." All that was needed to start a *real country* revival was, as he put it, "another Billy Joe Shaver, or Kris Kristofferson, or somebody like that."

In the interim, country radio was dominated by glossy, echoing pop vocals, synthesizers and keyboards, adult-contemporary lightness and cringeworthy dance crazes—much like rock and virtually every other genre. While male singers wore gigantic cowboy hats and cheap plaid button-downs and seemed to be imitating one another, women, especially platinum-selling women, faced relentless criticism and scrutiny for their appearance and vocal abilities. Reba McEntire showed up to the 1993 CMAs in a sparkling red velvet dress with a plunging neckline that barely covered her nipples*; when she stepped out to perform, the crowd audibly gasped. The dress became the most talked-about country music story of the year, landing her on newspaper and magazine front pages, and McEntire still fields questions about it today. Women were policed for their actions, too, of course, including from their own bandmates. Porter Wagoner said of Dolly

* A plane carrying McEntire's band and tour manager crashed in March 1991, killing all aboard. McEntire was not on board. Waylon Jennings later told her: "I know what it can do to you."

Parton that "I don't believe a country girl singer would do the things in the manner she's done them. Like the Playboy thing. Do you think Kitty Wells would do that?"

The awards and publicity machines started to dump millions into the harmless "hunk in a hat" types—typically a tanned mid-twenties cowboy type with an impenetrable Southern accent, catnip for American women country fans, anathema to the rest of the world.* Garth Brooks and Billy Ray Cyrus, who worshiped Waylon, sported black cowboy hats and plaid shirts and battled alongside McEntire and the Judds for chart domination, Cyrus with his "Achy Breaky Heart" and its accompanying dance craze, Brooks with what one country artist called "sappy...ballads that...sounded more like Kansas or Styx than they did Hank Williams or Ray Price." Brooks appeared at the Grand Ole Opry in October 1990, just as his "Friends in Low Places" was becoming a career-making anthem. One observer had been at a 1960s Johnny Cash performance there, in which audience members "stomped their feet on those wooden floors, and the sound...was unbelievable." But when Brooks made his return as a superstar, the Opry House reaction was somehow more energetic.

In the wake of the Brooks explosion,** which resulted in millions in sales for his debut album alone, publishers increasingly pressured songwriters to find likely hits, which led to more cowriting. Veteran hit writers were required to "cowrite" with up-and-coming artists (read: give up 50 percent of their credit for nothing). That in turn led to more desperate copycatting, retreads of last season's hits. No

---

* A 2022 viral photo featured a sign reading: SINGING POP MUSIC IN A SOUTHERN ACCENT DOESN'T MAKE IT COUNTRY.

** "When I first got to Nashville, I saw a billboard on the side of a bus for Garth Brooks or somebody like that," recalled Jack White. "You would *never* have seen that in the rock & roll world at the time, with its ridiculous rules about 'selling out.' To me, it was a real eye-opener."

longer could songwriters get stars to record written lyrics like Willie Nelson did in the '60s; now A-listers only wanted to hear demos. By the mid-nineties, most successful scribes worked nine to five in offices on Music Row, where few took vacations, lest their songs get overlooked in a pitch meeting. One hitmaker would take weeks just to come up with a verse melody; today, few publishers can afford to be that patient with staff. The larger, more successful publishers had been using their profits since the outlaw heyday to snap up mom-and-pop operations, giving them massive catalogs to license for film and TV or for new recordings, reducing the need to risk investing in new material. "It went from a comfortable, people-oriented company to a strictly money-oriented [one]," lamented an ex-publishing employee. While songwriters were still welcome to drop by Music Row's ground-floor label and publishing offices, no longer did one see guitars slung over shoulders of passengers disembarking at the Greyhound station. The musicians who wanted to "make it" instead got off in LA or Seattle. Nashville, worried about getting pushed off Top 40 radio by grunge or alternative, went hard.

"Nashville is a good town for someone who will toe the line," said songwriter David Olney.

Already, overdubs were making studio recordings feel less "live" and rendered almost anything on the radio pretty rote. Songs were being recorded at specific tempos and with changes depending on the season and produced with one market in mind: Dallas, from which an astonishing 40 percent of country sales originated. Sharon Vaughn, writer of the leadoff track for *Outlaws!* and an Oak Ridge Boys hit, struggled to stay on the radio. "It's a very difficult line to walk because if you're writing for strictly commercial purposes, it gets vapid," she says. "Today, songs are recorded because of the relationship the writer has with the producer or they write with the artist, either one. The whole procedure has changed."

Country's share of the radio market peaked at 16.6 percent in 1992, during which music generated $2 billion in economic activity for Nashville, but would fall to under 10 percent within four years, while the number of country stations would peak at 2,613 before dropping by nearly one hundred within a year. With the market shrinking, stars, including Waylon Jennings, personally visited stations to record promo spots and interviews to remind programmers and DJs of their existence.

"I got hired for a lot of things early on because I had rock sensibilities," said producer Mike Clute. "I probably made louder snares than probably anybody had heard in country before, with big, upfront vocals." Clute lamented that each record with a Nashville artist in his stable meant starting over on selling them to country radio and TV. "When bands and artists establish themselves, you get to the top, but next year, you're old news. With Diamond Rio, we had big hits, a dozen number one records instead of forty like Brooks & Dunn, but they were still able to go play and make a nice living. They weren't filling stadiums, though."

Certainly, the session musicians who had been working without a break for decades weren't complaining. Said one insider: "You could see how the effort of some of them was diminishing, how well they kept up their instruments or if they even bothered to tune up."

No longer controlled by record company handlers or restricted by television and newspaper censorship, artists turned on one another in public. Dwight Yoakam, the "anti-Nashville," honky-tonk "cowpunk" singer called his competitors, particularly the Oak Ridge Boys, "B-grade pop-schlock horseshit"; the fallout from that smear may have contributed to his losing every CMA Award he's ever been nominated for. Garth Brooks, surprisingly, was on Team Yoakam. He protested that "we've strayed away from country and got more into pop." In the early 1990s, however, Garth embraced

Big Brother, perfecting a kind of mass-market Southern pop that facilitated 157 million sales, making him the top-selling solo artist in any genre. Such was his ubiquitousness in the nineties, his debut album, without ever topping the country charts, was one of the bestselling records in the genre *every* year from 1989 through 1994. "What interests the country music listener today isn't what interests the country music listener in the sixties and seventies," he said. "Songs like, 'I Lost My Wife at the Truck Stop' and 'My Dog Got Ran Over Today.'" Brooks may have been exacerbating the issue with his sing-along radio bait, also known as "sippy-cup country" for its easily digestible lyrics, but he did make several stands in the face of corporate censorship. His promotional spot for "The Thunder Rolls" told the story of an abused wife who ultimately turns on her husband. Despite his popularity, the leading country music channels banned the video. He further pushed the envelope in 1993, at a time when few in country music were out of the closet, by discussing his sister's homosexuality in a television interview with Barbara Walters.

George Strait started out as an urban cowboy in the wake of the musical fad created by the film's success, eventually solidified a pop-country sound, and often sounds like a more polished Willie Nelson. Strait said of his own music that it was "about as rocked up and popped up as you can get and still pass it along to the country market," but these blurred lines had no effect on mainstream pop audiences. The Judds, a country-bluegrass revival act with electric guitars and wailing blues-rock vocals, had fourteen chart-toppers in a decade—not one cracked the pop charts. Country's decline in pop fortunes created a domino effect of lowered revenues for record labels, of course, but also anemic marketing budgets and smaller airplay royalties for songwriters. Radio stations, desperate to slow the attrition of listenership, excised older tunes from playlists and instead looped the week's Top 10. When that didn't work, they sold out to Clear Channel, a corporation that vastly expanded its empire in the '90s.

The year *Honky Tonk Heroes* hit airwaves, a smash country single might rack up eighty thousand sales; by the mid-'90s, that number would get an artist *dropped*. Six figures became the bare minimum. One artist, Mark Wills, was axed by his label shortly after his gold-selling single spent eight weeks atop the charts. The media turned to alternative rock and hip-hop for its quota of music interviews and features, and when it stooped to writing about C&W at all, *Billboard* dedicated more than eight in every ten articles on country to major label artists. Show bookings, too, were taken over by major conglomerates, with only 5 percent of bookers and promoters remaining independent, a complete 180 degrees from 1985, when 95 percent were indies.

But while country radio songs narrowed in style in the '80s and '90s, in the 2000s, the sound began to broaden again. The themes, too, were deeper and often darker; one hit single was about an alcohol binge that caused the narrator to miss their son's birthday. Meanwhile, new artists who had grown up on the Highwaymen and its individual members started to arrive in Music City. Tootsie's became a tourist destination, as were open mics at the Bluebird Cafe, where Brooks was "discovered." With free beer and burgers for performers, the Station Inn, which opened during the outlaw heyday, lured in songwriters fresh off the Greyhounds, giving them a path to reach indie record companies, which had also sprung up in town, looking for "authentic" country voices. The film *The Thing Called Love*, a fictionalized account of budding country singer-songwriters in Nashville, used a re-created Bluebird as its backdrop but ironically replaced the headshots of aspirants lining the real club's walls with those of Tanya Tucker and Garth Brooks. "The gatekeepers are tightening up at the gates," grumbled one songwriter. "In a perfect world, talent would be all you need. But like any other business, there's politics to consider."

In the late '70s, Cary Baker, a student at the University of Illinois, visited New York to see CBGB, the supposed birthplace of punk. But upon his return to the Midwest, he fell hard for a local cover band that played Bob Wills and Waylon Jennings. By 1979, Baker was working in A&R for Ovation Records in Chicago, which took its marching orders from the Nashville branch. After booking country rocker Joe Sun into a punk venue, Baker brought some Ovation staffers out to see Sun do his "thing," which was more "Bruce Springsteen than Clint Black." The staffers weren't sure what to make of this new sound until Baker jokingly called it "alternative country." One coworker turned to the others and loudly repeated the phrase, to much guffawing.

Baker then joined I.R.S. Records during the period that one of its artists, college radio favorite R.E.M., was in the Nashville studio where *Waylon & Willie* and Cash's *A Believer Sings the Truth* had been cut. "One might not have thought of R.E.M. as an Americana prototype band, but there were country songs ('Rockville' and 'Driver 8' come to mind) which were unwittingly laying the groundwork for a new genre," Baker recalls. The genre was, as he had coincidentally suggested, alt-country.

In the '90s, as Brooks peaked and R.E.M. became the biggest band in America, Missouri's Uncle Tupelo was creating alt-country, or "insurgent country," as they called it. Leaders Jay Farrar and Jeff Tweedy combined outlaw, folk, and Neil Young–style hard rock or punk arrangements, and despite not being the first band to combine country and, as one writer noted, "a certain DIY, anti-establishment aesthetic," Uncle Tupelo was the right band at the right time, releasing their first album, *No Depression*, between Nirvana's *Nevermind* and Pearl Jam's *Ten*, at the apex of alternative. The alt-country/Americana music magazine *No Depression* named itself after the group; its subtitle read: "The Alternative Country (Whatever That Is) Quarterly."*

Uncle Tupelo was the antithesis of Garth Brooks, and not just because they had the opposite commercial impact. "There's something wrong when Garth Brooks lists his major influence as Journey," Tweedy snarked, attacking their shared affinity for formulaic lyrics, robotic melodies that could've been churned out by computers, and live shows with wireless mics, programmed light displays, and fireworks for a homogenized, hick crowd.** Instead, the idea of fame nauseated Uncle Tupelo—Tweedy later imagined his band learning the news of their big break: "Oh no, *Rolling Stone* wants to interview us. Who gets to tell Jay? 'Oh great,'" he imagined Farrar saying sarcastically, "'*Rolling Stone*, is Madonna going to be on the cover?'"

Farrar and Tweedy, who grew up together in Missouri, had started Uncle Tupelo as a bar band, and they were so poorly paid and underfunded through their day jobs or parents that if a proprietor asked for their demo before booking them, they would need to go buy a blank Maxell cassette and rerecord it on a boombox. "We were conscious of the juxtaposition of putting a loud electric guitar next to acoustic folk-oriented songs," said Farrar, "but at the time we didn't feel like we were really doing anything that different" than the Byrds or Carter Family. "Merle Haggard never imagined Uncle Tupelo," said Farrar, "but he made that possible, too." They recorded Waylon's "Are You Sure Hank Done It This Way?" They even covered the Carters in front

* The Australian roots music magazine *Rhythms* launched in 1992, and today runs cover stories such as "New Queens of Outlaw Country."

** One reviewer, not unkindly, called Brooks's live show "part Kiss and part glam rodeo."

of Johnny Cash, who let out a cheer, when they opened for him at a California bar.* When they met Rick Danko from The Band, he told the group: "You sound desperate. You should always sound desperate. Don't lose that." Tweedy composed a tribute to Hank Williams's publisher Acuff-Rose, and Farrar wrote about the "halls of shame," an apparent dig at the exploitative major labels that had bilked and ruined generations of artists. Their first album came out on a label so small, the $3,500 advance didn't even cover recording expenses.

Both Farrar and Tweedy disdained the corporate record companies and recorded three of their four records for an indie. Although independent labels had no reach beyond a few record store clerks and music critics, there was a surprising upside: a fanbase of diehards who constantly spread the word. One band member marveled that, as he scanned the audience, he spotted both seniors with gray beards and college kids singing along.** Yet when Farrar left Uncle Tupelo as press coverage for their major label debut exploded, Tweedy expressed shock that his partner had not seen their success as a *good* thing. Soon, however, both songwriters played the money men off each other to land deals with their new outfits. Farrar started Son Volt and Tweedy gathered the remnants of Uncle Tupelo to form Wilco, ironically ending up with the same A&R rep at Warner Brothers. Joe McEwen, according to Tweedy, listened to Wilco's first record and gushed, "This is going to be a great way to set up Jay's record."

Thanks in part to the label's support, Farrar easily won the first battle. Son Volt's 1995 debut, *Trace*, recorded with vintage amps, acoustic guitars, and minimal overdubs, outsold the "country-tinged pop" of Wilco's *A.M.* and even produced a radio hit. In another universe

---

* Tweedy on meeting the man himself: "What was there to say to Johnny Cash? It was like talking to the Empire State Building or a bald eagle."

** The band played a pro-choice benefit in Boston in 1993 as part of a live compilation to benefit anti-rape, pro-choice, and women's healthcare organizations.

where alt-country was as popular as alternative rock, *A.M.* would've been a radio hit. Instead, *Trace* cracked the *Billboard* 200 and garnered praise for its "classic honky tonk and rock & roll." Wilco regrouped a year later for *Being There*, with the songs evenly split between their former country sound and new forays into hard-driving rock, serving as an alt-country update of Dylan's *Bringing It All Back Home*, and opened for Johnny Cash. When Wilco was dropped by Warner Brothers/Reprise in 2001, the group was able to brilliantly milk the shocking news for maximum publicity. After virtually every media outlet covered the story, David Kahne, responsible for the dismissal, said he would've put out their next album, which he had already paid the band for, "if Wilco had insisted," but said that he didn't think it would sell anyway. That contradiction backfired further on executives and led Nonesuch Records to release *Yankee Hotel Foxtrot*. It proved to be Wilco's breakthrough, gold-selling hit. Nonesuch, ironically, is a subsidiary of Warner, which meant the parent company paid for *Yankee* twice.

"Wilco gave me this permission to freely explore what creative chaos can sound like," says Beau Janke of Them Coulee Boys. "Wilco," he adds, "made the road map for live bands: persistence, talent, don't be a dick, and be your most brutally honest self... whoever the fuck that is."

Jay Farrar, with the on-again-off-again Son Volt and his solo work, has stuck with the alt-country sound—and the indie labels who took him in after he left "the world-domineering Warner Bros. conglomerate," as Pitchfork termed it, while Wilco embraced experimental, even ambient noise. Then COVID-19 hit. Jeff Tweedy spent the early months of the outbreak locked down, writing country music "to console myself," he said, and in 2021, Wilco recorded *Cruel Country*, a return to their "alt" origins. At their induction into the Austin City Limits Hall of Fame, the band brought up a slew of special guests, including Margo Price, Jason Isbell, and Rosanne Cash. Alt-country, Cash suggested, lived on through a group of "heartland laborers in the tower of song, with thick skins and open hearts... subversive without being destructive." This music, she said, can shatter "us and heals us at the same time."

When asked their opinions on country generally, teen fans of Garth Brooks, Rodney Crowell, and Uncle Tupelo ironically said: "I hate that shit." (As young people outpaced their parents on record purchases, Music Row tried to reach them without success, to show them that those acts *were* country.) Mike Heidorn of Uncle Tupelo told the *L.A. Times*: "It's a thrilling thing to feel that you got to be a part of the actual tradition of sharing this particular knowledge with people that might not have come to it as quickly or maybe would have not even been introduced to it at all. I just remember this overwhelming feeling that Jay and I would talk about getting from listening to folk music and country music, and speaking for myself personally, it was like having the veil pulled back and realizing that the world has always been weird.

"When people choose to express themselves with music," he went on, "it can also be completely untamed. It's not always shaped by fashion or commercial viability or anything like that; people just want to express themselves with words and noise and sound. That's what I think we were discovering in Uncle Tupelo."

"Their impact is measurable," wrote one fan. "They made it OK for Suburban White kids to like Country music."

One group still practicing alt-country, combining hard Southern rock sounds with outlaw attitudes, is Lukas Nelson & Promise of the Real. The band may be a little uncomfortable with the label—"Thanks for coming out and supporting the Americana, uh, situation," Nelson said onstage at the 2022 Americana Fest—but with the combination of Nelson's heritage, origins in Austin, hard-hitting live sets that can include Kris Kristofferson covers and lyrics like "out here in the country, forever is a four-letter word," production work by Dave Cobb,* and a number one album despite lack of airplay, the band fits snugly in the alternative side of Nashville. When Lukas sings, "Just outside Austin / I think I fell in love with you again," one might picture his father singing to country music itself.

Country-punk artists blended both styles, and, according to Neko Case, Johnny Cash "kicked that off." Cash, for his part, welcomed the new style he'd helped launch. "Alternative Country had to happen," he said, "because the record business is in danger of plasticization. You don't have to live in Nashville to record a country song—in fact, I'm not even sure it helps." Says relative newcomer Tyler Childers, "Why would you move to the largest growing and developing city in the nation to write country songs about rural life?"

Music City itself changed during alt-country's rise. Broadway's "peep shows, dope, and transients" gave way to celebrity-owned bars crowding out the dives, with the exception of Tootsie's, Willie Nelson's old stomping grounds. Nashville became a buzzy, gentrified tourist destination with a 40 percent population density increase and a football team within sight of the Ryman. In 2006, the Music City Walk of Fame opened, which honored Nashville's former idols. It, along with the city's museums, whitewashes the genre's controversies and censorship.

Songwriter Bob McDill, who had been around since 1970, nearly got into a screaming match with RCA staffers who confronted him in the company's men's room, demanding to know why he'd used *redneck,* a pejorative, in a song. Waylon Jennings had made a hit of McDill's "Amanda" in 1979, which included the word *hillbilly,* and

* Not to be confused with DJ David Cobb, credited with coining the term *Music City.*

McDill didn't recall any problem with *that*. McDill learned Music Row loved breakup songs, but mentioning the kids of a divorced couple would've got him booted from the building. Record companies removed the word *damn* from singles; even Garth Brooks was vulnerable to censorship or, in this case, self-censorship. He decided to leave out the third verse from "Friends in Low Places," his 1990 blockbuster, so radio stations would be more likely to play it. ("Just wait 'til I finish this glass / Then sweet little lady, I'll head back to the bar / And you can kiss my ass.") When Mindy McCready's feminist "Guys Do It All the Time" hit radio, its battle-of-the-sexes lyrics were given a pass because of its infectious pop-groove and dance-floor-ready mix, and the song went to number one. Songwriter Gretchen Peters convinced Nashville "Independence Day," truthfully a child's-eye view of her mother escaping a violent marriage, was as patriotic as its on-the-nose title implied; Martina McBride got her cover of the song and its music video on FM radio and CMT, respectively, and "Independence Day" went on to win the CMA Song of the Year honor for 1995. Far-right talking head Sean Hannity later used Gretchen Peters's "Independence Day" in his shows as a way to stir patriotic feelings, apparently unaware of its true meaning.

Then in 2003, Music Row came out of the shadows to eat one of its own. When the Dixie Chicks were performing in London on their European tour, singer Natalie Maines stopped midway through the show to say: "Just so you know, we're ashamed the president of the United States is from Texas."

Chet Flippo, who popularized the term *outlaw* and wrote the liner notes for *Wanted! The Outlaws*, encouraged country fans to abandon the group. "Memo to Natalie Maines," he wrote in his CMT.com column. "You're an artist? And you have a message? Hey, put it in a song. We'll listen to that. But, otherwise—shut up and sing." After an outpouring of such sentiment, a survey found that more than six in ten country fans would no longer listen to the band. Radio stations blacklisted the Dixie Chicks' then-number-one single and it quickly fell from its perch.

Unbeknownst to outsiders, Johnny Cash woke up from a medically induced coma in March to learn the Iraq invasion had begun, and muttered "no, no, no" in agony. He was mostly alone in his view—the war was supported by a majority of Americans. Toby Keith put out a pro-war song about kicking ass and taking names "the American way," but because it didn't choose the side of a specific political party, it became a crossover anthem. As the Iraq invasion turned into America's longest war and a boondoggle, Keith insisted he was a Democrat and supported the Afghanistan war but not the Iraq invasion. Nonetheless, when Keith muttered about Kristofferson's "liberal" politics backstage at a Willie Nelson tribute, Kris got in his face. "Have you ever taken another man's life and then cashed the check your country gave you for doing it?" As stunned onlookers stared, Keith shook his head. "No, you have not," Kristofferson went on. "So shut the fuck up!" When asked about this story the day it leaked and went viral, Kristofferson seemed more concerned with how the quote had spread rather than confirming or denying its accuracy.

Amidst the divisiveness, the Dixie Chicks waited three years before recording new music. Johnny Cash's producer Rick Rubin helmed the aptly titled *Taking the Long Way*, released amid deep dissatisfaction with President Bush, and despite a hotly discussed *Entertainment Weekly* cover for which the band appeared nude, tagged all over with faux-handwritten insults like "Dixie Sluts" and supportive phrases like "Free Speech." Wrote *Billboard*: "The group has finally re-emerged stronger, more defiant and more creatively ambitious than ever." However, despite a number one debut on the country and pop charts, *Long Way* got little airplay, especially in the South, where the Iraq War remained popular. Executives would warn liberal acts: "Do you want to get on some right-wing guy's radar? Because that's what killed the Dixie Chicks." The group, which eventually dropped the word *Dixie* from its name, didn't release another album for fourteen years.

At about the time Wilco abandoned alt-country, Shooter Jennings decided to join his father on tour. Metallica's James Hetfield had invited Waylon to play the 1996 Lollapalooza, and Shooter, then seventeen, was the only one in the family who saw the benefit. (Waylon accepted the gig after confusing it with "The Lola Falana Show," a dance program canceled in the seventies.) Waylon figured no one would know who he was, so if nothing else, his appearances would at least please his kid, who'd been through so much. "I remember, he kept saying, 'That's my boy!' onstage," Shooter said. "And I said, 'Dad, stop!' I was singing onstage for the first time in Doc Martens, cargo shorts, a Nine Inch Nails shirt—and playing piano." The boy who impressed his father with his drumming prowess at age three and guitar work at six and who used to fall asleep to his dad's music while Waylon was away had formed a band with high school friends, but no one in Nashville cared about Waylon's progeny—especially if he insisted on playing loud, Nails-inspired, metal-tinged country.*

Another decade passed. It had been twenty years since the birth of the Highwaymen. Country music, as *GQ* put it, became "the musical equivalent of Walmart—monolithic, cheap, and eroding the soul of small-town America." But there were still neglected rock fans with a soft spot for country out there, and Nashville wasn't catering to them.

* "Look at Bob Dylan," Shooter later said. "He's retained such a sense of mystery that it's allowed him to have cast a wide net."

These middle-class buyers had the same levels of rock fandom as the 1970s music geeks who professed to hate country but collected progressive country records. Gradually, the outlaw movement was reborn as an alternative to modern Nashville, a kind of gateway drug to "good" old country music.

Reenter Shooter Jennings. Shooter split up his hard rockin' country band and went solo, listening closely to his father's records for the first time, and, after discovering that the outlaw style came naturally, he and Dave Cobb recorded the Stones-influenced *Put the "O" Back in Country* in 2005, their debuts as artist and producer, respectively. The album was so inspiring to Outlaw aficionados, that half brother Terry Jennings heard it and immediately launched a publishing company. Shooter called in Jessi, George Jones, and Hank Williams Jr. for backing vocals, which helped the CD just miss the country Top 20. To give a boost to faltering single "4th of July," Shooter stopped in Manhattan for interviews and a performance at CBGB with Jessi as an unannounced duet partner. It may have been the birthplace of punk, but CBGB (which stood for "Country Bluegrass Blues") had also hosted the sold-out Uncle Tupelo show that put the alt-country pioneers on the industry's radar. Shooter then played a larger concert nearby as an opener for Lee Ann Womack while, a few dozen blocks away, the Grand Ole Opry held its eightieth anniversary concert at Carnegie Hall. In the lead-up to these New York shows, Shooter Jennings lamented carrying his father's torch seemingly by himself. It wasn't much of an exaggeration—or bravado.

"All I'm saying is, bring the energy back to country music," he explained. "You know that ain't country music you've been listenin' to. I miss the realness. We had such a fruitful era in the '70s. Now where is all that? Where are the Merles, the Waylons, and the Willies?" Shooter noticed that the success of Garth Brooks in the '90s led to retreads, "bro country," and "hat acts," phony cowboys more beloved for their looks than their tunes. He stuck to the rebellious, anti-Nashville country music he loved, with diminishing returns. In 2010, he played for a dozen people in Houston, even though he had just released a heavily hyped album narrated by Stephen King. He got yelled at for his anti-war sentiments, but behind the scenes, he had been "playing ball with the country establishment," as *Spin* put it, to no avail.

After years of championing the cause of the outlaws, Shooter, who is Cash's godson, got his widest exposure portraying one of them in the Cash biopic *Walk the Line*—his own father. Then he switched gears and began offering his producing services. Soon after, he met a singer-songwriter and activist who changed his life.

Brandi Carlile started out busking in Seattle's famed Pike Place Market, offering everyone who stopped a flyer for her shows. She caught the live performance bug as a child and started playing for free—not even free *drinks*—just to tame the beast. She hit Nashville just as women singer-songwriters were showing up to auditions and hearing: "Oh, but we wanted to hire a *man*." Miraculously, Carlile's music reached the major labels and resulted in one Top 10 album in 2012, but she returned with a release on indie ATO Records three years later. Johnny Cash's producer, Rick Rubin, had offered her her first record contract; she had auditioned for a Grand Ole Opry offshoot with Cash's "Tennessee Flat Top Box"; recorded "Folsom Prison Blues" for a tribute to the Man in Black; and played a Carter Family song on late-night television. Finally, her career was bolstered by a tribute album with Kris Kristofferson and other stars covering her music.

She and Shooter Jennings immediately bonded over their love for 1980s culture. "The '80s get so white-washed in roots music,"

Carlile told *Spin*, "because we still sing about the Dust Bowl and train-hopping like it's a thing that we do. He was like 'Fuck that, we all played the same video games and all wore Hammer pants. Why can't we sing about our actual childhood and what actually raised us and still be country and roots?'...And it was the really innocent beginnings of a really honest friendship."

Carlile, who is gay and recalls that her "first act of 'baby activism' was fighting my way through religious protestors to an Indigo Girls concert," and Jennings, who had kids Alabama and Waylon with actor Drea de Matteo, chatted all night. "All I knew was when I was in a room with him, it made me happy," Carlile said. "It made me inspired, made me laugh and made me talk about important things. I knew somehow I had to get him in the room while I was making the album. I didn't even know he was a producer."

Bringing on Shooter, as well as coproducer Dave Cobb, did have significant disadvantages. While Cobb had a convincing track record, Shooter had little experience in hitmaking, and Carlile definitely needed a hit after a decade without one. But she had gone in the opposite direction—going from working with a top hitmaker to handling everything, including the hiring, firing, and office management work it took to facilitate record production. There was nothing to lose. When they arrived at RCA Studio A in late 2017, they were told Carlile's label wanted them to focus on "getting drum sounds," really perfecting the songs' radio potential. Instead, Cobb broke out the tequila and played classic rock records to set the mood while Shooter paced, mulling over every note to come. Between Jennings and Cobb, Carlile found the middle ground.

"It was a really compelling change to be just a performer again," she said. "Because I had come from a background of working with producers in a way that was kind of high pressure, I had it in my head that there was a way to make records and a way to play live shows, and they were not the same way. And Dave Cobb was not impressed with that theory and wanted to challenge my belief on that, and really brought out my live performances on this record." Phil and Tim Hanseroth, better known as "the Twins," her fellow Brandi Carlile Band members, silently bristled over the raw nature of the sessions and having to sometimes get it all right on take one. Cobb and Jennings pretended not to notice, pushing for Carlile to hit ever-higher notes to see how far she could take her singing talent and to write a worthy successor to "The Story," written by Phil Hanseroth.

"Especially vocal," said Cobb, not reading the tension in the room. "You haven't had a vocal moment as good as 'The Story' since 'The Story.'" (That song had been produced by T Bone Burnett—and he, too, had forced it out of her.)

Carlile tried to respectfully demur. At home, she fumed about the situation—the record didn't need one more song *and* she was offended by Cobb's comment. But her wife wouldn't take her side. "If you're honest with yourself, though," said Catherine Carlile, "*do* you have a vocal moment as good as 'The Story'?"

After showing up to the studio with their newly purchased gear to cut the record, Cobb told Brandi and the Twins to remove their too-polished instruments from the building. He wanted worn and battered instruments, so the sound of authenticity would cut through the digital "tape." "He took our confidence away and replaced it with vulnerability, discomfort, and tension," Carlile said. "And those things are what essentially made the performance happen."

To show her what he had in mind, Cobb blasted Elvis's "An American Trilogy," written by Mickey Newbury of "Luckenbach" lyrics fame, a medley that includes "Dixie" and a Bahamian lullaby. Cobb asked Carlile to pay attention to the heavy-handed chords, over-the-top instrumentation, and the way it wrenched emotion from listeners. Carlile woke up the following morning with a new song swirling at the forefront of her mind. "There are so many people feeling misrepresented," she explained. "So many people feeling unloved. Boys feeling marginalized and forced into these kinds of awkward shapes of masculinity that they do or don't belong in.... The song is just for people that feel under-represented, unloved, or illegal."

With no one scheduled to be in the studio that day, Carlile grabbed a cellist, one of ten people living in her Nashville home, and hailed a rideshare to the studio to lay down the new track. She thought of Iraq, Syria, Donald Trump, little girls dreaming of occupying the White House, and, above all, her Christian faith, and directed her cellist to perform a soaring but tasteful backing track. "In fact," she wrote, "every single thing I mentioned...has been impacted negatively by Christianity in one way or the other.... I, too, have been impacted negatively by it. But something mystical brings me back time and time again to the revolutionary gospel of forgiveness."

"I played her one of the greatest songs of all time," Cobb marveled, "and then she wrote one of the greatest written since that one."

Says musician Jens Staff, "While the other side seems like it's 'put this beat in, sing verse chorus verse chorus with a twang, throw a solo in the song somewhere, and call it good,' whether or not the words hold any meaning more than what pop country wants to hear," Carlile and the Twins are focused on giving each element of the song a chance to breathe and tell the *artists* how it should be recorded.

Contrary to what executives would have suggested for a potential "hit," Shooter and Brandi, a dynamic voice and introspective songwriter, tamped down the twanginess and washed the melodies in rock orchestration. The string arrangement came thanks to Paul Buckmaster, who had turned David Bowie and Elton John into stars, and Carlile looked for a cross between Elton and The Band's Levon Helm on another track. "When I fell in love with Elton John, I was 11 years old, and I was *fixated*.... I knew every name, every statistic, shoe sizes, and Paul Buckmaster... was really responsible for so much of what Elton's music was during that time." With references to another closeted gay '70s icon, Freddie Mercury, "The Joke" and the rest of the album *By the Way, I Forgive You* come off as a cross between "gay men British pop singers and the Grand Ole Opry," hardly what country radio wanted. In an era with radio stations seeking longer listens and not necessarily new listeners, the Carlile-Cobb-Jennings team was making a play for album buyers. It worked. *By the Way* hit the *Billboard* Top 5 and won half of the six Grammy Awards it was nominated for.

That year, Tyler Childers won Best Emerging Artist at the Americana Music Awards. In his acceptance speech, he said: "As a man who identifies as a country music singer, I feel Americana ain't no part of nothing and is a distraction from the issues that we're facing on a bigger level as country music singers. It kind of feels like purgatory." Carlile objected. To her, it sounded dismissive of those in the LGBTQ+ community, long shut out of the Nashville establishment. "I was just tired of being reminded that I may never fully belong," she explained.

Before the release of *By the Way*, Carlile had believed "making records was more of a formal documentation of what you do, and that you should keep the drama at bay." But her production team, including Dave Cobb, asked her to forget radio, forget restrictive song lengths and dramatics, and unleash everything without regard for commercial success. The album, marveled National Public Radio's Ann Powers, "takes Carlile into a new space of risk-taking—as well as the emotional stratosphere." After appearances on late-night TV and *The Howard Stern Show*, it was a performance of "The Joke" at the 2019 Grammys, for which she earned a standing ovation from the industry-heavy crowd, that truly seemed to ring the bell. Following the broadcast, her concert audiences more than doubled in size, from about 2,400 to 5,600 attendees per show. With COVID-19, Carlile had to cut her tour dates down dramatically, but she still managed to average about 9,000 tickets nightly.

The industry opened itself up more to LGBTQ+ people in the 2010s and 2020s, too, both in reaction to Carlile and as simply a product of the times. When Mike Huckabee, the homophobic former governor of Arkansas, joined the board of the Country Music Association in 2018, an upswell of anger among insiders like the co-president of Monument Records led to his resignation within twenty-four hours. Orville Peck, a rainbow-masked cowboy singer inspired by Johnny Cash, duetted on the Cash-Carter duet "Jackson" with a drag queen. "I grew up with country music all around me," one fan told Peck. "But it wasn't until I listened to you that I felt like I could embrace that side of my culture because I felt really outside of it growing up." Melissa Carper, a gay folk musician from the South who often sports a Bill Monroe hat, only listened to pre-WWII records or Americana music that attempts to re-create it, and didn't even bother to try for a major label deal when she hit Nashville. "That always seemed to be a different world, and increasingly the kind of music that I saw on mainstream country radio; that's not what I do, so I just never thought about it." She came out to her family and was surprised to find acceptance. "They were able to let go of that belief that they had," she recalls. Since her first records were released and Brandi Carlile's fame exploded, more people approach Melissa Carper to tell her, one, they love her music, and two, that they love that she identifies with the same social groups, which are not known for a love of country music.

Another LGBTQ+ artist echoes this, saying: "We're so lucky to live in the day we live in now where we can love who we wanna love and be with who we wanna be with."

"Communities are so important," says Carlile. "You should be able to choose which one you're a part of.

"Is it a philosophy?" she asked rhetorically about her music. "Is it country music for liberals? I don't know, but I know it's me."

CHAPTER ELEVEN

THE NEW HIGHWAYMEN

Country music is the white man's blues. That's all it is.

—Hank Williams Jr.

Combine the sounds of Otis Redding, Wilson Pickett, and Aretha Franklin and you've got Jason Isbell, a 28-year-old reviving Southern musical history.

—Andy Langer, in *Esquire*, July 26, 2007

I like running off people who are closed-minded. I'm not trying to sway them to one side politically, I'm just trying to tell them my story.

—Jason Isbell, in the *L.A. Times*, October 9, 2023

Growing up in rural, hard-core Republican Green Hill, Alabama, Jason Isbell should have become an ultra-conservative. "There was a pretty big religious undertone to everything down there," he says. "Guilt, guilt, guilt, shame, shame shame." His grandfather and great-uncles played at Pentecostal services, but Isbell was mainly raised in the Church of Christ his mother attended, where only "human voices" were allowed. However, he says, "it wasn't the kind of house where we blamed our problems on people who are different from us." When his first adult band noticed an audience member holding up a Confederate flag, the entire group stopped playing to shout: "Get the fuck out with that!" As he later sang, "The right thing's always the hardest thing to do."

Isbell recalls learning to play guitar with the amp cranked, attempting to drown out his parents' arguments. He started writing songs at age twelve, not long after discovering Johnny Cash and '70s rockers among his father's LPs. Isbell first hit the Grand Ole Opry stage as a guitarist in 1995, when he was all of sixteen and already getting drunk on the regular.* He couldn't find his groove, however, even when FAME, a Muscle Shoals studio, hired him as an in-house songwriter at $250 a week. He tried copying Lucinda Williams's lyrics but said his own versions were so bad, no one caught on. Those early musings detailed heartbreak and heavy alcohol consumption, two major themes of country music, but the finished songs didn't excite him. Then, at long last, on tour, he discovered "the real America." He saw how society's outcasts, particularly the Indigenous people starved of social resources, were truly "living." He thought he'd grown up below the poverty line, in a trailer, under the direction of his house painter, tool man, Pentecostal preacher father, as with all his friends and neighbors, but this stunned him into speechlessness. The baby-faced six-foot-one, chubby white singer with short hair couldn't put a label on it, being a "dumb redneck," as Justin Townes Earle jokingly dubbed him. He later determined that he'd seen and experienced the economic effects of systemic racism. Sun-battered faces begging for change, couples with chapped lips and gizzard-thin necks tugging

* "First time I was ever drunk was right over there," he said from the stage at Shoals Fest 2022. "It was 1994 and I was drinkin' Zimas."

pit bulls along the expressway, silent campsites underneath overpasses. "The A/C hasn't worked in 20 years / Probably never made a single person cold / but I can't say the same for me / I've done it many times," he sang. He admitted: "I'm a white man living in a white man's world."

In his early twenties, he joined the Drive-By Truckers, half-jokingly dubbed "country music for Democrats." DBT, cofounded by Patterson Hood, son of the bassist on Willie's *Phases and Stages*, often included lyrical call-outs of poverty and systemic racism, and their music was hard rocking, stark, and heart-wrenching, especially live. During the height of the Iraq War, with the Dixie Chicks still blacklisted, Isbell wrote: "What did they say when they shipped you away / To fight somebody's Hollywood war?" Asked whether Music Row executives cared about his opinions, he said, "[Music Row] and I have avoided each other in dressing rooms since the beginning of time."

He wrote the classic 2003 story song "Decoration Day" only four days into his tenure with the Truckers. "When I wrote those first songs... like 'Outfit' and 'Decoration Day,' those were strong songs, very strong songs," he said in 2013. "But had I been in the position of writing an entire album at that point in time, I don't think the whole album would have been of that kind of quality." He often mocked the dog-beer-and-truck clichés in country songs, especially when introducing "Speed Trap Town" in concert, a song narrated by the son of a cop who pulls women over to demand sex in exchange for letting them out of tickets.

He didn't even *drink* beer. He had been booted from the Truckers for guzzling up to a fifth of Jack Daniel's on the daily and doing bumps of cocaine to stay awake enough to drink even more—"I was just an asshole too many times," he admitted.* He almost lost

* Not long after Isbell's firing, the Drive-By Truckers teamed up for a tour with Booker T. Jones, Willie Nelson's *Stardust* producer.

future wife Amanda Shires when he spiraled out of control on his "one more night of partying" before supposed sobriety. In 2012, the writer of "Hurricanes & Hand Grenades"* got sober at a Nashville clinic to save himself and his growing family. Like Waylon, he quit cocaine and woke up from his last binge to discover he had neglected his career in favor of rock star posturing. (Referencing a Waylon song, he jokingly tweeted: "Damnit Waylon I can't just take back the weed and the cocaine. It didn't come from WalMart. There's not a receipt.") During early tours, he often competed for coherence with loud commentary from televised football games. After Isbell grumbled his way through one set, a fan politely chastised him for not thanking the audience for coming. Now he does so religiously, often multiple times per show. "There are things I have to pay attention to now that I never had to pay attention to before," he says, partly kidding. "Scheduling. Other people's feelings... instead of just reacting all the time, which is what you're doing when you're living that part of the rock 'n' roll lifestyle."

Ironically, in his late thirties he recommitted to the goal he had at twenty-one of making real, no-holds-barred, anti-corporate country-rock, like his predecessors tried to do.** He wrote of real-life tragedies like the murder of actor Lana Clarkson by producer Phil Spector, the paradox of escaping a small town for the dangerous but more fulfilling wider world, and the death of an acquaintance in the Iraq War, as well as covering classic western-style songs like Guy Clark's "Desperados Waiting for a Train," a hit for the Highwaymen. Isbell dedicated himself to music that challenged his audience and

---

* A reference to two New Orleans cocktails.

** One told him that with his pedal steel guitar player behind him and "old drinking music" on the set list, he was "too rock 'n' roll for country and too country for rock 'n' roll."

himself, saying: "Some things you have to refuse, not because of other people's image of you but because it will gradually erode you."

The year he got sober, Isbell released *Southeastern*. The Dave Cobb–helmed record was originally intended to be solo acoustic, but backed by his band, the 400 Unit,* and inspired by Rosanne Cash and other heroes, Isbell instead sang in Cobb's Nashville home studio live into a classic RCA BK-5A mic with the emotional drive of someone given a second and final chance to say something. "This time I want to remember it all," he told the *New York Times*. "I just followed the songs, there wasn't really any concept going into the writing of the record," he later recalled. "I think they work best when I try to document what's going on in my life and if I'm creating a character try and follow that character and allow the character to behave in a natural way. And if I'm writing something where I'm actually the first-person narrator in the song then I just try to explain to myself how I feel about the world. . . .

"I had moved from Muscle Shoals to Nashville," he said of the title, *Southeastern*. "Being here for a little while, I can see a kind of community that is still around underground—independent music, punk rock, Americana—that's very separate from Music Row and the kind of music mill that pumps out Top 40 country music. . . . For the most part, you're either working on that side of the tracks or this one." He also said Cobb encouraged him to sing and play live to tape, which Waylon and Buddy both tried on their first days in Nashville, to guffawing. "It makes it a little bit more powerful emotionally," Isbell says.

Now, according to *Americana UK*, the best Americana album ever and one of *Rolling Stone*'s 500 Greatest Albums of All Time, *Southeastern*, detailing Isbell's post-rehab life, broke through to the pop and country charts in 2013 thanks to "Cover Me Up," a sex-soaked song in

* Growing up, he recalled, "if you were crazy, you went to the 400 Unit."

the "Help Me Make It Through the Night" vein that sent country fans swooning. "I sobered up and I swore off that stuff / forever this time," he sang, but most listeners were focused on the erotically charged lines "Girl, leave your boots by the bed / we ain't leaving this room." It helped that Isbell embraced the Alcoholics Anonymous motto of "rigorous honesty" and concentrated on perfecting the lyrics, without dressing them up in emotionally wrought guitar solos. "I realized that if I'm going to stand out, I need to use my instrument to express myself rather than to show people my technical ability," he said. "Once I got sober...I had something to talk about that wasn't just your typical love song or rock 'n' roll song. I had a story to tell.... We, as a country, got into a lot of trouble because people would rather be angry than admit to being afraid. You don't grow that way. Until I went through the recovery process, I wasn't very good at it at all. And I still work on it daily." In 2022, he looked back, saying: "I wanted an excuse to disconnect, and once that excuse was gone, I had to start the process of figuring out why I needed to connect in the first place."

His subsequent creative explosion led to high *Billboard* 200 positions, especially for an independent record, and, although *Southeastern* didn't make the country list, his following three albums all went to number one there and into the pop Top 10. In 2016 and 2018, his albums won all four Grammys they were nominated for. As one cohost joked at the 2022 Americana Music Awards: "Even though he's not here and not nominated, Jason Isbell will probably win an award tonight."

Isbell had proved to fellow outsider artists that, in the internet era, records could be cheaply made, lucrative without a corporation taking most of the profits, and that one didn't need radio to break through, just solid word of mouth and fantastic material. When a casual acquaintance—and longtime fan—needed an electric guitar overdub to complete his album, he called Isbell. "I rang up Jason, and he came over with his Duesenberg guitar," says Derek Hoke. "He's a true musician. Went out of his way to play the right parts and really bring my songs to life. No ego. No bullshit."

In 2021, Morgan Wallen, the most discussed country singer of the 2020s, released a version of "Cover Me Up." Wallen, who had expressed disdain for hip-hop and suggested he was a natural C&W musician because he naturally "sounded country," made headlines earlier in the year not for his music but for using the "n-word" in a home-shot video.

"Racism is real. It is unacceptable. And it has no place at The Grand Ole Opry," said that program's organizers in response. The industry was still arguing over 2019's "Old Town Road," a young, queer, Black man's rap-country breakout, and *Billboard*'s removal of the song from the country chart. The outcry over *Billboard*'s action forced the industry onto the defensive, and spurred insiders to "cancel" anyone who made Black musicians feel unwelcome. Wallen, effectively blacklisted from country radio and disqualified from the Country Music Awards, rallied conservatives and anti-"woke" reactionaries and rebuilt his audience among white adults who didn't normally listen to country. He performed with an African American rapper at Nashville's Bridgestone Arena for a Martin Luther King Jr. Day concert. His album shot to number one and remained there for weeks, becoming the bestselling record of 2021 in *any* genre. Wallen told Black morning show host Michael Strahan that he agreed racism was prevalent on Music Row: "It would seem that way," he said, but quickly added: "I haven't really sat and thought about that." The "proud" redneck obliquely said he would have made different decisions but wasn't letting it weigh him down.

Following a PR blitz involving collaborations with Black rappers, interviews about hip-hop artists he admired, the hiring of a Black multi-instrumentalist, and rumored six-figure charitable contributions,

Wallen started to reappear in the news and on radio playlists once more, and mere months into his "cancellation," announced an eight-month tour. NBC News termed his resurgence a huge disappointment. "Perhaps his future as a crossover act was in doubt, but his status as country's biggest star never wavered," wrote Kelefa Sanneh.

The Black country singer Mickey Guyton was unsurprised. "I mean, I was called a 'fucking nigger,'" she said, claiming to have received page after page of racist messages merely for claiming to be a country artist. She was running up against a historically homogenized genre—only four Black women had ever charted on *Billboard*'s country charts.

An African American country fan who got dirty looks at concerts and thought Music Row's marketing was geared toward "conservative white people" launched the Black Opry. Initially a one-off, private guitar pull in Nashville, the Black Opry caught fire in the media in 2021 and became a touring revue covered in the pages of *Rolling Stone*. "When people asked me what kind of music I played," said Black Opry performer Joy Clark, "it's always like, 'Good music? Music that sounds good?'" But after a year of the revue and a few mentions on CMT, the Black Opry had made little progress getting through to Nashville's marketing machine. Said founder Holly G.: "The real struggle is gonna be to convince these institutions that it's not me they need to talk to—it's their fans. It's their fans that are the problem, it's their fans that are making things unsafe. And they don't want to upset their fans because they don't want the money to stop coming in." Brandi Carlile wasn't surprised that women, LGBTQ+ people, and people of color were struggling to break in. "There's still a giant metallic steel door shut to country," she said. "Somebody's going to get that thing opened. And, when they do, we're all going to come running in."

The anti-diversity blowback peaked in 2023, when Bud Light released a pro–Gay Pride ad campaign, and Kid Rock shot up a case of

Bud Light beer. Morgan Wallen fans tweeted images showing supposedly empty Bud Light lines at Wallen's shows. Jason Isbell responded that his tour rider was now "all" Bud Light. "I don't drink any of it, I just shoot it," he joked. "But I buy it first so Anheuser-Busch gets the money. Much like what Kid Rock did, except I don't get another person off-screen to shoot for me, and I don't miss." (When he then got criticized on Twitter by a user calling himself "Sturgill Jennings" for trying to be "the people's champion," Isbell tweeted back: "And you sir are neither Sturgill nor Jennings.")

When the Grand Ole Opry invited Morgan Wallen to perform on a 2022 broadcast, coincidentally the fifty-fifth anniversary of Charley Pride's color-barrier-smashing debut, Isbell was waiting. He tweeted: "Last night you had a choice—either upset one guy and his 'team,' or break the hearts of a legion of aspiring Black country artists. You chose wrong and I'm real sad for a lot of my friends today. Not surprised though. Just sad." Black singer-songwriters, including Yola, echoed his sentiments, calling the move "a backslide" after the Opry's previous statement about racism. "This town is really not for us," said queer woman of color Joy Oladokun. Some were not so fatalistic. Wrote Rissi Palmer: "Systems only work when we continue to participate in them. The moment we stop and divest, they lose their power. . . . Money and power is all this industry understands and respects. . . . I can't say this enough: let's stop running into a burning building. Let's create platforms and systems that celebrate and welcome us. Anyone that wants to participate in that, they can come sit w/ me."

"I think it's hilarious that people assume that making somebody less famous is like cutting their fucking dick off!" said Isbell. "We're not calling for the man's head! We're just going, 'This guy is an idiot. And he does not deserve to be put on a pedestal. So let's take him off the pedestal and put him back down on the sidewalk with everybody else.'"

Isbell suggested that Music Row was mostly to blame, as they had already put too many marketing dollars behind Wallen to drop him. If he had his druthers, however, Isbell would have picked someone else, probably a Black woman, to be blessed with a promotional onslaught. Shortly before his own version went gold, Isbell donated the $53,000 he received in royalties for Wallen's version of Isbell's "Cover Me Up" to the Nashville NAACP.

Isbell has been at "war against the way nostalgia has been weaponized," one critic suggested, and how systemic sexism and racism seemed unbreakable in Nashville. In his lyrics for the 2018 film *A Star Is Born*, he suggested, "maybe it's time to let the old ways die," and in 2023, he released a song with the verse: "Jamie found a boyfriend / With smiling eyes and dark skin / And her daddy never spoke another word to her again."

Isbell used his status as a popular artist to help push Black women on the conservative industry.* His sold-out, eight-show Ryman run in 2021 featured a different opening act each night—and all but one was a Black woman country singer. Mickey Guyton, Adia Victoria, and more artists who released records that year performed for their largest-ever audiences in Nashville, including executives who had overlooked them for not being the classic faces of Country Music Television.

One Isbell fan discovered Victoria, Joy Oladokun, and Brittney Spencer through the Ryman shows, and called Spencer as "country as

* While most celebrities, especially in country music, have assistants or an employee at the record label running their social media accounts, Isbell is unbossed and uncensored online. "My therapist tells me that if I argue with people on Twitter, then I don't have to do it with people I know and love and care about at home," he told *Spin*. He promised to release cover records with special guests if Democrats won two Georgia Senates in 2020 and the 2022 Texas gubernatorial contest, suggesting he would have done Billy Joe Shaver and Willie Nelson originals for the latter.

Reba" and said she doubted "that there's anything she can't sing." But after Oladokun's opening set, in which the singer mentioned Black Lives Matter, the fan encountered an irate white man in the lobby. "He was screaming for the manager of the Ryman," she writes. "I mean, if Jason had said it, would he have act[ed] the same? Doubtful."

"I have no problem making the audience a little uncomfortable," Isbell said, practically gleeful about putting his mostly white fanbase on their toes. "Piss off all the assholes and pretty soon you have a nice, safe, fun crowd at all the gigs." Later, he added: "Just wait till they see Adia, if they're squirming now." Around this time, Adia Victoria, who was working at an Amazon warehouse to make ends meet, met Willie Nelson backstage at Nelson's Luck Reunion festival. (When he signed her lucky red stage boots, Victoria "retired" them.) "I definitely felt more like an outsider before COVID happened, ironically," Victoria says. "I've found more of a sense of community during the pandemic with Jason Isbell, Margo Price, Ally Russell, Brandi Carlile, and I guess I'm just a lot less socially fearful."

The moment seemed to have arrived, for Victoria and her contemporaries—and not just because they were overdue, but because powerful voices had noticed they were marginalized. Victoria says, "Those of us working in these rootsy, American-ish [styles] have been so tokenized and fetishized and isolated for so long." Onstage, she told stories of giving her record to her label and hearing that they couldn't understand a Southern Black woman's obsession with magnolia trees. She half-jokingly warned fans about the Nashville takeover by a "bedazzled, bedeviled and be-drunked cluster of Caucasian bachelorettes" leaving Jason Aldean's bar and rampaging straight toward "Kid Rock's big ass honky tonk."

Mickey Guyton, too, seemed poised to break out for a century before the Isbell opening spot. After moving from LA to Nashville in 2011, she auditioned for and won a contract with Universal Music

Group, creating a new category: a Black woman on a major Music City label. Kris Kristofferson and Darius Rucker, a Black rock singer who had successfully transitioned to country pop, helped her celebrate both it and the Obama presidency just weeks later at a White House performance. The president of the United States shared a famous quote from Charley Pride: "There is enough room in country music for everybody."

But Guyton, frequently mislabeled as a straight-up R&B singer, didn't feel accepted then or within the following decade. Under pressure to live up to historic labels and working relentlessly on simply fine-tuning her sound, she developed a drinking problem. Even after "Old Town Road" launched gay Black hip-hop/country artist Lil Nas X to fame, Guyton still fretted over sounding "too R&B." She was right to be worried—even the country-rap songs that became pop blockbusters, like a Tim McGraw and Nelly collaboration, failed to make most country station playlists. "Your songs need to be extremely country-sounding, because you're a Black woman and people are going to think you're not authentic," her label allegedly told her.*

"I wish they would have given listeners a bit more credit," she said.

After her husband suggested that she wasn't telling enough true-to-her stories in song, Guyton changed direction. The next chorus she wrote became "Black Like Me": "If you think we live in the land of the free / you should try to be Black like me." In 2020, Mickey Guyton released it as her first single on Universal/Capitol Nashville, smack-dab in the middle of a galvanizing protest movement spurred by the police murder of George Floyd. It detailed a youth spent feeling like an outcast and, as a minority woman in Nashville,

* Neko Case believes it's silly to demand authenticity from country artists. "That's what large entities" want poor consumers to believe, she says.

a career *proving* she was one. Capitol had delayed the release of the song until after the COVID-19 pandemic; employees at Spotify contacted the label to ask why it had been postponed. The truth, according to one newspaper, was that executives feared it would get completely ignored by country radio and be a waste of marketing money. Guyton had put out a pair of EPs but had yet to complete an album, which may have tamped down the label's expectations. But when Spotify hyped Guyton's track honoring police shooting victim Ahmaud Arbery, UMG finally posted "Black Like Me" on the streaming service. Despite being informally dubbed "country music's song of the year," "Black Like Me" didn't chart. However, it miraculously landed Guyton a Best Country Solo Performance Grammy nod, the first for a Black woman, and at age thirty-eight she finally found a label to release her debut album. "Thank God that Black don't crack," she joked.

"I can't think of a better song to make history with than 'Black Like Me' and I hope that I can continue to help open doors for other women and people who look like me," she said.

When white men reacted to her tweet with the "n-word," Guyton responded: "This is exactly who country music is. I've witnessed it for 10 gd years." She sustained the momentum, however, receiving an invitation to cohost the Academy of Country Music Awards with white male superstar Keith Urban and *TIME*'s 2022 Breakthrough Artist of the Year honor. A few Black people were even spotted at her set at the Ryman. But it wasn't enough. After being named Country Music Television's Breakout Artist of the Year, she announced in a quivering voice that she would make it her life's mission to "show that country music really is everyone's music."

"None of these people should be available to open for me," said Isbell. "They should all be too big for that."

While women of color dominated the 2021 and 2022 Americana Music Awards and Jimmie Allen became the second-ever Black Best New Artist honoree at the CMAs, cracks began to show in the alt-country world. The CMAs banned the Confederate flag and, practically in the same breath, confirmed that Morgan Wallen would cohost its 2022 awards show. Meanwhile, artists continue to be fearful of reprisals from conservative audiences, particularly in terms of radio requests.

Jimmie Allen may have inspired the most word-of-mouth buzz after the 2021 CMAs, but Chris Stapleton, possibly the most popular current country artist, swept the awards.

Like Kris Kristofferson, Stapleton, a Kentucky-born miner's son and star student and football player, hid behind his long hair, was described as soft-spoken, and had to build up a long track record as a songwriter before someone would give him a shot as a solo artist. He suggested that out of one thousand songs he wrote, perhaps ten were high quality. It took numerous rejections and a handful of hit singles by other artists before he landed a deal to make what became *Traveller* in 2015. But he didn't complain about the wait, the rejections, or even, as others in the alt-country movement did, the two facets of Nashville: the corporate radio sound and the rawer, independent-minded movement that pushed back against it. "If you don't like sushi, you don't go around all day telling everybody how much you hate sushi, and telling everybody who likes sushi to hate sushi," he said. "Music is supposed to be joyful and move people, and however that gets accomplished for different people, it's all good."

Nashville, though, hadn't known what to do with him: "I don't probably sing like a traditional country singer," he admitted. "I'm just trying to be the best version of that that I can be, whether that's playing a song that leans into blues or a song that leans into R&B or a song that leans into really distinctly outlaw country. I love all that music. And I don't feel limited to playing one type of song."

However, it wasn't until the year he turned thirty-seven that Nashville finally assented to an outlaw country record from him. Earlier, he had heard Sturgill Simpson's psych-country breakthrough *Metamodern Sounds* and discovered producer Dave Cobb. "Sonically, I didn't know that something like that could still exist," Stapleton said. "I thought it was something we had lost to modern techniques, technology, something. He's not afraid to make a record that doesn't sound like what else is going on.... He says, 'I want to make it sound like whatever *this* is supposed to sound like.' And that's a radical thought process."

After tracking down Cobb, he was amazed to discover that alt-country's leading producer knew *him*. "We met and talked and he had unlimited knowledge of me," said Stapleton. "We had a lot of musical tastes and addictions to guitars and gear in common—it was like a guy I'd known forever."

Of his first single, he says: "It shot straight up to number 46. That song died and my dad died pretty much the same week. My wife bought me a 1979 Jeep Cherokee. We were in Phoenix, Arizona, and she said let's get the hell outta here. And this was the first song I wrote." That song was "Traveller," ostensibly about the road, followed by "Daddy Doesn't Pray Anymore," about his father's cancer diagnosis. "My heartbeat's rhythm is a lonesome sound," he wrote. "Just like the rubber turnin' on the ground." Starting with that piece, the working songwriter would be the one singing his songs.

Cobb marveled at the music and shepherded Stapleton away from radio-friendly touches. (Later, even after his success, Stapleton would still have to endure the CEO of Universal Music requesting that he fine-tune his material to the pop-country sound of the company's other country acts.) "The records are so minimal," says Cobb. "It's like there's no filter between his thoughts, his voice and the performance on the record... what you're hearing on record is him and him saying whatever he wants to say...."

Stapleton and Cobb agreed to a recording style that had once been the norm, right up until the Highwaymen heyday: playing live in the studio. "That vocal you hear on the record is what he's saying at that moment," Cobb noted, "and that's very unusual for making records." Recorded in a single weeklong burst at RCA Studio A, Stapleton's debut set the tone with "Outlaw State of Mind," and included "Tennessee Whiskey," originally cut by Outlaw David Allan Coe. *Traveller* had been all originals until Cobb caught Stapleton playing "Whiskey" at a soundcheck and suggested they give it a one-time run-through in the studio.

"Chris Stapleton's astounding talent has been the worst kept secret on Music Row since what, 2010?" one critic cracked, before calling *Traveller* potentially the 2015 Record of the Year. Isbell threw him a bone and had him open a sold-out Ryman show. Without a radio single, though, it appeared *Traveller* was destined for the bargain bin. Then Stapleton caught a break. He was asked to duet on "Tennessee Whiskey" with Justin Timberlake for a segment at the CMAs. Stapleton won four awards in an upset and, a week later, *Traveller* leapt from the lower depths of the charts to become the first country record to top the *Billboard* 200 in four years. Insiders were stunned that a record of mostly original, stark, mournful tunes, coupled with Stapleton's age, bushy beard, and subdued but powerful performance style could shift units. "Stapleton's songs are both rhythmic and nuanced, perhaps a by-product of years spent writing for others," *Billboard* speculated. "They feature a cast of characters that remain likable even as they rush headlong into pursuit of ruin, fortune or chance." Stapleton, says Rory Kaplan, a development executive and one-time band director for Michael Jackson, gave the industry "hope that people still like real music, songwriters, and value performers that connect—as that's what music should do, give you an emotional experience!"*

Despite the angry, violent, anti-hero characters and gentle melodies, *Traveller* went on to become the bestselling country record of the 2010s and has been certified platinum ten times over. Coincidentally, it had been about the time he began working alongside Mickey Raphael that everything began to change.

Raphael, the harmonica phenom who joined Willie Nelson & the Family as a teenager and became a touring member of the Highwaymen, had established himself as the go-to country music harmonica player, especially for those who considered themselves *songwriters* first and foremost. When artists who skirted the country genre like Emmylou Harris, B.B. King, or Rosanne Cash wanted to make a record that fully embraced the label, they called Raphael. Stapleton's second effort, *From a Room: Volume 1*, was highlighted by a gentle cover of "The Last Thing I Needed First Thing This Morning," Willie Nelson's hit from 1982, on which Stapleton asked Raphael to feel free to either copy himself or let 'er rip. (One essayist wrote in rapt wonder: "Listen to the way his harmonica trails off in defeat after Stapleton sings about an alarm clock that rang two hours late.") *Volume 1*, with Dave Cobb returning to produce, almost topped the pop album charts in 2017, and Stapleton had his largest-ever sales week. With Stapleton so popular the Waffle House chain gave him a trophy for the most plays on its jukeboxes, Raphael couldn't resist hitting the road with

* He adds: "There's a reason why Steven Tyler, Don Henley, Sheryl Crow and many others migrate to Nashville to work with great songwriters."

him to promote *From a Room*—but then Nelson called: the Big Boss had booked new dates.* Stapleton, Raphael dryly suggested, would probably survive without him for a spell. (Raphael was also busy with another potential New Highwaymen member: Jason Isbell. The harmonica player appears on Isbell's 2023 album *Weathervanes*; he's been guesting with Isbell on shows and records since at least 2015.)

In June 2015, Stapleton effectively filled in for Waylon Jennings at his own tribute concert, appearing alongside Kris Kristofferson and Willie Nelson, as well as Kacey Musgraves and Ryan Bingham, on the Austin City Limits program *Outlaw: Celebrating the Music of Waylon Jennings*. Stapleton, whose first-born is named Waylon, kicked it off with "I Ain't Living Long Like This," a signature Waylon tune about trying to outrun one's demons—and the law—and duetted with Willie on "My Heroes Have Always Been Cowboys," the song Sharon Vaughn played for Waylon over and over again. Stapleton takes the stage at his shows shortly after Kristofferson's "Bobby McGee" and/or Waylon's "Ramblin' Man" blare over the PA, and he once played a funky, almost downright-nasty, and danceable "Folsom Prison Blues" as a live duet with his wife, Morgane, and went viral for it when it was rediscovered by social media users seven years later.

In 2022, Stapleton wrote a Grammy-winning single for Willie with Rodney Crowell. Then, with the headliner and opener reversed, Nelson toured with Stapleton's All-American Roadshow. At an arena concert in New Orleans, Stapleton scanned the crowd and cooed: "It's always amazing to me when we go into places like this, I don't know

* Nelson didn't rehearse or give notes, and hadn't used set lists since the day he took Larry Butler's band into an impromptu "Under the Double Eagle" without permission—all of which appealed to his harpist. "He starts the song, and once we hear the intro, we come right in and we know what's going on. The set follows a certain template; he starts off with 'Whiskey River,' and... I can't remember what happens after that, but his intro is the only cue."

if it's sold out tonight or what... sometimes I'd play places and there wouldn't be a soul there.

"I never got to see Aretha Franklin live and I always regretted that when she passed away recently," he says. "You make these plans, you're like, 'I'm gonna go see him when he comes around next year' or 'I'll see this person...' and then you lose a lot of history musically.... I never got to see Waylon Jennings play or Johnny Cash... [but] I played some shows with Haggard and Willie." He snapped up the unemployed Robby Turner, the Highwaymen's steel guitarist and a Waylor stretching all the way back to the *Outlaws* compilation. "I kind of have a history of doing that a little bit, [recording with my] heroes," Stapleton said. "I like to draw that bridge a little bit musically, and if it means I can coerce some heroes into participating in music with me... why wouldn't you do that if you could?

"Every time I get to play with Willie Nelson, it's the greatest treat in the whole wide world," he said.

He even brought Willie and Muscle Shoals full circle by recording a Dylan song with Nelson in the hamlet. Getting sober, and with his own exhibit at the Country Music Hall of Fame, Stapleton's name began to ring out as a possible leader for a New Highwaymen. As *Indy Week* noted: "He's now at the fore of a wave of artists keeping contemporary country honest."

More specifically, a wave of outlaw country.

The public had been primed by *Crazy Heart,* a 2009 indie film starring Jeff Bridges, friend to Kris Kristofferson. Great performances and songs gave CPR to the tired story of a down-on-his-luck boozer and grizzled outlaw country singer, whom writer-director Scott Cooper envisioned as the fifth Highwayman. In turn, Bridges drew on his experiences on the *Heaven's Gate* set, in which he and Kristofferson jammed on country classics.

On the set of *Crazy Heart*, Bridges, in spirit if not costume, found Ryan Bingham in the open door of the van he lived out of. Bingham told him he was a country songwriter and the actor went straight to soundtrack producer T Bone Burnett about his "discovery." Burnett surprisingly kept in touch with the young songwriter and, one day, near the end of production, Bingham plunked himself down on T Bone's coffee table and said he had an idea for a song. He couldn't meet T Bone's eyes, but he did work up the courage to play him "The Weary Kind." It became the centerpiece of the film, as well as of Bingham's Top 20 pop album and near-country chart-topper, *Junky Star*.

Bingham, known as "the cowboy" among friends, is a former rodeo bull rider. Before breaking in with *Crazy Heart*, he developed a cult following among fellow musicians and outlaw lovers, although he often played to about a dozen people, even in Austin, his adopted hometown. His first show with screaming fans came after the film's release, when he played in Fort Worth and he and guitarist Jesse Dayton had to cover their ears after each song. Soon, Bingham was opening for Willie Nelson on a starlit night at the Greek in LA and duetting with him on "On the Road Again" at another gig, and in 2018, Bingham's guitarist Charlie Sexton joined host Jimmy Fallon and actors Ben Dickey and Ethan Hawke to dress up as the Highwaymen and sing "On the Road Again" on *The Tonight Show*.

"What I've always respected about all of those guys was the honesty and the integrity of the songs," says Bingham of the supergroup. "Not being scared to say what is on your mind and buck up to the establishment, even if you might not make some people happy or ruffle feathers."

In COVID lockdown and unable to tour, Bingham covered Brandi Carlile's "The Joke" and generally laid low. However, around the same time, he created his own Dripping Springs Reunion with the backing of the Live Nation concert ticketing agency. The festival's location? Luckenbach, Texas.

Other outlaw artists who would fit seamlessly into the New Highwaymen may not have Bingham's star wattage—or even that of the original bandmembers at their nadirs. Jamey Johnson, who became a member of the Grand Ole Opry in 2022, idolized the originals, and Waylon's son Terry thanked Johnson in his memoir for keeping his dad's music out there. "Without people like me out there covering their songs, they just stop," said Johnson. "If nobody was singing Johnny Cash, there's a whole generation that would grow up without Johnny Cash. And if you ask me, that's not gonna be a good world. I just view myself as a torch that's passing down from one generation to the next, and if I could be used in that way, maybe that's a good purpose." To back up this assertion, Johnson joined Hank Williams Jr. and Shooter Jennings on Sirius/XM's Outlaw Country channel for a medley of Waylon classics, including the Cash-Jennings collab "There Ain't No Good Chain Gang," and closing with "Are You Sure Hank Done It This Way?" Willie Nelson made sure Johnson joined Chris Stapleton, Kris Kristofferson, Emmylou Harris, Margo Price, and other country stars at the Nelson tribute show at Nashville's Bridgestone arena.

Johnson, though, has been mostly out of the recording studio and thus off fans' radar since 2012. In 2016, in a supposedly tongue-in-cheek collaboration with George Strait, the duo sang about their record companies throwing their tapes in the trash for not fitting "the format," pointing out that's exactly what happened to Cash, Waylon, and others. Johnson doubled down with a 2022 duet with Julie Roberts called "Music City's Killing Me," produced by Shooter Jennings. Says Roberts: "When I first started recording this project, I went out to L.A. to record. I didn't feel like I fit in here anymore and I didn't know where I belonged," she said of Nashville. "In a way, Music City had worn me out. But I knew Shooter and Jamey got me."

Gary Allan is another outsider artist who ran into the wall that is Nashville and paid the price. Allan is, according to his PR, a "modern day outlaw" who has written songs about Johnny Cash and for Willie Nelson, calls Kris Kristofferson a hero, and whose big break came through a Waylon Jennings cover. He told *Rolling Stone* he believed conglomerates had rigged country radio, as they had pop stations, offering a sparse selection of derivative tunes written by the same few songwriting teams who used a mathematical approach to creating melodies. He speculated that the labels would soon scour TikTok and other social media apps for teenagers they could mold and completely control. Independent-minded artists might, like Waylon, fight back against songs they found too pop-y or might want to put out a stark, depressing concept album. "It's going to be really hard for us to have another Guns N' Roses or people with attitude who don't like the labels and want to buck the system," he concluded.

Like Johnson, Allan went M.I.A. for years after his 2013 comments about sterile country radio. After he suggested that Clear Channel and Cumulus snapping up independent radio stations and controlling so much of the market led to homogenized, teen-focused station playlists, he tried to backpedal. In later comments, he clarified that he thought the industry changed, but not necessarily in a bad way; however, he couldn't help but throw in a dig. "You used to be able to turn on the radio and you knew instantly it was a country station just by listening to it," he said. "Now you've got to leave it there for a second to figure it out."

The previous year, Allan had had a number one single and a number one album on both the pop and country charts. Since his comments about country radio, he has not had a Top 40 hit on any chart. In the interim, he cowrote a song with Chris Stapleton, but even that didn't get him back into heavy rotation. Subsequently, he worked with several one-named songwriters (usually a sign of commercial focus) on radio-ready tunes, but nothing clicked. "Look," he quoted a Universal Music Group Nashville staffer telling him, "during the bro-country thing, we just didn't think that you were going to fit in. So, we're kind of dragging our feet until we get through this."

By 2021, he had apparently accepted his fate. In an interview on his website, he spoke about having taken some hard hits from his label, Universal.

"I gave them a record that I thought still had something to play on the radio. But, you know, maybe there are shinier objects, or I'm too old. Shit, I'm wondering if I even need a record label right now. There's so many other avenues, and I've never got to make a record without radio in the back of my head. To make a record without even considering them would be so much fun." Allan expected that his music would continue to buck the slick, saccharine-pop style of competition TV shows about music: "They can't walk you through a night of emotion, which is what country is supposed to be," he said.

"Waylon wrote and played the way he wanted and refused to let anyone change that about him. He was considered an outlaw but was really just being himself and not what someone told him he should be." Allan wanted to return to his roots and to the career he'd once envisaged for himself, which he said he had modeled after Willie Nelson's. Later in 2021, he seemed to luck out when Nelson announced him as an opening act.

Shooter Jennings and Dave Cobb were instrumental in discovering perhaps the pivotal "new" outlaw.

"Eight years ago today, I plopped down on my couch after a bullshit gig, for bullshit pay, for a bunch of ungrateful despondent tourists in Nashville," musician Ed Ward recalled in 2022. "Said 'fuck this shit,' and turned on my TV."

The *Conan* late-night show was on, and host Conan O'Brien was introducing his musical guest, Sturgill Simpson. Ward folded his arms and harrumphed as the opening riff for Simpson's "Living the Dream" blared through his speakers. *Great*, he thought. *Some asshole trying to sound country*. But when Simpson opened his mouth, Ward felt a chill shoot through him, and sat up straight, as if "1990 naked Elle Macpherson had just walked in the room," he said. He had both of Simpson's records downloaded on his computer before the first chorus.

"That moment meant a lot to me," he recalls today. "It was when the whole 'I don't need Nashville' thought entered my brain."

Simpson hails from Kentucky—as does Chris Stapleton and arguably country itself—and a family of amateur musicians. "Back home, playing music is never anything you imagine you can do for a living," he said. "It's what you do after work." Despite reports that he had been the first male member of the clan not to follow his father into the coal mines, his father was actually a narcotics detective and head of security at the governor's mansion. Luckily, the elder Mr. Simpson was not tyrannical. "From a young age, when I showed interest and an inclination in music, he probably supported it more than anybody," said Sturgill. "He bought me my first guitar." Nonetheless, Sturgill appeared to be following his father into a position of authority, heading straight from high school graduation weekend into the US Navy, where he felt he could put some distance between himself and an OxyContin dependency. Instead, he would leave after a few years following a reported drinking binge, and may have tried heroin then or soon after his discharge. "You get on the boat, you get off the boat and you binge drink," he said of the navy. "That was it for almost three years. I didn't pick up a guitar the entire time I was in."

After hearing a Bill Monroe song he loved from childhood on the radio, he discovered that his once squeaky singing had matured into a deep yet smooth, barrel-chested *voice*. That led to him revisiting his youth love of both punk rock and bluegrass and found he could blend them into unique songs. "I want all that dirt and grime and life-sauce," Simpson said of his newly crafted soulful, outlaw-bluegrass style. "A lot of my favorite old soul records have it, but you don't hear it on country records anymore."

When his neighbors complained about his loud electric guitar, he found that he enjoyed the sound he was getting from an acoustic, despite stripped-down sounds being deemed "uncool" at the time. He soon lit out east again, this time for Tennessee.

"I drove down to Nashville at a time when pop-country was saturating," he recalled with some bitterness. "I couldn't find anybody who wanted to play with me."

After a year palling around with a bottle of whiskey, he surrendered, taking a job on the Utah railroad with an $80,000 salary. The role, though, was so physically demanding and creatively draining that he again stopped playing guitar. His girlfriend Sarah Tackett saw the life fade from his eyes. She gave Sturgill a tape recorder, thinking it might force him to at least make demos. It almost worked, but they were in Utah—how well would demo tapes make out in that remote place?

Tackett, though, was relentless. Her machinations included sending the tapes to radio stations and bringing guitars to a bar with Sturgill so he'd have no excuse not to play if a slot opened up. In 2010, Sarah convinced Sturgill to give Nashville one last shot. The couple, by then married, sold everything they owned except an acoustic guitar. It was the peak of "bro country," the era of easygoing, easy-on-the-eyes All-American boys, but Simpson was mostly listening to bluegrass and folkie John Prine. "I moved here primarily to seek those out, and I just hung out at The Station Inn for Jam Night on Sundays." One supporter later described Sturgill at the time as "a wholly unassuming fellow dressed unremarkably in a black sweater and jeans," contrasting his stage appearance with those of the traditional Nashvillian—"pseudo cowboys and fraudulent rodeo girls"—and a voice "that could halt warships." With their support, he scraped by, especially after giving up some of his fees to cover the expenses of his opening acts. He compiled a mailing list of hundreds of Music Row names, none of whom he had permission to write to, and sent them all a missive introducing himself and including a link to a sampling of his first band's music online. All but one person ignored him. After he posted a video of himself playing at a local club to his YouTube page, the clip made its way to Shooter Jennings.

After reveling in Simpson's recorded performance together, Cobb and Shooter attended a Billy Joe Shaver concert. Waiting for the headliner to go on, Jennings glanced over to see Simpson mixed in with the crowd. He urged Cobb to go over and introduce himself to Sturgill as a producer. Cobb marched straight over and offered to help the young songwriter create his first album. "I'm thankful for the rest of my life," Simpson said. "My manager got an email from Dave that night, at three in the morning, saying, 'I wanna make a record with Sturgill.'"

Despite Cobb's involvement, Simpson refused to consider signing to a Nashville label. He'd made it this far without Music Row, he decided, and not a single executive had approached him to express interest or at least tell him they enjoyed his music. Since Monument, Kris Kristofferson's original label, and other indies sold in the 1990s, there were few options outside the system, and an indie artist might as well have been a skunk-scented busker, blocking one's office door. Instead, Simpson plunged his savings into creating his self-released debut, *High Top Mountain*. "Nobody touched it," Simpson lamented. "It was too country for the hipsters and too country for the pop-country labels."

Released the same day as Isbell's Cobb-produced *Southeastern*, *High Top* was full of "straight-ahead Waylon-isms," one writer noted. Another said it "channels the spirit of Waylon Jennings and the traditional devotion of Jamey Johnson." Said *Country Standard Time*: "The first time you hear Sturgill sing you may feel like you've heard a ghost—the ghost of Waylon Jennings, that is. Although his voice isn't as low as Jennings' was," they added, it's in the "vocal range ballpark. Better still, the Kentucky native sings wonderfully honest country songs." AllMusic mentioned Jennings seven times in its single-paragraph review, noting that Simpson riffed on Waylon's early '70s sound and neglected post-1978 work.

Simpson took issue with that review and others like it that suggested *High Top* was "some kind of tribute to Waylon Jennings." While he did later admit to making "a Waylon Jennings record," he never intended to *sound* like Jennings—he heard Waylon's music, he said, after developing his own singing voice. Simpson so frequently defended himself on this point that he decided to incorporate a tongue-in-cheek Jennings cover into his nightly set list.

"I think people really want somebody right now to sound like Waylon Jennings. It makes me feel like I haven't done a very good job of really getting my voice down.... But there's a hell of a lot worse things you can be told than 'Hey man, you sound like Waylon Jennings.' I'll take it as a compliment, even when I'm burnt the fuck out hearing it."

Merle Haggard didn't get the memo. He said in listening to Sturgill "you hear a lot of Waylon. He's got something going energy-wise that I haven't seen in a long time." Shooter clarified: "Sturgill isn't imitating at all, and he sounds like my favorite era of my dad, the Seventies, when he would sing quieter and more conversational."

Perhaps Sturgill doth protest too much. After all, he worked with steel guitarist Robby Turner of the Waylors, and Dave Cobb, who had produced a posthumous Waylon record. Kris Kristofferson, too, loved Simpson and took him under his wing. "That's the best thing I've heard since The Beatles," he said. Of Haggard, who called bro-country a "screwing on a tailgate, no substance, bunch of shit to me," Simpson said, "getting to hang out with him and Kristofferson and pick their brains is an important reminder of why I do this in the first place."

In an attempt to promote *High Top*, which the music industry treated as an amusing anomaly—an outlaw country record in the twenty-first century!—he agreed to a canned interview with the Country Music Association's self-congratulatory magazine. "What can you tell us about yourself that we'd never guess about you?" went one generic question. Simpson answered: "I'm plotting your destruction."

In advance of *High Top Mountain*, he played to booking agents who asked if he owned some newer footwear. At the album release party, he opened a large bill of local acts at the Basement East. He estimates that ten people showed, although, crucially, one would later become his booking agent. Jonathan Levine, on vacation from California, couldn't believe his luck in discovering Simpson. Without thinking, he leapt onto the stage as Sturgill undid his guitar strap, startling the singer. "I want to work with you," Levine blurted out.

"To me, that was the greatest night of my Nashville experience, because that guy changed my fucking life," Simpson says of Levine. "It was so gratifying to have somebody of that stature come up and say, 'I recognize and believe in what you're doing, I see the potential,' after being rejected for a solid year-and-a-half by everybody in this town."

He landed a tour with Dwight Yoakam, then the Zac Brown Band, heading off potentially hostile crowds by immediately bashing Nashville. We "actually play country music," he told them, and backed this up by delivering raw lyrics about railroads and coal, not beer and pickups. In an in-depth feature, the *Times* called Simpson the "alternative to Alt-Country," suggesting he was pulling the independent and new outlaw movements back from the cowpunk cliff and simply reclaiming straightforward country music from the corporate machine. Simpson, though, welcomes all comers. "I want people to focus on listening, not the image," he said. "And I want to play to everyone: rednecks, dubstep kids, punk rockers, and people who like as-real-as-it-gets country music." One music fan wrote of their conversion to country: "Maturity brought a new perspective, a realization that only a fool would define themselves in such black and whites. And with that new perspective came a newfound appreciation for musicians like Willie Nelson, Waylon Jennings, Johnny Cash, Kris Kristofferson and The Highwaymen." The country music she was exposed to mainly consisted of treacly, repetitive radio-friendly redneck tunes, "but last year I was introduced to Sturgill Simpson's second album *Metamodern Sounds in Country Music*, with the title ironically spitting in the face of my beliefs that country would die with The Highwaymen."

With his sophomore record, Simpson found thousands of new such fans, despite *Metamodern*'s infinitesimal marketing budget. "People will connect, and they'll spread it for you," he said. "You don't need radio. You don't need some big machine throwing it out there. I'm living proof of that." A year later, he suggested he wouldn't have done it any other way, despite the financial losses, "because as a direct result I got to make a country album about metaphysics and turtles and drugs."

Regarding "Turtles All the Way Down," Cobb recalled its recording process in dramatic, hushed tones: "The room is so small, and we're all playing together—I'm playing nylon [string guitar] on that song, and Sturgill's playing acoustic . . . his guitar player's next to us and the bass and drums and we're in one room. It just seemed like it flowed out of everybody." That process, somehow both stripped down and indulging in technological advances such as voice echo effects, resulted in *Metamodern Sounds*. The band cracked twenty-first-century country music right down the middle. Now, country is only pre-*Metamodern* and post-*Metamodern*. Nonetheless, and for all its goofy charm, it's been treated as neither a groundbreaking record nor a turning point in America's growing and profound adoration for the genre.

Like the record its title references—*Modern Sounds in Country and Western Music*, the Ray Charles blockbuster from 1961 that mixed C&W with R&B/soul—Simpson's sophomore effort aimed straight for music lovers who missed the sounds of the Highwaymen or hated country and "the god-awful right-wing kiddie pop coming out of Nashville." The lyrics, too, were simpler and often emotionally resonant: "I'd give anything to go back," he sang on a hidden bonus track, "Days I was young / All the way back to Pan Bowl / I sit down on the lake bed / Stare at the sun."

"When I moved to Nashville," he said, "I put out a very traditional country record because that's just what you do. I had a bunch of very traditional country songs. Next thing you know, you're a country singer." But, he said, he wasn't really interested in genres, only interested in crafting concept albums a la Willie Nelson.

Instead, he fell back on the no-holds-barred music of his younger years, tastes that he shared with Dave Cobb. With uninhibited references to Buddhism and mind-expanding psychedelics, and backed only by a grassroots, no-frills marketing campaign, *Metamodern Sounds* received heavy promotion from industry vets, prestigious media outlets like NPR, multiple late-night TV appearances, and festival shows in an "Old Five and Dimers Like Me" shirt (a reference to the Billy Joe Shaver song made famous by Waylon Jennings), and crossed over to a mainstream audience that avoided Luke Bryan and Garth Brooks like they were covering the *Blue's Clues* theme. Even the notoriously highfalutin *Pitchfork*, after laying their trademark snootiness on thick, praised Simpson for his soft-spoken delivery, for his avoidance of the standard tropes of Nashville, and for refusing to give listeners clear, simplistic answers or endings to his stories, all contrary to what country radio required. FM stations unsurprisingly ignored *Metamodern*, joking that it was "from outer space." It didn't stop the train driving word of mouth, however.

Metamodern Sounds nearly broke through to the country Top 10 in its debut week, and eventually went gold for sales of half a million copies, astonishing for an indie record, and all the more so considering it was "almost completely ignored by Music Row," as *Nashville Scene* pointed out. Simpson had apparently complained online: "I'm having a baby in June and if there is any hopes of me feeding it AND still playing music after the release of this album I have no choice but to go even further into debt to pay a publicist and use major, distributed, accredited, journalism outlets for an announcement like this." Atlantic Records, which closed its country division in 1975 but returned to Nashville in 1991, pounced on Simpson. Execs there naively wondered, if Sturgill could break through to pop audiences without radio hits or even an *indie* label backing him, what could they accomplish with a little PR?

"But [at] a major label, the people that worry about bottom lines and quarterly reports, they'll never understand why my career really happened, because that's not the world they navigate," said Simpson. Although he signed with them, he told Atlantic he would not make a third outlaw country album. His next effort became an almost deliberately impenetrable, orchestral, about-face. As he once said: "Show me a stable artist and I'll show you some boring art."

Only one fan saw it coming. Working in a Nashville guitar shop when *Metamodern* was on the charts, the fan watched Simpson march across the store to a red Telecaster-style axe that the shop had custom-built. Turning it over in his hands, Simpson muttered about how much he missed playing balls-to-the-wall electric guitar, which wouldn't have been evident from his latest record. It reminded one shop employee of the moment Bob Dylan "went electric," having stopped by a British guitar store in a scene from the documentary *Dont Look Back*, filmed during Dylan's final acoustic tour.

Johnny Cash's engineer David "Fergie" Ferguson was at a card game in Nashville when Sturgill Simpson, whom he did not know, walked in. The two instantly fell into a deep conversation about music. Producer Dan Auerbach, who was hosting the game, told Simpson: "You oughta work with Fergie on the record." What started out as a simple country album with Cash's engineer supporting a self-producing Simpson turned into a surprisingly controversial release. "I thought it was hilarious when 'Brace for Impact' was released, and people said I had abandoned country, even though the song is dripping with pedal steel," said Simpson. *A Sailor's Guide to Earth* debuted at number three on the *Billboard* 200, but online badmouthing pushed it down to the ninety-third spot within five weeks.

"I don't think he wants to repeat himself," says Fergie, now a coproducer. "He had a vision of what this was gonna be, and he just had his kid, his first son, and it was kind of a 'welcome to Earth' for him. He had a vision and it didn't take that long to make the record.... He was pretty good at coming up with stuff on the floor."

With his third LP, Simpson made history as the first artist to receive Country Album and Rock Album Grammy nominations for the same release. But the CMAs, which evolved out of the DJ convention that launched Waylon and Willie on country radio, didn't nominate it. So, Simpson brought his acoustic guitar to the 2017 awards ceremony at Nashville's Bridgestone Arena. He hung around outside, though, busking for donations to the American Civil Liberties Union—his trophy for the Best Country Album Grammy in plain view in the guitar case. He propped up a sign reading FASCISM SUCKS, which also noted he wouldn't take requests but would accept questions. "Finally made it, guys, big show," he deadpanned. He mentioned he couldn't get into the sold-out event, "so I thought I'd come down and play some country music." He got half a line into his first song before giving up, drowned out by a preacher with a megaphone.

"I just want to play music. And I'd learned I'd been commodified," Simpson said of his breakthrough. He bought a Ford Bronco for a few hundred bucks so he wouldn't have to grocery shop in his tour bus. He played relentless shows, singing the same songs for weeks straight, and then stopped playing the "old favorites" of a few years prior, such as "Life Ain't Fair and the World Is Mean," a semi-autobiographical swipe at an executive who thought Simpson was too raw for radio. That's not to say he had learned to let go. When interviewers brought up Dave Cobb's production work and the "outlaw" sound, he might say: "Those songs were carved out when we were on the road, with my band. He got all the credit and career from it, but that's my album. Anybody that's heard my last few records, I think it's pretty fucking clear."

By 2018, Simpson was completely burnt out, increasing his drinking and substance abuse, scarfing down unhealthy food, and verging on a nervous breakdown in a Nowheresville motel. "I was just medicating from . . . " he said, trailing off. "I finally had the family I always wanted, but then you're gone nine months out of the year. And then I had two kids, and I literally missed the first year of their lives, and I just refuse to do that anymore. So, this tour is [a] way for us to go out and show this music and the creation the respect it deserves. But then, I don't know that I'll ever do this again."

He decided to record only at recording studios without interns—a way, perhaps, of spotting an impersonal, corporate culture—and sticking to Nashville's off–Music Row facilities, as the Outlaws had done before him. In 2020, he recorded a pair of bluegrass albums at the Butcher Shoppe, a studio partly owned by singer-songwriter John Prine, which was previously exactly what it sounds like. After Prine passed away and the business closed, Simpson said wistfully of the space, "It was like sitting in your grandparent[s'] nicotine-stained den. It didn't feel like a studio, which is why I loved it so much."

Simpson and Ferguson had previously used the Butcher Shoppe to give fellow Kentuckian Tyler Childers, then twenty-six, a shot at the title. Childers, who is from Johnson County, where Chris Stapleton grew up, and whose father, like Stapleton's, worked in the coal mines, put out two records under Simpson and Ferguson's tutelage, the latter of which topped the country chart. However, it was when he put out traditional bluegrass-fiddle albums that Childers came into his own. He surprise-released *Long Violent History* in 2020, the title and content of which was a commentary on systemic racism and police officers in America. In a video message to fans to help clear up any confusion about his purpose, he implored listeners to support Black Lives Matter. "If we didn't need to be reminded, there would be justice for Breonna Taylor . . . and countless others."*

---

* When criticized online for releasing a song about gay love, he said: "By being vocal in the small ways that I have, it might give some of those people that are sitting on the fence wondering exactly how they should feel about it . . . it might push them in a direction of realizing that maybe the people around them and how they think isn't all that there is."

He says: "Everybody always talks about the state of country music and puts down commercial country and [says] 'something's gotta be done' and 'we need to be elevating artists that are doing more traditional country.' We're our own thing, it's a new time, and I don't know what it's called but I've been calling it country, y'know?"

"Tyler's records were the most surprising," says coproducer Fergie Ferguson, noting that one never knows who fame will choose. "The world latched on to Tyler. That [first] record's sold over a million copies. It's hard to sell a million records."

Emboldened by all his successes, Sturgill Simpson stopped talking to his record company, a subsidiary of Atlantic, and suggested he had deliberately released albums that were so inscrutable, esoteric, and experimental that the company couldn't market it. *Here's an album of thunderous rock music I wrote for my kid to enjoy*, he seemed to say. Country music blogs were furious about the new direction: "But this isn't an 'outlaw' move, this is an asshole move," one wrote. "Simpson talks about how money has corrupted the music system. But he himself admits to using his major label deal to abscond with a huge signing bonus to pay his way through life, and then purposely dogging their efforts to recoup their investment." The blog pointed out that Elektra also had Brandi Carlile and that Simpson's previous label, the fledgling Thirty Tigers, didn't tie artists to multi-album deals or keep their masters hostage, as RCA had done with Waylon. Nonetheless, Simpson claimed Elektra, which had started as a small folk label, wouldn't relinquish their control over him.

"I'm done working for them," he said. "I'm done giving babies away. I equate it to, if you owned a fucking dry cleaners, and it took off, and somebody showed up like, 'Hey, we want to buy your dry cleaners. You can sit here and run the counter, but we'll keep all the money.' Like, what other business model would anybody fucking think that makes sense in?" He added: "I can go back to just doing it myself better than they do.... Because they don't know what the fuck to do with me."

When the Country Music Association instructed artists not to talk about guns or gun control in the wake of one of the worst mass shootings in history, which took place at a Las Vegas country concert, Simpson snapped. "Nobody needs a machine gun, coming from a guy who owns a few guns," he said.* He also said that he supported gay marriage, despised "fascist" President Donald Trump, and suggested that the prison-industrial complex re-enslaved African Americans. "Hegemony and fascism is alive and well in Nashville, Tennessee, thank you very much," he said. On Facebook, he asked the Academy of Country Music to "drop all the formulaic cannon fodder bullshit they've been pumping down rural America's throat for the last 30 years along with all the high school pageantry, meat parade award show bullshit and start dedicating their programs to more actual Country Music." As for getting snubbed for ACM awards, he told a fan it was better this way: "Dodged a corny bullet. Plus, it highlights their own hegemonic, transparent corruption/irrelevance. It's all working perfectly."

His comments about the CMAs and ACMs—organizations often seen as crowning winners of popularity contests—touched off a wave of publicity, mostly the negative kind. "Simpson is attempting a... trick with the music business, simultaneously attacking it and exploiting it for his own ends," one interviewer suggested. However, after some Music Row insiders privately thanked him for kicking executives in their proverbial balls, Simpson doubled down. "As I type this, meetings and conversations are taking place on Music Row to ensure I

* Jason Isbell has also fundraised for anti–gun violence initiatives.

am blackballed from the industry and that's perfectly fine with me," he wrote on social media. "I'm not sure how you can blackball somebody you don't acknowledge in the first place anyway," he added. "Yet, even though they mostly go out of their way to ignore artists like myself and Jason Isbell, I assure you they are more than aware of our existence.... Our last albums went to #1 without any help from the Mainstream Country Music establishment, and our next albums will too."

Isbell agreed. Music Row, the Grammys, and the Country Music Association were all shaking in their $900 cowboy boots over the success of antiestablishment artists, and taking fewer risks on new talent. Labels were spending sometimes as little as $20,000 to produce records in the '70s, then up to $200,000 on the front end in the '90s, and today, companies spend "as little as possible to make the record," says producer Mike Clute. "They need artists on the chart the quickest, safest way," he adds, "so you start taking less risks." Signing with a major label meant a nice upfront advance, but, as one artist noted, "when you sign a record deal, you should assume that's the last check you'll see." That made going the independent route more enticing for people like Simpson, Isbell, and Carlile.

Simpson suggested that buyers, too, realized the powers-that-be had rigged the system and were turning on the country music establishment. "Perhaps Country Music, especially Nashville, should wake up too before it's too late," he said. "My advice to anybody coming to Nashville is don't come to Nashville. Just get a van and start playing everywhere else." His outbursts inspired several even fresher artists in town. Singer-songwriter Colter Wall called Nashville "a song factory" and Brent Cobb name-checked Simpson in his 2022 single "When Country Came Back to Town," which, as one might surmise from the title, is about the "real" country artists, according to Cobb. He not only named Simpson as a torchbearer for the genre but singled out *High Top Mountain* for special mention.

Simpson claimed to be writing a guide to the music industry, helping up-and-comers navigate the "horseshit" they'll have to duck, thrown by corporate hacks. He considered releasing it while still in the biz, then decided to wait until he quit, which wouldn't be long in coming. He claimed he would retire after a five-album cycle telling the "Sturgill Simpson" story, implying he had created a fictional character with his own name, and quoted a Kris Kristofferson song ("he's a walking contradiction") to slyly suggest he might be fibbing. Finally, he deleted his entire social media presence.

He recorded one more "outlaw" record, this time at "Cowboy" Jack's studio, and decided he'd about had enough of being Sturgill. A vocal cord hemorrhage seemed to strengthen his commitment to quitting his solo career. Simpson has said: "Going forward, I'd like to form a proper band with some people who I really love and respect musically, and be a part of something truly democratic in terms of creativity," he told *Rolling Stone*. "Not having to stand up there behind my name would allow me to be even more vulnerable, in a way." Just before recording his fifth album, Simpson made an offhand remark at the CMAs suggesting he might form the Highwaymen, Part Two, with Jason Isbell and Chris Stapleton, and a woman this time, perhaps a Kristofferson acolyte like Margo Price or Simpson collaborator Angel Olsen, to complete the quartet. His coproducer, who had worked with the Highwaymen on tour, wasn't sure about that combo. "I would say somebody like Jamey Johnson," said Fergie Ferguson. "Isbell or somebody," he added, "although he's a little clean."

The world got a preview of the possible revamped Highwaymen in 2018, when Simpson appeared as a surprise guest during Stapleton's *Saturday Night Live* performance. Their bond seemed to tighten further when a *Garden & Gun* cover story on Simpson and Haggard got bumped in favor of one about Chris Stapleton. Simpson railed against the magazine: "The editor later claimed in a completely bullshit email apology to both Merle's publicist and ours (Chris and I share the same publicist) that they didn't get any good shots that day." Stapleton took them to task, too. "Merle was in the hospital when they did that," he said. "It wasn't cool."

The New Highwaymen concept, however, is complicated by the fact that someone else thought of the same thing, only with a new twist.

CHAPTER TWELVE

THE HIGHWOMEN

> We want to open more doors for women... maybe it's not through radio, it could be through so many different happenings.
>
> —Natalie Hemby

While everyone was speculating about who would form a Highwaymen 2.0, nobody noticed Brandi Carlile and Amanda Shires cooking something up.

In 2012, Carlile recruited Kris Kristofferson to star in a video promoting her album *Bear Creek*. The following year, she appeared with Willie Nelson on *To All the Girls...*, his CD of duets, which became his highest charting album in two dozen years. Then, in 2016, as part of a tribute to Joni Mitchell, she and Kristofferson duetted in Los Angeles. Despite numerous flubs from Kristofferson, suffering from the effects of a tick-borne illness, Carlile swooned. "One of the great honors of our career [was] to back up the songwriter to beat all songwriters," she wrote of her band's performance. Finally, in 2019, she and Amanda Shires made an announcement that stunned the music world.

"In 2016, I had this idea and took me a couple of years to put it into words," says Shires. "And when I did put it into words, it was to our friend and producer Dave Cobb, and I told him, 'We're gonna start a band, and we're gonna be called the Highwomen.'" Cobb, who produced her husband, applauded the idea of a four-woman Highwaymen, and suggested another artist as cofounder: Brandi Carlile. Shires then approached Carlile backstage after a show.

"Join the *Highwaymen*?" Carlile responded, incredulous.

"Before we called ourselves the Highwomen, we talked to the Highwaymen," says Carlile. Her first call was to her coproducer, Shooter Jennings, then she phoned "the living ones and then the kids of Johnny and Waylon, and everyone gave us their blessing and loved the idea," she adds. "Willie got involved, and Kris was so lovely about it." (Waylon would have been delighted; his decades-old comment that "a woman president would be great . . . because of what she don't have, and that's a male ego" went viral around this time.) "You know who loves the Highwomen and has given them a lot of support?" Carlile asked one audience. "The Highway*men*," she said.

At home, Carlile made bacon on the barbecue grill for Shires, and they sat down at the fireplace to knock out a song that worked best with two voices: "Mamas Don't Let Your Babies Grow Up to Be Cowboys," from *Waylon and Willie*. As for their self-penned songs, Shires said, they came chop chop. "One of the first things we tasked ourselves with—was writing that to tell the stories of women and the progress and the regress, I guess, at times. Brandi started it, and then I swung it back to her, and then she swirled it back to me. And we kept going back and forth until we had it to perfect."

It helped that Shires, who hails from Lubbock, Texas, had decades of experience, having found her calling as a child, when she spotted a fiddle in a pawnshop window and felt it was meant to be hers forever. During a violin lesson in sixth grade, when her teacher told her he wanted to challenge her with something, he pulled out an old Texas fiddle tune by Bob Wills, "a two-step, a Spanish song," as she told Steve Earle. "Now I know what I want to do," she said after playing it. "I know my passion." Within a few months, she was playing with some of the legends of the Texas music scene, including ninety-year-old men inexperienced in awestruck adolescent girls picking their brains. Seeing Bobbie play with Willie Nelson & the Family, she suddenly understood that a woman could be a "sideman." On the bus one night while on tour backing Billy Joe Shaver, Shires quietly eked out a vocal to one of her originals. When she finished singing for Shaver, "he told me that my songs were good. He told me to quit being a side player and go be a songwriter."

With Shaver's nudge, she moved to Nashville in the mid-2000s, when she was in her twenties. In Music City, the tattoo-covered, wisecracking Texan ran into a culture jazzed about President Bush and not interested in women artists. She was undeterred, creatively. "I learned that waiting for bolts of inspiration is not going to help you when you're trying to keep your pencil sharp," she said. "So, I do some kind of writing every day."*

"She was a great songwriter and singer, but she was terrified" after some bad experiences, says her now-husband Jason Isbell. "Not everybody treated her with respect, and a lot of people made her feel small." Shires, who has a master's in poetry, attended the CMAs wearing a shirt that read MAMA WANTS TO CHANGE THAT NASHVILLE SOUND, a reference to an Isbell lyric about her. (The following line is: "But they're never gonna let her.")

Shires dreamed up the Highwomen during a drive between tour stops, when she and Mercy, her toddler with Isbell, sat through more than twenty country radio songs. Mercy rang the station with a request: "I'd like to hear a song, you know, where a girl sings," she said.

Unbeknownst to the toddler, country radio DJs were following rigid guidelines. "If you want to make ratings in Country radio, take

---

* "Everybody has a Bob Dylan phase for life," she said of songwriting. "It all just goes from there."

females out," one consultant warned. Roughly three-quarters of listeners who stuck around country channels for fifteen minutes, a crucial ratings marker, were women, "and women like male artists," he noted.

Shires mulled asking Kacey Musgraves, Yola, Margo Price, Gillian Welch, and even R&B star Janelle Monáe to join, and finally settled on Maren Morris and Natalie Hemby. Shires had met Morris at a Texas festival show when Morris was eleven, singing "Blue Moon of Kentucky" at a post-show campfire—Shires today deadpans: "She hasn't gotten any taller."

Morris, initially a full-time songwriter, released her first single, "My Church," in 2016. "Country music is my religion in a way," she explained. "That's what I grew up listening to. When you think about Johnny Cash's 'Sunday Morning Coming Down' and Hank Williams—where do I even begin with his catalog?—it's church to me." Morris wavered between the country of her solo debut and her pop breakthrough with a 2018 EDM single. Asked about whether the lines between country and pop were blurring, Morris said: "Every generation has been accused of ruining country music, even the outlaw era of Waylon and Willie. Country is evolving. It's always evolving. You'll always have purists no matter what." Nonetheless, she would forgo "bells, whistles, 808s, genre-stretching ambition for its own sake" for the group and continue it on her next record. She joined the Highwomen in 2019, the year she topped the country and adult contemporary charts with the same song, and soon became "the most-played woman on country radio" and the first woman in eight years with a multi-week number one country single. One male artist tweeted: "Ooh, can we not make it another eight years till a woman repeats at No. 1?"

Morris used her pop stardom to push for systemic change, starting with her pro-immigrant, pro-Black equality anthem "Better Than We Found It." After winning the 2020 CMA Female Vocalist of the

Year award, she singled out several Black women country singers and said they were "as country as it gets." Partly to break a taboo in country music and partly because, in a much more blatantly sexist era, Dolly Parton had done it, she posed topless with cowboy hat askew in *Playboy.* Days prior to her interview with the magazine, Morris's second album broke the record for most weekly streams by a woman country artist. "They" had told her, a la the Dixie Chicks, to not rock the boat, and certainly not challenge the conservative establishment's anti-feminist, conservative positions. Instead, Morris used the *Playboy* platform to castigate the music industry for playing women off one another for hype: "Actually, this is their issue, not ours," she imagined saying to her fellow artists. "It's not our fault there are so few slots that we turn on each other." On her subsequent record, she fully embraced country, incorporating dobros and recording in a barn on singer-songwriter Sheryl Crow's Nashville farm. "I was so nice till I woke up," she sang on the title track. "I was polite till I spoke up." Hemby, who knew Morris already as a longtime country song cowriter, said: "I am grateful that she stayed in Nashville—we need her."

The Highwomen, like their forebears, were hitmakers, Grammy winners, and gold-selling songwriters—and, since they were outgunning the competition commercially, *Rolling Stone* suggested that "the timing couldn't be worse for such a left-field group project. But for this quartet, the collective mission took precedent over any individual pursuits." Their first gig was a brilliant coup: the July 2019 Newport Folk Festival, a nod, in part, to both Dylan "going electric" there in 1965 and Cash introducing Kristofferson to the public four years later. To help sell the booking, Carlile agreed to handle booking Newport's first-ever all-women headliners, including Dolly Parton.

"We know about Cash, Hank, Merle, Waylon and George," Carlile wrote in her memoir. "We know all these men were delightfully self-destructive drug addicts, *some* even convicted criminals who left their wives and kids on multiple occasions. Total hell-raisers, yet we literally sing their songs in church! Our undying love and reverence for these men (mine included) rivals any religious deity I can think of," she said, but it bothered her that older women weren't afforded the same fresh start in the business, nor were their exploits celebrated in tongue-in-cheek songs, certainly not in Nashville and arguably not in the music industry, period. The fact that they were women served as an unspoken rebuttal to Music Row publishers, too, which tried to pair them with fellow women cowriters or announce they were hiring a "female writer" to add authenticity. "Why is male country music like 'hot girls in teeny tiny shorts I will make you my wife, bear my children, front porch, family values, casseroles,'" read one fan's viral tweet, and "female country music is like 'oops I killed my husband.'" The Highwaymen, Carlile believed, could change the conversation about country music's women and women in general.

Their first strike was to rewrite "Highwayman" to be about different characters—*women* characters. "I was a highwayman / along the coach roads I did ride" became "I was a highwoman / and a mother from my youth." Original author Jimmy Webb allowed Carlile and Shires to replace the starships and robbers with assassinated civil rights activists and doctors who get put to death for witchcraft. Shires said of the song in 2023, "I believe even as all this stuff keeps happening, there's still a place for hope, and when people are feeling hopeless, we gotta reach out to one another." Carlile explained, "We are saying, 'We are country artists,' and we are going to ask they include us. And if they do or don't, either way it will tell a story about feminism in rural American music."

For Shires, the goal of the group was to rewrite country music *and* women's history. The song titles tell the story: "My Only Child" and "My Name Can't Be Mama" for starters. "Crowded Table," a utopian vision of a label-free society and "a place by the fire for everyone," went on to win the Grammy for Best Country Song. Hemby brought in a tune she'd been working on, "Redesigning Women," with a title riffing on an empowerment-minded TV show from her youth, and lyrics about "trying to run our world and clean up the kitchen." While knocking it out in the studio, producer Dave Cobb called out: "That's a fucking hit. There's no excuse why this can't be on the radio." Cobb was wrong, however. The song didn't break into the country Top 40. In fact, no Highwomen single has.

Cobb wasn't the only man in the studio, either. The Twins from Carlile's solo band popped in and Jason Isbell cowrote a song and played guitar. Isbell, who has a Bob Dylan tattoo, added a Highwomen ankle tat and, when the internet chatter started to center around whether a group of female harmony singers could really be "country," weighed in without restraint. The choice of Isbell seems obvious in light of his relationship with Shires, who said the two got together because they "bonded so much first on songs, craft, and words," but he has multiple connections to the group. Like Hemby, he cowrote songs for the 2019 blockbuster *A Star Is Born*, and Brandi Carlile has co-headlined with him. As one woman studio guest observed: "There are a few penises here, but a whole lot more balls."

The Highwomen was recorded live to tape in RCA Studio A, where Shires realized the group's harmonies really gelled on digital tape. "It makes it feel like a collective," she said, "like other people might sing along."

"When we sing these out," Hemby echoed, "it's great because we're all singing the lead. And it was kind of intentional in that way."

Hemby had as much to gain from the group as Kristofferson did from the Highwaymen. "Even as a songwriter, it's so hard to get songs cut or played on the radio," she told NPR. "Because there's still this talk of... 'we've got a girl like her already.' And it's like, well, you have 10 boys who all sound alike, and all their names are Luke."

Programmers had told her the real reason she wasn't getting airplay was because women vocalists, with natural, rural country vocals, were not selling because country wasn't popular with women, which was "a bunch of lies," according to Shires. Surveys suggest women were more drawn to country than men by a margin greater than 10 percent, and country is the preferred genre for adults under fifty-five in the United States. Other data suggested that more than three-quarters of listeners polled wanted "equal" plays from women and men, but contradictory evidence also indicated less than half wanted more female voices. Perversely, only about 15 percent of the music on country radio is made by women, and there are few women among the crews, promoters, and producers.

However, "the Highwomen's LP isn't a kiss-off to Music Row," as *Rolling Stone* points out. "Rather, it's an invitation to turn a corner on inclusivity." That didn't stop Morris from getting into a tiff with Brittany Aldean, wife of pop-country star Jason Aldean, who posted a message supporting her parents for not "changing" her gender. "It's so easy to, like, not be a scumbag human? Sell your clip-ins and zip it, Insurrection Barbie," Morris tweeted. "Check on your gay friends," she told fans. "Anyone that is in country music and had to look at that bullshit today and feel subhuman." Thousands booed Morris's name at Aldean's next concert, and Fox News personality Tucker Carlson called her a "lunatic."* Morris, who has chastised Morgan Wallen for racism, admitted that her "allyship has to be more proactive and not reactive." She added: "I think there's crumbs that are given out to people to make it feel like there's progress. But once you've awakened to it—how the system protects itself—you can't close your eyes again. So, you kind of have to be the squeaky wheel."

* After the broadcast, a shirt Morris produced reading LUNATIC COUNTRY MUSIC PERSON generated $100,000-plus in funds for pro-transgender causes.

Cris Lacy, an executive at Warner Music, defended her company's unbalanced roster by saying they had lost out on bidding wars with other labels for female artists, which suggested women were becoming more sought-after than men in Nashville. "That's what's so crazy about all of this," said Lacy. "Women are so interesting. You have so many stories to tell, and they're so open with their feelings, so raw and so honest, and it's heartbreaking that this is a piece that's missing when we shut them out."

In keeping with the trend in Nashville, several songs on *The Highwomen*, even the feminist anthems, were cowritten with men. Rodney Clawson got involved with the group after Dave Cobb told Natalie Hemby, who often cowrites with Clawson, that he thought the group "needed an up-tempo song and they were cutting the next week," says Clawson. He was deeply honored to be asked to participate in *The Highwomen*, in part because he'd been a fan of the members of the Highwaymen. "Johnny Cash was such an icon," he says. "I'm old enough to remember watching his TV show." Hemby says, for her part, that one thing that fascinates her about country music is that, no matter what movements come along to reshape the genre, its roots always return to the forefront. The Highwomen, she says, are naturally evolving but, at the same time, "trying to get back to our roots."

Shires, like her husband, has weighed in on the left side of politically sensitive subjects. Their song for the Highwomen record, "If She Ever Leaves Me,"* has erroneously been called the first gay country song—Willie's "Cowboys Are Frequently, Secretly Fond of Each Other" beat it by a dozen years. Of "If She Ever," Carlile says: "When I first heard it, I just couldn't believe it was written by straight people because it's so insightful. Not everyone can relate to it, but *God* can I relate to it!" In 2020, Shires and Isbell released "The Problem," Shires's

* Shires joked that her cowriter was "Jason Isbell Shires."

autobiographical song about a couple deciding to get an abortion to end an ectopic pregnancy, which took her ten years to write. Heading off potential criticism, Shires said that her bodily autonomy is given to her by God, not lawmakers or the healthcare industry. "Where are our Nashville folks?" Shires wrote after the song's release. "I want Garth Brooks out there telling people that women's health is a priority." Asked if an updated version, released after the reversal of *Roe v. Wade*, could backfire, Shires shrugged. "Fuck it," she said. "Who needs a career if we have no rights to our bodies?"*

In 2020, shortly before the COVID-19 pandemic, Shires played a show in Billings, Montana. She closed with "Highwomen," and, as the women in the crowd sang at the top of their lungs, she squatted down before one fan leaning against the railing. Shires wrapped her arm around the stranger's shoulder and kept the mic between them. Together, "surrounded by other women singing along," the fan said, she felt certain "every single one of us could feel the power of the music despite the absolute shitstorm brewing in the world."

Morris said "all are welcome" to sing with the Highwomen, and Shires agrees. "It was never going to be limited to just four folks," she says. Carlile clarified: "It's not a band. It's a movement. The Highwomen is not just four people. It's not a compilation disc."

To back this up, in 2020, Shires invited Brittney Spencer, a Black woman with an explosive range, to join the Highwomen, at least as a special guest. Spencer grew up on the Dixie Chicks and Beyoncé in Baltimore. Before her discovery, she had been living out of her car and playing Johnny Cash on Nashville's bustling streets for tips. She was blown away that Music City songwriters would just sit around with a guitar, tell stories behind the songs, and pass the axe around.

* The video shoot for "The Problem" was as wrenching as the writing had been, and Isbell had to keep Shires from having a complete breakdown by playing Van Halen riffs until she cracked up.

Music Row snubbed a track she composed for a songwriting competition that addressed the industry's stonewalling on racial justice. "It's not easy being a Black woman in an industry that's learning how to have Black women," she said. "There are a lot of Black artists coming into Nashville. . . . We're bringing culture, we're not just bringing complexion." She tried to get on the radio by writing a paean to country stations, but it didn't click. "I tried to take a different approach and say to country radio, 'Hey, I love you so much. Why don't you love us [women]?' "

When Morris and Shires discovered her YouTube cover of "Crowded Table," they helped change her life overnight, inviting her to guest with them onstage, as well as to duet with Shires and Isbell on a track at Columbia Studio A, now leased to Dave Cobb, and to open for Morris at a Nashville stadium. In 2023, for a three-day Carlile-centered festival at the Gorge in Washington state, the Highwomen regrouped with Brittney Spencer and Allison Russell as guest vocalists for their first-ever full, headlining set. (Among the highlights: a soaring version of "Always on My Mind," Willie's biggest hit, Amanda Shires's blazing fiddle on Dylan's anti-racist anthem "Hurricane," a sing-along of "Mamas Don't Let Your Babies," with Carlile taking the verses, and two versions of "Redesigning Women.")

Yola believes there is a huge new wave of women of color coming and occasionally breaking into Nashville. At one point in her youth, she had been briefly unhoused and didn't find solo success until well into her thirties. Executives, producers, and fellow musicians alike saw her "as a tool," she said. "Everyone had a plan for me, but I never had space to have a plan for myself." The British powerhouse was told by an executive that he didn't think a Black woman could find success singing rock music, but she landed a role as Sister Rosetta Tharpe* in

* Johnny Cash's idol.

the 2022 movie *Elvis*. Her mother had warned her about the dangers she might face playing country music, "but to me that was all the more reason I should be able to take up this space." In interviews promoting her disco-flavored second album and the country single "Hold On," recorded with the Highwomen and Jason Isbell, Yola stressed the importance of being able to work across genres and said, "'Hold On' is asking the next gen to take up space, to be visible and to show what it looks like to be young, gifted and black."

Other possible Highwomen include white outlaw singer Margo Price and Black Canadian multi-instrumentalist Allison Russell.

Price, who started out as a Dylan obsessive—"the way he sang wasn't perfect, but it was honest," she wrote—and named her kids after characters in "Desolation Row," and, through him, discovered Kristofferson and Jessi Colter, started out busking, singing anti-drinking, anti–Iraq War songs, playing in a band with Sturgill Simpson, and dreaming of headlining the Ryman. She endured compliments like "You play like a man!" Her first session was at Sun Studios, where she heard and fell for Waylon Jennings records. But when record companies listened to her demos, they would say: "We already have two girls," and her electric guitar–drenched and fiddle-filled music has long been called too badass for country, too country for rock. "I don't like modern, I like 'vintage,'" she told Sony Music execs. Simpson helped put her on the map by producing her 2020 record, but dates opening for Chris Stapleton to promote it were canceled due to the pandemic.

Russell's own description of her debut album's themes sounds just like a Highwomen CD: "resilience, survival, transcendence, the redemptive power of art, community, connection, and chosen family... from a new home made in Nashville." At the 2022 Americana Awards, Carlile was seen side stage, literally jumping for joy when Russell won a top prize. Russell said of her road to success: "Brandi Carlile made phone calls for me, championed me."

Price, who produced Jessi Colter's 2023 comeback album, covered Kris Kristofferson, and posted a video of herself smoking pot with "Okie from Muskogee" playing, could fit in either a New Highwaymen or an expanded Highwomen, and Russell, Yola, and Spencer are available to appear on the second Highwomen record, which Shires says is in the draft stage.* Morris, meanwhile, claimed in 2023 that she's quitting country music, and released a new single that seemed to confirm it, with lyrics like "The rot at the roots is the root of the problem / But you wanna blame it on me."

Strangely, there's one artist not often included in these discussions who fits cleanly into the Highwomen and is, like Nelson in the mid-'80s, near her commercial peak: Kacey Musgraves. Her first album, with its refreshing blend of dance beats and acoustic guitars, confounded country radio programmers, but her initial headline tour nearly sold out on critical praise alone. She swept several years of Grammys "despite being too pop for country and too modish for Americana," as one historian noted. Leslie Fram, a senior vice president at Country Music Television, wrote: "I just don't know how, as a format, we are not embarrassed that Kacey Musgraves won album of the year—she won country album of the year, yes, but overall album of the year, too (at the Grammys as well as CMAs)—and our format ignored her. I don't understand how that happens." Journalist Lisa Robinson suggested Musgraves "still is considered something of an 'outlaw' in Nashville because she sang about smoking pot and gay marriage." Indeed, the president of her label told her she could record and release whatever material she chose, but quit shortly thereafter, leaving her without a champion at the company. But, she told Robinson, "I

* Carlile had previously stated that another Highwomen record would only happen if the people demanded it. The first album, she suggested, was for the fans and not to "serve our careers."

was already doing...what I wanted to do, so no one could come in and change it. Not that I would have let them anyway."

Musgraves went on: "Every measure of success in country music is based on whether you're getting support from country radio. Critical acclaim, Grammys, even the quality of the music—none of it matters....And when it comes to that mindset, women do not get the same support when it comes to radio play or festival billing."

She claimed to have been scolded by executives after a radio programmer claimed Musgraves hadn't been pleasant enough. Regarding the possibility the Me Too movement had helped shift that conversation, she said she hadn't noticed any changes in Nashville. The country industry continued to use formulas for releasing records, a practice it began in the Windows 95 era, when publishers offered searchable databases of lyrics so producers and performers could find a theme, say, "ex-wives" or "dogs," that had generated other hits. In the studio, the producers received directives from executives that gradually shifted their focus "toward the way a record sounds at the expense of the quality of the song." In the '90s and 2000s, A&R representatives sat listening to piles of demo tapes from staff writers to uncover something palatable to radio and instead learned songwriters were banging out nothing but "introspective, heavy ballads about middle-aged women in search of their identity." Where, record company employees wondered, were the boppers that would get people humming along to their radios? Execs scrutinized the shortlists for their artists' potential CDs, making sure the beats per minute varied to cover a lively range of tempos.

Worse, it was getting harder for artists to make a living; two associations and each of the major labels were trying to freeze royalty rates through 2027, and bands were reportedly losing money on tours, even before paying booking fees and reimbursing themselves for food. And with compositions often taking years to reach top-level performers through the Music Row system, generic, or "evergreen" pieces, rather than topical or unique songs, were more likely to get recorded and released.

On paper, Chris Stapleton may not have a lot in common with Kacey Musgraves, but looking beneath the surface of their lyrics and melodies, there is not only an antiestablishment bent to their songs and an affinity for marijuana but also a love of Willie Nelson, who has been arrested at least four times for marijuana offenses. (After one Nelson bust, Mickey Raphael joked: "He feels great—he said he lost six ounces!" Nelson has long pushed for national marijuana legalization but says America must also reckon with disproportionately arresting and sentencing Black marijuana users.)* Stapleton noted that one couldn't get much more country than songs about weed and women.

Musgraves has the Texas twang and attitude of past country stars but has not compromised her principles, mocking the beauty pageants, small town gossip, anti-individualism, and greed in American life. After opening for Willie Nelson, she had the idea for a duet with the legend himself.

Musgraves had discovered Nelson's demo of "Are You Sure?" on YouTube; after being recorded by Ray Price, the song had fallen into obscurity. So, Musgraves was stunned when, after shyly mentioning it to Nelson, he peered at her for a second, said "This song?," and instantly plucked it on Trigger. Willie then insisted they record it together. "I don't think there's another artist, really, that embodies American music like he does... very few," she said. "Ray Charles, Dolly Parton. I mean, there are some. Johnny Cash is one. . . . " She then released

* Even Merle Haggard and Johnny Cash smoked and boasted about it in song.

Star-Crossed, a breakup album with one "acknowledgement"—"thank you to me," she wrote—and that one writer called "side one from *Phases and Stages*" across a whole record. With her then-husband, Musgraves previously cut "To June This Morning," an unrecorded Johnny Cash poem, and Musgraves did *Waylon & Willie* closer "The Wurlitzer Prize" with Chris Stapleton at the concert *Outlaw: Celebrating the Music of Waylon Jennings*. She completed her Highwaymen quadfecta at a Willie Nelson show in 2017, slipping onstage to sing backup with Kristofferson, whom she praised for having written "For the Good Times," what, in her view, "might be the saddest song of all time." Musgraves, whose humor is of the rural deadpan variety, seemed to be giggling and beaming throughout the three-song gospel medley, including Hank Williams's "I Saw the Light" and Nelson's own "Roll Me Up and Smoke Me When I Die," a pro-pot song she seemed to know by heart.

Despite all his success, Dave Cobb continues to work as an alt-country producer, helming Chris Stapleton's 2023 album and Dillon Carmichael's 2018 "hard-nosed Outlaw country" debut. Waylon Jennings was Carmichael's chief inspiration for the record. "What I've always loved about Waylon is how his voice, and songwriting, was so raw," he says. "It came straight from the heart and you can feel it in every note."

Although Cobb grew up going to a church that had a steel guitarist every Sunday, fell in love with the Muscle Shoals sound, and subsequently became an accomplished guitar player himself, like Atkins, he abandoned performance. Although he's often found playing along with the band or showing them a chord in the recording studio itself, he nonetheless has no interest in touring or being part of a group. "Always, my favorite part of being in a band was making records," he told *Paste*. "Producing was really the natural extension, to continue feeling like you're in a band and getting to stay home—always feeling like you're in a different band. For me, the point of creation with songwriting and recording is always the most fun. I kind of get to live a lot of my fantasies by doing this every day." To him, it's important that a record mystify the listener—one should be utterly transfixed and wonder if the music had been beamed from an alien planet.

If a new Highwaymen never arrives, at least there's a worthy substitute in Old Crow Medicine Show, a band Cobb produced in in 2018. Created out of rural Appalachia in 1998 as a kind of Uncle Tupelo–style punk-bluegrass ensemble, OCMS has become the rare act to break through to country success with word of mouth rather than radio support. The band got its big break less than three months after relocating to Nashville. First, they were given a spot busking outside the Opry, where Marty Stuart stumbled upon them. The singer, who helped unite the Highwaymen, had become a major solo act through his "hillbilly rock" in the '90s, and as an ambassador to the Opry, he could immediately invite Old Crow to perform on the show. Secor and other members of the band were barely in their twenties and didn't even have a record deal. Despite this extraordinary break, they remained unconvinced about Nashville.

"This town is shitty," Secor told a reporter that week. "This town is everything that the mountain is not. This town is full of money. This town has no kinship. This town has no brotherly love. But this town is where we are, and we have never been in the wrong place."

At the Ryman, mere days into the new millennium and with only four minutes allotted to them, they cranked out a "jug-based romp" and were stunned to be greeted by an immediate standing ovation. It had been years since country audiences had heard a new band playing old school fiddle music, sans keyboards or electric guitars. Much later but partly due to this performance, Stuart had the band play his TV show and invited them to join the Opry. Coupled with their offer to Jamey Johnson, the Opry seemed to be trying to counter criticism from Merle Haggard, who called the institution "that sacred cow devoted to filling the pockets of a bunch of anonymous bastards who don't know doodle-shit about country music or what it means to those of us who love it."

Frontman Ketch Secor said Old Crow's number one influence was Bob Dylan, "more than any book or song or story or play. The work and the recorded work of Bob Dylan . . . and then the other people that really influenced me tend to be the same people who influenced Bob Dylan.

"I think bands like us, Mumford and Sons, and Gillian Welch and David Rawlings are sort of doing what he has done before, in that we take our own experiences and observations and put them into songs made of traditional, American roots form. That form is still a great vehicle for songs, whether the song is about love, the Iraq War or anything else."

Old Crow's "Wagon Wheel" had grown out of a Bob Dylan session for the *Pat Garrett & Billy the Kid* soundtrack, with Dylan horsing around and repeating a two-line chorus until the take collapsed. Secor discovered the song as a teenager while listening to a bootleg, and couldn't get the mind-numbing chorus out of his brain. While snowbound at a New Hampshire boarding school, he daydreamed about the South and added a few verses about hitchhiking that were reminiscent of "Bobby McGee." OCMS had to get Dylan's permission to add verses to the fragment and record it at RCA Studio B for their debut.* The single sold glacially but went platinum mostly through downloads, one of the rare alt-country singles to hit that mark.**

In 2016, OCMS celebrated the fiftieth anniversary of *Blonde on Blonde* in a headline set at the Ryman, recorded a song-for-song live cover album on Columbia, and toured internationally performing Dylan's first Nashville record in its entirety. ("Did you ever hear so much *e-nun-ci-a-tion* at a Bob Dylan concert?" Secor joked.) OCMS punked up the songs, added high-velocity fiddle solos, and even let their drummer perform one number solo. The encore would typically consist of four extra songs, including "Knockin' on Heaven's Door" and "Wagon Wheel," perhaps the most recognizable Dylan tune, at least to millennials.

When they were working with Cobb on their sixth record, Secor said the band decided to switch things up: "Because we were working with Dave, we wanted to pull out some of our more, I guess, rockin' sounds and do less of a roots music or old-time acoustic record.

"We were in a big room, RCA Studio A as opposed to Studio B, and a lot of times the music kind of matches the space."*** When *Billboard* asked further about the choice to use a dreaded electric guitar, Secor cracked: "It was in Bob Wills' band, so it's good enough for me." After appearing on *CMT Crossroads* with Kesha, a Top 40 singer, Secor admitted he didn't even hate mainstream music anymore. "I'm

---

* Indie country star Charley Crockett dipped into the same *Pat Garrett* outtakes to build a 2022 song.

** Darius Rucker heard the song via his daughter's school band. He hadn't appreciated it in the *Pat Garrett* guise or in the OCMS version, but he thought it might work with his voice. His version, with Lady Antebellum on backing vocals, reached the pop Top 20, was certified Diamond, and made Rucker the first Black man to be played on country radio in years.

*** Studio B was older and warmer while Studio A could feel "narrow" but offer a brighter, crisper sound, as Waylon once noted.

kind of a natural skeptic about pop music, but Kesha showed me you really can get to the top of pop music and retain a sense of passion and an understanding of the craft," he said.

"I feel like the city, this is our time," Cobb said. "Nashville is what London was in the '60s musically, what LA was in the '70s—I think Nashville is that now. And that's why I came. Music drew me here and the people drew me here."

CHAPTER THIRTEEN

THE ROAD GOES ON FOREVER

Music's going to die out. You either keep going and you fail, or you stop while you're ahead.

—Zach Bryan

Nashville is afraid of change. I think they think that . . . to try and bring something new to the music and throw off some of the shackles is going to destroy the old country, what they call the true country . . . they can't do that.

—Waylon Jennings

I had a list of rules I made up one time. It says: Tell the truth; sing with passion; work with laughter; love with heart. Those are good to start with anyway.

—Kris Kristofferson

Country music isn't a guitar, it isn't a banjo, it isn't a melody, it isn't a lyric. It's a feeling.

—Waylon Jennings

If I was everything people made me out to be, I'd have been dead long ago.

—Waylon Jennings

In 2021, a post on the music community subreddit titled "County [*sic*] music has become insufurable [*sic*]" turned into a discussion of all the great country music out there—as long as one ignores Country Music Television, the radio, and the "twang pop" the record companies are marketing most vociferously, of course.

"I believe country music used to be a good genre of music," said the original poster. "You had artists like Johnny Cash, Merle Haggard. . . . They made good music that made you feel something, now what do we have. We have absolute dog shit, country was never my favorite genre of music but I still appreciated it. The new country literally fits the stereotype of what country music is, they sing about being red necks drinking beer and fucking hookers."*

Users responded by recommending great indie artists, including Isbell, Musgraves, Carlile, Shires, Margo Price, and Morgan Wade. One person quoted singer Steve Earle: "The country coming out of Nashville today is just hip-hop for people who are afraid of black people." Another user recommended Simpson: "That man changed my mind about country, now I don't dislike country, just bad country."

Zach Bryan, 2022's most popular new discovery, set a new record for the longest-running country single on the pop charts by a male artist and then debuted at number one on the *Billboard* 200 the next year. While pegged as a country singer, he avoids the label, mainly listens to Springsteen and "weird indie music," and says, "Anything I've learned and grown from came from Isbell."** He also says he'll never accept a CMA award. His contemporary, Charley Crockett, left Sony instead of refining his country-blues style, refined as a subway

---

* Fans of an outlaw music blog agreed: variations on the statement "country died with Waylon and Johnny" appear in comments almost daily.

** He broke attendance records even after disparaging Ticketmaster in a live album title and switching to the AXS ticketing service.

musician in New York, for pop-country radio programmers. "The game you have to play to write a hit and break through with radio is just wack," he said. He twice evaded prison, including once for transporting five pounds of weed, survived emergency heart surgery, and signed with Nashville's tiny Thirty Tigers, home of Sturgill Simpson. His producer, Mark Neill, urged him to become a student of Waylon Jennings. "Waylon took George Jones country and the R&B of the time," said Neill, "and put them on a blind date. He was trying to merge Motown with the Carter Family." And while Crockett admits to loving Willie, whom he's opened for, he has another favorite: "Bob Dylan broke all the rules. He's so much more of an outlaw than anyone's ever given him credit for."

Country Music Hall of Famer Eddie Bayers says: "Some people say they didn't like country music but they like Keith Urban. It's all silly to me." Indeed, surveys stretching back to 2011 and the rebirth of the outlaw movement confirm that most Americans *do* like country; it is the most popular radio format, with more than one-third of all stations dedicated to it. Far from "the redneck with the three rusted-out Chevys in the driveway," three-quarters of country music fans are homeowners and half of Americans with six-figure incomes listen to the genre. However, actual sales have declined, in keeping with an industry-wide problem.

"If I have the number one record, I'm selling 26,000 records," says producer Mike Clute, who moved to Nashville in 1985. Back then, he says, hitting the top spot usually meant "more like 200,000 records." Nonetheless, three of the ten biggest-selling records of 2021 were country albums, including the number one spot, a feat the genre achieved in 2020 and 2018, as well. Nashville music publishing operations collected $1.1 billion in revenue in 2017, beating out New York and LA. A majority of American adults listen to country music at least once a week. Country itself is more popular on streaming services than other forms of music, and young people make up a substantial majority of fans, both bellwethers. In another sign that alt-country or outlaw-infused music is gaining in popularity, more than eight in ten people who listen to country also listen to rock, 5 percent more than those who say they like pop music, too. More country fans are out there than perhaps at any time in history, as well, with a 54 percent growth rate in young adult fans since 2006, with nonwhite listeners making up seven of every ten fans. "Who cares about crossovers?" said songwriter Bob McDill. "We're selling more than pop anyway."

Pop is so anathema to what alt-country and the outlaw mentality is about, musicians don't even want Grammy nods in the category. After Kacey Musgraves's 2021 album was ruled ineligible for country categories by the Grammys, one music blogger wrote: "She isn't cutting songs that sound like everybody else's songs, but that doesn't mean they aren't country. It just means that they are country through *her* lens." Perhaps the problem, then, is that Musgraves doesn't fit in with country *culture*. "I mean, my music has never been straight-up one hundred percent one thing or the other," she admits. "And I think all the best music is that way. I mean, when you listen to Willie Nelson . . . or the Beatles, or whoever, they kind of end up creating their own genre." She added: "Willie is a Texas and country artist, but he is also so many other things."

As with Musgraves and Sturgill Simpson, singer-songwriters took flak in the 2020s for "going pop" when they changed direction for highly anticipated follow-ups. But the problem isn't just with straight country artists making places for the nightclub dance floors. Rina Sawayama, a Japanese-British artist, combined nü-metal, R&B/dance, and rock on her 2020 debut, and then got thrashed by fans and critics for her radio-friendly follow-up. Sawayama explained: "The past couple of years I've been listening to lots of female country singers and wanted to write a euphoric and tongue-in-cheek country-pop song.

Country music at its core to me represents comfort, brilliant storytelling, and authentic expression of the writer's reality."

Brandi Carlile complained about being nominated in the Pop instead of Country or Americana categories at the 2022 Grammys. After all, Americana was the second choice of the people who came up with the chart category—the first, "Crucial Country," was meant to be a diss of dispensable radio-friendly pop. "I think there's gatekeeping when country music mixes with pop," says Carlile. "That's just history repeating itself."

"The importance of staying and working within Americana is greater than just me," Carlile wrote. "I feel great responsibility in representing marginalized queer people in rural America who are raised on country and roots music but are repeatedly and systematically rejected by the correlating culture. Every rung I can sling my gay sequined boot up on top of gets queer people a little higher on the ladder to being seen as just a bit more human in the great American roots landscape."

She believed that being nominated as a pop artist for a country record was par for the course for queer people, used to being marginalized or left out altogether from Music Row. k.d. lang, a gay woman, had been so captivating as a country singer in the late eighties, she persuaded Owen Bradley to come out of retirement to produce her. But country radio did not appreciate her, even after she won multiple Grammys, and when she appeared in an anti-meat campaign by the People for the Ethical Treatment of Animals and came out of the closet, country stations banned her songs.

Americana, as musician Dave Alvin joked, didn't create a lot of jobs for jet pilots and limo drivers, although it has slowly grown into a formidable cultural force. In 2001, when the conference and the Americana Music Convention was in its infancy, publicist Cary Baker suggested there might be a mere handful of PR people among the 350 attendees. Over the next decade, however, "AmericanaFest," as it became known, expanded to multiple venues across four days and added sold-out nightly performances with Brandi Carlile headlining. "I go today and find myself among 35 to 50 publicists—and a corresponding expansion in the . . . diversity of artists," says Baker. "It's certainly come a long way from when I thought I spotted 'alt-country' at Joe Sun's 1980 Chicago gig. Turns out that's exactly what it was. And frankly, those who guffawed that night are no longer working in this biz!"

The Highwaymen didn't disappear with the rise of alt-country or their breakup in 1996.

Thanks to the blockbuster Highwaymen album, Kris Kristofferson and Johnny Cash both caught the attention of Mercury Records. The exec who signed them to solo deals disputed the idea both were headed for the bargain bin: "If Johnny Cash is over, country music is over," he said.

Kristofferson, despite cranking out *more* than one album per year on average at his peak, didn't release anything between 1981 and *Highwayman* in 1985. Monument had become part of Columbia's distribution arm before being crushed in the "corporate meat grinder" and shunted aside for moneymaking subsidiaries. Mercury enlisted Chips Moman, coming off the successes "Highwayman" and "Always on My Mind," but Kristofferson didn't seem to care about getting a single on the charts. He wanted to talk about Nicaragua and El Salvador, left-leaning governments criticized by President Reagan.* Kristofferson

* Reagan called country "one of only a very few forms that we can claim as purely American."

wrote "Sandinista," an ode to the leftist guerrilla movement, and "They Killed Him," which Bob Dylan and the Highwaymen both covered, about Mahatma Gandhi. Johnny Cash, himself pro-Sandinista, joined Kristofferson at a New York show to belt out Dylan's "Masters of War."

Perhaps chastened by becoming a parent twice more in the lead-up to *Repossessed*, Kristofferson attempted to make amends with the ghost of his father through "The Heart," a sentimental ballad and Top 20 hit for Lacy J. Dalton. (When asked about whether his father tried to keep him locked into a rigid lifestyle, Kris said: "No, my father was a great guy, a great spirit. Any shackles I had on were put on by me, by expectations I put on myself.") He went to Nicaragua to visit a captured American soldier—the only US national to do so—and was driven around by the country's president and flown in a rickety Soviet chopper that had him gripping his seat. When he got back, he played benefits for convicted murderer Leonard Peltier and fired back at more conservative fans who picketed him or demanded refunds by the hundreds. He enjoyed bright spots, including the chain restaurant Bobby McGee's, which launched in 1971 and peaked in the '80s with two dozen locations. But without radio play, Kristofferson's music dropped off the radar. "I've tried to be more self-sufficient as I've gotten older," he said. "I'd like to not worry about whether they're going to sell my next album. . . . " By the early '90s, he had dismissed his band to save on expenses and was either opening for Johnny Cash or playing cruises, once disembarking a ship two hours before it crashed, leaving an eighty-five-foot gap in the hull.

It wasn't until the 1996 film *Lone Star*, in which Kristofferson played a murderous, bribe-taking border town sheriff, became a sleeper hit that his acting career took off again. Marvel's *Blade*, costarring Kristofferson as the vampire title character's mentor, followed, and it was successful enough to jumpstart a franchise and spawn multiple, profitable sequels, which are what most casual fans recognize Kristofferson from today. He might have become a major movie star again but for the fact that he kept turning down offers to play Abraham Lincoln in a period piece over the quality of the script or stopped accepting narrator roles, although he did for the Dylan biopic *I'm Not There*. He began to mount a musical comeback in 1999, when an album he made with Nelson, Jennings, and Billy Joe Shaver of Shaver's songs was finally released and when Kristofferson recorded stripped-down versions of some of his classics at Waylon's Arlyn Studios. Award shows and specials began luring in older viewers by pairing him with up-and-comers or high-draw performers, including Margo Price, Darius Rucker, Willie, and Barbra Streisand. During a live TV appearance from Nashville, he stopped "Help Me Make It Through the Night" due to a misplaced guitar capo, and, to the mute horror of producers, restarted it.

Over the next decade, he racked up songwriting awards, including the Americana Music Association's free speech honor, an induction into the Country Music Hall of Fame, and the Grammy Lifetime Achievement Award. At one ceremony, he grinned, saying: "Nashville saved my life. . . . I never regretted coming here . . . it was like bliss being around all these people who were doing what I love to do." Margo Price fulfilled a dream when she got to play her concert staple, "Me and Bobby McGee," with the song's writer: "I actually had the pleasure of singing that song with him at Newport, and all because Patti Smith was stuck in traffic. She was supposed to do it, so they hit me up like ten minutes before," she says. "I got to hang out with him, go on his bus, and smoke joints with him. . . . " Before handing him the Johnny Cash Visionary Award from CMT, Rosanne Cash called Kristofferson "the living artistic link" to her father and said the two were "closer than brothers." Kristofferson marveled: "I was thinking back to when I first met him, and if I ever thought that I'd be getting an award with his name on it, it would have carried me through a lot of hard times." In a *Vogue* interview, superstar Taylor Swift called Kristofferson her true inspiration, career-wise. "I got to meet him last year, and he's just one of those people who has been in this business for years but you can tell it hasn't chewed him up and spit him out. He just seemed like the human embodiment of gratitude."*

He paced backstage before shows, especially at sold-out, six-thousand-attendee gigs like one in Ireland, saying that he'd never outboxed stage fright. As his voice and memory declined in the 2010s, and following a diagnosis of Lyme disease, Kristofferson stopped touring. (At one late-period gig in Arizona, he called up Jessi Colter for "Bobby McGee," but both flubbed the lyrics.) But he still performed live and recorded sporadically. He and his longtime wife, Lisa, live in Hawaii, not far from Willie's winter compound. "We marry what we need," he said. "I married a lawyer, and Willie married a makeup artist!" As for Mauians, Kristofferson says, "When people come looking for me, they've never heard of me. That's just great." Today, Lukas Nelson, Morgan Wade, and Tyler Childers regularly cover Kristofferson. "Seeing people who can transform the thing you made and make it bigger than it was" gives him great pride. Says Steve Earle of the post-outlaw antiestablishment artists: "We were all essentially folkies who followed Kristofferson to Nashville. No offense, but they were traditional writers who happened to be incredibly good, transcendent."

"Traditional" songwriter Willie Nelson came roaring back as a major live draw in the 1980s. After hearing Bob Dylan complain onstage in 1985 that no one was paying attention to American farmers, Nelson created Farm Aid, through which he has used his rabid concert

* Swift's battles with RCA, Willie and Waylon's old label, are legendary. She ended up quitting the label before her first record came out, an unheard-of decision on Music Row. When it came out on another label, it rose to the top of the *Billboard* 200.

following to deliver aid for family farms, down by 75 percent from a peak the decade he was born. Kristofferson was aboard from day one, having recently started working with the United Farm Workers movement. The Highwaymen appeared at the first Farm Aid concert before eighty thousand fans, as well as at the July 4th picnics, which returned to Luckenbach and Austin beginning in 1984. The former pig farmer's enthusiasm for independent tillers inspired the supergroup to reunite annually.

However, the party seemed over, turn out the lights, for his personal life. His marriage to Connie collapsed, two of Bobbie's children died six months apart, and then, on Christmas Day 1991, his son, Billy, hung himself.* Amid it all, the IRS was in the process of investigating Nelson's finances, including suspiciously low profits from the picnics. Agents surrounded him on the fairway of his golf course in 1990—one imagines him quipping: "You're late. I already lost my shirt this round"—and hit him with a $5 million case over unpaid taxes. But Waylon claimed Nelson "never learns anything" from all his trials and tribulations. Shooter described him as having a wall around him, only penetrated when someone yelled, "Fuck you, Willie, answer the question!" at him. "You'll never quite fully get that picture," said Shooter.

As always, family, friends—who bought the golf course from the government and resold it to Nelson—and music are what pulled him through. Realizing he had no one else to blame for his deep funk, Nelson checked out of the three-star hotels and began sleeping exclusively on his bus, surrounded himself with only "positive people," and announced that he hoped to go broke before death came a-knocking. He toured minor league stadiums with Bob Dylan as co-headliner, trying to "stay out of the corporate amphitheaters." He also announced

* He has called Billy's suicide his chief regret.

he would stop any fight, regardless of risk, by throwing himself in the middle and daring them to hit *the* Willie Nelson.* All the "positive" vibes may have worked; in 2014, after a twenty-eight-year drought, Nelson returned to the top of the country album charts.**

Willie, his two youngest children, and his fourth wife moved back to Abbott. The honeymoon was truncated by several invasions of their privacy, including one drunk-driving crash that miraculously resulted in a single fatality: the family porch. Nelson kept a bunch of trusty sidekicks handy: a sawed-off shotgun, .22 rifle with a scope, and another rifle, this one double-barreled, that had lyrics from "Red Headed Stranger" engraved on it. (He also had a knife with his face engraved on the handle.) The family later decamped for Austin, and in 2013, Willie assembled his sprawling clan for a show in New York honoring his eightieth birthday, and the patriarch, going on last after hours of performances by his children and special guests, blazed through one of his finest sets in ages.

Mark Rothbaum, fall guy in Waylon's drug bust, still "manages" Willie, one of the few from the Outlaw heyday still around. Bee Spears, bassist for the Family beginning in 1968, died in 2011, retired guitar player Jody Payne passed away two years later, and Paul English, who had a stroke in 2010 and cut back to playing only a few songs per night, died of pneumonia. He never quit, calling his relationship with Willie Nelson the most important of his life.*** Until the end, he was often spotted escorting Bobbie Nelson to and from her stage piano and the bus.

---

* "If I hurt your feelings, I'm sorry," he once told Woody Harrelson. "But if I made you mad, fuck you."

** It was his first record after his return to Columbia Records, too.

*** English had lived several lifetimes, once losing $500,000 in a year on the stock market but eventually earning it all back through touring.

Willie and Bobbie returned to the Methodist Church they'd grown up in to buy and reopen it. (It was the same one he had to quit in the fifties after a preacher told him he would have to choose between teaching Sunday school and "playing in beer joints.") They had to enter the ribbon cutting through surging crowds.

"I'm thinking the whole 'Willie Nelson & Family' phenomenon begins right here with those two siblings," said a fellow musician.

"When the two of them play 'Uncloudy Day' together, they're going back in time a little bit," said Willie's daughter Paula. Bobbie agreed: "It's a little bit like going in for Communion and praying."

At one of their last shows together, in Luck, Texas, Willie's frontier town built for the *Red Headed Stranger* film, the siblings emerged from COVID-19 quarantine and, with Bobbie in high heels and pounding away at the piano in perfect time on "Down Yonder," drew tears from family standing side-stage.

"The most fruitful sibling relationship in music history" sadly ended in 2022, when Bobbie died at age ninety-one. A year later, Amanda Shires sent an email announcing an album of duets she and Nelson completed before the latter's passing. "'Loving You' is the only song Bobbie Nelson ever wrote on her own," Shires noted. "It doesn't have any words, but when you hear the melody, you know what the song is about: family. Love of family, God, and music guided Bobbie through decades of struggle and triumph, chaos and peace.

"She made a path for women, for mothers even, in the male-dominated music business. You can read her incredible story in the book 'Me and Sister Bobbie.' You should, but you can hear who Bobbie was when you listen to her play the piano."

After Bobbie's death, Willie's son Micah asked if he should cancel the July 4, 2022, Austin stadium picnic with Jason Isbell and Allison Russell. His father, though, needed the pick-me-up. Nelson played with just Micah, better known by his musical alias Particle

Kid,* on guitar, Paul's brother on drums, and a bass player, and he's essentially been performing that way, in a Beto O'Rourke or "I Stand with Ukraine" T-shirt, strumming on Trigger, ever since.

When COVID-19 first spread across the country, Willie returned to Austin, his physical and spiritual home, which has evolved into a tech mecca. "I think if you ask some New Yorkers and Californians who are moving here now, you'd find a couple who'd say, 'Austin is great, but not as great as it was a month ago,'" he said.** There, in lockdown, he and his sons recorded *Family Bible*, comprising rerecorded Nelson's gospel songs, including the title track, which he called "probably the first truly good and lasting song I'd ever written." He may have signed over the eventual million-seller for $50, but it set him on the path to outsider glory.

"He was very timeless in his way of writing," Lukas said of his father. "It sounds more like an ancient text than it does a song. 'Your heart has been forewarned, all men will lie to you. Your mind cannot conceive.' It sounds like if she came stumbling into a cave, she could read it chiseled in the walls, from thousands of years ago."

He didn't write new songs. He wanted to play the old ones live again. "When I've been home a little too long and start saying hello to the walls," he wrote, "everyone knows I can't wait to get back on the road." He quoted Billy Joe Shaver, saying: "'Moving is the closest thing to being free.' I believe that. It's that old cowboy trail-riding thing."

* The name came about because Nelson, high on marijuana, tried to call Micah the "prodigal son."

** Austin, which bills itself as the "Live Music Capital of the World," continues to challenge Nashville for the title of "Home" of country music. The CMT Awards were moved from Nashville to Austin for the 2023 ceremony.

Bobbie Nelson agreed. She believed that when Willie is unable to perform, his health will quickly fade. "Those songs contain a spirit that keeps us positive," she said.

Off the road, he narrowly escaped a bout of COVID-19 and another, equally serious experience. "We were watching the sunset," his wife, Annie, recalled. "And these little lights started to zip across the sky. The first one kind of flashed past in the distance. Then there was a second, which went by a little closer. All of a sudden, the light went right past us—like, two feet over Will's head." Children had found some neglected semiautomatic rifles with tracer bullets, and were firing them from the valley below. "Dude," Annie wanted to tell the kids. "You don't want to be the one that kills Willie Nelson. Especially in Texas."

Nelson, as with any other topic, claimed to be sanguine on his eventual passing. "Who was it, Seneca, the thinker, that said you should look at death and comedy with the same expression of countenance?" He joked: "Some negative thinkers assume I won't make it another four decades, but my advice is not to bet against me or Keith Richards."

Most major country acts are on the record as loving Willie Nelson's music, including up-and-coming outlaws like Tyler Childers, who has spoken about how *Red Headed Stranger* influenced him. He, Ryan Bingham, Chris Stapleton, Margo Price, Yola, and Sturgill Simpson have all played his Outlaw Music Festival, and share a stripped-down style.* Nelson still has no love for Music Row: "I knew this was a cold-blooded business back forty years ago.... With these big corporations, it's only gotten colder." After a moment, he added: "The only thing those bean counters respect is beans."

* Nelson came to the attention of the TikTok generation in 2022, albeit indirectly, after the Patsy Cline version of "Crazy" went viral on the app. It's also apparently very popular in lesbian bars with jukeboxes.

He scoffs at discussions of his legacy. One day, he writes, "my music will fade away to a soft, distant song, and then it will be no more...which is why the point of our lives is not just to become famous or even to produce lasting work."

"Being true to what is unique about himself, he connects each of us to the best parts of ourselves," wrote one collaborator. Ray Price, who gave Nelson his big break, said, "I lived with Hank Williams the last year of his life, and he was just like Willie. His secret was he could walk out onstage and just be himself, and that's what it's all about."

The alt-country movement lives on in Lukas Nelson + the Promise of the Real and Wilco, arguably America's best rock band.* (The latter's predecessor, Uncle Tupelo is, as Mike Heidorn put it, "bigger now than ever.... I guess death is a great career move.") Outlaw country itself lives on through its and the Willie's Roadhouse channels on Sirius/XM, as well as through the Outlaw Music Festival and the Outlaw Country Cruise, at which Shooter Jennings appeared.** Shooter still has connections with his father's music, which seeps into his professional life. He finished several songs his father had left incomplete, recorded a duet about Texas with Kris Kristofferson, Kacey Musgraves, and others, and in 2016 hired the grandson of Waylors bassist Jerry "Jigger" Bridges as his manager. He clicked with legendary singer Tanya Tucker, "the only woman Waylon called 'hoss,'" and he

* In 2013, Wilco teamed with Ryan Bingham, Bob Dylan, and My Morning Jacket for the Americana Festival of Music tour.

** The cruise has hit the high seas from Miami for several years running. Past weeklong outings starred Jessi Colter, Kris Kristofferson, Son Volt, Emmylou Harris, and Steve Earle, who released his own prison record.

and Brandi Carlile produced an album for Tucker with minimal overdubs, to keep it sounding vintage, true, and pure country. "I spit it out and Brandi unscrambles it," Tucker explained. ("She came into my life at just the right time," Tucker said, then paused for effect. "It might've been better a little earlier.") "Without Tanya Tucker, there'd be no Highwomen," Carlile told a Washington State crowd. "She paved the way for some of the most badass women in country music."

Soon after working with Tucker, Shooter announced he would probably never tour again. He joked on his outlaw radio show that he was focusing on "waging war against the forces of Bro-Country."

"Hey, pretty boy in the baseball hat / You couldn't hit country with a baseball bat" went the widely disseminated lines of his "Outlaw You." He called out name-droppers who have been taught how to look like outlaws by the country music image machine, but their new, expensive boots give them away. "You can't buy true," he sang.

Fans attacked Jennings for using his dad's outlaw life to increase his own bona fides,* while Shooter claimed the song was a joke, mainly intended to amuse Jamey Johnson and other, *actual* outlaw musicians. "It seemed like somebody needed to come in and poke some fun at the posers," he told CMT.

The alt-country world, however, was thrilled at the takedown. "This is a shot right to the gut of Music Row, and specifically, this crop of 'New Outlaws' (Justin Moore, Josh Thompson, etc.) invading country music," one blogger proclaimed. While Shooter's fans didn't expect the song—or any song—would end Music Row's preponderance for phony, commercial country, they thought it might become a rallying cry for fans and artists: "Pop isn't going anywhere in country music,

* Another Jennings relative, grandson Whey Jennings, collaborated on a cover of "Highwayman" with Johnny Cash's grandson Thomas Gabriel in late 2021; the YouTube video garnered more than a million views in just a few weeks.

folks. It's always been there, and always will be. What we can fight for is balance, equality, and choice."

After the third Highwaymen album, Cash was "the walking definition of cool" and "one of the last real deal country stars" but most listeners had forgotten him. As journalist Paul Hemphill predicted in his 1970 book *The Nashville Sound*, Cash and his crew were on the way out, to be replaced by handsome, exuberant ass-kissers who saw dollar signs. Cash sniped back in the mid-'90s: "The 'country' music establishment, including 'country' radio and the 'Country' Music Association, does after all seem to have decided that whatever 'country' is, some of us aren't." He suggested that if he ever "lost" his audience, he'd just get rid of the suits and strip his band back to three members to do an acoustic "Give My Love to Rose."

After his controversial dismissal from Columbia, Cash signed with Mercury Records, which pitted him with his Sun Records producer Jack Clement. Cash wanted a bare-bones backing band, while Clement pushed for a pop country sound. In the end, the Mercury albums were overproduced and cloying, and Cash lashed out after learning the label shipped only five hundred copies of one record. "I have not turned my back on Nashville," he announced. "I don't know if they turned their back on me. Doesn't really matter, I wasn't doing anything there anyway but going through the motions."

On February 27, 1993, with Cash freshly out of rehab after another relapse, he headlined a show at the one-thousand-seat-capacity Rhythm Cafe in Santa Ana, California, with Uncle Tupelo opening. Backstage, he received a visit from twenty-nine-year-old producer Rick Rubin, who wanted to cut a CD for Rubin's fledgling label, American Recordings. Cash had reasons to both be suspicious—could he look *any* more pathetic signing with the unknown label—and jump at the chance. As cofounder of the storied Def Jam hip-hop label, Rubin had helmed the rock-rap of the Beastie Boys and the recent Red Hot Chili Peppers CD, one of the most popular of the previous year, at Warner Bros. But, he admitted, "I have no technical ability, and I know nothing about music." He gave Cash the "hard sell," suggesting that the jowly, haggard Cash had fallen into irrelevance, and that taking away the synthesizers and programmed drums could recapture his old fanbase. "You'll come to my house, take a guitar and start singing. You'll sing every song you love, and somewhere in there we'll find a trigger song that will tell us we're headed in the right direction," said Rubin. Bringing out a solid new song, "Drive On," and adapting the traditional "Delia's Gone," about murdering a woman, indeed gave Cash a new vibrancy.

"I can't see nothing wrong with this," said Marty Stuart. "This is as pure as it gets."

That made the hair on Cash's neck stand up. He had dreamed about recording a stark album called "Late and Alone"—this would fulfill the prophecy. Still, though, he resisted, demanding that Rubin accept his engineer, David "Fergie" Ferguson, into his home to monitor the sessions.

"There was nothing to hide behind," Cash said. "And that was scary. I had nothing to lose and everything to gain."

It wasn't much of an exaggeration—he didn't even sign the deal with Rubin's American Recordings label until *after* the album was completed. Luckily, *American Recordings* became his first taste of success since *Highwayman*, garnering a perfect five-star rating from *Rolling Stone*; winning the Grammy for Best Contemporary Folk Album; and helping to birth Americana, as the category was later retitled. It was his most heartfelt album since the gospel years and the starkest major country release by anyone since *Red Headed Stranger*, yet a hundred thousand young people turned out for his solo acoustic set from a stool at the Glastonbury Festival. "How does it feel to be cool again?" a reporter wanted to know.

"Rick came along at exactly the right time," said Rosanne Cash, who also took the independent route after a commercial downturn. "Dad was depressed, discouraged. It was a powerful thing that happened between them, and Dad was completely revitalized and back to his old enthusiastic self."

The second American Recordings album, *Unchained*, was meant to "offend Johnny Cash fans," according to the Man himself. It "felt a lot like the Memphis days" to the reinvigorated Cash, especially with Tom Petty & the Heartbreakers, Kerry Marx, Marty Stuart, and a woman engineer, Sylvia Massy, aboard. Johnny had to mutter to himself: "Get off the stage, Cash," and try not to hide behind his crafted persona. But, once again, radio and Music Row ignored the CD. When *Unchained* won the Best Country Album Grammy in an upset, Rubin ran a full-page *Billboard* magazine ad that featured a close-up of Cash flipping the bird at a San Quentin cameraman: "American Recordings and Johnny Cash would like to acknowledge the Nashville music establishment and country radio for your support," it read.

Cash was the only Highwayman riding high, critically and commercially thanks to *American Recordings*. "The drug days are over for sure," Waylon said. "But me and Johnny Cash are still gettin' mean if we want to." Despite their apparent falling out, the two would record together sporadically until the end. In the studio, the elderly Cash would occasionally look at the fifty-something Jennings and intone: "Beats pickin' cotton."

With Rubin as close collaborator, the last decade of Cash's life was his most creatively fulfilling, although it wasn't without its troubles. Temporarily blind due to an illness, he struggled to get a handle on the Nick Cave song "The Mercy Seat," even with Cave in the studio to guide him through the lyrics. Fergie had to suggest punching in a word at a time in the overdubbing session until Cash felt he had each syllable down. Cave said he watched as Cash sat down to sing and transformed "into a higher being. Like all the songs he does, he made it his own. He's a great interpreter of songs."*

For *American IV*, the plan was to record at Rubin's LA home studio again. "Please listen to these songs every day, so when it comes time to cut them, you'll be confident," Rubin wrote in a January 2002 note accompanying a cassette of original versions. That tape included "Hurt," a Trent Reznor song for his band Nine Inch Nails. Rubin had been pushing for "Hurt" for years, putting it on previous cassettes for the Man in Black. Cash preferred the Byrds' biblical "Turn! Turn! Turn!" and Depeche Mode's "Personal Jesus," which Cash seemed to misinterpret as a gospel song, over the uber-heavy, industrial-metal dread of the Reznor song. Reznor's music, like that of the artists Rubin produced, including the Beastie Boys, was too "urban" for him. But Cash realized "Hurt" had a powerful anti-drug message, and the finished Cash take, with acoustic guitar and piano, stripped the song back to the raw core Cash had been trying to dig down to.

The song needed a video for the record to have a hope of reaching young people; however, Cash had done few. As Waylon put it: "Videos mean you have to be good-looking," and indeed, the original "Hurt"

* Nick Cave recalls the moment: "Johnny has his hands out in front of him like a ghost or specter or something as he descends the stairs, led by his wife, June Carter Cash. I later find out that he has a condition where he is temporarily blinded when he goes indoors from sunlight. He keeps saying in a weird, shaky voice, *Are you there, Nick? Are you there, Nick?* And I'm thinking, *Oh my God,* because Johnny seems seriously debilitated, and *how the fuck is he going to sing a song?* I'm here, Johnny, I say. I'm here." "These are the things that can't be taken away from you," Cave said. "It doesn't matter what anyone says, 'Johnny Cash recorded my song.'"

video was set to star Johnny Depp and Beck. Instead, an almost disturbing, stark promo was produced, which included eerie moments where June Carter stood on the stairs of their Tennessee home and gazed at John expressionlessly, as if having become an angel unable to interfere in her husband's affairs. In the video's climactic moment, with a trembling hand, Cash poured an entire bottle of red wine onto a table with a bountiful feast.

Despite June, Johnny, and Rick Rubin's uneasiness with the morbid video, acclaim for it was otherwise instant and universal, including from Trent Reznor, Rosanne Cash, and MTV viewers who flooded the network's request line. "Hurt" is now considered the greatest country music video of all time, and the single often tops or comes close to topping the list for cover songs across all genres. Soon after, Cash was named the number one country act of all time—the Highwaymen were number two. Perhaps the most satisfying result of its success, though, was *American IV* sweeping the year's CMAs.

Lost in the hubbub over "Hurt," however, was the title track, "The Man Comes Around," which Cash handwrote as a long, poetic screed. It had been years since he had written something with its depth and power, and its dreamlike proselytizing served as a career capper, his last great song. *I hope this is the one the kids know in fifty years*, he said.

American IV far surpassed the previous records on the charts, nearly topping the country album charts and narrowly missing the pop Top 20. It, and the *American Recordings* collectively, brought Cash back to public attention and inspired other aging singers, including Tanya Tucker, to cross genres and try songs by bands like Nine Inch Nails. But, Cash said, "I might finally be at the point where I would only be singing for myself. I'm a lucky man."

Cash, described as "forever restless," and who once said he wanted to "keel over and die onstage" during "Sunday Mornin' Comin'

Down,"* had quietly reduced his touring schedule in the '70s, following an unrelated accident in which five-year-old son John Carter fractured his skull. Then, shortly after the final Highwaymen show in 1996, Cash felt his energy flagging—every day. He "looked 50 years older," according to his former bassist. His voice had never recovered from the drug days, and he had always struggled to fulfill contractually obligated ninety-minute sets. Just before a US tour, he had to relearn the lyrics to "A Boy Named Sue," which he performed every night but had lately screwed up. "He didn't plan it out to be his last show," keyboardist Earl Poole Ball said of the final stop in Michigan. "He was gonna go on a book tour after that show. But what happened was that he was needing yellow tape to be put down from his dressing room to the stage. Whatever illness he was starting to manifest manifested then." That night in Flint, Cash reached over for a guitar pick and collapsed, unable to raise himself again.

Cash canceled the book events and retired from touring. He settled in Port Richey, Florida, in a modest house June had inherited from her parents. Their home sat next to a riverside dock and, beneath a small orange grove, Cash would sit and watch the boats drift by, strumming absent-mindedly on his guitar. "I'm sure when John was younger he was restless and tortured, but when I met him he seemed so incredibly centered that it rubbed off on everyone around him," said musician Jesse Dayton, who played guitar for each of the Highwaymen. In his final years, Cash was jocular, a kidder, and an absolute optimist, no longer "the wild outlaw we see in those early pictures and film clips, although that vibe was still part of him," just beneath the surface. Willie Nelson claimed that, when the Man in Black couldn't sleep, he would call and ask for some fresh jokes.

* He told audiences he still sang "Sunday Morning" "because it helps me reflect on where I've been and where I'm going."

Regarding Willie, John said: "When we started out, we both had the same attitude toward Nashville and things, and they had the same attitude towards him as they did me. He gets mad at me and I get mad at him, but we made a pact a long time ago. Most of our trouble has been caused by people around us, not between me and him. Before we get mad enough to kill one another we'll talk about it first."

Despite their early uneasiness with each other, Cash and Nelson eventually became something approaching friends. In the '90s, Cash put out a solo album that began with the self-penned track "A Backstage Pass," a supposed peek behind the curtain at a Willie & the Family concert. While, on the surface, the song seems to be a comical tribute to Nelson's fame, and the "wackos and weirdoes and dingbats and dodoes" it attracted, it could also be seen as a jealous artist mocking a competitor. In 1998, they made peace for *VH1 Storytellers*. The two oddballs, recorded by Rick Rubin, ribbed one another while blazing through "On the Road Again," "Folsom," and "Family Bible," a common ground song for two Christian-raised, family-focused warhorses. Not long after the taping, Cash, wracked with tremors from Parkinson's disease, invited Nelson to Jamaica for golf on the Cash-Carter course. "He's got more lives than a cat," Nelson wrote before the visit. "It's way too early to be writing him off." It was the last time he saw John and June.

After a bypass operation, Cash was briefly dead on the operating table. He basked in a warm light until he was rudely shaken awake. Although initially unhappy to be alive, he eventually returned to his quietly optimistic self, crying over touching moments in movies or a sweet love note from the wife he spent every waking moment with.* Well into his later life, he would open his eyes each morning and say,

---

* They kept separate bedrooms, which Cash joked was the "secret to a happy marriage."

"Good morning, Lord," and when he rose to his feet, add: "Praise God." After Cash was honored at the Kennedy Center, his daughters confronted him and aired long-standing grievances about his neglect during their childhoods. (Once, Johnny called Kathy from the hospital and demanded a six-pack of beer and pills; when she refused, he yelled: "Piss on you, then!" and hung up on her.) Later, he reunited with Rosanne for a surprise guest spot at Carnegie Hall. As the two harmonized, Rosanne said, "All the old pain dissolved. . . . I got something from my dad that I'd been trying to get since I was about six years old."

At home, as June sank into prescription drug abuse and spoke only in short, incomplete bursts, John encouraged her to finish her solo album. When June had gone to the Mayo Clinic, a doctor told her that her biggest issue was being the wife of Johnny Cash. But, despite several brief splits over his temper, drug use, and affairs, the two remained married. Says Jesse Dayton: "One day when June came over to the studio . . . he put everything on hold and went up to her and gave her a hug and a kiss on the cheek and said, 'I've missed you; so glad you're here.'" At that point, they had been married for almost thirty years.

In the spring of 2003, Cash wrote in his diary: "Now she's an angel."* Although he said at her grave, "I'm coming, baby," after the funeral, he told his son he planned to head straight back to the studio. When Rick Rubin called to check on him, Cash, on a staggering forty prescription drugs, told his producer: "My faith is unshakable!" and suggested he was full-speed ahead on his career. In his final performance, at the Carter Family Fold near his home in Florida, he played for half an hour, saying: "The spirit of June Carter overshadows me

* As confidants worried about his mental health, Cash added a bit of levity to his diary by drawing a portrait of himself as a Disney character, accompanied by the self-parody: "Hello, I'm Mickey Mouse."

tonight." Afterward, Rosanne moved in with her father, who consoled her and his other daughters by suggesting: "When a parent dies, you take on all of their good qualities."

At the end, it was Cash's eyesight that truly depressed his spirit. When he couldn't travel to the MTV Music Video Awards to represent "Hurt"* or read from his overflowing library, his spirits seemed to turn. The man who believed that life's purpose was to "sing with all your heart as long as you can" kept recording in his cabin with Fergie until the last days of his life. After he was gone, John Carter Cash did something his father surely would've cheered: he tossed the old man's wheelchair into the lake.

Kris Kristofferson eulogized J. R. Cash as "the best of America—we're not going to see his like again." Asked to cry on camera for an artistic photography exhibition the following year, he let the tears flow, saying they came easily when he thought of his mentor. Rosanne, who had said she could "almost live in a world without Johnny Cash because he will always be with us," preferred to let the silence speak, including a seventy-one-second soundless track at the end of her 2006 album *Black Cadillac*—one for each year her mother, father, and stepmother had lived. Those who worked to keep him down in life became fair-weather friends in death: in 2007, Cash received a posthumous pardon for his 1965 public drunkenness arrest in Mississippi,** ahead of the first Johnny Cash Flower Pickin' Festival in Oktibbeha County, and today, there is a one-room museum dedicated to Cash outside the walls of Folsom Prison.

---

* "I demand a recount," said singer Justin Timberlake, whose song swept the ceremony.

** Although Cash wrote a song suggesting he had been busted for "picking flowers" along the side of the road, Marshall Grant confirmed the arrest came about because a wasted Man in Black had been discovered rooting around in a private citizen's flowerbed.

Three years after Cash's passing, *American V: A Hundred Highways* debuted atop the *Billboard* 200. It finally, fully restored the commercial standing he'd enjoyed with *Folsom Prison* and *San Quentin*.*

While in lockdown during the COVID-19 outbreak, Willie Nelson wrote: "While you're sitting at home, it's natural to think about friends you'd like to see and give a hug. High on my list would be my fellow Highwaymen.... They called us a country supergroup, but mainly we were old friends who loved making music together."

Says Kerry Marx, a guitarist in Cash's band: "I think it was a positive experience for him. He enjoyed singing with those guys." However, says Marx, Cash "had health issues then, so his state of mind was pretty much affected by that."

Despite the near constant ego battles and drama in the Highwaymen, after their split in 1996, Cash actually grew closer to each of them. "I miss those criminals, er, guys," he joked onstage. While recording the final Highwaymen album, he said, "Between the four of us Highwaymen, we got 135 years on the road. God's almost let us live forever."

The only Highwayman to have declined in renown is Waylon Jennings.

He never physically or emotionally recovered from a heart attack scare on tour in Orange County, California, in 1988. He was hospitalized after learning that his arteries were clogged and he would need a bypass. When Cash visited, Waylon suggested John looked flushed and encouraged him to get checked out; it turned out Cash's arteries were blocked, as well, and he needed emergency surgery. Nurses put

* It took four further years for Rubin to complete *American VI: Ain't No Grave*, recorded at the same time, but when it finally came out, it went Top 3.

them in the same room and the press went batshit with rumors that the men were at death's door.

"Can we keep this low-key?" Waylon asked pleadingly.

"No, sir," Cash said. "If we both kick the bucket, I wanna make sure I get the headline, not you."

Upon checking out, they held an impromptu press conference outside, arm in arm. Although they would each live another dozen years, both left Orange County greatly affected. "For all Waylon's determination to lead a robust and productive life," wrote Colter years later, "for all the strength of his undiminished spirit, his stamina was permanently compromised. Physically, he would never be the same again."

Jennings wrote a song about missing "my wild days" for Cash to sing on the final Highwaymen album, and ended up recording it with him as a duet. Waylon also updated his "Are You Sure Hank Done It This Way?" to say "If Ole Hank Could See Us Now," with cutting lines like: "Well Nashville's got too rich to sing the blues / They've traded in their cowboy boots for high-heeled Gucci shoes," and "It's still a long hard road but you know you're at the top / When the CMA awards you for crossin' over pop." It served as a centerpiece of the concept album *A Man Called Hoss*, essentially a ten-track autobiography. On it, "the Bob Dylan of country music"—a reference to Waylon's shyness—paid tribute to Cash and Colter. "Rough and Rowdy Days," Jennings's final classic, detailed his friendship with Cash and thanked his wife for saving him: "Girl you came along, and just in time / To show me the way / While I was wadin' through / My rough and rowdy days."

Onstage and off, he continued to irritate the establishment, specifically the CMAs, which he called "a joke" rigged by record companies. After he refused to listen to Epic's advice on the sound of a 1992 album, the label buried it. On September 23, 1998, he was set to appear on *The Late Late Show* with host Tom Snyder. After learning he had been mistaken in assuming he would be the only guest that hour, he threatened to leave if not brought on immediately. After stewing for over half an hour, he motioned for Jessi to follow him out to the idling town car. Snyder, laughing, had to fill eighteen minutes of airtime at the end of the show with cutaways to an empty chair. The incident spurred talk shows to put comedians or potential backup interviewees working elsewhere in the building on speed dial, but endeared him to 1990s country stars like Billy Ray Cyrus.*

"The real deal" kept touring. He joked to David Letterman: "I've been on the road since Kitty Wells was a Girl Scout. I don't like getting there, but once I get there, I enjoy playing…getting that immediate feedback."** Willie urged him to "keep going." Attendance was thin, shows were inconsistent, and he would often appear flustered or frustrated, especially when he took to sitting on a stool due to his mobility issues. Outside, under hot lights, he struggled. Inundated with bugs attracted to the stage lights at one outdoor performance, Waylon exclaimed: "These goddamn bugs are coming in shifts!"

"You can play the coliseums and the big auditoriums and after a while the audience starts to look like chairs instead of people," he said, rationalizing the honky-tonks and theater shows. "You can't get that one-on-one thing with people."

When he started getting dizzy spells on tour, he thought: "Maybe it's from riding the bus."

---

* Jennings, after listening to a TV host warble Roy Acuff in 1994, joked that he happened to be "looking for a replacement for Billy Ray Cyrus."

** Jennings and the other guests on *Late Night* had too much fun, bumping Samuel L. Jackson from the program. It may sound like Jennings was more powerful and popular than he was at the time—it would be years before Jackson became the biggest box office earner of all time.

Still, he wouldn't fly for a long time, and in his later years, he took only what he called "forced" flights, when he had no other option. He almost died in such back-to-back "forced" charters. He had rented a single-engine plane against his better judgment, thinking of Buddy booking himself a similar-sized aircraft. When its lights failed, Jennings grudgingly took a second charter. When that ran out of gas and the pilots warned Jennings of an imminent crash, he reminded them of who he was, what he'd been through, and that, if they were going down, he'd make sure to beat the hell out of them before touchdown. Miraculously, the plane landed on a runway lit by only a trio of bulbs. "Waylon, you can breathe now, we're on the ground," Bee Spears told him.

When Willie Nelson learned from Shooter that Waylon was only "hanging in there," he said: "Tell him to come out and do some shows with me. I'll write him a bad check."

"We're brothers from somewhere," Waylon said, "and we're together, right or wrong, to the end, and ain't nobody gonna separate us."

They duetted together on their hits at a show in Phoenix, near where Waylon had moved, finding Nashville too chilly in more ways than one. "A new life inspired by a former life," Jessi Colter called it, referring to how her husband, following the day the music died, had started over in Arizona, and had been sucked back into music "thanks to the wild enthusiasm of the college kids."

"I saw him once," one fan wrote on YouTube. "I came through a blizzard to get there. I saw a horrible wreck [where] someone died." At the gig, the fan started trying to snap pictures of Waylon, but a security guard kept blocking her. Jennings began to pose for her while he sang, and the security guard noticed and stormed off.

In the mid-'90s, he put together a series of Nashville Network TV specials called *Waylon Jennings and Friends*, which guest-starred the individual Highwaymen. For one episode, Jennings brought on Danny Dawson, a young African American guitarist and vocalist from Georgia, who had been inspired to become a country music singer after seeing Charley Pride. Dawson then toured as Waylon's opener. Ronny Light, Waylon's 1970s producer, went on to coproduce Dawson's debut, but an RCA deal fell through.

At the end of the nineties, Waylon was physically a shambles due to a triple bypass, blood circulation issues, diabetes, and carpal tunnel surgery. His feet were always too cold, an issue that began on the bus during the Winter Dance Party tour. Eventually, he developed an infection in his left foot, the same one that had been damaged in a childhood fall and caused his lifelong lean. Doctors told him they would have to partially amputate it to improve his circulation and keep him alive. Perhaps worse, he needed to retire from touring. First, though, he brought Jessi, Travis Tritt, and more modern artists to the Ryman on January 6, 2000, for a last hurrah: *Never Say Die: The Concert Film*. It became his final major appearance. He took the stage in a sleeveless leather vest, dark sunglasses, and trademark cowboy hat, and opened with the defiant "Never Say Die," and rolled through "Good Hearted Woman" and a Kris Kristofferson cover. He wound down the main set with "I've Always Been Crazy" and "Goin' Down Rockin'." At the conclusion of the encore of "The Weight" and "Can't You See," played on his white 1953 Fender Telecaster guitar with a "leather-bound, hand-carved cover," Jennings nodded to the crowd, unable to rise from his seat. They gave him a standing ovation.

The guitar was another sign Jennings was forever drawn back into the fifties, the era of *Rebel Without a Cause*, leather jackets, and barroom brawls, his rise through the Texas music business, and his friendship with Buddy Holly. In the nineties, Holly's protégé played a twangy, electrified, jolly "Peggy Sue" on *Late Night with David*

Letterman, and he and Mark Knopfler closed out a Buddy Holly tribute album, which surprisingly hit the country Top 20, performing "Learning the Game," which Holly had tape-recorded in his New York living room to an audience of one, Waylon Jennings, shortly before they left for the Winter Dance Party tour. But Waylon never recovered from either Holly's death or, more specifically, joking that he hoped Holly's plane crashed.

"I was so afraid for many years that somebody was going to find out I said that," he told Country Music Television before his final Nashville concert. "Somehow, I blamed myself. Compounding that was the guilty feeling that I was still alive. I hadn't contributed anything to the world at that time compared to Buddy. Why would he die and not me?"

When asked about how he recovered from the death of Jerry Garcia, his partner in the Grateful Dead, Bob Weir answered: "I tell you what, I'm not sure if I ever did. I['d] think... 'What am I gonna do? I'm gonna hit the road, that's what Jerry would've wanted me to do.' And I did, I stayed on the road for a long time after Jerry checked out. And you know, by the time I finally came home and my wounds were all licked, I was okay.... I guess I processed the grief to a greater extent than not just by playing."

Waylon figured out what his destiny was, and it wasn't to be Buddy Holly's guilt-stricken bassist. He realized that Holly had picked him to play bass not because he could be a great musician but rather a great singer-songwriter. Jennings applied Holly's ideas to the country music he'd grown up on, and so it's fitting that his last-ever studio recording was Holly's "Well All Right," cut with the surviving Crickets for another tribute CD.* (After his death, Kristofferson, Cowboy

* After his death, Jennings's vocals from a separate session would be added to a preexisting Patsy Cline recording to make a duet and a tribute to both singers.

Jack, Norah Jones, and the surviving Crickets contributed to a Waylon tribute album.)

"All the fussing and fighting over who gets played on the radio or headlines the state fairs don't amount to much more than a range war," Jennings said. "I think you just make your music, you do the best you can with that, and that's what you'll be remembered for."

"My friends," Jennings wrote, closing out his memoir. "The town is big enough for all of us."

Shortly before Waylon's death, he received a call from Johnny Cash. The two men spoke for only a few minutes, but the call ended with both men saying "I love you." On February 13, 2002, the devil finally came back for the man it missed on the runway four decades earlier. "I remember the morning that he died. They called my phone and I had been out all night at the Standard hammered, and I didn't answer," Shooter Jennings recalled. "I didn't have any kind of premonition, but I remember it. I didn't answer 'cause I was too hungover. Two hours later, he died."

Reeling from his death, his widow managed to get through "Storms Never Last" at the funeral. The subsequent, public memorial in Nashville served as the last hurrah of the Highwaymen—one of their number had passed and Cash decided against traveling from his winter home due to his own health issues, but Kristofferson was there. He told the crowd: "If I ever thought I would be singing to honor Waylon in the Ryman Auditorium, it might have helped me through some hard spots," he said, echoing comments he made after receiving an award named after Cash. Emmylou Harris, Charley Pride, and Waylon's godson Hank Williams Jr. also appeared. Eulogizing Jennings, Nelson wrote: "When it came to taking on the country music establishment, he had the guts and self-confidence to lead the way. If it weren't for Waylon, I might still be back in Nashville looking to please the wrong people." As stipulated in his father's will, Shooter and his metal band did "I've Always Been Crazy" at the event's climax.

"I miss Waylon," singer Marshall Chapman wrote a few years on. "Somehow, the universe seems a little tilted without him."

"Waylon was the coolest of the outlaws," said Jesse Dayton. "Willie was and is operating on a universal Zen level.... Kris is literally a genius... a poet in his heart of hearts who is on par with all the literally greatest.... Johnny, after finally tempering his addiction issues, became a champion for the underdog and had a glowing spiritual aura surrounding him...." But in the end, Dayton wrote, "Waylon was, and will always be, at least to me, the coolest man to ever sing country music.... Waylon was like part Elvis, part outlaw Josey Wales, and part the wildest horse that even the most experienced ol' cowboy could never take." At an unofficial tribute show of his own, Dayton had broken down in tears playing "Dreaming My Dreams with You," perhaps Waylon's most touching love song.

Despite keeping the flying "W" for "Waylon" on the old Hillbilly Central building,* Music City ignores the savior of the business; although Cash and Kristofferson are on Nashville's Walk of Fame, there is no star for Waylon or Willie. In 2010, Waymore's brother James filled in a gap that Nashville should have plugged, creating a Waylon museum near the Waylon Jennings Free RV Park in the brothers' hometown.

"You know, we never did advertise," James says of the Littlefield shrine. "My computer's a number two pencil, and I'm old school everything. We've had people from Japan, China, Australia, Switzerland, all

---

* Sometime after Glaser Sound Studios, the former "Hillbilly Central," merged with another operation in 1984, a remodeling team tore open the walls to reveal dozens of ounces of cocaine and pills hidden there.

over Canada, and all over the United States. We had a tour come from Germany...and there was forty-five of 'em. Some of the stories we tell," he joked, "they're the first time I've ever heard 'em." Today, the Waylon Jennings Museum at Waymore's Liquor Store hosts weddings, which it has done for couples from as far-flung as New Zealand.

Breakout star Colby Acuff spent part of the COVID-19 pandemic listening to the outlaw catalog on vinyl, going down a musical rabbit hole,* and got really "into Waylon Jennings albums, and with the life that we were living at the time, I could really relate with a lot of his songs." In 2021, Acuff had a dream in which he was visited by Jennings, Haggard, and his other musical idols, and he found "himself" pleading with them for advice after the coronavirus canceled his first tour and nuked his income. "And as Waylon started walking away, he just said: 'Hoss, we all had to do it that way.' They left, and I woke up and I wrote the song" "Once in a Lifetime," which became his debut single. "The outlaws were honky tonk legends," Acuff said, "and I'm here to make sure that legends are not forgotten."**

That year, Shannon McNally released the first major Waylon Jennings tribute album. At the time, she had been dropped from Capitol Records for her twang and had all but given up. "I wasn't too country for country radio; country radio didn't think I was country enough. I was always too something: too young, too old, too pretty,

* Musician David Byrne notes that seven in every ten songs played or sold are catalog/an older recording.

** Months later, Jesse Daniel and Jodi Lyford, two other up-and-coming outlaw artists, covered the Billy Joe Shaver–Waylon Jennings cowrite "You Asked Me To," giving new life to a Top 10 single that had helped put both men on the map nearly half a century earlier.

not sexy enough, too smart, not smart enough." She said she wanted to do a record of Waylon songs because his story was getting lumped in with racist white bearded country acts lost to history, "because that just wasn't Waylon." McNally had not really broken out as a star and, when a friend asked what she would do with creative freedom success might allow, McNally instantly responded: "An album of Waylon."

When she put out feelers to make sure she could get the necessary permissions to cover certain songs, the delighted author of "Lonesome, On'ry and Mean" wrote back: "You're a girl!" With the green light from songwriters, McNally brought in Lukas Nelson for a duet and hired Fred Newell, a Waylor, and J. T. Cure and Derek Mixon of Chris Stapleton's band for *The Waylon Sessions*, recorded in Nashville. On day one, however, she was hit with the immensity of the project and waves of nausea bowled her over. As the first take rolled without her, she recovered and sang "Pretend I Never Happened" without a hitch.

The Highwaymen got called outlaws, McNally claimed, simply for bucking conservative Music Row. "Willie and Waylon, Kris Kristofferson, Billy Joe Shaver, those guys were really decent human beings," she said. "They partied, but they weren't trapped in their own thoughts. And that's what being an outlaw is. It's a no-brainer for a certain type of woman."

Newell had been playing in an amalgam of the Waylors and a tribute act, the Waymore's Blues Band, and eventually helped form Waymore's Outlaws with Tommy Townsend. In 2014, Shooter linked up with Waymore's Outlaws, who opened for him and brought him on for Waylon covers. Although he's promised to quit touring solo, Shooter spent two years as Brandi Carlile's touring pianist and still plays one-off shows with the Waymore's; when Shooter is busy working with Carlile, Townsend takes lead vocals, having learned from his old producers, Jerry Bridges and Waylon himself. "Waylon and Jerry always took their time to direct me on how to phrase lines, listen to pitch, and pocket, and I would always try my best to impress them," he says.

"I feel really responsible for his legacy," said Shooter. "I knew him so well to know how much he cared about country music and about music in general—boundless music and experimentation and the progressiveness of music. I feel I have an obligation I'll never lose."

After Buddy Holly's death, Waylon had the same sense of responsibility come crashing down on his shoulders. At first, though, he resisted making music altogether. "I was just trying to figure out what to do with myself, you know? I was a completely changed person. I quit for a while—I wouldn't even play a guitar, I wouldn't pick it up." When he finally did, and eventually had to choose between the music he wanted to make and record company protocols, he compromised, but the sense that he was wasting the gift bestowed upon him—and that Buddy's ghost might be grimacing from above—pushed him to decide: *Well, if I'm not gonna do it on my terms, it ain't worth the devil's bargain.*

Waylon could have coasted, kept performing surefire minor hits written by record company men, but he stubbornly stuck to his guns, and thus we have "Are You Sure Hank Done It This Way?," "Dreaming My Dreams," "Bob Wills," "My Rough and Rowdy Days," and "This Time." He bottomed out and got another shot at the title. After, he said he wanted people to remember "that a person . . . can make it and blow it and hit bottom doing drugs, and come back and be able to survive that and do something worthwhile." He grew into the man he saw in Holly: "He was laughing all the time, but he had another side to him too," said Jennings. "You didn't want to mess with him, that was it."

He finally made peace with the past on October 6, 1995. At the Mason City, Iowa, airport, where calculations near the runway determined that half an inch of snow covered the ground, and the crisp fall air and seventeen-mile-per-hour wind gusts nipped at Clear Lake, visibility rose to over four miles. Relieved air traffic controllers green-lit flights out of the regional hub, but everyone was sticking around for a country music concert. Waylon Jennings, who toured exclusively by bus, and had previously passed through Clear Lake on one concert itinerary, was on his way. When his bus puttered to a stop and couldn't be immediately resuscitated, Jennings saw it as yet another sign of the curse visiting him: *I hope your bus breaks down.*

"I'm not sure if I'd have known that when they were booking this what I might have said," he told a reporter outside. "I'd have stopped for a minute because I kinda dodged all of that all my life. . . .* It's just a mixed bunch of emotions. You are never ready for someone dying and you feel guilty."

Johnny Cash wrote: "There's no way around grief and loss: you can dodge all you want, but sooner or later you just have to go into it, through it, and, hopefully, come out the other side." However, he added, "the world you find there will never be the same as the one you left."

"I think he's still sensitive to this whole thing, and I think there might even be some guilt that he wasn't on the plane," said Jeff Nicholas, the ballroom's then-owner, "but I guess he felt it was time to come back."

Waylon Jennings's cowboy boots stepped tentatively into the Surf Ballroom for the first time in three dozen years for a press conference. After telling someone, "I'm looking for my youth . . . but she's gone," he was asked about Holly's own struggles in Nashville. "He got a dose of Nashville early," Jennings said. "They had a bluegrass band backing Buddy Holly singing rock and roll. He went nuts and went home. I

---

* He had avoided seeing the widely distributed wire photo of the wreckage until accidentally coming across it during the twenty-fifth anniversary.

learned that if it sounds different, that's good." He said that Buddy Holly, as well as Don Was, who had produced the recent Highwaymen album, taught him about living in the pocket: "What I call the pocket is when you get that rhythm and you don't stop," he said. "You can't go anywhere but right."

Prompted by repeated questions, Jennings pointed to the spot behind the curtain where he stood when Holly approached him, asking if he'd go grab some hot dogs, since Buddy couldn't have done so without being mobbed by teenagers. "I came back and we separated and him laughing..." Jennings said, his voice drifting off. "When I came by the chair [over there] he was leaning against the wall by where you go upstairs. And he was laughing at me because I wasn't going on the plane."

On the strength of the national publicity and despite Jennings's fallen stature, the twenty-two-hundred-seat ballroom nearly sold out by showtime. It was, the owner said, fitting, seeing as how everyone said the decades-old bar owed its success predominantly to the legend of Holly's final concert there. "Waylon had a part in that too," Nicholas said. "It means a lot to a lot of people that he's coming back."

ACKNOWLEDGMENTS

Thank-yous

Alex Glass and the team at Alex Glass Literary Management.
Ben Schafer, Carrie Napolitano, Fred Francis, and everyone at Hachette Book Group.
Erika Wiese, Marco Ceglie, Wylie Stecklow, Kurt Opprecht, Andrew Boyd, Dan Katz, Tom Hill, Marquela Stevenson, Diane Fairbanks, Terry Linton, Dana Fairbanks, Cathy Phillips, Scott Fairbanks, Ula Uberesen, Emily Farris, Conor Donohue, Tiana Nobile, Katie Lyon-Hart, Zachary Belway, Yasin Frank Southall, Betsy Phillips, Lisa Wade, Colleen Kane, Stephanie Renee Kauffman, Melissa Gramstad, Johnny Sansone, Jessi Colter, Lukas Nelson, Brittney Spencer, Marissa R. Moss, Ricky Valido, Barbara Sudduth Newsome, Jon Shults, Sebastian Timm, Randy O'Brien, and J. Brandon Maughon.
The Americana Music Association, Country Music Hall of Fame, Lmnl Lit, the Garden District Book Shop, Blue Cypress Books, Lionheart Prints, Mo's Art Supply & Framing, the Buddy Holly Center, and Waymore's Museum and Drive-Thru Liquor.

Interview subjects and those who helped facilitate interviews

Kay Ashbrook, Nicole Atkins, Cary Baker, Earle Poole Ball, Adam Barnes, Jon Bauer, Eddie Bayers, Cory Branan, Amy Butler, C. Craig Campell/Campbell Entertainment Group, Dillon Carmichael, Brandi Carlile, Melissa Carper, Kelly Carter, Marco Ceglie, Marshall Chapman, Carl A. Chauvin, Rodney Clawson, Gary Clevenger, Mike

Clute, John Cowling, Dan Daley, Sherry Davis, Chris DeCubellis, Chris DeStefanis, Kristin Diable, Conor Donohue, Andrew Duhon, Kari Estrin, Katie Fike, Parker Forsell, Joe Galante, Jon Grau, Susan Hamilton, Terry Hamilton, Marianne Helin, Robert Hilburn, Derek Hoke, John Holman, James Jennings, Whey Jennings, Andrew Joyce, Colleen Kane, Rory Kaplan, Kris Kristofferson, Lisa Kristofferson, H. J. Lally, Don Larson, Jim Lauderdale, Anita R. Lay, Bob Lee, Peter Levin, Caleb Lewis, Linda Gail Lewis, Gloria Lovel Brewster, Todd Markland, Kerry Marx, Katherine Maurer, Barry Mazor, Kathie McCathie, Shannon McNally, Kevin Moran, Raelyn Nelson, Justin Osborne/SUSTO, Sara Sadowski Pforr, PD Poindexter, Chris Powell, Norbert Putnam, Michelle Reese, Tony Roberts, Thomas Rondeau, Bryan Ros, Georgee "Girl George" Royce, Allison Russell, John Sebastian, Di Shaw, Joe A. Shaw, Jens Staff/Them Coulee Boys, Jody Stephens, Nora Jane Struthers, Tommy Townsend, Lucian K. Truscott IV, Tanya Tucker, Ricky Valido, Sharon Vaughn, Patricia Viars, Adia Victoria, Peter Walsh, Steve Warren, Ashley Wells, Glenn White, John Buck Wilkin, Coleman Williams, a.k.a. "IV," Barry Winters, and Ayana Woodard.

NOTES

A Note on Sources

I consulted hundreds of articles, books, DVDs, LPs, CD liner notes, and interviews to gather material for this book. Here are the ones I ended up sourcing, chapter by chapter.

Introduction

Greg Weatherby, "The Outlaw at 50: Our 1988 Interview with Waylon Jennings," *Spin*, June 15, 2020, accessed November 29, 2023, https://www.spin.com/2020/06/the-outlaw-at-50-our-1988-interview-with-waylon-jennings/.

Jesse Dayton, *Beaumonster: A Memoir* (New York: Hachette Books, 2021), 76.

Willie Nelson with Bud Shrake, *Willie: An Autobiography* (New York: Simon & Schuster, 1988), 158.

Kelefa Sanneh, *Major Labels: A History of Popular Music in Seven Genres* (New York: Penguin, 2021), 173, 215.

John Milward, *Americanaland: Where Country & Western Met Rock 'n' Roll* (Urbana: University of Illinois Press, 2021), 44.

Albert Cunniff, *Waylon Jennings* (New York: Zebra, 1985), 10.

Dan Daley, *Nashville's Unwritten Rules: Inside the Business of Country Music* (Overlook Books, 1999), 131–133, 146.

Marshall Chapman, *They Came to Nashville* (Nashville: Vanderbilt University Press, 2010), 111, 212.

John Lomax III, *Nashville Music City USA* (New York: Abrams, Inc., 1985), 33–34.

Chet Flippo, "Waylon Jennings: 'If I Was Everything People Make Me Out, I'd a Been Dead Long Ago,'" *Creem*, July 1973, 34.

Billboard Staff, "No Budging Beyoncé from Hot 100 No. 1," *Billboard*, February 23, 2006, accessed November 29, 2023, https://www.billboard.com/music/music-news/no-budging-beyonce-from-hot-100-no-1-59610/.

Bill Pearis, "Lavender Country's Patrick Haggerty Has Died," *BrooklynVegan*, October 31, 2022, accessed November 29, 2023, https://www.brooklynvegan.com/lavender-countrys-patrick-haggerty-has-died/.

Bloodshot Records, "Country music 'belongs to us all, but lest we forget, country music is a product of inequality and doesn't exist to glorify the powerful,'" Facebook.com, October 5, 2020, accessed November 29, 2023, https://www

.facebook.com/BloodshotRecords/posts/pfbid09RDNWzHDhbexk2UTiiC7ai9KCvXBBdgG7zKx3pR7VrNZvnaxhr33Zn4xFh5zqbfwl.

R. Serge Denisoff, *Waylon: A Biography* (Knoxville: University of Tennessee Press, 1983), 299.

Prologue

Willie Nelson with Turk Pipkin, *The Tao of Willie* (Gotham Books, 2006), 183.

Waylon Jennings with Lenny Kaye, *Waylon: An Autobiography* (New York: Warner Books, 1996), 6, 12–13, 26, 48–49, 51–52, 55, 57–58, 63, 67, 72–75.

Tony Byworth, liner notes to *Singer of Sad Sad Songs, Taker/Tulsa, Good Hearted Woman,* and *Ladies Love Outlaws* (Morello Records, 2021), CD box set.

"HD* The True Buddy Holly Story," interview with Dion, YouTube, February 2, 2015, accessed February 20, 2022, youtu.be/HIxwW3NbAx4.

Denisoff, *Waylon,* 61–62, 68, 70, 72–74.

Bob Dylan, "Bob Dylan: Nobel Lecture," Nobel Foundation, June 5, 2017, accessed November 29, 2023, https://www.nobelprize.org/prizes/literature/2016/dylan/lecture/.

Gary Clevenger, email interview, June 12, 2022.

Terry Jennings, *Waylon: Tales of My Outlaw Dad* (New York: Hachette Books, 2016), 7, 16.

Barbara Sudduth Newsom interview by Gary Clevenger, date unknown.

Sanneh, *Major Labels*, 164.

"The Time Waylon Jennings Got Fired for Playing Little Richard (RIP)," Saving Country Music, May 9, 2020, accessed November 29, 2023, https://www.savingcountrymusic.com/the-time-waylon-jennings-got-fired-for-playing-little-richard/.

Robert Hilburn, *Johnny Cash: The Life* (New York: Little, Brown and Company, 2013), 297.

Weatherby, "The Outlaw."

Transcript from the *Dinah Shore* show, circa 1975, quoted in Denisoff, *Waylon*, 238.

Cunniff, *Waylon Jennings*, 22, 28, 37, 43.

Lomax, *Nashville*, 150.

JR, "The Waylon Jennings Years at KLLL (Part Five)," KLLL.com/The Internet Archive Wayback Machine, April 16, 2014, accessed November 29, 2023, https://web.archive.org/web/20140714155659/http://www.klll.com/pages/18144181.php?pid=395032.

"Stars of Rock 'n' Roll Troupe Die in Crash Which Claims 4 Lives," *Bulletin* (Bend, Oregon), February 3, 1959, page A1, accessed November 29, 2023, https://news.google.com/newspapers?id=flNYAAAAIBAJ&pg=6401%2C3799730.

Sumit Singh, "How an Aircraft Crash Became Known as the Day the Music Died," *Simple Flying*, February 4, 2021, accessed November 29, 2023, https:

//simpleflying.com/how-an-aircraft-crash-became-known-as-the-day-the-music-died/.

"The RIAA/NEA's Songs of the Century," DavesMusicDatabase, March 7, 2021, accessed November 29, 2023, http://davesmusicdatabase.blogspot.com/2012/03/riaaneas-top-365-songs-of-20th-century.html.

Spring Sault, "Waylon Jennings Was Forever Haunted by His Last Words to Buddy Holly," *Texas Hill Country*, April 11, 2019, accessed December 5, 2021, https://texashillcountry.com/waylon-jennings-last-words-buddy-holly/.

Kris Kristofferson, personal interview, April 10, 2009.

Don Giller, "Johnny Cash & Waylon Jennings Collection on Letterman, 1983–1995," YouTube, accessed January 5, 2022, https://www.youtube.com/watch?v=pfAKhjGAA-0.

Chapter One

Nelson with Pipkin, *The Tao of Willie*, 9, 11, 19, 37–38, 46, 55, 77.

Chapman, *They Came to Nashville*, 253.

Joe Nick Patoski, *Willie Nelson: An Epic Life* (New York: Little, Brown and Company, 2008), 15, 35–36, 56, 85, 93, 95, 101–102, 112, 129, 139, 144, 157, 159, 220.

Rob Ruggiero, "Warrant Brings Houston a Special Slice of Cherry Pie—Plus Eddie Trunk!," *Houston Press*, June 22, 2021, accessed November 29, 2023, https://www.houstonpress.com/music/things-to-do-see-warrant-lita-ford-bulletboys-and-emcee-eddie-trunk-at-warehouse-live-11579948.

Leon Beck, "Larry Butler's Memories of Willie," *Texas Hot Country Magazine*, undated, accessed November 29, 2023, http://www.texashotcountrymagazine.com/articles/larry-butler-s-memories-of-willie.

Milward, *Americanaland*, 26, 44–45, 62–63, 65.

Jason Woodbury, "Van Morrison, Three Chords and the Truth," *Pitchfork*, October 31, 2019, accessed November 29, 2023, https://pitchfork.com/reviews/albums/van-morrison-three-chords-and-the-truth/.

Jim D'Ville, "Uke Lesson: 3 Chords and the Truth—Country Songwriting Legend Harlan Howard," *Ukulele Magazine*, February 19, 2020, accessed November 29, 2023, https://ukulelemagazine.com/stories/uke-lesson-3-chords-and-the-truth-country-songwriting-legend-harlan-howard.

Jennings with Kaye, *Waylon*, 142–143, 178–179, 194.

"Harlan Howard Quotes," BrainyQuote.com, undated, accessed November 29, 2023, https://www.brainyquote.com/authors/harlan-howard-quotes.

Amanda Petrusich, "Willie Nelson Understands," *New Yorker*, November 8, 2020, accessed November 29, 2023, https://www.newyorker.com/culture/the-new-yorker-interview/willie-nelson-understands.

Nelson with Shrake, *Willie*, 52–53, 81, 111, 118, 129, 140, 150.

Willie Nelson with Larry McMurtry, *The Facts of Life: And Other Dirty Jokes* (New York: Random House, 2003), 10, 12–14, 29, 41, 47, 84, 92.

"22 Best Willie Nelson Quotes," *American Songwriter*, undated, accessed November 29, 2023, https://americansongwriter.com/the-22-best-willie-nelson-quotes/.

Willie Nelson and Bobbie Nelson with David Ritz, *Me and Sister Bobbie: True Tales of the Family Band* (New York: Penguin Random House, 2020), 15.

Bill C. Malone, *Country Music: Second Revised Edition* (Austin: University of Texas Press, 2002), 303.

Heymarkarms, "The Genius and Mystery of Willie Nelson," Longreads, September 4, 2014, accessed November 29, 2023, https://longreads.com/2014/09/04/the-genius-and-mystery-of-willie-nelson/.

Patrick Doyle, "All Roads Lead to Willie Nelson: *Rolling Stone*'s Definitive Profile of the Country Icon," *Rolling Stone*, September 2, 2014, accessed November 29, 2023, http://www.rollingstone.com/music/features/all-roads-lead-to-willie-nelson-rolling-stones-definitive-profile-of-the-country-icon-20140902.

biggestkkfan, "American Revolutions: The Highwaymen," 1995, Country Music Television, directed by Don Was, accessed January 2, 2022, https://youtu.be/wbxFy5DB6Rc.

Willie Nelson with David Ritz, *It's a Long Story* (New York: Little, Brown & Co., 2015), 124–26, 131, 142, 144–145, 147, 164, 357.

Don Cusic, "Nashville Recording Industry," *Tennessee Encyclopedia*, October 8, 2017, accessed December 5, 2021, https://tennesseeencyclopedia.net/entries/nashville-recording-industry/.

Colin Escott, *The Grand Ole Opry: The Making of an American Icon* (New York: Center Street, 2006), xi–xii, 117, 151–152.

Andrew Grant Jackson, *1973: Rock at the Crossroads* (New York: Thomas Dunne, 2019), 132, 134.

Tyler Mahan Coe, "CR016/PH02—Owen Bradley's Nashville Sound," *Cocaine & Rhinestones* (podcast), May 4, 2021, accessed November 29, 2023, https://cocaineandrhinestones.com/owen-bradley-nashville-sound.

John Markert, *Making Music in Music City: Conversations with Nashville Music Industry Professionals* (Knoxville: University of Tennessee Press, 2021), 2–3, 101.

Sanneh, *Major Labels*, 158, 163, 167.

Robert Palmer, "Nashville Sound: Country Music in Decline," *New York Times*, September 17, 1985, A1, https://www.nytimes.com/1985/09/17/arts/nashville-sound-country-music-in-decline.html.

Paul Du Noyer, *The Illustrated Encyclopedia of Music, First Edition* (London: Flame Tree Publishing, 2004), 14.

Weatherby, "The Outlaw."

Brian Allison, Elizabeth Elkins, and Vanessa Olivarez, eds., *Hidden History of Music Row* (Charleston: History Press, 2020), 10, 52.

Rachel DeSantis, "Willie Nelson Recounts Past Suicide Attempt—and How Friend Paul English Supported Him After—in New Memoir," *People*, September 16, 2022, accessed November 29, 2023, https://people.com/country/willie-nelson-recounts-past-suicide-attempt-book-excerpt/.

Addie Moore, "How Faron Young Helped Launch Willie Nelson's Career with 'Hello Walls,'" *Wide Open Country*, April 28, 2022, accessed November 29, 2023, https://www.wideopencountry.com/hello-walls-country-classics-revisited/.

"Patsy Cline," Spotify.com, accessed November 29, 2023, https://open.spotify.com/artist/7dNsHhGeGU5MV01r06O8gK.

Lorie Liebig, "Here's the Real Reason the Grand Ole Opry Won't Reinstate Hank Williams," *The Boot*, February 17, 2020, accessed November 29, 2023, https://theboot.com/hank-williams-kicked-out-grand-ole-opry-wont-be-reinstated/.

Paul Sexton, "Patsy Cline: 10 Dramatic Quotes," UDiscoverMusic.com, July 17, 2014, accessed November 29, 2023, https://www.udiscovermusic.com/stories/patsy-cline-ten-dramatic-quotes/.

"The Patsy Cline Story," Dr. Progresso, undated, accessed November 29, 2023, https://web.archive.org/web/20120306035446/http://www.holeintheweb.com/drp/bhd/PatsyCline.htm.

Ellis Nassour, *Honky Tonk Angel: An Intimate Story of Patsy Cline* (Chicago: Chicago Review Press, 2008), 165.

Addie Moore, "Dottie West: A Country Music Success Story with a Tragic Ending," *Wide Open Country*, March 17, 2020, accessed November 29, 2023, https://www.wideopencountry.com/dottie-west/.

Miranda Raye, "Patsy Cline Nearly Died Twice Before Fatal Plane Crash," *Classic Country Music*, February 5, 2019, accessed November 29, 2023, https://classiccountrymusic.com/patsy-cline-nearly-died-twice-before-fatal-plane-crash/.

Linda Wertheimer, "Patsy Cline's 'Crazy' Changed the Sound of Country Music," NPR.org, September 4, 2000, accessed November 29, 2023, https://www.npr.org/2000/09/04/1081575/crazy.

Tim Ott, "How Patsy Cline and Willie Nelson Teamed Up for Her Hit Song 'Crazy,'" Biography.com, December 15, 2020, accessed November 29, 2023, https://www.biography.com/news/patsy-cline-willie-nelson-crazy-song.

Dayton Duncan and Ken Burns, *Country Music* (New York: Penguin Random House, 2019), 240, 347–348.

Lynden Orr, Abby Wills, and Madison Comstock, "The Nashville Sound," Country Music Project, February 25, 2015, accessed November 29, 2023, https://sites.dwrl.utexas.edu/countrymusic/the-history/the-nashville-sound/.

Lomax, *Nashville*, 110.

"Shirley Nelson," *Springfield News-Leader*/Legacy.com, February 2, 2010, accessed November 29, 2023, https://www.legacy.com/us/obituaries/news-leader/name/shirley-nelson-obituary?id=48899405.

Willie Nelson interview by Steve Fishell, liner notes to *Crazy: The Demo Sessions*, Sugar Hill, 2003, CD.

Willie Nelson interview, *The Highwaymen Live*, 2016, DVD, Sony Entertainment, bonus features/interview feature.

"Knowing of Your Own Death," Professional Theatre at Southern University / Bard.org, undated, accessed November 29, 2023, https://www.bard.org/study-guides/knowing-of-your-own-death/.

Kaleena Fraga, "How Did Patsy Cline Die? Inside the Plane Crash That Killed a Country Music Icon," AllThatIsInteresting.com, August 3, 2022, accessed November 29, 2023, https://allthatsinteresting.com/patsy-cline-death.

Untitled, unsigned, rootsrockweirdo.tumblr.com, March 8, 2013, accessed November 29, 2023, https://rootsrockweirdo.tumblr.com/post/44863825811/the-death-of-jack-anglin-on-march-7-1963-one.

Chapter Two

Randy Lewis, "Bob Dylan's Songwriting Looks Back to the Ancients," October 14, 2016, accessed November 29, 2023, https://www.vnews.com/Revolutionary-poet-Bob-Dylan-upended-foundations-of-pop-with-his-literate-lyrics-5389077.

Sean Wilentz, "Mystic Nights," *Oxford American* 58, Fall 2007, accessed November 29, 2023, https://main.oxfordamerican.org/magazine/item/186-mystic-nights.

Norbert Putnam, *Music Lessons: A Musical Memoir* (Thimbleton House Media, 2017), 24, 71, 73, 154.

Laura Hostelley, "Throwback to the Time Kris Kristofferson Was a Janitor," Sounds Like Nashville, June 22, 2017, accessed November 29, 2023, https://www.soundslikenashville.com/news/throwback-kris-kristofferson-janitor/.

Stephen Miller, *Kris Kristofferson: The Wild American* (London: Omnibus Press, 2009), 12, 16–17, 29, 48, 50, 54–55, 59, 63, 65, 79, 87–90, 94.

Blake Stilwell, "Famous Veteran: Kris Kristofferson," Military.com, April 19, 2013, accessed November 29, 2023, https://www.military.com/veteran-jobs/career-advice/military-transition/famous-veteran-kris-kristofferson.html.

John Spong, "That '70s Show," *Texas Monthly*, April 2012, accessed November 29, 2023, https://www.texasmonthly.com/arts-entertainment/that-70s-show/.

Duncan and Burns, *Country Music*, 325, 328–329, 332, 338–340.

Spencer Leigh, "Kris Kristofferson," SpencerLeigh.com, June 28, 2004, accessed November 29, 2023, https://web.archive.org/web/20120415001040/http://www.spencerleigh.demon.co.uk/Interview_Kristofferson.htm.

Daryl Sanders, *That Thin, Wild Mercury Sound: Dylan, Nashville and the Making of Blonde on Blonde* (Chicago: Chicago Review Press, 2019), 99, 131.

Douglas McPherson, "Kris Kristofferson," *Country Music Magazine*, August/September 2018, accessed December 8, 2022, https://www.facebook.com/groups/WillieHNelson/permalink/10158300717086950/?locale=bg_BG&paipv=0&eav=AfasY_bq0hsglOuhqDrj8rQf4tC4OPMcWIIPRHMRoPL20yBwxhxFvIt48J8K9CCKtxs&_rdr.

"Survival Skills with Kris Kristofferson," *Men's Journal*, December 4, 2017, accessed November 29, 2023, https://www.mensjournal.com/health-fitness/survival-skills-with-kris-kristofferson-20130709/.

John Buck Willkin, phone interview, July 10, 2022.

John Carter Cash, *The House of Cash: The Legacies of My Father, Johnny Cash* (San Rafael: Insight Edition, 2011), 137.

Allison, Elkins, and Olivarez, *Hidden History*, 59–60, 92, 129.

Kay Ashbrook, personal communication, July 12, 2022.

Katherine Maurer, personal communication, July 25, 2022.

David Bowman, "Kris Kristofferson," Salon.com, September 24, 1999, accessed November 29, 2023, https://www.salon.com/1999/09/24/kristofferson/.

Rita Coolidge, *Delta Lady* (New York: HarperCollins Publishers, 2016), 148–149.

"Kris Kristofferson: Vietnam Blues (1966)," Alpha History, 2018, accessed November 29, 2023, https://alphahistory.com/vietnamwar/kris-kristofferson-vietnam-blues-1966/.

Milward, *Americanaland*, 26, 96, 103–104, 134.

Bob Dylan, *Bringing It All Back Home* (Columbia Records, 1965), BobDylan.com, liner notes, accessed November 29, 2023, https://www.bobdylan.com/albums/bringing-it-all-back-home/.

Dave Henderson, *Touched by the Hand of Bob: Epiphanal Bob Dylan Experiences from a Buick 6* (Pewsey, UK: Black Book Company, 1999), 7, 35, 159, 163.

Harvey Kubernick, "Bob Dylan's 'Nashville Skyline' Turns 50 This Spring," Music Connection, April 24, 2019, accessed November 29, 2023, https://www.musicconnection.com/bob-dylans-nashville-skyline-turns-50-this-spring/.

Michael Kosser, *How Nashville Became Music City, U.S.A.* (Milwaukee: Hal Leonard Corporation, 2006), 150.

Daryl Sanders, "Looking Back on Bob Dylan's *Blonde on Blonde*, the Record That Changed Nashville," *Nashville Scene*, May 5, 2011, accessed November 29, 2023, https://www.nashvillescene.com/news/looking-back-on-bob-dylans-i-blonde-on-blonde-i-the-record-that-changed-nashville/article_c17cc27e-b6e4-5794-901c-e2e7ce4c5cb9.html.

Lomax, *Nashville*, 8, 39, 163–164.

Christer Svensson, "Dylan's Harp Keys," Dylanchords, undated, accessed November 29, 2023, https://dylanchords.com/node/1851.

Olof Bojorner, "Still on the Road 1966," Bjorner.com, March 3, 2017 and January 27, 2021, accessed November 29 and 30, 2023, http://www.bjorner.com/DSN01225%20(66).htm#DSN1280 and http://www.bjorner.com/DSN01225%20(66).htm#DSN1281.

Wilfrid Mellers, "Bob Dylan: Freedom and Responsibility," in *Bob Dylan: The Early Years: A Retrospective*, ed. Craig McGregor (New York: William Morrow and Company, 1972), 402–403.

Bob Spitz, *Dylan: A Biography* (New York: W. W. Norton & Company, 1989), 337.

Clinton Heylin, *Bob Dylan: Behind the Shades Revisited* (Perennial Currents, 2003), 241.

Robert Hilburn, "Pop Music: The Impact of Dylan's Music 'Widened the Scope of Possibilities,'" *L.A. Times*, May 19, 1991, accessed November 30, 2023, http://articles.latimes.com/1991-05-19/entertainment/ca-3173_1_bob-dylan-song.

Scott Bunn, "Sad-Eyed Lady of the Lowlands," Recliner Notes, December 15, 2021, accessed November 30, 2023, https://reclinernotes.com/2021/12/15/sad-eyed-lady-of-the-lowlands/.

Peter Guralnick, *Looking to Get Lost: Adventures in Music & Writing* (New York: Little, Brown & Company, 2020), 204, 212.

Michael McCall, "Freedom's Just Another Word," *Nashville Scene*, September 18, 2003, accessed November 30, 2023, https://www.nashvillescene.com/arts_culture/freedom-s-not-just-another-word/article_7dc31fa9-c247-577a-99a4-3264ea737ca2.html.

Robbie Robertson, *Testimony* (New York: Crown Archetype, 2016), 212–213.

"Inside Bob Dylan's 'Blonde on Blonde': Rock's First Great Double Album," *Rolling Stone*, May 16, 2016, accessed November 30, 2023, https://www.rollingstone.com/music/music-news/inside-bob-dylans-blonde-on-blonde-rocks-first-great-double-album-164769/.

"Blonde on Blonde," Bob Dylan Commentaries, undated, accessed November 30, 2023, http://www.bobdylancommentaries.com/blonde-on-blonde/.

"Bob Dylan Roots: Loudon Wainwright," dead link, http://bobdylanroots.com/wainwr.html.

Daley, *Nashville's Unwritten Rules*, 123–125, 138, 237–238.

A. D. Amorosi, "Bob Dylan, 'Travelin' Thru, Featuring Johnny Cash: The Bootleg Series Vol. 15,'" *Flood*, November 15, 2019, accessed November 30, 2023, https://floodmagazine.com/71480/bob-dylan-travelin-thru-featuring-johnny-cash-the-bootleg-series-vol-15/.

Scott Carrier, "Kris Kristofferson: What I've Learned," *Esquire*, January 29, 2007, accessed November 30, 2023, https://www.esquire.com/entertainment/interviews/a1283/learned-kris-kristofferson-0599/.

Ron Thibodeaux, "He Made It Through the Night," *New Orleans Times-Picayune*, November 29, 2006, accessed November 30, 2023, https://web.archive.org/web/20070930185002/http://www.nola.com/music/t-p/index.ssf?%2Fbase%2Fentertainment-0%2F116478236147900.xml&coll=1.

Chapman, *They Came to Nashville*, 9, 11, 22, 27.

Mary Hurd, *Kris Kristofferson: Country Highwayman* (Roman and Littlefeld, 2015), 23.

Kris Kristofferson, quoted in Hilburn, *Johnny Cash*, 365, 387.

The Highwaymen—DVD, bonus features/interview with Kris Kristofferson and interview with Willie Nelson.

"How Kris Kristofferson Convinced Johnny Cash to Record His Songs," PBS / *American Masters* / WNET, season 30, episode 7, accessed November 30, 2023, https:

//www.pbs.org/wnet/americanmasters/the-highwaymen-how-kris-kristofferson-convinced-cash-to-record-his-songs/7311/.

Katie Foley, "This Music Legend Stole a Helicopter and Landed It at Johnny Cash's House," We Are the Mighty, accessed November 30, 2023, https://www.wearethemighty.com/popular/kris-kristofferson-army/.

Philip Norman, "Johnny Cash: 'I Was Evil. I Really Was'—a Classic Interview from the Vaults," *The Guardian*, February 28, 2012, accessed November 30, 2023, https://www.theguardian.com/music/2012/feb/28/johnny-cash-classic-interview.

"The Great Story Behind 'Sunday Morning Coming Down,'" *Wide Open Country*, June 27, 2022, accessed November 30, 2023, https://www.wideopencountry.com/sunday-morning-coming-down-story-behind-song/.

"Kris Kristofferson Clears Up Stories About Helicopter Visit to Johnny Cash," WENN, ContactMusic.com, July 19, 2011, accessed November 30, 2023, https://www.contactmusic.com/kris-kristofferson/news/kris-kristofferson-clears-up-stories-about-helicopter-visit-to-johnny-cash_1233132.

Andrew Joyce, personal communication, July 11, 2022.

Joe Leydon, "Kris Kristofferson Is a Son of Nashville," Cowboys and Indians, December 30, 2105, accessed November 30, 2023, https://www.cowboysindians.com/2015/12/kris-kristofferson-is-a-son-of-nashville/.

"Help Me Make It Through the Night by Sammi Smith," SongFacts.com, undated, accessed November 30, 2023, https://www.songfacts.com/facts/sammi-smith/help-me-make-it-through-the-night.

Jennings with Kaye, *Waylon*, 199.

Chet Flippo, "Waylon Jennings Gets off the Grind-'Em-Out Circuit," *Rolling Stone*, December 6, 1973, accessed November 30, 2023, https://www.rollingstone.com/music/music-news/waylon-jennings-gets-off-the-grind-em-out-circuit-249302/.

Martha Hume, *You're So Cold I'm Turning Blue: Martha Hume's Guide to the Greatest in Country Music* (New York: Viking Press, 1982), 198.

"Sammi Smith and Her Story with 'Help Me Make It Through the Night,'" Country Thang Daily, August 2, 2023, accessed November 30, 2023, https://www.countrythangdaily.com/sammi-smith-through-night/.

Mikal Gilmore, *The Highwaymen—Live*, liner notes.

biggestkkfan, "The Highwaymen in the studio, 1995 (CMT documentary)," YouTube Video, June 3, 2019, accessed November 30, 2023, https://youtu.be/wbxFy5DB6Rc.

Chris Neal, "Elder Statesman Kris Kristofferson Grows into His Voice," *Nashville Scene*, January 21, 2010, accessed November 30, 2023, https://www.nashvillescene.com/music/elder-statesman-kris-kristofferson-grows-into-his-voice/article_f6df128f-23ed-583e-9577-13347dc74c12.html.

Jack Hurst, "Kristofferson Beats the Devil," *Tennessean*, September 6, 1970, 3–S, 8–S, accessed November 30, 2023, https://www.newspapers.com/clip/73300490/tennesseean-feature/.

Paul Zollo, "Behind the Song: 'Me and Bobby McGee' by Kris Kristofferson & Fred Foster," *American Songwriter*, undated, accessed November 30, 2023, https://americansongwriter.com/me-and-bobbie-mcgee-by-kris-kristofferson/.

Andrew Langer, "Lone Star: Kris Kristofferson, Walking Tall down 'This Old Road,'" *Austin Chronicle*, February 24, 2006, accessed November 30, 2023, https://www.austinchronicle.com/music/2006-02-24/341985/.

Kyle "Trigger" Coroneos, "Kristofferson Coming Down: Landing a Helicopter on Cash's Lawn," Saving Country Music, April 23, 2014, accessed November 30, 2023, https://www.savingcountrymusic.com/kris-kristofferson-coming-down-landing-a-helicopter-on-johnny-cashs-lawn/.

Jamie Loftus, "The Dirty Side of Five Children's Authors," *Boston Globe*, January 30, 2015, accessed November 30, 2023, https://webcache.googleusercontent.com/search?q=cache:VOj4y_8mA4QJ:www.bdcwire.com/dirty-side-of-childrens-authors/&hl=en&gl=us.

Johnny Cash with Patrick Carr, *Cash: The Autobiography* (San Francisco: Harper San Francisco, 1997), 90, 205.

Norbert Putnam, personal interview, July 25, 2022.

Malone, *Country Music*, 303, 306.

"Life with Bob Dylan, 1989–2006," *Uncut*, February 15, 2015, accessed November 30, 2023, https://www.uncut.co.uk/features/life-with-bob-dylan-1989-2006-30130/.

George Cantor, *Pop Culture Landmarks: A Traveler's Guide* (Detroit: Visible Ink, 1995), 146–147.

Markert, *Making Music*, 3–4.

Escott, *The Grand Ole Opry*, 146.

David Cantwell, "12 Classic Country Albums Turning 50 in 2020," *Rolling Stone*, March 3, 2020, accessed November 30, 2023, https://au.rollingstone.com/music/music-lists/great-country-albums-turning-50-in-2020-8084/kris-kristofferson-kristofferson-8095/.

Carter Cash, *The House of Cash*, 76.

Anita Lay, "Kris Kristofferson Appreciation Group—Official," Facebook.com, October 12, 2022, accessed November 30, 2023, https://www.facebook.com/groups/kriskristoffersonappreciation/posts/2071560949716715/.

Paul Hendrickson, "Janis Joplin: A Cry Cutting Through Time," *Washington Post*, May 5, 1998, accessed November 30, 2023, https://web.archive.org/web/20190621160450/http://www.washingtonpost.com/wp-srv/style/features/joplin.htm.

Randy Lewis, "Bob Neuwirth Remembered by His Friends T Bone Burnett, Steven Soles and David Mansfield," *Variety*, June 4, 2022, accessed November 30, 2023, https://variety.com/2022/music/news/bob-neuwirth-remembered-t-bone-burnett-david-mansfield-steven-soles-rolling-thunder-1235284946/.

Lucian K. Truscott, personal communication, May 31, 2022.

"Watch Kris Kristofferson Tell Story Behind Janis Joplin Recording 'Me and Bobby McGee,'" *Outsider*, May 5, 2021, accessed November 30, 2023, https://outsider.com/news/country-music/watch-kris-kristofferson-tell-story-behind-janis-joplin-recording-me-and-bobby-mcgee/.

"Kris Kristofferson," JanisJoplin.net, undated, accessed November 30, 2023, https://www.janisjoplin.net/life/friends/kris-kristofferson/.

Bob Dylan, "Read Bob Dylan's Complete Riveting Musicares Speech," *Rolling Stone*, February 9, 2015, accessed November 30, 2023, https://www.rollingstone.com/music/music-news/read-bob-dylans-complete-riveting-musicares-speech-240728/.

Jennings with Kaye, *Waylon*, 200.

Stephen L. Betts, "Flashback: Johnny Cash Puts His Stamp on 'Sunday Morning Coming Down,'" *Rolling Stone*, February 25, 2020, https://www.rollingstone.com/music/music-country/johnny-cash-sunday-morning-coming-down-kris-kristofferson-958048/.

The Johnny Cash TV Show 1969–1971, Sony Columbia Legacy, commentary track on DVD, 2007.

Michael Stewart Foley, *Citizen Cash* (New York: Basic Books, 2021), 80.

Noel Murray, "The Best of the Johnny Cash TV Show 1969–1971," *Onion A.V. Club*, October 3, 2007, accessed November 30, 2023, https://www.avclub.com/the-best-of-the-johnny-cash-tv-show-1969-1971-1798203094.

Chapter Three

Johnny Cash, quoted in "The Johnny Cash Trail," Folsom Cash Trail, March 5, 2023, accessed November 19, 2023, https://folsomcasharttrail.com/the-trail/blog/why-i-wear-black-johnny-cash-quotes-and-the-stories-behind-them.

Johnny Cash, quoted in "Johnny Cash > Quotes > Quotable Quote," Goodreads.com, undated, accessed November 30, 2023, https://www.goodreads.com/quotes/168622-i-wore-black-because-i-liked-it-i-still-do, https://www.goodreads.com/quotes/120567-there-s-a-lot-of-things-blamed-on-me-that-never, and https://www.goodreads.com/quotes/668018-it-s-good-to-know-who-hates-you-and-it-is.

Carter Cash, *The House of Cash*, 13.

Hilburn, *Johnny Cash*, 5, 8, 16, 23, 42, 47, 137, 165, 172, 185–186, 188–193, 203–205, 207, 220, 225, 227, 316, 319, 322, 325–326, 331, 335, 422.

Duncan and Burns, *Country Music*, 184–185, 187, 193, 199, 201, 224, 244–245, 304–306, 309, 328.

Stewart Foley, *Citizen Cash*, 37, 53, 73, 86, 148, 159, 163, 189–190, 195.

Norman, "Johnny Cash."

Peter Guralnick, *Johnny Cash: The Last Interview and Other Conversations* (Brooklyn: Melville House Publishing, 2021), x–xi, 38, 64, 205–208, 211.

Alan Light, *Johnny Cash: The Life and Legacy* (New York: Smithsonian Books / Random House, 2018), 42, 49, 100, 104–105, 115–116, 125.

Cash with Carr, *Cash*, 7, 53, 111, 143, 153, 158, 160–163, 165, 169, 199–200, 274, 279–280.

Michael Streissguth, *Johnny Cash at Folsom Prison: The Making of a Masterpiece* (University Press of Mississippi, 2019), xi, 8–9, 48, 75, 86.

Chris Lehmann, "Johnny Cash Was Not a Politician," *New Republic*, December 7, 2021, accessed November 30, 2023, https://newrepublic.com/article/164638/johnny-cash-not-politician-citizen-cash-biography-review.

Marshall Grant with Chris Zar, *I Was There When It Happened* (Nashville: Cumberland House Publishing, Inc., 2006), 32, 76, 110, 139.

Joe McGasko, "Johnny Cash: 10 Things You Might Not Know About the Country Icon," Biography.com, December 10, 2020, accessed November 30, 2023, https://www.biography.com/news/johnny-cash-10-interesting-facts.

"Johnny Cash," Bear Family Records, undated, accessed November 30, 2023, https://www.bear-family.com/cash-johnny/.

Milward, *Americanaland*, 40, 59, 65.

Denisoff, *Waylon*, 21, 23, 133, 152, 291.

Laura Rice, "Johnny Cash's First Wife Was Vivian Liberto. A Documentary Finally Tells Her Story," *Texas Standard,* July 24, 2020, accessed November 30, 2023, https://www.texasstandard.org/stories/johnny-cashs-first-wife-was-vivian-liberto-a-documentary-finally-tells-her-story/.

"Johnny Cash & Waylon," YouTube Video.

Robert Hilburn, "Johnny Cash's Dark California Days," *L.A. Times*, October 12, 2013, accessed November 30, 2023, https://www.latimes.com/entertainment/music/posts/la-et-ms-johnny-cash-calif-story.html.

Roseanne Cash, *Composed* (New York: Viking, 2010), 159.

Trish Long, "The Man in Black(mail)," *El Paso Times / Tales from the Morgue*, April 25, 2008, accessed November 30, 2023, https://elpasotimes.typepad.com/morgue/2008/04/the-man-in-blac.html.

Chris Foy, "Johnny Cash's Long Struggle with Drugs and Sobriety," *FHE Health*, August 27, 2018, accessed November 30, 2023, https://fherehab.com/news/johnny-cashs-struggle-with-addiction/.

"October 5th, 1965: Johnny Cash Arrested Again . . . ," undated, accessed November 30, 2023, https://gaslightrecords.com/news/johnny-cash-arrested-again.

Richard Skanse, "Johnny Cash Talks Love, God and Murder," *Rolling Stone*, July 5, 2000, accessed November 30, 2023, https://www.rollingstone.com/music/music-news/johnny-cash-talks-love-god-and-murder-199957/.

Emma Foster, "EXCLUSIVE: How Johnny Cash Downed 100 Pills Daily Chased by a Case of Beer and Smashed Then Mistress June Carter's Cadillac into Telephone Pole, Knocked Out His Teeth and Was Refused Treatment Because Doctors Said He Was 'Bad News,'" *Daily Mail* (UK), June 21, 2017, accessed November 30, 2023, https://www.dailymail.co.uk/news/article-4622964/Johnny-Cash-downed-100-pills-smashed-June-Carter-Cadillac.html.

Dean Goodman, "Johnny Cash's Son Opens Up on Parents' Addictions," Reuters, August 9, 2007, accessed November 30, 2023, https://www.reuters.com/article/us-cash/johnny-cashs-son-opens-up-on-parents-addictions-idUSN3046078520070531.

June Carter Cash, *From the Heart* (Hoboken: Prentice Hall, 1987), 59, 66–68.

Escott, *The Grand Ole Opry*, 160–161.

Hurd, *Kris Kristofferson*, 83–84.

Lomax, *Nashville*, 38, 97.

"Country Hall of Fame Elects Kenny Rogers, Bobby Bare, Jack Clement," CMT, April 10, 2013, accessed January 1, 2022, https://www.cmt.com/news/3o589n/country-hall-of-fame-elects-kenny-rogers-bobby-bare-jack-clement.

Allison Stewart, "At Folsom Prison, Johnny Cash Found His Cause," *Washington Post*, May 28, 2018, accessed November 30, 2023, https://www.washingtonpost.com/national/at-folsom-prison-johnny-cash-found-his-cause/2018/05/28/740124ca-4f03-11e8-84a0-458a1aa9ac0a_story.html.

Michael Stewart Foley, "Johnny Cash Is a Hero to Americans on the Left and Right. But His Music Took a Side," Slate.com, December 7, 2021, accessed November 30, 2023, https://slate.com/news-and-politics/2021/12/johnny-cash-politics-blood-sweat-and-tears.html.

Joel Whitburn, *The Billboard Book of Top 40 Country Hits* (Billboard Books, 1996), 68, 121.

"Johnny Cash Setlist," Setlist.fm, January 4, 2014, accessed November 30, 2023, https://www.setlist.fm/setlist/johnny-cash/1968/folsom-state-prison-folsom-ca-63c5ba4f.html.

Eduardo Cuevas and Chelcey Adami, "Remembering Glen Sherley, the Convict Who Inspired Cash and Died in Gonzales," *The Californian*, May 11, 2018, accessed November 30, 2023, https://www.thecalifornian.com/story/news/2018/05/11/convict-musician-inspired-johnny-cash-died-gonzales-40-years-ago/600653002/.

Tommy Winfrey, "Merle Haggard: San Quentin Parolee, Music Icon," *San Quentin News*, May 1, 2016, accessed November 30, 2023, https://sanquentinnews.com/merle-haggard-san-quentin-parolee-music-icon/.

Wes Langeler, "On This Date: Merle Haggard Witnessed the 'Power of Johnny Cash' as an Inmate at San Quentin Prison," Newsbreak.com, January 1, 2022, accessed November 30, 2023, https://www.newsbreak.com/news/2474760880007-on-this-date-merle-haggard-witnessed-the-power-of-johnny-cash-as-an-inmate-at-san-quentin-prison.

Michael Streissguth, "Merle Haggard's Lost Interview: Country Icon on Johnny Cash, Prison Life," *Rolling Stone*, January 4, 2017, accessed November 30, 2023, https://www.rollingstone.com/music/music-country/merle-haggards-lost-interview-country-icon-on-johnny-cash-prison-life-193183/.

Abargale, "Merle Haggard live with Johnny Cash," YouTube Video, April 6, 2016, accessed November 30, 2023, https://www.youtube.com/watch?v=G-QoqVFB1kY.

Jennings with Kaye, *Waylon*, 144, 354.

Stephen M. Deusner, "Johnny Cash at Folsom Prison: Legacy Edition," *Pitchfork*, October 23, 2008, accessed December 1, 2023, https://pitchfork.com/reviews/albums/12331-johnny-cash-at-folsom-prison-legacy-edition/.

"Johnny Cash," SOS Children's Villages Canada, August 18, 2013, accessed December 1, 2023, https://www.soschildrensvillages.ca/johnny-cash.

Stephen L. Betts, "Flashback: Kris Kristofferson's Awkward CMA Win," *Rolling Stone*, July 16, 2014, accessed December 1, 2023, https://www.rollingstone.com/music/music-country/flashback-kris-kristoffersons-awkward-cma-win-78903/.

Miller, *Kris Kristofferson*, 91.

Matthew Leimkuehler, "Nearly 50 Years After His First Trophy, Trailblazing Charley Pride Returns to the CMA Awards," *Nashville Tennessean*, November 10, 2020, accessed December 1, 2023, https://www.tennessean.com/story/entertainment/music/2020/11/10/charley-pride-cma-awards-willie-nelson-lifetime-achievement-interview/6136710002/.

"Charley Pride Setlist," Florida Strawberry Festival, Plant City, Florida, March 9, 2018, Guestpectacular.com, accessed December 1, 2023, https://guestpectacular.com/artists/charley-pride/events/2018-03-09/united-states/plant-city/wish-farms-soundstage.

Eric Greene, "53 Years Ago, Charley Pride Breaks the Country Color Barrier," WUPE.com / WUPE FM, January 7, 2020, accessed December 1, 2023, https://wupe.com/53-years-ago-charley-pride-breaks-the-country-color-barrier/.

Charley Pride, "Country Music: Charley Pride," Time-Life Records STW-101, 1981, 12-inch vinyl, liner notes by Charles K. Wolfe.

Kristin M. Hall, "Charley Pride Overcame Racial Barriers as Country Music Star," ABC27News.com / Associated Press, December 12, 2020, accessed December 1, 2023, https://www.abc27.com/news/entertainment/charley-pride-overcame-racial-barriers-as-country-music-star/.

"Cash Box Top 100 Singles, February 5, 1972," TropicalGlen.com, archived November 15, 2017, accessed December 1, 2023, https://web.archive.org/web/20171115015342/http://tropicalglen.com/Archives/70s_files/19720205.html.

biggestkkfan, "Kris Kristofferson—CMA Award 1970," YouTube Video, August 12, 2011, accessed December 1, 2023, https://www.youtube.com/watch?v=-VOCJYFe93A.

Chapter Four

Willie Nelson with Turk Pipkin, *The Tao of Willie* (New York: Gotham Books, 2006), xiv, 24, 39, 49, 57–58, 67, 81, 128.

Doyle, "All Roads."

"Kris Kristofferson ticket," eBay.com, 2021, dead link, https://www.ebay.com/sch/i.html?_from=R40&_nkw=Kris+Kristofferson+ticket+Lincoln+Center+for+the+Performing+Arts&_sacat=0&rt=nc&LH_Complete=1.

"Kris Kristofferson Album: 'Live at the Philharmonic,'" BestCountrySingers.com, undated, accessed December 1, 2023, http://www.bestcountrysingers.com/kris-kristofferson/albums/prk-ipC117757.html.

Daley, *Nashville's Unwritten Rules*, 228.

William Ruhlmann, "Border Lord," AllMusic.com, undated, accessed December 1, 2023, https://www.allmusic.com/album/border-lord-mw0000179382.

Leigh, "Kris Kristofferson."

Graeme Thomson, "Kris Kristofferson: 'I'm Sure I Made Some Stupid Mistakes . . . ,'" *Uncut*, June 22, 2016, accessed December 1, 2023, https://www.uncut.co.uk/features/kris-kristofferson-im-sure-made-stupid-mistakes-77521/2/.

Norbert Putnam, personal interview, July 25, 2022.

Duncan and Burns, *Country Music*, 348, 385.

Bowman, "Kris Kristofferson."

Jakob Greene, "Kris Kristofferson & Rita Coolidge—1972-05-11 Dublin (National Stadium) [historical document]," July 31, 2021, accessed December 1, 2023, https://www.guitars101.com/threads/kris-kristofferson-rita-coolidge-1972-05-11-dublin-national-stadium-historical-document.764027/#post-3616888.

"Rita Coolidge—Southern Museum of Music Artist Hall of Fame Spotlight," Southern Museum of Music, undated, accessed December 1, 2023, https://www.southernmuseumofmusic.com/Spotlight/00-C/Rita-Coolidge.htm.

Coolidge, *Delta Lady*, 18, 21–22, 34, 42–43, 140, 144–145, 147, 209.

"Rita Coolidge," Biography.com, undated, May 27, 2020, accessed December 1, 2023, https://www.biography.com/musician/rita-coolidge.

"Never a Great Singer, Kris Kristofferson Has Had an Amazing Career Nonetheless," *Pittsburgh-Post Gazette*, June 10, 2010, accessed December 1, 2023, https://www.post-gazette.com/ae/music/2010/06/10/Never-a-great-singer-Kris-Kristofferson-has-had-an-amazing-career-nonetheless/stories/201006100491.

Michael Cavacini, "Interview with Rita Coolidge," *The Aquarian*, July 3, 2019, accessed December 1, 2023, https://www.theaquarian.com/2019/07/03/interview-with-rita-coolidge/.

"CASH BOX Top 100 Singles—May 15, 1971," accessed December 1, 2023, https://tropicalglen.com/Archives/70s_files/19710515.html.

Gene Daniell, "Kris Kristofferson," Geni.com, July 8, 2022, accessed December 1, 2023, https://www.geni.com/people/Kris-Kristofferson/6000000002905502106.

Gdino, "MG Henry Christopher Kristofferson," FindAGrave.com, August 14, 2017, accessed December 1, 2023, https://www.findagrave.com/memorial/182380883/henry-christopher-kristofferson.

Miller, *Kris Kristofferson*, 47, 67, 81, 88, 99, 101, 117, 119, 124, 145, 151–152, 229, 246.

"Rita Coolidge," *Billboard*, undated, accessed December 1, 2023, https://www.billboard.com/artist/rita-coolidge/.

William Ruhlmann, "Full Moon," AllMusic.com, undated, accessed December 1, 2023, https://www.allmusic.com/album/full-moon-mw0000887412.

Douglas McPherson, "Kris Kristofferson," *Country Music Magazine*, August/September 2018.

Patoski, *Willie Nelson*, 153, 169, 184, 190, 204–205, 208, 211, 236, 258.

Kris Kristofferson, personal interview, April 10, 2009.

Milward, *Americanaland*, 44, 106–107, 160–161.

Ree Hines, "Willie Nelson Says He'd Chop His Signature Hair Before Parting with This Prized Possession," November 11, 2021, accessed December 2, 2023, https://www.today.com/popculture/willie-nelson-says-he-d-chop-his-signature-hair-parting-t238665.

Anita Lay, "Kris Kristofferson—Busted Flat in Baton Rouge," Facebook Group comment, Facebook.com, April 3, 2023, accessed December 2, 2023, https://www.facebook.com/groups/1197170037067806/posts/6068486599936101?comment_id=6070026799782081.

Leigh, "Kris Kristofferson."

Spong, "That '70s."

Nelson with Ritz, *It's a Long Story*, 176–177, 181, 187, 189, 202, 207–208, 215, 219, 223, 226, 231–232.

"Outlaws & Armadillos: Country's Roaring '70s (temporary exhibit)," photographed by the author, Country Music Hall of Fame, Nashville, TN, June 17, 2021.

Nelson with Shrake, *Willie*, 14, 30, 126, 163–164, 169, 185–186, 257–258, 306.

Nelson with McMurtry, *The Facts of Life*, 97–98, 100, 117, 161.

Cheryl McCall, "Willie Nelson: Yesterday's Outlaw," *People*, September 1, 1980, accessed December 2, 2023, https://people.com/archive/cover-story-willie-nelson-yesterdays-outlaw-vol-14-no-9/.

"Texas County Population Estimates, 1971–74, Arranged in Alphabetical Order," Texas State Library and Archives Commission, June 6, 2018, accessed December 2, 2023, https://www.tsl.texas.gov/ref/abouttx/popcnty71-74.html.

Nelson and Nelson with Ritz, *Me and Sister Bobbie*, 193, 200, 209, 212, 215–216.

Joe Nick Patoski, *Austin to ATX: The Hippies, Pickers, Slackers & Geeks Who Transformed the Capital of Texas* (College Station: Texas A&M University Press, 2019), 19, 56, 59.

Jennings with Kaye, *Waylon*, 6, 130, 193.

Karen Mizoguchi, "Willie Nelson Recalls Having to Admit Cheating to Wife When Mistress Had Their Baby: I 'Was Caught,'" *People*, September 18, 2020, accessed December 2, 2023, https://people.com/country/willie-nelson-admitted-affair-to-wife-when-mistress-had-their-baby/.

Gary Cartwright, *Turn Out the Lights: Chronicles of Texas in the '80s and '90s* (University of Texas Press, 2000), page unidentified.

John Spong, "Willie Nelson's Daughter Paula on Gunfights, the Devil, and Sister Bobbie," *Texas Monthly*, April 27, 2022, accessed November 23, 2022, https://www.texasmonthly.com/podcast/willie-nelsons-daughter-paula-on-gunfights-the-devil-and-sister-bobbie/.

Michael Corcoran, "Willie Nelson's Performance at Armadillo World Headquarters (1972) '#1 Most Significant in Austin Music History,'" StillIsStillMoving.com, September 22, 2014, accessed December 2, 2023, https://stillisstillmoving.com/willienelson/willie-nelsons-performance-at-armadillo-world-headquarters-1972-1-most-significant-in-austin-music-history/.

Dave Thomas, "40 Years Ago, Dripping Springs Reunion Helped Create Austin's Musical Identity," *Austin American-Statesman*, June 24, 2016, accessed December 2, 2023, https://www.statesman.com/story/entertainment/music/2016/06/24/40-years-ago-dripping-springs-reunion-helped-create-austins-musical-identity/10225070007/.

Don Roth and Jan Reid, "The Coming of Redneck Hip," *Texas Monthly*, November 1973, 75, accessed December 2, 2023, https://books.google.com/books?id=KywEAAAAMBAJ&q=%22shotgun%20willie%22&pg=PA75#v=snippet&q=%22shotgun%20willie%22&f=false.

Denisoff, *Waylon*, 206, 240, 264.

Kinky Friedman, introduction to Nelson with Pipkin, *The Tao of Willie*, xii–xiii.

"Black Rose," Genius.com, undated, accessed December 2, 2023, https://genius.com/Billy-joe-shaver-black-rose-lyrics.

Sanneh, *Major Labels*, 178.

Weatherby, "The Outlaw."

Joe Nick Patoski, "Willie Nelson and the Birth of the Austin Music Scene," *Texas Almanac 2012–2013*, accessed December 2, 2023, https://www.texasalmanac.com/articles/willie-nelson-and-the-birth-of-the-austin-music-scene.

Briana Edwards, "The Real Story of How Austin Became Known as the Live Music Capital of the World," Click2Houston.com, August 12, 2020, accessed December 2, 2023, https://www.click2houston.com/news/texas/2020/08/13/the-real-story-of-how-austin-became-known-as-the-live-music-capital-of-the-world/.

Alicia Dietrich, "The Way Back: Willie at the Armadillo," *Alcade*, March 1, 2014, accessed December 2, 2023, https://alcalde.texasexes.org/2014/03/the-way-back-willie-at-the-armadillo/.

"Roger Sovine to Retire from BMI," BMI.com, October 12, 2000, accessed December 2, 2023, https://www.bmi.com/news/entry/20001013_roger_sovine_to_retire_from_bmi.

Norbert Putnam, personal interview, July 25, 2022.

Ed Ward, "Troublemaker," *Austin Chronicle*, December 29, 2006, accessed December 2, 2023, https://www.austinchronicle.com/music/2006-12-29/432091/.

Berry Shank, *Dissonant Identities: The Rock 'n' Roll Scene in Austin, Texas* (Middletown: Wesleyan University Press, 2011), 53–56.

Arlo Guthrie, Facebook.com, June 27, 2022, accessed June 27, 2022, https://www.facebook.com/arloguthrie.

Willie Nelson Setlist at Abilene Civic Center, Abilene, TX, USA, September 11, 1972, setlist.fm, accessed December 2, 2023, https://www.setlist.fm/setlist/willie-nelson/1972/abilene-civic-center-abilene-tx-5bfc13a0.html.

"How Willie Nelson Changed Music in Austin, TX," LTCornerPub.com, undated, accessed June 28, 2022, dead link, https://ltcornerpub.com/how-willie-nelson-changed-music-in-austin-tx/.

Kara Pound, "Willie Nelson's Harmonica Player Opens Up About Life on the Road," *St. Augustine Record*, May 9, 2014, accessed December 2, 2023, https://www.staugustine.com/story/entertainment/local/2014/05/09/willie-nelsons-harmonica-player-opens-about-life-road/16117893007/.

Jody Rosen, "Willie Nelson's Long Encore," *New York Times Magazine*, August 21, 2022, 26, 28, accessed December 2, 2023, https://www.nytimes.com/2022/08/17/magazine/willie-nelson.html.

"English, Robert Paul, Sr. (1932–2020)," Texas Historical Association, April 8, 2021, accessed December 2, 2023, https://www.tshaonline.org/handbook/entries/english-robert-paul-sr.

Ed Ward, "Willie Nelson: Rednecks, Thai Sticks, and Lone Star Beer," *Creem*, October 1975, 40.

Allie Hinds, "The History of Willie's Picnic," NBC-DFW, June 29, 2012, accessed December 2, 2023, https://www.nbcdfw.com/local/willies-picnic-through-the-years/1921807/.

Cunniff, *Waylon Jennings*, 112, 125.

John Sebastian, personal interview, July 4, 2022.

Dave Thomas, "The (Almost) Definitive Chronology of Willie's Fourth of July Picnics," *Austin American-Statesman*, May 21, 2012, accessed December 2, 2023, https://www.statesman.com/story/entertainment/music/2016/12/21/the-almost-definitive-chronology-of-willies-fourth-of-july-picnics/10219364007/.

Dayton, *Beaumonster*, 81–83.

Tim Cumming, "'Releasing This Has Destroyed Miles,'" *The Guardian*, October 16, 2003, accessed December 2, 2023, https://www.theguardian.com/music/2003/oct/17/2.

Grant Jackson, *1973*, 37, 132–133.

Ashley Kahn, "Jerry Wexler: The Man Who Invented Rhythm & Blues," *Rolling Stone*, August 15, 2008, accessed December 2, 2023, https://www.rollingstone.com/music/music-news/jerry-wexler-the-man-who-invented-rhythm-blues-245859/.

Jerry Wexler and David Ritz, *Rhythm and the Blues: A Life in American Music* (New York: Alfred A. Knopf, 1993), 31, 34, 37, 51, 67.

Barry Lazell, ed., *Rock Movers & Shakers: An A to Z of the People Who Made Rock Happen* (Garden City: Billboard Publications, 1989), 462.

"Donny Hathaway," AllMusic.com, undated, accessed December 2, 2023, https://www.allmusic.com/artist/donny-hathaway-mn0000182360.

Jan Reid, *The Improbable Rise of Redneck Rock* (Austin: University of Texas Press, 2004), 223–224, 228.

Michael Streissguth, *Outlaw: Waylon, Willie, Kris, and the Renegades of Nashville* (New York: HarperCollins), 41.

Lomax, *Nashville*, 103.

Joe Nick Patoski, "Watching Willie's Back," *Oxford American* 87, Winter 2014, January 13, 2015, accessed December 2, 2023, https://oxfordamerican.org/magazine/issue-87-winter-2014/watching-willie-apos-s-back.

David Courtney, Michael Hall, Rich Kienzle, Max Marshall, Joe Nick Patoski, John Spong, and Christian Wallace, "All 151 Willie Nelson Albums, Ranked," *Texas Monthly*, April 29, 2020, accessed December 3, 2023, https://www.texasmonthly.com/interactive/big-list-willie-nelson-albums-ranked/.

John Spong and Michael Hall, "Sister Bobbie Grounded Willie Nelson in His Music—and His Life," *Texas Monthly*, May 2022, accessed December 3, 2023, https://www.texasmonthly.com/arts-entertainment/bobbie-nelson-obituary/.

Ed Ward, "Shotgun Willie Makes Another Album," *Creem*, September 1, 1973, accessed December 3, 2023, https://archive.creem.com/article/1973/9/1/shotgun-willie-makes-another-album.

Chapman, *They Came to Nashville*, 104, 223–224, 226–227.

Jerry Wexler, "Advertisement," *Jet* 40, no. 4 (April 22, 1971): 34–35.

Jan Reid and Shawn Sahm, *Texas Tornado: The Times & Music of Doug Sahm* (Austin: University of Texas Press, 2010), 105.

Max McNabb, "How a Gunfight Earned Willie Nelson His Nickname of Shotgun Willie," *Texas Hill Country*, February 7, 2019, accessed December 3, 2023, https://texashillcountry.com/how-willie-nelson-got-nickname/.

Andrew Winistorfer, "Willie Nelson Got Free on 'Shotgun Willie,'" VinylMePlease.com, March 25, 2021, accessed December 3, 2023, https://www.vinylmeplease.com/blogs/magazine/willie-nelson-shotgun-willie-liner-notes.

Robert Christgau, "'Consumer Guide '70s: N' / Christgau's Record Guide: Rock Albums of the Seventies," RobertChristgau.com, accessed December 3, 2023, https://www.robertchristgau.com/get_chap.php?k=N&bk=70.

Don Roth and Jan Reid, "The Coming of Redneck Hip," *Texas Monthly*, November 1973, 1, 10, 75.

Gus Walker, "Willie Recites Lyrics as Well as Sings 'Em," *Arizona Republic*, July 8, 1973, accessed November 9, 2022, https://www.newspapers.com/image/?clipping_id=76281537&fcfToken=eyJhbGciOiJIUzI1NiIsInR5cCI6IkpXVCJ9.eyJmcmVlLXZpZXctaWQiOjExNzg3ODM0MywiaWF0IjoxNjMzMTMwNDk0LCJleHAiOjE2MzMyMTY4OTR9.9slxjdY9C9RZvEST6lAlGOK51oDb5HCcGaqiknFfftw.

Steve Ditlea, "Shotgun Willie," *Rolling Stone*, August 30, 1973, accessed November 9, 2022, https://www.rollingstone.com/music/albumreviews/shotgun-willie-19730830.

Gary Cartwright, *Turn Out the Lights: Chronicles of Texas in the '80s and '90s* (Austin: University of Texas Press, 2000), 278.

Willie Nelson, *Yesterday's Wine* (LP), RCA/Sony Music, 2017 printing / 1971 original recording and release, Stereo, FRM–4568.

Harold Bradley, quoted in Willie Nelson, "Crazy: The Demo Sessions," CD liner notes by Steve Fishell, 2003, Sugarhill Records.

Laura Flynn Tapia and Yoshie, *Muscle Shoals* (Charleston: Arcadia Publishing Library Editions, 2007), 104.

Willie Nelson, *Shotgun Willie* (LP), Atlantic Records, 1973, SD 7262.

Willie Nelson and Jerry Wexler, Encyclopedia of Alabama, undated, accessed December 3, 2023, https://encyclopediaofalabama.org/media/willie-nelson-and-jerry-wexler/.

Rolling Stones, *Get Yer Ya-Ya's Out* (LP), Decca/London, 1970.

"History," MuscleShoalsSoundStudio.org, undated, accessed December 3, 2023, https://muscleshoalssoundstudio.org/pages/history.

Heymarkarms, "The Genius."

Travis D. Stimeling, "'Phases and Stages, Circles and Cycles': Willie Nelson and the Concept Album," Cambridge University Press, September 21, 2011, accessed December 3, 2023, https://www.cambridge.org/core/journals/popular-music/article/abs/phases-and-stages-circles-and-cycles-willie-nelson-and-the-concept-album/A3466AFDA7F780D6189904A702126943.

Patterson Hood, liner notes for Drive-By Truckers, *Welcome 2 Club XIII*, CD, 2022, ATO Records.

Chet Flippo, "Phases and Stages," *Rolling Stone*, March 14, 1974, accessed December 3, 2023, https://www.rollingstone.com/music/music-album-reviews/phases-and-stages-255419/.

Stephen Thomas Erlewine, "Phases and Stages," AllMusic.com, undated, accessed December 3, 2023, https://www.allmusic.com/album/phases-and-stages-mw0000266616.

"Happy 45th: Willie Nelson, Phases and Stages," Rhino.com, March 6, 2019, accessed December 3, 2023, https://www.rhino.com/article/happy-45th-willie-nelson-phases-and-stages.

Chapter Five

Denisoff, *Waylon*, viii, 4, 12–14, 16, 28, 30–31, 83–84, 95, 108, 120, 131, 133, 135, 146–147, 150, 153, 157, 159, 162, 168–169, 180, 182, 184–185, 187, 190, 202, 208–210, 212, 221, 233, 210–211, 229, 244, 248–249, 295.

Cunniff, *Waylon Jennings*, 53–55, 62, 73–76, 81, 92–93, 98, 105, 110, 121, 127, 145, 180.

"The Songs of Waylon Jennings," EasyReaderNews.com, September 10, 2022, accessed November 25, 2022, https://easyreadernews.com/the-songs-of-waylon-jennings/.

Flippo, "Waylon Jennings."

Brian Boone, "The Tragic Real-Life Story of Waylon Jennings," *Grunge*, May 1, 2020, accessed December 3, 2023, https://www.grunge.com/206482/the-tragic-real-life-story-of-waylon-jennings/.

Jessi Colter with David Ritz, *An Outlaw and a Lady: A Memoir of Music, Life with Waylon, and the Faith That Brought Me Home* (Nashville: Thomas Nelson, 2017), 101–103, 120, 128, 136–138, 141, 170.

Jennings with Kaye, *Waylon*, 47, 66, 87, 89, 92, 109, 110, 147, 151, 153–155, 157–161, 163–167, 170–171, 174–175, 179–181, 188–189, 196–198, 222, 274, 326.
Giller, "Johnny Cash," YouTube.
"Johnny Cash and Waylon Jennings Once Hilariously Discussed Being Roommates on 'Late Show with David Letterman,'" Outsider.com, March 12, 2021, accessed December 3, 2023, https://www.outsider.com/entertainment/music/johnny-cash-waylon-jennings-hilariously-discussed-roommates-late-show-david-letterman/.
biggestkkfan, "The Highwaymen," YouTube, https://www.youtube.com/watch?v=wbxFy5DB6Rc&t=193s.
Cash with Carr, *Cash*, 167–168.
Grant with Zar, *I Was There*, 142.
Milward, *Americanaland*, 98, 168.
Norman, "Johnny Cash."
Dayton, *Beaumonster*, 29, 63, 74.
Tyler Mahan Coe, "Cocaine and Rhinestones: Billy Sherill's Nashville Sound," *Cocaine and Rhinestones* (podcast), December 7, 2021, https://cocaineandrhinestones.com/billy-sherrill.
"Waylon Jennings and the Cocaine Bear (Country History X)," SavingCountryMusic.com, May 11, 2021, accessed December 3, 2023, https://www.savingcountrymusic.com/waylon-jennings-and-the-cocaine-bear-country-history-x/.
Matty Wishnow, "Waylon Jennings: 'A Man Called Hoss,'" PastPri.me, undated, accessed December 3, 2023, https://www.pastpri.me/home/waylon-jennings-a-man-called-hoss.
T. Jennings, *Waylon*, 24, 82, 84–85, 89, 108–109.
Lomax, *Nashville*, 100, 123.
Grant Jackson, *1973*, 129, 133–135.
Spong, "That '70s."
Scott Feinberg, "'Awards Chatter' Podcast: 'Sopranos' Creator David Chase Finally Reveals What Happened to Tony (Exclusive)," *Hollywood Reporter*, November 2, 2021, accessed December 3, 2023, https://www.hollywoodreporter.com/feature/the-sopranos-david-chase-tony-ending-the-many-saints-of-newark-1235040185/.
Rich Kienzle, liner notes, Waylon Jennings, *Nashville Rebel* (CD), Legacy Recordings, 2006, 30, 39, 48, 66.
Duncan and Burns, *Country Music*, 359, 382–386.
Hume, *You're So Cold*, 12, 196.
Allison, Elkins, and Olivarez, *Hidden History*, 56.
Flippo, "Waylon Jennings Gets."
Weatherby, "The Outlaw."
Bob Lee, Crickets interview in Tucson, AZ, November 9, 1979, digital file provided by Gary Clevenger.
Sanneh, *Majory Labels*, 170.

Coe, "Cocaine."

Guralnick, 227, 229.

"CMT—100 Greatest Country Songs," undated, accessed January 6, 2022, https://cs.uwaterloo.ca/~dtompkin/music/list/Best7.html.

"Grammy Awards 1967," AwardsandShows.com, undated, accessed January 6, 2022, https://www.awardsandshows.com/features/grammy-awards-1967-242.html.

Whitburn, *The Billboard*, 162.

Joseph Carr and Alan Munde, *Prairie Nights to Neon Lights: The Story of Country Music in West Texas* (Texas Tech University Press, 1997), 156.

"10 Badass Waylon Jennings Moments," SavingCountryMusic.com, December 7, 2013, accessed December 3, 2023, https://www.savingcountrymusic.com/10-badass-waylon-jennings-moments/.

LeRoy Ashby, *With Amusement for All: A History of American Popular Culture Since 1830* (University Press of Kentucky, 2006), 418, 473.

Hurd, *Kris Kristofferson*, 88.

Nelson with McMurtry, *The Facts of Life*, 100, 102.

"The Time," SavingCountryMusic.com.

Chapman, *They Came to Nashville*, 11.

fullcyrkle, "Waylon Jennings," Ebay.com, auction listing, accessed July 31, 2022, https://www.ebay.com/sch/i.html?_fss=1&_saslop=1&_sasl=fullcyrkle&LH_SpecificSeller=1.

Patoski, *Willie Nelson*, 54, 185.

Nelson with Ritz, *It's a Long Story*, 171.

Nelson with Shrake, *Willie*, 158.

Nelson with Pipkin, *The Tao of Willie*, 187.

Hilburn, *Johnny Cash*, 307.

Waylon Jennings interview, in *The Highwaymen—Live* (DVD), special features.

Billy Joe Shaver, quoted in Michael Corcoran, "Billy Joe Shaver Wudn't Born No Yesterday," Michael Corcoran's Overserved, August 16, 2022, accessed December 3, 2023, https://michaelcorcoran.substack.com/p/billy-joe-shaver-wudnt-born-no-yesterday.

Billy Joe Shaver and Brad Reagan, *Honky Tonk Hero* (Austin: University of Texas Press, 2005), 34–35.

Addie Moore, "'Honky Tonk Heroes': Waylon Jennings' Billy Joe Shaver–Penned Outlaw Anthem," *Wide Open Country*, February 12, 2022, accessed December 3, 2023, https://www.wideopencountry.com/honky-tonk-heroes/.

Lost Highway: Beyond Nashville, BBC Films, February 23, 2003, directed by Ben Southwell, https://www.imdb.com/title/tt5927346/.

Streissguth, *Outlaw*, 143.

William Yardley, "Neil Reshen, 75, Dies; Manager Won 'Outlaw' Singers' Freedom," *New York Times*, December 15, 2014, A17.

Bruce Feiler, *Dreaming Out Loud: Garth Brooks, Wynona Judd and the Changing Face of Nashville* (New York: Avon Books, 1998), 172–173.

Bill Friskics-Warren, "Tompall Glaser, Country Artist in Outlaw Movement, Dies at 79," *New York Times*, August 17, 2013, B6.

Daley, *Nashville's Unwritten Rules*, 142.

Waylon Jennings, *The Essential Waylon Jennings* (CD), Legacy Recordings, 2008.

"Waylon Jennings Chart History (Hot Country Songs)," Billboard.com, undated, accessed December 3, 2023, https://www.billboard.com/artist/waylon-jennings/.

"Joe Galante Biography," PBS.org, undated, accessed December 3, 2023, https://www.pbs.org/kenburns/country-music/joe-galante-biography.

Joe Galante, personal communication, June 1, 2022.

Waylon Jennings—Live from Austin TX '84 (CD/DVD), New West Records, 2008, NW6154.

Chapter Six

Denisoff, *Waylon*, 12, 198, 226, 228, 280–281, 424.

Bradley "Budrock" Prewitt, quoted in Nelson with Shrake, *Willie*, 290.

John Sebastian, personal interview, July 4, 2022.

Allison, Elkins, and Olivarez, *Hidden History*, 98–99.

Jennings with Kaye, *Waylon*, 184, 187, 213–215, 222–223, 229, 234, 257.

Grant Jackson, *1973*, 136–137.

Waylon Jennings, *This Time*, Buddha Records (CD), expanded edition, 1999, tracks 11–15.

Waylon Jennings, *Waylon Live*, Sony Legacy (CD), 2003 deluxe expanded edition, disc one, track 14.

"10 Badass," SavingCountryMusic.com.

Fishell, "Crazy."

Malone, *Country Music*, 397–398.

Nelson with Ritz, *It's a Long Story*, 208, 241, 243–245, 262, 265–267, 355–356.

Nelson with Shrake, *Willie*, 67, 103, 178, 186, 200, 215, 225, 227, 249, 251, 269, 285, 288–289, 321.

Nelson and Nelson with Ritz, *Me and Sister Bobbie*, 219–220, 224–226.

Connie Nelson, quoted in Ingrid Croce, "The Buzz: One Degree of Separation with Willie Nelson's Wife," April 15, 2018, accessed December 4, 2023, https://vanguardculture.com/the-buzz-an-interview-with-willie-nelsons-wife-connie-nelson/.

Dayton, *Beaumonster*, 84.

"Audio Dallas Recording Studio," AudioDallas.com, undated, accessed December 4, 2023, https://audiodallas.com/.

Patoski, *Willie Nelson*, 60, 144, 183–184, 221, 256, 293, 297–298, 300, 321, 336, 338–339.

Nelson with Pipkin, *The Tao of Willie*, 24, 71, 99, 133, 135–136.

"Bruce Lundvall," IPL.org, undated, accessed December 4, 2023, https://www.ipl.org/essay/Born-To-Run-Analysis-FC9QYXVVG.

Yardley, "Neil Reshen."

Duncan and Burns, *Country Music*, 398, 407.

Joe Nick Patoski, "'Red Headed Stranger'—Willie Nelson (1975)," Library of Congress, 2009, accessed December 4, 2023, https://www.loc.gov/static/programs/national-recording-preservation-board/documents/Willie-RRHS.pdf.

Daley, *Nashville's Unwritten Rules*, 154–155, 292.

Kevin Moran, personal communication, February 14, 2023.

Chapman, *They Came to Nashville*, 228, 231.

Chet Flippo, "Matthew, Mark, Luke and Willie," *Texas Monthly*, September 1975, 30.

Casey Young, "Willie Nelson & Merle Haggard Went Through 52 Cases of Beer Backstage at a Festival in 1980," Whiskey Riff, August 27, 2023, accessed December 4, 2023, https://www.whiskeyriff.com/2023/08/27/willie-nelson-merle-haggard-went-through-52-cases-of-beer-backstage-at-a-festival-in-1980/.

Doyle, "All Roads."

Patoski, "Watching Willie's."

Cunniff, *Waylon Jennings*, 110, 129, 214.

Peter Blackstock, "Paul English, Longtime Willie Nelson Drummer, Dies," *Austin-American Statesman*, February 12, 2020, accessed December 4, 2023, https://www.statesman.com/story/entertainment/music/2020/02/12/paul-english-longtime-willie-nelson-drummer-dies/1720547007/.

Rachel Stone, "Willie Nelson's Best Friend, Paul English, Led a Quiet Family Life in Dallas," *Advocate-Lake Highlands*, September 23, 2021, accessed December 4, 2023, https://lakehighlands.advocatemag.com/2021/09/23/paul-english-me-and-grandpa-paul/.

Meagan Flynn, "Paul English, Willie Nelson's Best Friend, Drummer and Formidable Enforcer, Dies at 87," *Washington Post*, February 13, 2020, accessed December 4, 2023, https://www.washingtonpost.com/nation/2020/02/13/english-willie-died/.

Steve Loftin, "Bowtie Beauties—Procars on Chevy Chassis," Friends of the Professional Car Society, discussion forum, November 4, 2011, accessed December 4, 2023, https://professionalcarsociety.org/threads/bowtie-beauties-procars-on-chevy-chassis.3744/page-3.

René Zimmermann, Chevrolet Impala 1959 Stageway Limousine Willie Nelson—Zu vermieten, YouTube Video, March 2, 2014, accessed December 4, 2023, https://www.youtube.com/watch?v=TbZ0Zmnn53M.

Jacob H. Wolf, "Willie Nelson Gets Jailhouse Jumpin'," UPI.com, May 21, 1981, accessed December 4, 2023, https://www.upi.com/Archives/1981/05/21/Willie-Nelson-gets-jailhouse-jumpin/3263359265600/.

James Montgomery, "5 Amazing (and Possibly Apocryphal) Willie Nelson Stories," *Rolling Stone*, August 13, 2014, accessed December 4, 2023, https://www.rollingstone.com/music/music-country/5-amazing-and-possibly-apocryphal-willie-nelson-stories-236189/.

Milward, *Americanaland*, 170, 178–179.

Spong and Hall, "Sister Bobbie."

Booker T. Jones, interviewed in *This Is Pop: When Country Goes Pop*, Netflix, April 3, 2021, directed by Simon Ennis, https://www.imdb.com/title/tt14180666/.

Booker T. Jones, *Time Is Tight* (New York: Hachette, 2022), 232–235.

Robert Wilonsky, "Full Nelson," *Houston Press*, June 29, 1995, accessed December 4, 2023, https://www.houstonpress.com/music/full-nelson-6572165.

Ariel Swartley, "Stardust," *Rolling Stone,* June 29, 1978, accessed April 12, 2021, accessed December 4, 2023, https://www.rollingstone.com/music/music-country/stardust-94365/.

Robert Kemnitz, "Music," *Orange Coast* 4, no. 8 (August 1978): 67, accessed December 4, 2023, https://books.google.com/books?id=OV0EAAAAMBAJ&lpg=PA67&dq=%22stardust%22%20willie&pg=PA67#v=onepage&q=%22stardust%22%20willie&f=false.

Waylon Jennings, *Live from Austin, TX*, New West, track 10, 1989, 2006 (CD/DVD).

Weatherby, "The Outlaw."

Streissguth, *Outlaw*, 189–190, 223.

Colter with Ritz, *An Outlaw and a Lady*, 158–159.

Sharon Vaughn, phone interview, July 18, 2022.

Waylon Jennings, *US Festival 1983*, DVD, Shout! Factory, 2012.

Lost Highway: The Story of Country Music, BBC documentary, Part Three/"Beyond Nashville," 2003, interview with Chet Flippo.

Miller, *Kris Kristofferson*, 151.

Johnny Cash, quoted in Guralnick, *Johnny Cash*, 38.

T. Jennings, *Waylon*, 137.

Stephen Thomas Erlewine, "Waylon & Willie," AllMusic.com, undated, accessed December 4, 2023, https://www.allmusic.com/album/r575479.

Chapter Seven

"The Rhodes Scholar Who Is Reshaping Rock," *Detroit Free Press*, January 5, 1972, 16, accessed October 19, 2022, https://www.newspapers.com/newspage/99098421/.

Dan Jenkins, "Roll 1, Take 2: Semi-Tough," *Sports Illustrated*, November 7, 1977, accessed December 3, 2023, https://vault.si.com/vault/1977/11/07/roll-1-take-2-semitough.

John Buck Wilkin, phone interview, July 10, 2022.

Kris Kristofferson, quoted in Patoski, *Willie Nelson*, 210.

Coolidge, *Delta Lady*, 156, 169, 171, 181–182, 184–186.

Bob Zmuda and Lynn Margulies, *Andy Kaufman: The Truth, Finally* (Dallas: BenBella Books, 2014), 89, 92.

Cameron Crowe, "The Kristoffersons Make It," *Rolling Stone*, February 23, 1978, accessed December 3, 2023, https://www.rollingstone.com/music/music-news/the-kristoffersons-make-it-35828/.

Miller, *Kris Kristofferson*, 101, 105–106, 145, 156, 159, 163.

John Patterson, "I Was Killing Myself," *The Guardian*, March 4, 2008, accessed October 9, 2021, https://www.theguardian.com/music/2008/mar/04/popandrock.folk.

Roger Ebert, "A Star Is Born," RogerEbert.com, December 24, 1976, accessed December 3, 2023, https://www.rogerebert.com/reviews/a-star-is-born-1976.

"One Day at a Time by Lena Martell," Offical UK Charts Company / OfficialCharts.com, undated, accessed December 3, 2023, https://www.officialcharts.com/songs/lena-martell-one-day-at-a-time/.

Hume, *You're So Cold*, 198.

Allison, Elkins, and Olivarez, *Hidden History*, 80.

Light, *Johnny Cash*, 86, 105–106, 127, 147, 168.

Johnny Cash, quoted in Guralnick, *Johnny Cash*, 19, 48, 110.

Giller, "Johnny Cash," YouTube.

A. J. Samuels, "The Good, the Bad, and the Real Johnny Cash," *Culture Trip*, December 2, 2016, accessed December 3, 2023, https://theculturetrip.com/north-america/usa/arkansas/articles/the-good-the-bad-and-the-real-johnny-cash/.

Carter Cash, *The House of Cash*, 21, 60, 142–143.

Cash with Carr, *Cash*, 37–43, 123, 204–206, 211, 219, 233.

Norman, "Johnny Cash."

"'Crash' Classic Kept Faron Young at Art . . ." The Free Library, 2006, accessed December 3, 2023, https://www.thefreelibrary.com/%27CRASH%27+CLASSIC+KEPT+FARON+YOUNG+AT+ART..-a0145740964.

Stewart Foley, *Citizen Cash*, 154, 231, 249.

Casey Cep, "Johnny Cash's Gospel," *New Yorker*, February 9, 2020, accessed December 3, 2023, https://www.newyorker.com/books/page-turner/johnny-cashs-gospel.

Hilburn, *Johnny Cash*, 265, 384, 400, 435, 442–443, 459, 465, 513, 535–536.

Jack Whatley, "When Johnny Cash Met President Nixon and Didn't Hold Back: 'I Got a Few of My Own I Can Play for You,'" *Far Out*, June 20, 2020, accessed December 3, 2023, https://faroutmagazine.co.uk/johnny-cash-richard-nixon-man-in-black-1972/.

"'Truth'—the Story Behind the Johnny Cash Song Inspired by Muhammad Ali," SavingCountryMusic.com, June 4, 2016, accessed December 3, 2023, https://www.savingcountrymusic.com/truth-the-story-behind-the-johnny-cash-song-inspired-by-muhammad-ali/.

Duncan and Burns, *Country Music*, 261–262, 345, 349–350, 443, 445.

Tatiana Cirisano, "Johnny Cash's Family Condemns White Supremacist: Read Cash's 1964 Letter to Radio Stations," *Billboard*, August 18, 2017, accessed December 3, 2023, https://www.billboard.com/music/country/johnny-cash-letter-racist-radio-stations-family-condemns-white-supremacist-7934004/.

Tina Benitez-Eves, "Behind the Song Lyrics: 'Ragged Old Flag' by Johnny Cash," *American Songwriter*, February 3, 2022, accessed December 3, 2023, https://americansongwriter.com/ragged-old-flag-johnny-cash-behind-song-lyrics/.

Johnny Cash, *Man in Black* (Grand Rapids: Zondervan, 1975), 203–205, 209, 211, 213–215.

Milward, *Americanaland*, 50, 182–183.

"Gospel Road: A Story of Jesus," JohnnyCash.com, March 31, 1973, accessed December 3, 2023, https://www.johnnycash.com/film/gospel-road-a-story-of-jesus/.

Lesli White, "The Incredible Faith of Johnny Cash," BeliefNet.com, undated, accessed December 3, 2023, https://www.beliefnet.com/entertainment/celebrities/the-incredible-faith-of-johnny-cash.aspx.

Streissguth, *Johnny Cash*, 66–67, 91, 139.

Peter Gilstrap, "Johnny Cash and the Ballad of Glen Sherley," KCRW.com, May 3, 2018, accessed December 4, 2023, https://www.kcrw.com/music/articles/johnny-cash-and-the-ballad-of-glen-sherley.

Grant with Zar, *I Was There*, 154.

Lily Murphy, "Glen Sherley: When Johnny Cash Met the Man Inside Folsom Prison," FluxMagazine.com, undated, accessed December 4, 2023, https://www.fluxmagazine.com/glen-sherley-johnny-cash/.

C. Eric Banister, *Johnny Cash FAQ* (Rowman & Littlefield, 2014), accessed December 4, 2023, https://www.google.com/books/edition/Johnny_Cash_FAQ/-NCGDwAAQBAJ?hl=en&gbpv=1&dq=Glen+Sherley&pg=PT170&printsec=frontcover.

Cuevas and Adami, "Remembering Glen."

Skanse, "Johnny Cash."

"Johnny Cash Chart History," Billboard.com, undated, accessed December 4, 2023, https://www.billboard.com/artist/johnny-cash/.

"Johnny Cash, Arkansas Primary Source Sets," University of Arkansas/UAL, UALExhibits.org, dead link, https://ualrexhibits.org/primarysources/primary-source-set/johnny-cash/; see also: https://ualrexhibits.org/primarysources/primary-source-set/johnny-cash/.

McGasko, "Johnny Cash."

"17 of the Best and Most Memorable Johnny Cash Gospel Songs," Country Thang Daily, November 9, 2023, accessed December 4, 2023, https://www.countrythangdaily.com/johnny-cash-gospel-albums/.

Stephen Thomas Erlewine, *The Rambler*, AllMusic.com, undated, accessed December 4, 2023, https://www.allmusic.com/album/the-rambler-mw0000863670.

Julie Chadwick, *The Man Who Carried Cash: Saul Holiff, Johnny Cash and the Making of an American Icon* (Dundurn, 2017), 308–309.

Lomax, *Nashville*, 118, 124.

Frederic Dannen, *Hit Men: Power Brokers and Fast Money Inside the Music Business* (New York: Vintage Books, 1991), 4–27.

"This Day in History: 1986, Columbia Records Drops Country Legend Johnny Cash After 26 Years," History Channel / History.com, November 16, 2009, accessed December 4, 2023, https://www.history.com/this-day-in-history/columbia-records-drops-country-legend-johnny-cash-after-26-years.

Dayton, *Beaumonster*, 73.

Peter Lewry, "Back in Black," *Record Collector* 333, October 5, 2007, accessed January 20, 2022, https://recordcollectormag.com/articles/back-in-black.

Merle Haggard, quoted in Wes Langeler, "Merle Haggard Told a Record Exec He Was the "Dumbest Son of a B*tch" He Ever Met for Dropping Johnny Cash," Whiskey Riff, October 29, 2022, accessed December 4, 2023, https://www.whiskeyriff.com/2022/10/29/merle-haggard-told-a-record-exec-he-was-the-dumbest-son-of-a-btch-he-ever-met-for-dropping-johnny-cash/.

Sterling Whitaker, "Remember When Columbia Records Dropped Johnny Cash and Stunned Nashville?," TasteOfCountry.com, July 18, 2020, accessed December 4, 2023, https://tasteofcountry.com/columbia-records-dropped-johnny-cash/.

Ashley Cleveland, quoted in Chapman, *They Came to Nashville*, 186.

"Rosanne Cash, Chart History," Billboard.com, undated, accessed December 4, 2023, https://www.billboard.com/artist/rosanne-cash/.

Rosanne Cash, *King's Record Shop*, liner notes (back cover), Sony BMG Music Entertainment (CD), 2005.

Chapter Eight

Weatherby, "The Outlaw."

Andrew Dansby, "Waylon Jennings Dead at Sixty-Four," *Rolling Stone*, February 14, 2002, accessed December 4, 2023, https://www.rollingstone.com/music/music-news/waylon-jennings-dead-at-sixty-four-201572/.

Jennings with Kaye, *Waylon*, 225, 232, 236, 238–239, 245–246, 249–251, 253–255, 257, 259, 274, 276, 291, 294, 301–302.

Nelson with Shrake, *Willie*, 189, 258–259, 288–289.

Miranda Raye, "The Night Waylon Jennings Frantically Flushed Pills & Cocaine but the DEA Arrested Him Anyway," CountryRebel.com, accessed December 4, 2023, https://countryrebel.com/blogs/videos/the-night-waylon-jennings-frantically-flushed-pills-cocaine-but-the-dea-arrested-him-anyway/.

"Cocaine Bust: How Richie Albright Saved Waylon Jennings from Prison," SavingCountryMusic.com, February 11, 2021, accessed December 4, 2023, https://www.savingcountrymusic.com/cocaine-bust-how-richie-albright-saved-waylon-jennings-from-prison/.

Colter with Ritz, *An Outlaw and a Lady*, 142, 155, 161, 165–168, 178–179, 209–213, 219, 229–230.

Milward, *Americanaland*, 170.

Joe A. Shaw, personal communication, July 14, 2022.

Bill Conrad, "Waylon Jennings: Sex, Drugs & Rockabilly–Part 6/The End," *No Depression*, July 17, 2012, accessed December 4, 2023, https://www.nodepression.com/waylon-jennings-sex-drugs-rockabilly-part-6-the-end/.

Denisoff, *Waylon*, 270–271, 285, 288, 292, 299.

T. Jennings, *Waylon*, xx, 168, 187.

Cunniff, *Waylon Jennings*, 161, 167, 203, 223.

"Survival Skills," *Men's Journal*.

Jeremy Burchard, "5 True Stories That Capture Who Waylon Jennings Was as a Person," WideOpenCountry.com, February 13, 2017, accessed December 4, 2023, https://www.wideopencountry.com/5-true-stories-capture-waylon-jennings/.

"Old Friend, Waylon Jennings," *Song Meanings*, undated, accessed December 5, 2021, https://songmeanings.com/songs/view/3530822107858818568/.

Waylon Jennings, "A Long Time Ago," *I've Always Been Crazy*, 1978, RCA, LP, track 4.

"10 Badass," SavingCountryMusic.com.

Thomas, "The (Almost)."

Coolidge, *Delta Lady*, 18, 197–200.

Chris Hillman, *Time Between: My Life as a Byrd, Burrito Brother, and Beyond* (Bar None Music, 2020), 185.

Geoff Lane, quoted in Kylo-Patrick R. Hart, *Mediated Deviance and Social Otherness: Interrogating Influential Representations* (Cambridge Scholars Publishing, 2007), 183.

Ken Emerson, "Country Music-Confusion in Profusion," *New York Times*, November 18, 1979, D24, accessed December 4, 2023, https://www.nytimes.com/1979/11/18/archives/country-musicconfusion-in-profusion-country-music.html.

Emmalainen, "Waylon Jennings—Buddy Holly Medley—Live—1980," YouTube Video, Red Rocks Amphitheater, Denver, CO, 1980, May 3, 2016, accessed December 22, 2021, https://www.youtube.com/watch?v=Yb8rup5J5Cc.

Bob Dylan Center, excerpt from Bob Dylan interview with Edna Gunderson for *USA Today*, 1995, Facebook.com, October 25, 2022, accessed December 4, 2023, https://www.facebook.com/bobdylancenter/photos/a.851021611690096/5298106770314869.

Kris Kristofferson, personal interview, April 10, 2009.

Steven Bach, *Final Cut: Art, Money, and Ego in the Making of Heaven's Gate, the Film That Sank United Artists* (New York: Newmarket Press, 1999 edition), 6–8, 124, 184.

Miller, *Kris Kristofferson*, 111, 164, 166, 171–172, 186–187, 193, 203.

"Document—'Kris Kristofferson,' Transcript," Briscoe Center, June 19, 1977, accessed December 4, 2023, https://danratherjournalist.org/interviewer/whos-who/compilation-whos-who-interviews-transcripts/document-kris-kristofferson.

Hurd, 75, 77.

Zach Vasquez, "I've Never Seen…Heaven's Gate," *The Guardian*, June 10, 2020, accessed December 4, 2023, https://www.theguardian.com/film/2020/jun/10/ive-never-seen-heavens-gate.

Michael Bonner, "Michael Cimino Remembered + Kris Kristofferson on the Making of Heaven's Gate," *Uncut* (UK), July 4, 2016, accessed December 4, 2023, https://www.uncut.co.uk/features/michael-cimino-remembered-kris-kristofferson-making-heavens-gate-77697/.

“General Discussion: HEAVEN’S GATE Film & Score the Whole Cimino Thing,” *Film Score Monthly*, discussion forum, February 2, 2017, accessed December 4, 2023, https://www.filmscoremonthly.com/board/posts.cfm?threadID=118757&forumID=1&archive=0.

Bret Easton Ellis, “How Michael Cimino Destroyed Hollywood,” Unherd.com, March 19, 2022, accessed December 4, 2023, https://unherd.com/2022/03/how-hollywood-destroyed-michael-cimino/.

Stephen Prince, *A New Pot of Gold: Hollywood Under the Electronic Rainbow, 1980–1989* (University of California Press), 35.

Vincent Canby, “‘Heaven’s Gate,’ A Western by Cimino,” *New York Times*, November 19, 1980, C29.

Chris Barsanti, “Everybody Was Right About ‘Heaven’s Gate,’” *Pop Matters*, January 2, 2013, accessed December 4, 2023, https://www.popmatters.com/166341-everybody-was-right-about-heavens-gate-2495792035.html.

Bernard Drew, “‘Rollover’ Plays Dead,” *San Bernardino Sun*, December 12, 1981, B11, accessed December 4, 2023, https://cdnc.ucr.edu/?a=d&d=SBS19811212.1.29&srpos=6&e=—198-en—20—1—txt-txIN-%22Bernard+Drew%22+gannett-PAGE—1981—1.

“Kris Kristofferson (I),” IMDB.com, undated, accessed December 4, 2023, https://www.imdb.com/name/nm0001434/.

“Flashpoint,” BoxOfficeMojo.com, undated, accessed December 4, 2023, https://www.boxofficemojo.com/release/rl3226699265/weekend/.

Andrew P Street, “Kris Kristofferson Interview,” Andrew P Street Is the Internet, February 21, 2014, accessed December 4, 2023, https://andrewpstreet.com/2014/02/21/kris-kristofferson-interview/.

Susan King, “Still Trying to Shake Things Up,” *Los Angeles Times*, October 3, 1993, https://www.latimes.com/archives/la-xpm-1993-10-03-tv-41616-story.html.

“The Glaser Brothers—Chart History,” Billboard.com, undated, accessed December 4, 2023, https://www.billboard.com/artist/the-glaser-brothers/.

TV Guide 1787, June 27–July 3, 1987.

Norbert Putnam, personal interview, July 25, 2022.

Daley, *Nashville’s Unwritten Rules*, 184, 198, 210, 275, 277, 280, 309.

j crosby, “Kris Kristofferson: The AD Interview,” Aquarium Drunkard, November 4, 2009, accessed December 4, 2023, https://aquariumdrunkard.com/2009/11/04/kris-kristofferson-the-ad-interview/.

Sharon Hand, “‘The Winning Hand’ TV Special,” WorldRadioHistory.com, March 22, 1985, accessed December 4, 2023, https://www.worldradiohistory.com/hd2/IDX-Business/Music/Archive-RandR-IDX/IDX/80s/85/RR-1985-03-22-OCR-Page-0044.pdf.

biggestkkfan, “Love Is the Way—Kris Kristofferson with Johnny, Waylon and Willie (1983),” YouTube Video, December 17, 2016, accessed October 31, 2021, accessed December 4, 2023, https://www.youtube.com/watch?v=5731gWteJK8.

Roger Ebert, "Songwriter," RogerEbert.com, April 3, 1985, accessed December 4, 2023, https://www.rogerebert.com/reviews/songwriter-1985.

Nelson with Pipkin, *The Tao of Willie*, 50.

"Songwriter," *Rotten Tomatoes*, undated, accessed December 4, 2023, https://www.rottentomatoes.com/m/songwriter.

Chapter Nine

Alison Richter, "Harmonica Legend Mickey Raphael Reflects on the Highwaymen: 'It Was Like Mount Rushmore Onstage,'" MusicRadar.com, May 18, 2018, accessed December 4, 2023, https://www.musicradar.com/news/harmonica-legend-mickey-raphael-reflects-on-the-highwaymen-it-was-like-mount-rushmore-onstage.

Kahlil Gibran, "On Marriage," Poetry Foundation, undated, accessed December 4, 2023, https://www.poetryfoundation.org/poems/148576/on-marriage-5bff1692a81b0.

Noah Zender, "Finding Beauty in the Madness by Noah Zender," undated, SecondRightAnswer.com, accessed December 4, 2023, https://www.secondrightanswer.com/home/2021/12/8/finding-beauty-in-the-madness-by-noah-zender.

Henry C. Parke, "The Westerns of Willie Nelson," INSP.com, undated, accessed October 24, 2022, https://www.insp.com/blog/the-westerns-of-willie-nelson/.

Cunniff, *Waylon Jennings*, 146, 161, 167, 203, 223.

Denisoff, *Waylon*, 288, 299.

Joe Levy, "40 Years Later, Country Owes a Lot to 'Urban Cowboy': Here's Why," Billboard.com, August 13, 2020, accessed December 4, 2023, https://www.billboard.com/music/country/urban-cowboy-soundtrack-40th-anniversary-country-9432879/.

Melissa Brinks, "The Rise and Fall of the Urban Cowboy Craze," *Ranker*, June 1, 2019, https://www.ranker.com/list/the-urban-cowboy-moment-in-america/melissa-brinks.

Daley, *Nashville's Unwritten Rules*, 184, 198, 210, 275, 277, 280, 309.

Cash with Carr, *Cash*, 13, 117, 249, 273, 281, 304.

Duncan and Burns, *Country Music*, 442–443.

Escott, *The Grand Ole Opry*, 216.

Robert Palmer, "Nashville Sound: Country Music in Decline," *New York Times*, September 17, 1985, A1.

Lomax, *Nashville*, 68, 81.

Kurt Wolff, *Country Music: The Rough Guide*, ed. Orla Duane (London: Rough Guides Ltd., 2000), 360.

Colter with Ritz, *An Outlaw and a Lady*, 142, 155, 161, 165–168, 178–179, 209–213, 219, 229–230.

Giller, "Johnny Cash."

Nick Gostin, "Waylon Jennings' Son Says Dad Quit Drugs Cold Turkey: 'Betty Ford Didn't Get Me on It and She Can't Get Me off It,'" FoxNews.com, April 16, 2016, accessed December 4, 2023, https://www.foxnews.com/entertainment/waylon-jennings-son-says-dad-quit-drugs-cold-turkey-betty-ford-didnt-get-me-on-it-and-she-cant-get-me-off-it.

T. Jennings, *Waylon*, xx, 168, 187.

Weatherby, "The Outlaw."

Jennings with Kaye, *Waylon*, 274, 276, 291, 294, 301–302, 343–344, 346, 349–350, 354.

Duncan with Burns, *Country Music*, 442–443.

Patoski, *Willie Nelson*, 241, 325–326, 361, 392.

Arun Starkey, "Watch Johnny Cash Star in a Pair of Hilarious 1980s Commercials," FarOutMagazine.con, January 26, 2022, accessed December 4, 2023, https://faroutmagazine.co.uk/johnny-cash-hilarious-commercials/.

Hilburn, *Johnny Cash*, 471, 486–487, 503.

Eric Lensing, "Johnny Cash (1932–2003)," EncyclopediaOfArkansas.net, October 5, 2023, accessed December 4, 2023, https://encyclopediaofarkansas.net/entries/johnny-cash-9/.

"Johnny Cash Once Fought an Ostrich with a Stick: Story Behind the Bizarre Moment," *Outsider*, January 12, 2021, accessed December 4, 2023, https://www.outsider.com/entertainment/music/johnny-cash-once-fought-ostrich-with-stick-story-behind-bizarre-moment/.

Carter Cash, *The House of Cash*, 96–97, 100–101.

Light, *Johnny Cash*, 156.

"The Chicken in Black," JohnnyCash.com, January 1, 1984, accessed December 4, 2023, https://www.johnnycash.com/track/the-chicken-in-black/.

biggestkkfan, "The Highwaymen."

Grant with Zar, *I Was There*, 254.

Gilmore, *The Highwaymen—Live.*

"How the Highwaymen Became Family in Montreux," PBS.org / *American Masters*, Season 30, episode 7, undated, accessed December 4, 2023, https://www.pbs.org/wnet/americanmasters/the-highwaymen-how-the-highwaymen-became-family-in-montreux/7280/#.

Miller, *Kris Kristofferson*, 111, 166, 171–172, 178, 184, 187, 202–203.

Jack Hurst, "Willie Nelson's Manager Plays the Phone to Help the 'Destined,'" *Chicago Tribune*, December 15, 1985, accessed December 4, 2023, https://www.chicagotribune.com/news/ct-xpm-1985-12-15-8503260930-story.html.

Stephen Thomas Erlewine, "Tougher Than Leather," AllMusic.com, undated, accessed December 4, 2023, https://www.allmusic.com/album/tougher-than-leather-mw0000191185.

Nelson with Shrake, *Willie*, 122, 189, 258–259, 288–289.

Nelson with Pipkin, *The Tao of Willie*, 110–111, 159, 164.

Nelson with Ritz, *It's a Long Story*, 310–311, 320–321.

Montgomery, "5 Amazing."

"Car Hits Willie Nelson's Bus, Motorist Killed," UPI.com, April 1, 1990, accessed October 25, 2022, https://www.upi.com/Archives/1990/04/01/Car-hits-Willie-Nelsons-bus-motorist-killed/4321638946000/.

Marty Stuart, "Marty Stuart Brings the Song 'Highwayman' to Cash, Waylon, Wil…,'" Facebook.com, video, November 23, 2016, accessed December 4, 2023, https://www.facebook.com/watch/?ref=external&v=10154212718233163.

Miranda Raye, "Marty Stuart Tells the Story of How 'The Highwaymen' Saved Johnny Cash's Career," ClassicCountryMusic.com, September 27, 2017, accessed December 4, 2023, https://classiccountrymusic.com/marty-stuart-tells-the-story-of-how-the-highwaymen-saved-johnny-cashs-career/.

Amy Beeman, "The Untold Truth of the Highwaymen," Grunge.com, April 22, 2021, accessed December 4, 2023, https://www.grunge.com/389695/the-untold-truth-of-the-highwaymen/.

Joseph Hudak, "The Highwaymen," Willie Nelson and Friends Museum, May 20, 2016, accessed December 4, 2023, https://willienelsonmuseum.com/museum/highwaymen/.

David "Fergie" Ferguson, phone interview, September 23, 2022.

Chapman, *They Came to Nashville*, 235.

Dayton, *Beaumonster*, 232.

Philip Martin, "As Highwaymen, Four Legends Just Couldn't Match Solo Works," *Arkansas Democrat-Gazette*, June 19, 2016, accessed December 17, 2021, https://www.arkansasonline.com/news/2016/jun/19/as-highwaymen-four-legends-just-couldn-/.

Joseph Hudak, "The Highwaymen: The Fights and Friendship of Country's Great Supergroup," *Rolling Stone*, May 20, 2016, accessed December 4, 2023, https://www.rollingstone.com/music/music-country/the-highwaymen-the-fights-and-friendship-of-countrys-great-supergroup-184126/. *(Note, there are two different sources by Hudak with the same date; they are not the same text.)*

Nelson and Nelson with Ritz, *Me and Sister Bobbie*, 249.

Willie Nelson, *Willie Nelson's Letters to America* (Nashville: Harper Horizon, 2021), 160.

"The Highwaymen: 'The Mount Rushmore of Country Music,'" PBS.org, season 30, episode 7, undated, accessed December 4, 2023, https://www.pbs.org/wnet/americanmasters/highwaymen-highwaymen-mount-rushmore-country-music/7289/.

John "Bucky" Wilkin, personal communication, July 11, 2022.

Chapter Ten

Cash with Carr, *Cash*, 281, 289.

Bryan Di Salvatore, "Ornery," *New Yorker*, February 4, 1990, accessed December 4, 2023, https://www.newyorker.com/magazine/1990/02/12/ornery.

Ray Padgett, "Bob Dylan at the Ryman, 1969–2022, Flagging Down the Double E's," November 9, 2022, accessed December 4, 2023, https://dylanlive.substack.com/p/bob-dylan-at-the-ryman-1969-2022.

Casey Young, "Travis Tritt Shares Advice Johnny Cash Gave Him on Making It in the Music Industry: 'It's Called Mystique,'" Whiskey Riff, March 11, 2022, accessed December 4, 2023, https://www.whiskeyriff.com/2022/03/11/travis-tritt-shares-advice-johnny-cash-gave-him-on-making-it-in-the-music-industry-its-called-mystique/.

T. Jennings, *Waylon*, 30, 238.

Angela Stefano, "Reba McEntire Looks Back on That CMA Awards Red Dress," TheBoot.com, November 10, 2021, accessed December 4, 2023, https://theboot.com/reba-mcentire-cma-awards-red-dress/.

Monique Douty, "Reba McEntire's 1993 CMA Award Dress Caused a Fashion Stir: 'I Didn't Win an Award But I Did Make the Front Page,'" Cheatsheet.com, January 1, 2022, accessed December 4, 2023, https://www.cheatsheet.com/entertainment/reba-mcentire-1993-cma-award-dress-caused-fashion-stir-didnt-win-award-did-make-front-page.html/.

Scott Hinds, "20th Century Country Music," Facebook.com, discussion forum, June 7, 2023, accessed December 4, 2023, https://www.facebook.com/groups/918135608326763?multi_permalinks=2574184822721825&hoisted_section_header_type=recently_seen.

We Hate Pop Country, Facebook.com, October 7, 2022, accessed December 4, 2023, https://www.facebook.com/wehatepopcountry/posts/pfbid02PZ9NJ6zJe9uhiv4Rdq1SeP3tKyPpjGayDzKAFNagoqkx6svhpmZXf52ZFcSvhbdol.

Dayton, *Beaumonster*, 65, 98, 190.

Daley, *Nashville's Unwritten Rules*, 127–129, 136–137, 140–141, 166, 171, 173, 197, 220–221, 226, 251, 262, 282, 287, 293–294, 301.

Jack White, quoted in Stephen Deusner, "Only in Nashville," *The Nashvillian* 1, no. 1 (September 2022): 51.

Allison, Elkins, and Olivarez, *Hidden History*, 115–116, 120, 149.

Denisoff, *Waylon*, 276.

Markert, *Making Music*, 34–35, 55, 81, 159.

Mike Clute, phone interview, February 24, 2022.

CDX Nashville, "Sharon Vaughn Tells the Story of Walking into Waylon Jennings Office, Unannounced," YouTube Video, October 19, 2019, accessed December 4, 2023, https://www.youtube.com/watch?v=B2KG105NWZM.

Sharon Vaughn, phone interview, July 18, 2022.

Sanneh, *Major Labels*, 159, 176, 179, 184, 198.

Robert Deutsch, "Country Stars Who've Never Won a CMA Award," USAToday.com, November 5, 2013, accessed December 4, 2023, https://www.usatoday.com/picture-gallery/life/music/2012/10/29/country-stars-whove-never-won-a-cma-award/1667039/.

"Past Winners and Nominees," CMAAwards.com, undated, accessed December 4, 2023, https://cmaawards.com/past-winners-and-nominees/.

Escott, *The Grand Ole Opry*, 220–221.

Ethan Illers, Country Music Superstar Garth Brooks Breaks Entertainment Record for Nissan Stadium, WKRN.com, June 25, 2021, accessed December 4, 2023, https://www.wkrn.com/entertainment-news/country-music-superstar-garth-brooks-breaks-entertainment-record-for-nissan-stadium/.

"Year-End Charts—Top Country Albums," Billboard.com, 1994, accessed December 4, 2023, https://www.billboard.com/charts/year-end/1994/top-country-albums/.

"Garth Brooks Video Banned by 2 Channels," *Oklahoman,* accessed January 17, 2022, dead link, https://www.oklahoman.com/article/2355681/garth-brooks-video-banned-by-2-channels.

Richard Cromelin, "Hey, Garth, Let Your Sister Have a Turn," *L.A. Times,* July 14, 1994, accessed December 4, 2023, https://www.latimes.com/archives/la-xpm-1994-07-14-ca-15514-story.html.

Barry Mazor, "The Judds," Britannica.com, November 11, 2011, accessed December 4, 2023, https://www.britannica.com/topic/the-Judds.

Lomax, *Nashville,* 37.

"Clients," Sound Emporium Studios, undated, accessed December 4, 2023, https://www.soundemporiumstudios.com/clients/.

Jeff Tweedy, quoted in *Yankee Hotel Foxtrot (Super Deluxe Edition)*, CD, Disc 6, track 8, Nonesuch, 2022.

Jason Nickey, "89/93: An Anthology," Pitchfork.com, April 16, 2002, accessed December 4, 2023, https://pitchfork.com/reviews/albums/8345-8993-an-anthology/.

Old Roots, New Routes: The Cultural Politics of Alt.country Music, ed. Pamela Fox and Barbara Ching (Ann Arbor: University of Michigan Press, 2008), 192, 199, 207.

Jeff Tweedy, *Let's Go (So We Can Get Back)* (New York: Penguin Random House, 2018), 92, 96, 98, 101–102, 110, 122.

Jeff Tweedy, "Chit-Chat Check-In #18: A Clean Slate," email newsletter, December 31, 2021.

Milward, *Americanaland*, 213, 245.

Brian Baker, "10 Years Later, Uncle Tupelo Is Still Ahead of Its Time," Country Standard Time, March 2003, accessed December 4, 2023, https://www.countrystandardtime.com/d/article.asp?xid=829.

"Uncle Tupelo and Neil Young," Thrasher's Wheat, undated, accessed December 4, 2023, http://thrasherswheat.org/jammin/uncle_tupelo.htm.

Rick Danko, quoted in Allison Rapp, "The Piece of Advice Rick Danko Gave Jeff Tweedy," Ultimate Classic Rock, September 15, 2023, accessed November 13, 2023, https://ultimateclassicrock.com/jeff-tweedy-rick-danko-advice/.

Mark Deming, "Trace," AllMusic.com, undated, accessed December 4, 2023, https://www.allmusic.com/album/trace-mw0000176692.

Jeff Tweedy, email newsletters, September 7, 2023, and December 9, 2022.

Evan Schlansky, "Are Wilco Done with Nonesuch Records?," *No Depression*, undated, accessed December 4, 2023, https://americansongwriter.com/are-wilco-done-with-nonesuch-records/.

Beau Janke, personal communication, September 26, 2022.

"Wilco—Chart History," Billboard.com, undated, accessed December 4, 2023, https://www.billboard.com/artist/wilco/chart-history/.

Christopher F. Schiel, "Sebastapol," Pitchfork.com, December 3, 2001, accessed December 4, 2023, https://pitchfork.com/reviews/albums/2998-sebastapol/.

Eddie Fu, "Watch Wilco Play 'California Stars' with Jason Isbell, Rosanne Cash, and More at ACL Hall of Fame: Exclusive," *Consequence*, January 7, 2022, accessed December 4, 2023, https://consequence.net/2022/01/wilco-california-stars-acl-hall-of-fame-exclusive/.

"Uncle Tupelo—'No Depression' 30th Anniversary Released June 21st, 1990," *The Fat Angel Sings*, June 27, 2020, accessed December 5, 2023, https://thefatangelsings.com/tag/mike-heidorn/.

Brian L. Knight, "Music from America's Heartland: An Interview with Son Volt's Mike Heidorn," *Vermont Review*, undated, accessed December 5, 2023, https://vermontreview.tripod.com/Interviews/heidorn.htm.

Degen Pener, "EGOS & IDS; Who's Singing Now?," *New York Times*, November 14, 1993, section 9, p. 4, accessed December 5, 2023, https://www.nytimes.com/1993/11/14/style/egos-ids-who-s-singing-now.html.

L.A. Juergens, Facebook.com, Now Playing (private group), accessed December 5, 2023, https://www.facebook.com/groups/1476227915928068/user/100007008210319.

Neko Case, interviewed in *This Is Pop: When Country Goes Pop*, Netflix.

Johnny Cash, quoted in Light, *Johnny Cash*, 185.

Chapman, *They Came to Nashville*, 119, 184.

Wes Langeler, "Tyler Childers on Nashville: 'Why Move to the Largest Growing City in the Nation to Write Country Songs?,'" Whiskey Riff, October 7, 2020, accessed December 5, 2023, https://www.whiskeyriff.com/2020/10/07/tyler-childers-on-nashville-why-would-you-move-to-largest-growing-city-in-the-nation-to-write-country-songs/.

"Waylon Jennings," Billboard.com.

"Music Monday," HeadTale.com, June 13, 2016, accessed December 5, 2023, https://headtale.com/2016/06/13/music-monday-just-wait-til-i-finish-this-glassthen-sweet-little-ladyill-head-back-to-the-barand-you-can-kiss-my-ass/.

"Mindy McCready—Chart History," *Billboard*, undated, accessed December 5, 2023, https://www.billboard.com/artist/mindy-mccready/chart-history/.

Matt Bjorke, "The Top 30 Digital Country Singles: July 13, 2015," Roughstock.com, accessed December 5, 2023, https://roughstock.com/news/2015/07/36277-the-top-30-digital-country-singles-july-13-2015.

Joel Whitburn, *Hot Country Songs 1944 to 2008* (Record Research, Inc., 2008), 262.

J. R. Journey, "Single Review: Loretta Lynn—'The Pill,'" MyKindofCountry.com, April 19, 2010, accessed December 5, 2023, https://mykindofcountry.wordpress.com/2010/04/19/single-review-loretta-lynn-the-pill/.

Robert Windeler, "Loretta Lynn's 'Pill' Is Hard for Some Fans to Swallow," *People*, March 31, 1975, accessed December 5, 2023, https://people.com/archive/loretta-lynns-pill-is-hard-for-some-fans-to-swallow-vol-3-no-12/.

Carena Liptak, "Loretta Lynn's 'The Pill' May Have Gotten Banned, but She Had the Last Laugh," TheBoot.com, October 4, 2022, accessed December 5, 2023, https://theboot.com/loretta-lynn-the-pill-secret-history-of-country-music/.

Johnny Cash, quoted in Stewart Foley, *Citizen Cash*, 288.

Chet Flippo, "Nashville Skyline: Shut Up and Sing?," CMT.com, March 20, 2003, accessed December 5, 2023, http://www.cmt.com/news/1470672/nashville-skyline-shut-up-and-sing/.

"Remembering Kris Kristofferson and Toby Keith's Reportedly Legendary Argument on Willie Nelson's Birthday," Outsider.com, January 31, 2021, accessed December 5, 2023, https://outsider.com/news/country-music/remembering-kris-kristofferson-toby-keith-reportedly-legendary-argument-willie-nelsons-birthday/.

Kris Kristofferson, personal interview, April 10, 2009.

Kyle Anderson, "The Dixie Chicks' Nude EW Cover 10 Years Later: Emily Robison and Martie Maguire Reflect," EW.com, August 9, 2013, accessed December 5, 2023, https://ew.com/article/2013/08/09/dixie-chicks-nude-ew-cover-court-yard-hounds/.

Marisa R. Moss, "The Country Music Industry Is More Liberal Than It Lets On: Will More Start to Speak Up?," Billboard.com, June 5, 2018, accessed December 5, 2023, https://www.billboard.com/music/country/why-liberal-country-music-artists-executives-dont-speak-up-8458774/.

Paul Kingsbury, Michael McCall, and John W. Rumble, eds., *The Encyclopedia of Country Music, Second Edition* (Oxford: Oxford University Press, 2012), 592.

Weatherby, "The Outlaw."

Cunniff, *Waylon Jennings*, 155, 216.

Amy Young, "Shooter Jennings on Death, Politics, and the Family Business," *Phoenix New Times*, August 4, 2018, accessed December 5, 2023, https://www.phoenixnewtimes.com/music/country-musics-shooter-jennings-on-john-lennon-bob-dylan-and-nashville-vs-los-angeles-10665383.

Will Welch, "Meet Three Country Badasses Who Are Shaking Up the Nashville Establishment," GQ.com, January 7, 2016, accessed December 5, 2023, https://www.gq.com/story/meet-the-country-badasses-from-nashville.

"Shooter Jennings—Chart History," Billboard.com, undated, accessed December 5, 2023, https://www.billboard.com/artist/shooter-jennings/.

Author's personal observation, CBGB, New York, November 14, 2005.

Cole Haddon, "Music Straight Shooter," *San Antonio Current*, October 27, 2005, accessed December 5, 2023, https://www.sacurrent.com/sanantonio/music-straight-shooter/Content?oid=2274879.

Daniel Kohn, "Shooter Jennings: New Age Outlaw," *Spin*, September 30, 2021, accessed December 5, 2023, https://www.spin.com/featured/shooter-jennings-new-age-outlaw/.

Philip Trapp, "Tanya Tucker's Next Album Will Again Involve Brandi Carlile + Shooter Jennings," TasteofCountry.com, February 16, 2021, accessed December 5, 2023, https://tasteofcountry.com/tanya-tucker-next-album-brandi-carlile-shooter-jennings/.

Author's personal observation, Tanya Tucker and the Highwomen, Gorge Amphitheatre, Quincy, WA, June 11, 2023.

Jeffrey Brown, Alison Thoet, and Anne Azzi Davenport, "Grammy Nominee Brandi Carlile on Her Comeuppance and the Industry Barriers She Still Faces," PBS.org, December 17, 2021, accessed December 5, 2023, https://www.pbs.org/newshour/show/grammy-nominee-brandi-carlile-on-her-comeuppance-and-the-industry-barriers-she-still-faces.

Jonathan Bernstein, "Brandi Carlile: New Album 'I Forgive You' Is About Life 'Being F–king Hard,'" *Rolling Stone*, February 15, 2018, accessed December 5, 2023, https://www.rollingstone.com/music/music-country/brandi-carlile-new-album-i-forgive-you-is-about-life-being-f-king-hard-202472/.

Brandi Carlile, *Broken Horses: A Memoir* (New York: Crown, 2021), 35, 118–120, 221–225, 235, 251.

Gayle Thompson, "Brandi Carlile, Avett Brothers Duet on Country Classic on 'Letterman' [WATCH]," TheBoot.com, May 6, 2015, accessed December 5, 2023, https://theboot.com/brandi-carlile-avett-brothers-keep-on-the-sunny-side/.

Author's personal observation, 2022 Americana Music Awards, Ryman Auditorium, Nashville: September 14, 2022.

James McGuinn, "Album of the Week: Brandi Carlile, 'By the Way, I Forgive You,'" TheCurrent.org, February 12, 2018, accessed December 5, 2023, https://www.thecurrent.org/feature/2018/02/09/album-of-the-week-brandi-carlile-by-the-way-i-forgive-you.

Ann Powers, "Songs We Love: Brandi Carlile, 'The Joke,'" NPR.org, November 13, 2017, accessed December 5, 2023, https://www.npr.org/2017/11/13/563358018/songs-we-love-brandi-carlile-the-joke.

Jens Staff, personal communication, September 17, 2022.

By the Way I Forgive You marketing materials, Low Country Sound / Elektra Records, February 2018.

Chris Willman, "Mike Huckabee Resigns from Country Music Association Board as Nashville Firestorm Ignites," Variety.com, March 1, 2018, accessed December 5, 2023, https://variety.com/2018/music/news/mike-huckabee-resigns-country-music-foundation-nashville-controversy-1202714847/.

Katherine Turman, "Orville Peck on Horses, Masks, and Crying While Writing Music," *Vulture*, April 7, 2022, accessed December 5, 2023, https://www.vulture.com/2022/04/orville-peck-bronco-interview.html.

Marc Malkin, "Masked Singer Orville Peck on Being Openly Gay in Country Music: 'We've Always Been There,'" June 2, 2022, accessed November 22, 2022, https://variety.com/2022/music/news/orville-peck-country-music-gay-lgbtq-1235283119/.

Melissa Carper, personal interview, September 17, 2022.

Jeff Gage, "Tyler Childers, Rosanne Cash Sound Off at 2018 Americana Honors & Awards," *Rolling Stone*, September 13, 2018, accessed December 5, 2023, https://www.rollingstone.com/music/music-country/tyler-childers-rosanne-cash-sound-off-at-2018-americana-honors-awards-723621/.

Hudak, "The Highwaymen."

Gilmore, *The Highwaymen: Live*.

Chapter Eleven

Hank Williams Jr., quoted in Lomax, *Nashville*, 81. Also attributed to Hank Williams Sr. and Ray Charles.

Andy Langer, "The Muscle Shoals Sound (Featuring Jason Isbell)," *Esquire*, July 26, 2007, accessed November 16, 2022, https://www.esquire.com/entertainment/music/a3218/muscleshoals0807/.

Jason Isbell, quoted in Marissa R. Moss, "The Radical Empathy of Jason Isbell," *L.A. Times*, October 9, 2023, accessed November 13, 2023, https://www.latimes.com/entertainment-arts/music/story/2023-10-09/jason-isbell-grammys-weathervanes.

Jason Isbell and Amanda Shires, interviewed in *Jason Isbell: Running with Our Eyes Closed*, HBO Max, 2023, directed by Sam Jones.

"Jason Isbell Biography," Musictory.com, 2018, accessed December 5, 2023, http://www.musictory.com/music/Jason+Isbell/Biography.

Will Welch, "The GQ&A: Jason Isbell, the New King of Americana Music," GQ.com, January 7, 2016, accessed December 5, 2023, https://www.gq.com/story/jason-isbell-king-of-americana-music.

Jason Isbell, "Different Days," track 6, *Southeastern*, Southeastern Records, 2013 (CD/LP).

Patterson Hood, "Welcome to the Dirty South," liner notes for *The Complete Dirty South* by Drive-By Truckers. New West Records, 2004, 2023 (CD).

Steve Bells, "Jason Isbell Writes Songs to Sort Out His Baggage," TheMusic.au, July 17, 2015, accessed December 5, 2023, https://themusic.com.au/features/jason-isbell-steve-bell/ga2SlZSXlpk/17-07-15.

Dwight Garner, "Jason Isbell, Unloaded," *New York Times Magazine*, May 31, 2013, accessed December 5, 2023, https://www.nytimes.com/2013/06/02/magazine/jason-isbell-unloaded.html.

Jason Isbell and the 400 Unit, "Live at Red Rocks—Morrison, CO—8/1/2021," Bandcamp.com, April 26, 2022, mp3s, https://jasonisbell.bandcamp.com/album/live-at-red-rocks-morrison-co-8-1-2021.

Madeline Crone, "Pioneering Artist Jason Isbell Discusses the Evolving Role of His Guitar Throughout His Musical Journey," AmericanSongwriter.com, undated, accessed December 5, 2023, https://americansongwriter.com/pioneering-artist-jason-isbell-discusses-evolving-role-of-his-guitar-throughout-his-musical-journey/.

Elamin Abdelmahmoud, "Jason Isbell Is Tired of Country's Love Affair with White Nostalgia," BuzzFeedNews.com, December 16, 2021, accessed December 5, 2023, https://www.buzzfeednews.com/article/elaminabdelmahmoud/jason-isbell-ryman-country-music-mickey-guyton.

Jason Isbell, quoted in "Jim Beviglia, Behind the Song: 'Dress Blues' by Jason Isbell," AmericanSongwriter.com, accessed December 5, 2023, https://americansongwriter.com/dress-blues-jason-isbell-behind-the-song/.

Milward, *Americanaland*, 4, 234.

Jerrick Adams, "'Commiserating Is Underrated in Art: An Interview with Jason Isbell," PopMatters.com, June 11, 2013, accessed December 5, 2023, https://www.popmatters.com/172292-commiserating-is-underrated-in-art-an-interview-with-jason-isbell-2495750056.html.

Barbara Schultz, "Jason Isbell: Vocals Come First on 'Southeastern,'" MixOnline.com, May 1, 2013, accessed December 5, 2023, https://www.mixonline.com/recording/jason-isbell-vocals-come-first-southeastern-366412.

Lior Phillips, "'No Downside': Johnny Marr, Best Coast and Jason Isbell on How Sobriety Improves Music," *The Guardian*, June 2, 2020, accessed December 5, 2023, https://www.theguardian.com/music/2020/jun/02/no-downside-johnny-marr-best-coast-and-jason-isbell-on-how-sobriety-improves-music.

"2016 Grammy Awards: Complete List of Winners and Nominees," *L.A. Times*, December 7, 2015, accessed December 5, 2023, https://www.latimes.com/entertainment/music/posts/la-et-ms-grammys-2016-nominees-winners-list-story.html.

Nate Hertweck, "Jason Isbell and the 400 Unit Win Best Americana Album | 2018 Grammys," Grammy.com, January 29, 2018, accessed December 5, 2023, https://www.grammy.com/news/jason-isbell-and-400-unit-win-best-americana-album-2018-grammys-0.

Author's personal observation, Milk Carton Kids, Americana Music Awards 2022.

Markert, *Making Music*, 70, 81.

Derek Hoke, email interview, October 19, 2022.

Sanneh, *Major Labels*, 160, 182, 210, 214.

Steve Earle, quoted in Jonathan Bernstein, "Steve Earle Is Chasing Broadway Success—by Trying to Write a Mainstream Country Song," *Rolling Stone*, May 29, 2022, accessed December 5, 2023, https://www.rollingstone.com/music/music-country/steve-earle-broadway-jerry-jeff-walker-1355557/.

Paige Pfleger, "Black Musicians Question the Opry's Dedication to Anti-Racism After Morgan Wallen's Performance," WPLN.org, January 10, 2022, accessed December 5, 2023, https://wpln.org/post/black-musicians-question-the-oprys-dedication-to-anti-racism-after-morgan-wallens-performance/.

Joe Levy, "Inside the 'Old Town Road' Charts Decision," Billboard.com, September 19, 2019, accessed December 5, 2023, https://www.billboard.com/pro/inside-the-old-town-road-charts-decision/.

Jon Caramanica, "The Morgan Wallen Conundrum," *New York Times*, January 23, 2022, AR18.

Ben Sisario, "Morgan Wallen Tops Chart for a 10th Week," *New York Times*, March 23, 2021, C2.

"Year-End Charts Billboard 200 Albums," Billboard.com, undated, accessed December 5, 2023, https://www.billboard.com/charts/year-end/2021/top-billboard-200-albums/.

Elena Sheppard, "Morgan Wallen's Country Music Redemption Arc Is a Sad Sign of the Times," NBCNews.com, December 6, 2021, accessed December 5, 2023, https://www.nbcnews.com/think/opinion/morgan-wallen-s-country-music-redemption-arc-sad-sign-times-ncna1285479.

Olivia Roos, "Country Music's Reckoning: Black Women Forge Their Own Path in Whitewashed Industry," NBCNews.com, October 15, 2020, accessed December 5, 2023, https://www.nbcnews.com/news/nbcblk/country-music-s-reckoning-black-women-forge-their-own-path-n1243570.

Tressie McMillan Cottom, "The Black Vanguard in White Utopias," *Andscape*, December 31, 2021, accessed December 5, 2023, https://andscape.com/features/the-black-vanguard-in-white-utopias/.

Jon Freeman, "A Black Country Music Fan Didn't Feel Safe at Concerts. So She Started a Movement," *Rolling Stone*, February 17, 2022.

Ryan Smith, "Photo of Bud Light Booth with No Line at Morgan Wallen Concert Goes Viral," Newsweek.com, April 25, 2023, accessed December 5, 2023, https://www.newsweek.com/bud-light-photo-morgan-wallen-concert-viral-twitter-dylan-mulvaney-1796488.

Garrett Gravley, "Ahead of His Dallas Show, Jason Isbell Recalls Scaring Away UNT Students," Dallas Observer, April 26, 2023, accessed December 5, 2023, https://www.dallasobserver.com/music/jason-isbell-talks-about-scorsese-and-kid-rock-being-a-bad-shot-16442396.

Jason Isbell (@JasonIsbell), "And you sir are neither Sturgill nor Jennings," Twitter, July 21, 2023, 10:45pm, https://twitter.com/JasonIsbell/status/1682597601651179520.

Jessica Nicholson, "Jason Isbell, the Black Opry & More Condemn Morgan Wallen's Grand Ole Opry Performance," Billboard.com, January 10, 2022, accessed December 5, 2023, https://www.billboard.com/music/country/jason-isbell-slams-morgan-wallen-grand-ole-opry-performance-1235017092/.

Allison Russell (@outsidechild13), "So grateful for you and your advocacy, Holly. I feel heartbroken. I was so proud to debut @opry last May & overjoyed that @amythystkiah & @TheValerieJune also debuted in 2021—it felt like a long overdue shift toward greater inclusivity-beyond tokenism... this is such a backslide," Twitter, January 9, 2022, 9:02pm, https://twitter.com/outsidechild13/status/1480374494195859465.

Kevin Accettulla, "Grand Ole Opry Receives Backlash After 'Surprise' Morgan Wallen Appearance," WKRN.com, January 10, 2022, accessed December 5, 2023, https://www.wkrn.com/news/local-news/nashville/grand-ole-opry-receives-backlash-after-surprise-morgan-wallen-appearance/.

Chris DeVille, "Morgan Wallen's Grand Ole Opry Appearance Draws Criticism from Jason Isbell, Allison Russell, Joy Oladokun," Stereogum.com, January 10, 2022, accessed December 5, 2023, https://www.stereogum.com/2172387/morgan-wallen-grand-ole-opry-criticism/news/.

Rissi Palmer (@RissiPalmer), "Money and power is all this industry understands and respects. If you figure out how to make money and create power, guess who's knocking on your door? Black Wall streets were created AND destroyed for a reason, remember that," Twitter, January 10, 2022, 7:46am, https://twitter.com/RissiPalmer/status/1480536426781593600?s=20.

Rissi Palmer (@RissiPalmer), "I believe now is the time to watch and move. Watch how people are responding and reacting and move accordingly. Systems only work when we continue to participate in them. The moment we stop and divest, they lose their power..." Twitter, January 10, 2022, 7:32am, https://twitter.com/RissiPalmer/status/1480533091420708865.

"Tyler Childers, Jason Isbell Earn New Gold & Platinum Singles," SavingCountryMusic.com, February 20, 2022, accessed December 5, 2023, https://www.savingcountrymusic.com/tyler-childers-jason-isbell-earn-new-gold-platinum-singles/.

"Jason Isbell Donated $53,000 from Morgan Wallen Song Royalties," SavingCountryMusic.com, February 8, 2022, accessed December 5, 2023, https://www.savingcountrymusic.com/jason-isbell-donated-53000-from-morgan-wallen-song-royalties/.

Author's personal observation, Adia Victoria, UNO Lakefront Arena, New Orleans, LA, April 2, 2022.

Adia Victoria, personal interview, April 2, 2022.

Adia Victoria, Facebook.com, September 19, 2022, accessed December 5, 2023, https://www.facebook.com/adiavictoria/posts/pfbid0KpVccQZ4jMhuWZ4CKnwe1zJKFw8a7i5m8gp7HBPr7Nth7gbrSxWLnrMGoxJbJREkl.

Gwen Aviles, "Country Music Is Typically a White Space. Mickey Guyton Is Ready to Change It," NBC, July 25, 2020, accessed February 12, 2021, https://www.nbcnews.com/news/nbcblk/country-music-typically-white-space-mickey-guyton-ready-change-it-n1234821.

Thor Christensen, "Country Singer Mickey Guyton's 'Overnight Success' Was Years in the Making," *Dallas Morning News*, September 16, 2021, accessed December 5, 2023, https://www.dallasnews.com/arts-entertainment/music/2021/09/16/country-singer-mickey-guytons-overnight-success-was-years-in-the-making/.

Nancy Kruh, "Finding Her Voice, Mickey Guyton Stirs Hearts with 'Black Like Me': 'God Put It on My Heart,'" *People*, June 15, 2020, accessed December 23, 2021, https://people.com/country/mickey-guyton-reacts-black-like-me-single-response/.

Craig Shelburne, "With 'Black Like Me,' Mickey Guyton Makes Grammy History," *CMT*, November 4, 2020, accessed December 23, 2021, https://www.cmt.com/news/ef2s20/with-black-like-me-mickey-guyton-makes-grammy-history.

Tomás Mier, "Mickey Guyton Slams User for Calling Her Son the 'Ugliest' as Stars Rally Around: 'Shame on You,'" *People*, July 2, 2021, accessed December 5, 2023, https://people.com/parents/mickey-guyton-slams-racist-comment-about-son-stars-rally/.

Mickey Guyton (@MickeyGuyton), "When I read comments saying 'this is not who we are' I laugh because this is exactly who country music is. I've witnessed it for 10 gd years. You guys should just read some of the vile comments hurled at me on a daily basis. It's a cold hard truth to face but it is the truth," Twitter, February 3, 2021, 7:55am, https://twitter.com/MickeyGuyton/status/1356964476793180161.

Andrew R. Chow, "Mickey Guyton Is TIME's 2022 Breakthrough Artist of the Year," TIME.com, December 5, 2022, accessed December 5, 2023, https://time.com/6238732/mickey-guyton-breakthrough-artist-of-the-year-2022/.

Marcus K. Dowling, "2021 CMT Breakout Artist of the Year Honoree: Mickey Guyton," CMT.com, October 12, 2021, accessed December 5, 2023, http://www.cmt.com/news/1838253/2021-cmt-breakout-artist-of-the-year-honoree-mickey-guyton/.

Sebastian Posey, "Jimmie Allen Becomes Second Black Performer to Win CMA Awards New Artist of the Year," WKRN.com, November 10, 2021, accessed December 5, 2023, https://www.wkrn.com/news/cma-awards/jimmie-allen-becomes-second-black-performer-to-win-cma-awards-new-artist-of-the-year/.

Melinda Lorge, "'American Idol' Singer Goes to Hollywood After Morgan Wallen Cover [WATCH]," TasteofCountry.com, March 30, 2022, accessed December 5, 2023, https://tasteofcountry.com/american-idol-maurice-the-musician-morgan-wallen-whiskey-glasses/.

Alison Bonaguro, "Jason Isbell Shares His Sobering Truths," CMT, January 15, 2019, accessed December 5, 2023, https://www.cmt.com/news/9pt6tt/jason-isbell-shares-his-sobering-truths.

Author's personal observation, Jason Isbell and the 400 Unit, McFarland Park, Florence, AL, October 2, 2022.

Jason Isbell (@JasonIsbell), "Damnit Waylon I can't just take back the weed and the cocaine. It didn't come from WalMart. There's not a receipt," Twitter, July 1, 2023, 10:59am, dead link, https://twitter.com/JasonIsbell/status/1675172253607288832.

Kathie McCathie, personal communication, July 11, 2022.

Dayton, *Beaumonster*, 97–98, 101, 200–207, 232.

"Jason Isbell—Chart History," *Billboard*, undated, accessed December 5, 2023, https://www.billboard.com/artist/jason-isbell/chart-history/billboard-200.

Jonah Bayer, "Exit Interview: Jason Isbell on the Difference Between Being an Artist and Entertainer," *Spin*, December 20, 2021, accessed December 5, 2023, https://www.spin.com/2021/12/jason-isbell-georgia-blue-interview/.

Ryan Reichard, "Hear the Beautiful Ballad Chris Stapleton Wrote for Willie Nelson [Listen]," TasteofCountry.com, June 6, 2020, accessed December 5, 2023, https://tasteofcountry.com/willie-nelson-our-song-chris-stapleton/.

Chris Willman, "Willie Nelson Covers Everyone from Chris Stapleton to Charles Aznavour on 70th Album," *Variety*, February 21, 2020, accessed December 5, 2023, https://variety.com/2020/music/news/willie-nelson-release-70th-studio-album-april-1203510238/.

"Willie Nelson Releasing New LP 'A Beautiful Time' on 89th Birthday [WATCH]," *Rock Cellar Magazine*, February 10, 2022, accessed December 5, 2023, https://www.rockcellarmagazine.com/willie-nelson-a-beautiful-time-new-album-music-video-watch/.

Brett Martin, "Is Chris Stapleton the One Thing That America Can Agree On?," *GQ*, October 31, 2023, accessed December 5, 2023, https://www.gq.com/story/chris-stapleton-gq-hype.

Chris Stapleton, interviewed by Bobby Bones, *The Bobby Bones Show* (iHeart Radio FM, Nashville/syndicated), December 26, 2022.

Sharon Alfonsi, "'I'm Good at Being Me on Guitar': Chris Stapleton on His Life and Career," *CBS News / 60 Minutes*, January 16, 2022, accessed December 5, 2023, https://www.cbsnews.com/news/chris-stapleton-60-minutes-2022-01-16/.

Dacey Orr, "Dave Cobb: Building Southern Family One Record at a Time," *Paste*, February 9, 2016, accessed December 5, 2023, https://www.pastemagazine.com/music/dave-cobb-building-southern-family-one-record-at-a.

Author's personal observation, Chris Stapleton, Smoothie King Center, New Orleans, LA, October 22, 2022.

"Traveller—Chris Stapleton," ChrisStapleton.com, accessed December 5, 2023, https://www.chrisstapleton.com/song/traveller/.

Matthew Riley, "Inside the Recording Studio with Chris Stapleton and Producer Dave Cobb," *CBS News / 60 Minutes*, January 16, 2022, accessed December 5, 2023, https://www.cbsnews.com/news/chris-stapleton-dave-cobb-60-minutes-2022-01-16/.

Keith Caulfield, "Chris Stapleton Soars to No. 1 on Billboard 200 Albums Chart After CMAs," *Billboard*, November 9, 2015, accessed December 5, 2023, https://www.billboard.com/pro/chris-stapleton-soars-to-no-1-on-billboard-200-albums-chart/.

Caitlin White, "Country Songwriter Chris Stapleton Copes with Loss on Triumphant Solo Debut: Album Review," *Billboard*, May 12, 2015, accessed December 5, 2023, https://www.billboard.com/music/music-news/chris-stapleton-traveller-solo-debut-album-review-6561354/.

Rory Kaplan, personal communication, November 22, 2022.

"Decade-End Charts—Top Country Albums," *Billboard*, undated, accessed December 5, 2023, https://www.billboard.com/charts/decade-end/top-country-albums.

Tiffany Smithson Aaron, "2 Years After CMA Collaboration, Chris Stapleton & Justin Timberlake Reunite for 'Tennessee Whiskey' Duet," Country Rebel, September 24, 2017, accessed December 5, 2023, https://countryrebel.com/blogs/videos/2-years-after-cma-collaboration-chris-stapleton-justin-timberlake-reunite-for-tennessee-whiskey-duet/.

"Just Shut Up and Get Chris Stapleton's 'Traveller' Already," SavingCountryMusic.com, May 15, 2015, accessed December 5, 2023, https://www.savingcountrymusic.com/just-shut-up-and-get-chris-stapletons-traveller-already/.

Juli Thanki, "Jason Isbell Announces 4-Night Ryman Run," *Tennessean*, April 15, 2015, accessed November 13, 2023, https://www.tennessean.com/story/entertainment/music/2015/04/15/jason-isbell-announces-night-ryman-run/25841285/.

Jeff Clark, "Mickey Raphael Talks New Willie Album, Recording with Chris Stapleton," May 4, 2017, accessed December 5, 2023, https://www.sunherald.com/news/local/news-columns-blogs/by-the-way/article148621089.html.

Jonathan Bernstein, "Willie's Other Voice," *Oxford American* 104, Spring 2019, March 19, 2019, accessed December 5, 2023, https://main.oxfordamerican.org/magazine/item/1692-willies-other-voice.

Keith Caulfield, "Logic Scores His First No. 1 Album on Billboard 200 Chart with 'Everybody,'" *Billboard*, May 15, 2017, accessed December 5, 2023, https://www.billboard.com/pro/logic-everybody-album-billboard-200-no-1/.

Nelson with McMurtry, *The Facts of Life*, 47.

Vincent Harris, "Harmonica Player Mickey Raphael Talks Willie Nelson, His Career, and Set Lists," *Greenville Journal*, March 2, 2018, accessed December 5, 2023, https://greenvillejournal.com/arts-culture/harmonica-player-mickey-raphael-talks-willie-nelson-career-set-lists/.

Stephen Thomas Erlewine, "Weathervanes," *Pitchfork*, June 8, 2023, accessed December 5, 2023, https://pitchfork.com/reviews/albums/jason-isbell-and-the-400-unit-weathervanes/.

"Mickey Raphael on David Letterman Show, with Jason Isbell," StillIsStillMoving.com, April 27th, 2015, accessed December 5, 2023, https://stillisstillmoving.com/willienelson/mickey-raphael-on-david-letterman-show-with-jason-isbell/.

“Waylon Jennings Tribute,” ChrisStapleton.com, June 9, 2015, accessed December 5, 2023, https://www.chrisstapleton.com/waylon-jennings-tribute/.

LegacyRecordingsVEVO, “Chris Stapleton—I Ain’t Living Long Like This (Live),” YouTube Video, April 7, 2017, accessed December 5, 2023, https://www.youtube.com/watch?v=pFTedYeP-vQ.

Wes Langeler, “Chris Stapleton Reveals the Artists He Wishes He Could’ve Seen Perform: ‘I Never Got to See Waylon Jennings or Johnny Cash,’” *Newsbreak*, February 2, 2007, accessed December 5, 2023, https://www.newsbreak.com/news/2508626681699-chris-stapleton-reveals-the-artists-he-wishes-he-could-ve-seen-perform-i-never-got-to-see-waylon-jennings-or-johnny-cash.

Craig Jenkins, “Chris Stapleton Is Still Molding Country Music into His Own Image,” *Vulture*, November 12, 2020, accessed December 5, 2023, https://www.vulture.com/2020/11/chris-stapleton-interview-starting-over-album.html.

Bill Fetty, “Dare to Dream—Modern Country’s New Highwaymen,” Heavy Blog Is Heavy, March 30, 2017, accessed December 5, 2023, https://www.heavyblogisheavy.com/2017/03/30/dare-to-dream-modern-countrys-new-highwaymen/.

Jim Allen, “Willie Nelson, Kenny Chesney, Chris Stapleton: Three Very Different Generations of Country Songwriters in Three Days,” *Indy Week*, May 18, 2016, accessed December 5, 2023, https://indyweek.com/music/features/willie-nelson-kenny-chesney-chris-stapleton-three-different-generations-country-songwriters-three-days/.

Chris Stapleton (@ChrisStapleton), “Every time I get to play a show with @WillieNelson it’s the greatest treat in the whole wide world. Austin • 8.22.2021 [camera emoji]: @andybarron,” Twitter, August 23, 2021, 4:40pm, https://twitter.com/ChrisStapleton/status/1429921428598493199.

Chris Parton, “Dillon Carmichael Preps Debut Album ‘Hell on an Angel,’ Shares Title Track,” *Rolling Stone*, April 26, 2018, accessed December 5, 2023, https://www.rollingstone.com/music/music-country/dillon-carmichael-preps-debut-album-hell-on-an-angel-shares-title-track-630348/.

Dillon Carmichael, personal communication, July 18, 2022.

Juli Thanki, “Old Crow Medicine Show, Dave Cobb Team Up for New Album,” *Tennessean*, January 17, 2018, accessed December 5, 2023, https://www.tennessean.com/story/entertainment/music/2018/01/17/old-crow-medicine-show-dave-cobb-team-up-new-album/1040341001/.

Cole Premo, “Curiocity Interview: Ketch Secor of ‘Old Crow Medicine Show,’” CBS Minnesota, November 12, 2012.

SLN Staff Writer, “Marty Stuart to Celebrate 20 Year Anniversary as Grand Ole Opry Member on December 8,” November 29, 2012, accessed December 5, 2023, https://www.soundslikenashville.com/news/marty-stuart-to-celebrate-20-year-anniversary-as-grand-ole-opry-member-on-december-8/.

Jerry Holthouse, "Mandy Barnett Celebrates Being Newest Member of Grand Ole Opry," Nashville.com, November 3, 2021, https://www.nashville.com/mandy-barnett-celebrates-being-newest-member-of-grand-ole-opry/.

Matt Dellinger, "Hardcore Troubadours," *Oxford American*, March/April 2003, accessed January 3, 2022, https://web.archive.org/web/20131015144612/http://mattdellinger.com/articles/oldcrow.html.

"The Old Crow Medicine Show," tvdb.com, December 6, 2008, accessed December 5, 2023, https://thetvdb.com/series/the-marty-stuart-show/episodes/4466416.

Derek Halsey, "Old Crow Medicine Show," Mountaintimes.com, August 28, 2013, accessed December 5, 2023, https://www.wataugademocrat.com/mountaintimes/entertainment/music/old-crow-medicine-show/article_21109445-69a1-5403-89a5-1b62b23d8eaa.html.

Di Salvatore, "Ornery."

Robert Lewis, "Old Crow Medicine Show Make Old Bob Dylan New Again at NYC 'Blonde on Blonde' Concert," *Billboard*, May 25, 2017, accessed December 5, 2023, https://www.billboard.com/music/country/old-crow-medicine-show-bob-dylan-blonde-on-blonde-new-york-town-hall-concert-7809421/.

Andy Greene, "Darius Rucker on 'Wagon Wheel' and the Future of Hootie," *Rolling Stone*, July 19, 2013, accessed December 5, 2023, https://www.rollingstone.com/music/news/darius-rucker-on-wagon-wheel-and-the-future-of-hootie-20130719.

Cory Stromblad, "Darius Rucker Inspired to Record 'Wagon Wheel' in Unlikely Place," Taste of Country, January 21, 2013, accessed December 5, 2023, http://tasteofcountry.com/darius-rucker-wagon-wheel-inspiration/.

Paul Grein, "Chart Watch: Thanks Oscar. Love, Idina," *Yahoo Music*, March 12, 2014, accessed December 5, 2023, http://music.yahoo.com/blogs/music-news/chart-watch-thanks-oscar-love-idina-205147750.html.

Jennings with Kaye, *Waylon*, 132.

Gary Graff, "Old Crow Medicine Show Premieres 'Dixie Avenue,' Talks Newfound Love for Kesha," *Billboard*, March 8, 2018, https://www.billboard.com/music/rock/old-crow-medicine-show-volunteer-8238619/.

"Jeff Bridges Channels Waylon, Willie & Kris in 'Crazy Heart,'" ABC News, January 14, 2010, accessed December 5, 2023, https://abcnews.go.com/Entertainment/Movies/jeff-bridges-crazy-heart-channels-country-music-legends/story?id=9562943.

Michelle Reese, personal communication, July 12, 2022.

Andrew Mies, "Ryan Bingham Covers John Prine, Guy Clark, Brandi Carlile, & More," Whiskey Riff, January 12, 2022, https://www.whiskeyriff.com/2022/01/12/ryan-binghams-covers-john-prine-guy-clark-brandi-carlile-more/.

Rachel Rascoe, "Faster Than Sound: Ryan Bingham Warms Up His Western Festival," *Austin Chronicle*, April 19, 2019, accessed December 5, 2023, https://www.austinchronicle.com/music/2019-04-19/faster-than-sound-ryan-bingham-warms-up-his-western-festival/.

Wes Langeler, "Hank Williams Jr., Jamey Johnson & Shooter Jennings Perform Waylon Jennings Medley," *Newsbreak*, February 2, 2022, accessed December 5, 2023, https://www.newsbreak.com/news/2520861657746-hank-williams-jr-jamey-johnson-shooter-jennings-perform-waylon-jennings-medley.

Sirius XM, "Hank Williams Jr., Jamey Johnson & Shooter Jennings—Waylon Tribute Medley [LIVE @ SiriusXM]," YouTube Video, February 6, 2012, accessed February 26, 2022, https://www.youtube.com/watch?v=Hcx7OOJE3JE.

T. Jennings, *Waylon*, xxi.

"**POSTPONED**Willie Nelson & Family with special guest Gary Allan," ozarksamphitheater.com, August 16, 2021, accessed December 5, 2023, https://ozarksamphitheater.com/events/willie-nelson-family/.

Mario Tarradell, "Gary Allan Evolves as an Artist, Deals with Tragedy," *Dallas Morning News* / GaryAllan.com, October 21, 2010, accessed December 5, 2023, https://garyallan.com/2010/10/21/gary-allan-evolves-as-an-artist-deals-with-tragedy/.

"Gary Allan Lashes Out at Country Radio. Again," SavingCountrymusic.com, December 20, 2021, accessed December 5, 2023, https://www.savingcountrymusic.com/gary-allan-lashes-out-at-country-radio-again/.

"Gary Allan Calls Out Carrie Underwood and Taylor Swift," SavingCountryMusic.com, September 13, 2013, accessed December 5, 2023, https://www.savingcountrymusic.com/gary-allan-calls-out-carrie-underwood-and-taylor-swift-as-not-country/.

Antoinette Bueno, "Country Music Association Says Goodbye to Taylor Swift," *ET*, August 19, 2014, accessed December 5, 2023, https://www.etonline.com/music/150042_country_music_association_says_goodbye_to_taylor_swift.

Amanda Remling, "Taylor Swift Mocked at 2014 CMA Awards as Pop Star Celebrates Album Sales," November 6, 2014, accessed December 5, 2023, https://www.ibtimes.com/taylor-swift-mocked-2014-cma-awards-pop-star-celebrates-album-sales-1720150.

Elias Light, "Country Stars on Taylor Going Pop: 'Taylor Swift Can Do What Taylor Swift Wants to Do,'" *Billboard*, November 14, 2014, accessed December 5, 2023, https://www.billboard.com/music/country/country-stars-cma-red-carpet-taylor-swift-can-do-what-she-wants-6319506/.

"Gary Allan—Chart History," *Billboard*, undated, accessed December 5, 2023, https://www.billboard.com/artist/gary-allan/chart-history/tlp/.

Joseph Hudak, "Gary Allan Is Going Rogue," *Rolling Stone*, December 19, 2021, accessed December 5, 2023, https://www.rollingstone.com/music/music-country/gary-allan-country-radio-tiktok-1273409/.

Jimmie Tramel, "5 to Find: Music Artists Who Influenced Hard Rock–Bound Performer Gary Allan," *Tulsa World*, November 21, 2018, accessed December 5, 2023, https://tulsaworld.com/lifestyles/5-to-find-music-artists-who-influenced-hard

-rock-bound-performer-gary-allan/article_5b571345-68da-5f88-a069-1323abea8bc2.html.

Ward Davis, Facebook.com, September 10, 2022, accessed December 5, 2023, https://www.facebook.com/WardDavisOfficial/posts/641361737350099.

Steve Dougherty, "Sturgill Simpson Sings Country Metaphysics," *Wall Street Journal*, May 6, 2014, accessed December 5, 2023, https://www.wsj.com/articles/SB10001424052702304101504579543640189785928.

Adam Gold, "How Sturgill Simpson Conquered Country Without Music Row," *Nashville Scene*, October 27, 2016, accessed December 5, 2023, https://www.nashvillescene.com/music/coverstory/how-sturgill-simpson-conquered-country-without-music-row/article_ef4eb531-b0bd-56de-a757-85eb7a1c2500.html.

VolcanoDunker, "Sturgill, Seattle, Heroin, and the Navy," Reddit.com, November 27, 2019, accessed December 5, 2023, https://www.reddit.com/r/SturgillSimpson/comments/e2popa/sturgill_seattle_heroin_and_the_navy/.

Welch, "Meet Three."

Michael VenutoloMantovani, "That Time Sturgill Simpson Gave Me His Door Money," *Medium*, March 1, 2017, accessed December 8, 2021, https://medium.com/cuepoint/that-time-sturgill-simpson-gave-me-his-door-money-edf6198cbc0a.

Andrew Leahey, "5 Things We Learned from Sturgill Simpson's Interview with Foos Guitarist," *Rolling Stone*, July 31, 2015, accessed December 8, 2021, https://www.rollingstone.com/music/music-country/5-things-we-learned-from-sturgill-simpsons-interview-with-foos-guitarist-64483/.

"Label Guide: Monument," CVinyl.com, undated, accessed February 23, 2022, http://www.cvinyl.com/labelguides/monument.php.

Daley, *Nashville's Unwritten Rules*, 195, 200.

Erik Ernst, "CD Reviews: Jason Isbell, Alison Moyet, Walter Trout, Sturgill Simpson," *Milwaukee Journal Sentinel*, June 11, 2013, accessed December 5, 2023, https://archive.jsonline.com/entertainment/musicandnightlife/cd-reviews-jason-isbell-alison-moyet-walter-trout-sturgill-simpson-b9927487z1-211021241.html/.

Steven Hyden, "Sturgill Simpson Has a Lot to Get Off His Chest," *UPROXX*, February 20, 2020, accessed December 5, 2023, https://uproxx.com/indie/sturgill-simpson-interview-sound-and-fury-tour/.

LR Baggs, "Sturgill Simpson & Dave Cobb—Interview," YouTube Video, August 12, 2014, dead link.

"Dave Cobb Explained," everything.explained.today, undated, accessed December 5, 2023, https://everything.explained.today/Dave_Cobb/.

Dan MacIntosh, "Metamodern Sounds in Country Music (High Top Mountain, 2014)," Country Standard Time, accessed December 8, 2021, accessed December 5, 2023, https://www.countrystandardtime.com/d/cdreview.asp?xid=5441.

Stephen Thomas Erlewine, "High Top Mountain," Allmusic.com, June 1, 2013, accessed December 5, 2023, https://www.allmusic.com/album/high-top-mountain-mw0002529932.

"Don't Compare Sturgill Simpson to Waylon . . . Unless You're Merle Haggard. That's Probably Okay," SavingCountryMusic.com, August 4, 2015, accessed December 5, 2023, https://www.savingcountrymusic.com/dont-compare-sturgill-simpson-to-waylon-unless-youre-merle-haggard-thats-probably-okay/.

Shooter Jennings, quoted in Tommy Combs, "Sturgill Simpson Outlaw Music Fest," *OnStage Magazine*, July 15, 2018, accessed December 5, 2023, https://onstagemagazine.com/sturgill-simpson-outlaw-music-fest/.

"'Man of Steel' Robby Turner Hospitalized After Auto Accident," SavingCountryMusic.com, January 4, 2020, accessed December 5, 2023, https://www.savingcountrymusic.com/man-of-steel-robby-turner-hospitalized-after-auto-accident/.

"Merle Haggard Calls Modern Country 'Crap.' Says It's 'Screwing on a Pickup Tailgate,'" SavingCountryMusic.com, September 3, 2015, accessed December 5, 2023, https://www.savingcountrymusic.com/merle-haggard-calls-modern-country-crap-says-its-screwing-on-a-pickup-tailgate/.

Jon Caramanica, "Sturgill Simpson, a Genuine Alternative to Alt Country," *New York Times*, March 31, 2016, accessed December 5, 2023, https://www.nytimes.com/2016/04/03/arts/music/sturgill-simpson-a-genuine-alternative-to-alt-country.html.

Matt Hendrickson, "Sturgill Simpson: Country Philosopher," *Garden & Gun*, April/May 2014, accessed December 5, 2023, https://gardenandgun.com/articles/sturgill-simpson-country-philosopher/.

Kory Thibeault, "Sturgill Simpson Continues to Show Why He's Country Music's Next Great Talent," Showbams, April 24, 2015, accessed December 5, 2023, https://showbams.com/2015/04/24/sturgill-simpson-continues-to-show-why-hes-country-musics-next-great-talent/.

Will Welch, "The GQ&A: Sturgill Simpson, Country Music's Psychedelic Warrior-Philosopher," *GQ*, January 7, 2016, accessed December 5, 2023, https://www.gq.com/story/sturgill-simpson-country-music-interview.

Lauren Lewek, Facebook.com, April 20, 2023, accessed December 5, 2023, https://www.facebook.com/photo/?fbid=10232138588630410.

Stephen M. Deusner, "Metamodern Sounds in Country Music," *Pitchfork*, May 16, 2014, accessed December 5, 2023, https://pitchfork.com/reviews/albums/19386-sturgill-simpson-metamodern-sounds-in-country-music/.

Sturgill Simpson, comment on "Sturgill Simpson's 'Metamodern Sounds in Country Music,'" SavingCountryMusic.com, February 23, 2014, accessed December 5, 2023, https://www.savingcountrymusic.com/sturgill-simpson-to-release-metamodern-sounds-in-country-music/.

Matthew Leimkuehler, "Sturgill Simpson on the 'Nicotine-Stained Den' in Nashville Where He Cut Albums," *Nashville Tennessean*, January 3, 2022, accessed December

5, 2023, https://www.tennessean.com/story/entertainment/music/2022/01/03/sturgill-simpson-nicotine-stained-den-butcher-shoppe-where-he-recorded-beloved-albums/9076167002/.

Steve Warren, personal communication, July 13, 2022.

David "Fergie" Ferguson, phone interview, September 23, 2022.

"Billboard 200," Billboard.com, June 6, 2016, accessed December 5, 2023, https://www.billboard.com/charts/billboard-200/2016-06-10/.

"The Butcher Shoppe," Discogs, undated, accessed December 5, 2023, https://www.discogs.com/label/507990-The-Butcher-Shoppe.

"The Butcher Shoppe EP," Della Mae, undated, accessed December 5, 2023, https://www.dellamae.com/the-butcher-shoppe-ep.

Wes Langeler, "Watch Sturgill Simpson Cover Waylon Jennings' 'Waymore's Blues' Back in 2014," Whiskey Riff, May 25, 2022, accessed December 6, 2023, https://www.whiskeyriff.com/2022/05/25/watch-sturgill-simpson-cover-waylon-jennings-waymores-blues-back-in-2014/.

James Barber, "Navy Vet Sturgill Simpson's Middle Finger to Nashville," Military.com, July 23, 2019, accessed December 6, 2023, https://www.military.com/daily-news/2019/07/23/navy-vet-sturgill-simpsons-middle-finger-nashville.html.

Kentucky Country Music, "Sturgill Simpson Busking in Nashville at CMA Awards," YouTube Video, November 8, 2017, accessed December 6, 2023, https://www.youtube.com/watch?v=-LrKYpAgT3s.

Ann Powers, "Tyler Childers Pushes Back on Southern Values and Our 'Long, Violent History,'" NPR.org, September 18, 2020, accessed December 6, 2023, https://www.npr.org/sections/we-insist-a-timeline-of-protest-music-in-2020/2020/09/18/914469882/tyler-childers-pushes-back-on-southern-values-and-our-long-violent-history.

"Tyler Childers Playing New Songs Has Us Thinking a New Album Is Coming," *Outsider*, March 2, 2022, accessed December 6, 2023, https://www.outsider.com/entertainment/music/tyler-childers-playing-new-songs-has-us-thinking-new-album-coming/.

Angela Stefano, "Tyler Childers Hopes 'Long Violent History' Makes Listeners Think, Then Act," *The Boot*, September 18, 2020, accessed December 6, 2023, https://theboot.com/tyler-childers-long-violent-history-statement/.

Rachel DeSantis, "Tyler Childers 'Honored' That His 'In Your Love' Music Video Has Encouraged Fans to Come Out: 'The Power of Music,'" *People*, September 19, 2023, accessed December 6, 2023, https://people.com/tyler-childers-honored-music-video-encouraged-fans-to-come-out-7971420.

"Sturgill Simpson Isn't Being Outlaw. He's Just Being an Asshole," SavingCountryMusic.com, February 21, 2020, accessed December 6, 2023, https://www.savingcountrymusic.com/sturgill-simpson-isnt-being-outlaw-hes-just-being-an-asshole/.

Mike Devlin, "Sturgill Simpson Lets His Music Do the Talking," *Times Colonist*, August 18, 2016, accessed December 6, 2023, https://www.timescolonist.com/entertainment/sturgill-simpson-lets-his-music-do-the-talking-4639845.

Colin Larkin, ed., *The Guinness Who's Who of Fifties Music, First Edition* (Guinness Publishing, 1993), 121.

Travis Waldron, "The True Spirit of Country Music Is Sturgill Simpson Calling Trump 'A Fascist F**king Pig,'" *Huffington Post*, November 9, 2017, accessed December 6, 2023, https://www.huffpost.com/entry/sturgill-simpson-country-music-awards_n_5a045f75e4b03deac08b993c.

Leesa Cross-Smith, "Ain't Half Bad," *Oxford American* 99, Winter 2017, November 21, 2017, accessed December 6, 2023, https://oxfordamerican.org/magazine/issue-99-winter-2017/ain-t-half-bad.

Joseph Hudak, "Sturgill Simpson: I Will Be 'Blackballed from the Industry,'" *Rolling Stone*, August 30, 2016, accessed December 14, 2021, https://www.rollingstone.com/music/music-country/sturgill-simpson-i-will-be-blackballed-from-the-industry-251686/.

Juli Thanki, "Sturgill Simpson Rips Academy of Country Music, Vows to Leave Nashville," *Tennessean*, August 29, 2016, accessed December 6, 2023, https://www.tennessean.com/story/entertainment/music/2016/08/29/sturgill-simpson-rips-academy-country-music-over-merle-haggard-award/89561586/.

Mike Clute, phone interview, February 24, 2022.

Ari Herstand, "How to Crack TikTok for Musicians (from the Major Label Experts)," Ari's Take, May 19, 2022, accessed December 6, 2023, https://aristake.com how-to-crack-tiktok-for-musicians/.

Ari Herstand, @aris.take, TikTok, https://www.tiktok.com/@aris.take.

Brady Cox, "Brent Cobb Namechecks Tyler Childers, Sturgill Simpson, Luke Combs, & More on Unreleased 'When Country Came Back to Town,'" Whiskey Riff, February 14, 2022, accessed December 6, 2023, https://www.whiskeyriff.com/2022/02/14/brent-cobb-namechecks-tyler-childers-sturgill-simpson-luke-combs-more-on-unreleased-when-country-came-back-to-town/.

"Sturgill Simpson Deletes Social Media Feeds After Leaving Cryptic Message," SavingCountryMusic.com, November 1, 2017, accessed December 6, 2023, https://www.savingcountrymusic.com/sturgill-simpson-deletes-social-media-feeds-after-leaving-cryptic-message/.

Steven Hyden, "Is the Latest Sturgill Simpson Album Also the Last? An Investigation," August 24, 2021, accessed December 6, 2023, https://uproxx.com/indie/sturgill-simpson-the-ballad-of-dood-and-juanita/.

Caleb Lewis, personal communication, July 12, 2022.

Chapter Twelve

Ray Rahman, "Kris Kristofferson Smashes Guitar in Brandi Carlile's 'That Wasn't Me' Video: Watch It Here," *Entertainment Weekly*, June 5, 2012, accessed December

6, 2023, https://ew.com/article/2012/06/05/brandi-carlile-kris-kristofferson-video/.

Brandi Carlile, "2nd night with Kris Kristofferson. One of the great honors of our career to back up the songwriter to beat all songwriters. 'freedom's just another word for nothing left to lose.' xobc," Facebook.com, November 12, 2016, accessed December 6, 2023, https://www.facebook.com/brandicarlile/photos/a.10150501814683414/10153891677408414/?type=3&locale2=zh_CN.

"Country's New Supergroup 'The Highwomen' Unite to Make Way for Unsung Female Artists," NPR.org, September 15, 2019, accessed December 6, 2023, https://www.npr.org/transcripts/760562412.

Author's personal observation, Amanda Shires, Saenger Theater, Mobile, AL, October 24, 2023.

Joseph Hudak, "Brandi Carlile, Maren Morris Talk Highwomen Project," *Rolling Stone*, June 11, 2019, accessed December 6, 2023, https://www.rollingstone.com/music/music-country/highwomen-brandi-carlile-maren-morris-amanda-shires-natalie-hemby-847032/.

Carlile, *Broken Horses*, 280.

Brandi Carlile, personal interview, September 17, 2022.

Steve Earle, The Steve Earle Show, interview with Amanda Shires, Outlaw Country Sirius/XM radio, July 30, 2022. 8:15-8:20pm; see also: https://www.facebook.com/watch/?v=783966896139202.

cuntrytrash, @cuntrytrash, January 11, 2023, accessed December 6, 2023, https://www.tiktok.com/@cuntrytrash/video/7187435813314121003.

Alex Hopper, "The Origin of the Highwaymen," *American Songwriter*, undated 2023, accessed December 6, 2023, https://americansongwriter.com/the-origin-of-the-highwaymen/.

Cat Woods, "Amanda Shires Delivers a Sultry Take on Country, Rock, and Folk on New Album 'Take It Like a Man,'" *Shondaland*, August 4, 2022, accessed December 6, 2023, https://www.shondaland.com/inspire/a40799290/amanda-shires-delivers-a-sultry-take-on-country-rock-and-folk-on-new-album-take-it-like-a-man/.

John Cowling, personal communication, July 11, 2022.

Natalie Weiner, "Country Music Is a Man's World. The Highwomen Want to Change That," *New York Times*, September 5, 2019, C5.

Brandon Gaille, "46 Curious Country Music Demographics," BrandonGaile.com, May 9, 2016, accessed December 6, 2023, https://brandongaille.com/46-curious-country-music-demographics/.

Share of Consumers Who Are Fans of Music in the United States as of February 2019, by Gender, Statista, January 8, 2021, accessed December 6, 2023, https://www.statista.com/statistics/976638/music-fans-in-the-us-gender/.

Kelley King and Emily Falvey, "Part 2—Women and Girls in Music Production," accessed December 6, 2023, https://www.giveanote.org/blog/2022/06/part-2-women-and-girls-in-music-production/.

Chris Willman, "CMT Throws a Data Party to Prove Country Fans Really Do Want More Female Voices," *Variety*, February 20, 2020, accessed December 6, 2023, https://variety.com/2020/music/news/cmt-women-country-music-equal-play-data-presentation-1203507846/.

Jada E. Watson, "Inequality on Country Radio: 2019 in Review," Song-Data, February 17, 2020, accessed December 6, 2023, https://songdata.ca/wp-content/uploads/2020/02/SongData-Watson-Inequality-Country-Airplay-2019-in-Review.pdf.

McMillan Cottom, "The Black."

Rodney Clawson, personal communication, August 30, 2022.

Billy Dukes, "The Highwomen Interview: Where Have All the Mothers Gone?," TasteofCountry.com, October 4, 2019, accessed December 6, 2023, https//tasteofcountry.com/the-highwomen-interview-where-have-all-the-mothers-gone/.

Author's personal observation, The Highwomen, Gorge Amphitheatre, Quincy, WA, June 11, 2023.

Hilary Hughes, "Amanda Shires on Why She Tackled Abortion Rights with 'Our Problem,'" *Entertainment Weekly*, January 22, 2021, accessed December 6, 2023, https://ew.com/music/amanda-shires-our-problem-interview/.

CMT.com Staff, "Without Naming It, Amanda Shires and Jason Isbell Focus on 'The Problem,'" CMT, November 9, 2020, accessed December 6, 2023, https://www.cmt.com/news/xj0gr5/amanda-shires-the-problem-video.

HJ Lally, personal communication, July 11, 2022.

Lia Beck, "Why Maren Morris Is Really Quitting Country Music: 'It's Burning Itself Down,'" BestLifeOnline.com, September 18, 2023, accessed December 6, 2023, https://bestlifeonline.com/maren-morris-quitting-country-music-news/.

Author's personal observation, Brittney Spencer, McFarland Park, Florence, AL, October 1, 2022.

Michale Broerman, "Amanda Shires Joined by Brittney Spencer, Jason Isbell in Studio for 'Lonely at Night [Video],'" Live for Live Music, October 19, 2022, accessed December 6, 2023, https://liveforlivemusic.com/news/amanda-shires-brittney-spencer-jason-isbell-lonely-at-night/.

Matt Hendrickson, "Brittney Spencer's New Nashville Sound," *Garden & Gun*, April/May 2022, accessed December 6, 2023, https://gardenandgun.com/articles/brittney-spencers-new-nashville-sound/.

Chris Willman, "How Yola Got Her Groove Back: Why America Is Falling for Bristol's Greatest Soul-Country-Pop Export," *Variety*, July 19, 2021, accessed December 6, 2023, https://variety.com/2021/music/news/yola-feature-interview-stand-for-myself-sister-rosetta-1235022238/.

Yola, quoted in Joe Vitagliano, "Yola: A Bitch Is Back," *American Songwriter*, July/August 2021, 59.

Margo Price, personal interview, November 30, 2022.

Margo Price, *Maybe We'll Make It* (Austin: University of Texas Press, 2020), 28, 30, 75, 89, 95, 177, 226, 242, 249, 252.

Allison Russell, Carnegie Hall, New York, program for Songs of Our Native Daughters, November 4, 2022.

Author's personal observation, 2022 Americana Music Awards, Ryman Auditorium, Nashville, September 14, 2022.

Marissa R. Moss, "The Highwomen: In the Studio with Country's Ballsiest New Supergroup," *Rolling Stone*, July 19, 2019, accessed December 6, 2023, https://www.rollingstone.com/music/music-country/the-highwomen-interview-brandi-carlile-maren-morris-860629/.

Ashley Iasimone, "Maren Morris and Cassadee Pope Call Out Jason Aldean's Wife Brittany over Transphobic Comments," *Billboard*, August 27, 2022, accessed December 6, 2023, https://www.billboard.com/music/music-news/jason-aldean-wife-brittany-transphobic-post-reactions-1235131821/.

Mitchel Peters, "Maren Morris' 'Lunatic Country Music Person' T-Shirt Raises Over $100K for Transgender Causes," *Billboard,* September 3, 2022, accessed December 6, 2023, https://www.billboard.com/music/music-news/maren-morris-lunatic-country-music-person-charity-t-shirt-tucker-carlson-1235134700/.

Joe Coscarelli, "Sinking Headlines and Bearing Fruit in Nashville," *New York Times*, January 16, 2022, AR10.

Father Nathan Monk, "Dear Jason Aldean, I grew up in Nashville. I'm as Southerner as fried chicken and collard greens. On my Dad's side, we are from Louisiana and Texas, and Mississippi on my Mother's side. I was born in Louisiana, raised in Tennessee, and spent much of my adult life in a small town on the Gulf Coast. What really upsets me about what you have done here is that I know you know better," Facebook.com, July 24, 2023, accessed December 6, 2023, https://www.facebook.com/fathernathan/posts/pfbid021EqnRkFB7Pg46BMo8d5aSpcSTa8PH8FpM9q7ApYDT2XVvffxm25Zs7SQKsPwFUzel.

Brittney Spencer @BrittNicx, "You can hold my hand When you need to let go [yellow heart emoji] @TheHighwomen." Twitter, October 10, 2020, 3:18pm. https://twitter.com/BrittNicx/status/1315023849340252166.

Sanneh, *Major Labels*, 182–183.

"Billboard Box Score," *Billboard,* May 16, 2015, 124.

"Kacey Musgraves Charms a Sold-Out Bluebird Theater (Photos)," *Denver Post,* April 22, 2016, accessed December 6, 2023, https://www.denverpost.com/2016/04/22/kacey-musgraves-charms-a-sold-out-bluebird-theater-photos/.

WENN Rights Ltd, "Kacey Musgraves Kicks Off Her 'Same Trailer Different Park' Tour to a Sold-Out Crowd at Bowery Ballroom Featuring: Kacey Musgra," Alamy, September 18, 2013, accessed December 6, 2023, https://www.alamy.com/stock-photo-kacey-musgraves-kicks-off-her-same-trailer-different-park-tour-to-70941986.html.

Milward, *Americanaland*, 2.

Lisa Robinson, *Nobody Ever Asked Me About the Girls: Women, Music, and Fame* (New York: Henry Holt and Company, 2020), 73, 172–173.

Daley, *Nashville's Unwritten Rules*, 175, 179, 182–183, 202.

Doyle, "All Roads."

Nelson, 165, 167.

Marissa R. Moss and Robert Crawford, "20 Best Country Songs to Play While Getting High," *Rolling Stone Australia*, April 20, 2021, https://au.rollingstone.com/music/music-lists/country-songs-weed-getting-high-9800/chris-stapleton-might-as-well-get-stoned-9807/.

Alfonsi, "'I'm Good.'"

John Spong, "Kacey Musgraves on Making "Real-Ass" Country Music with Willie Nelson," *Texas Monthly*, April 20, 2022, accessed December 6, 2023, https://www.texasmonthly.com/podcast/kacey-musgraves-one-by-willie/.

Steve Sullivan, *Encyclopedia of Great Popular Song Recordings, Volume 3* (Rowman and Littlefield, 2017), 461.

Miranda Raye, "Willie Nelson, Kris Kristofferson, & Kacey Musgraves Team Up for Gospel Medley in 2017," *Country Music Nation*, August 21, 2017, accessed December 6, 2023, https://countrymusicnation.com/willie-nelson-kris-kristofferson-kacey-musgraves-team-up-for-gospel-medley-in-2017.

"Willie Nelson Setlist, Shrine Auditorium, Los Angeles, CA," Setlist.fm, August 17, 2017, accessed December 6, 2023, https://www.setlist.fm/setlist/willie-nelson/2017/shrine-auditorium-los-angeles-ca-6be54ea6.html.

Chapter Thirteen

Waylon Jennings, interview with Dinah Shore, quoted in Denisoff, *Waylon*, 237.

Denisoff, *Waylon*, 242, 303.

Jack White, quoted in Stephen Deusner, "Only in Nashville," *Nashvillan* 1, no. 1 (September 2022): 46.

Kris Kristofferson, quoted in "Douglas McPherson," *Country Music Magazine*, August/September 2018.

Robert Abernathy, "'First Time Feelin' (Song #7)," Robert Abernathy Music, May 2, 2017, accessed December 6, 2023, https://robertabernathy.com/blogs/sticks-and-stones-014e3f74-c982-4826-a6ca-06d3e4dde263/posts/4694354/first-time-feelin.

Waylon Jennings, quoted in Flippo, "Waylon Jennings," *Creem*.

Cox, "Brent Cobb."

Simon Hattenstone, "Steve Earle: 'My Wife Left Me for a Younger, Skinnier, Less Talented Singer,'" *The Guardian*, June 14, 2017, accessed December 6, 2023, https://www.theguardian.com/music/2017/jun/14/steve-earle-so-you-wanna-be-an-outlaw-interview.

Staff, "Steve Earle Thinks Modern Country Stars Make 'Hip Hop for People Who Are Afraid of Black People,'" *Far Out*, July 28, 2017, accessed December 6, 2023, https://faroutmagazine.co.uk/steve-earle-thinks-modern-country-stars-make-hip-hop-for-people-who-are-afraid-of-black-people/.

MathematicianHot5452, "County music has become insufurable," Reddit.com, r/Music, December 27, 2021, accessed December 6, 2023, https://www.reddit.com/r/Music/comments/rq25dy/county_music_has_become_insufurable/.

Xander Zellner, "Every Country Music Record Broken on the Hot 100 in 2023: From Morgan Wallen to Oliver Anthony Music & More," *Billboard*, September 5, 2023, accessed December 6, 2023, https://www.billboard.com/lists/country-music-records-hot-100-morgan-wallen-oliver-anthony/most-distinct-runs-at-no-1-for-a-song-on-the-hot-100/.

Jon Caramanica, "Heartfelt Songs by an Uneasy Star," *New York Times*, September 25, 2023, AR13.

Zach Bryan (@zachlanebryan), "Anything I've learned and grown from came from Isbell, a man I will respect and listen to until I die," Twitter, November 28, 2022, 5:18pm, https://twitter.com/zachlanebryan/status/1597369423102242816.

James Rettig, "Zach Bryan Shares Christmas Message About Concert Ticket Prices, Drops Surprise Live Album *All My Homies Hate Ticketmaster (Live from Red Rocks)*," *Stereogum*, December 25, 2022, accessed December 6, 2023, https://www.stereogum.com/2209169/zach-bryan-concert-ticket-prices-message-live-album/news/.

Keith Spera, "Who Holds the Smoothie King Center Concert Attendance Record? As of Saturday, Zach Bryan," *New Orleans Times-Picayune*, May 23, 2023, accessed December 6, 2023, https://www.nola.com/entertainment_life/music/country-singer-zach-bryan-breaks-smoothie-king-center-record/article_98131e30-f8b9-11ed-9730-43ec69f4e45e.html.

Andrew Mies, "Zach Bryan on the CMA Awards: 'I Don't and Will Never Want to Be Considered,'" Whiskey Riff, October 17, 2023, accessed December 6, 2023, https://www.whiskeyriff.com/2023/10/17/zach-bryan-on-the-cma-awards-i-dont-and-will-never-want-to-be-considered/.

Matt Hendrickson, "Charley Crockett's Lone Star Turn," *Garden & Gun* (October–November 2022): 35, https://gardenandgun.com/articles/charley-crocketts-lone-star-turn/.

John Spong, "The Long Ride of Charley Crockett," *Texas Monthly*, May 15, 2023, accessed December 6, 2023, https://www.texasmonthly.com/arts-entertainment/the-long-ride-of-charley-crockett/.

Eddie Bayers, personal communication, February 24, 2022.

"Country Music Statistics: All About the Fans," Grizzly Rose, April 23, 2018, accessed December 6, 2023, https://grizzlyrose.com/country-music-statistics/.

"North Dakota's Newest Grammy Winner," *Grand Forks Herald*, March 10, 2011, accessed February 21, 2022, https://www.grandforksherald.com/lifestyle/arts-entertainment/north-dakotas-newest-grammy-winner.

Markert, *Making Music*, xi.

"CMA: Millennials Remain Main Driver of Country Music Growth," Insider Radio, February 1, 2019, accessed December 6, 2023, https://www.insideradio.com/cma-millennials-remain-main-driver-of-country-music-growth/article_fd9154e2-25f1-11e9-9b3d-c7034b8f54b6.html.

Daley, *Nashville's Unwritten Rules*, 126, 143.

Alison Bonaguro, "Opinion: Has Kacey Musgraves Been Snubbed?," Holler, October 13, 2021, accessed December 6, 2023, https://holler.country/feature/the-case-for-kacey.

Chris Riemenschneider, "Kacey Musgraves Is Happy to Take Her Sad Divorce Record on the Road, Starting in St. Paul," *Star-Tribune*, January 16, 2022, accessed December 6, 2023, https://www.startribune.com/kacey-musgraves-is-happy-to-take-her-sad-divorce-record-on-the-road-starting-in-st-paul/600136487/.

Spong, "Kacey Musgraves."

Matthew Strauss, "Rina Sawayama Announces New Album Hold the Girl, Shares New Song 'This Hell': Listen," *Pitchfork*, May 18, 2022, accessed December 6, 2023, https://pitchfork.com/news/rina-sawayama-announces-new-album-hold-the-girl-shares-new-song-this-hell-listen/.

Milward, *Americanaland*, 1, 4, 226–227, 243, 251.

Brandi Carlile, interviewed in *This Is Pop: When Country Goes Pop*.

Cary Baker, personal communication, June 2, 2022.

Amanda Williams and Avery Jessa Chapnick, "Americana Musician Brandi Carlile Thinks Genre Matters," The 1A / WAMU / NPR, December 15, 2021, accessed December 6, 2023, https://the1a.org/segments/brandi-carlile-country-grammys/.

"Stations Ban K.D. Lang over Her Beef with Meat," *Orlando Sentinel*, July 4, 1990, accessed December 6, 2023, https://www.orlandosentinel.com/1990/07/04/stations-ban-kd-lang-over-her-beef-with-meat/.

Brown, Thoet, and Davenport, "Grammy Nominee."

Sanneh, *Major Labels*, 154, 179.

Stewart Foley, *Citizen Cash*, 278.

Miller, *Kris Kristofferson*, 196–197, 200–201, 212, 229, 235, 239.

McMillan Cottom, "The Black."

"Lacy J. Dalton Singles," Allmusic.com, undated, accessed December 6, 2023, https://www.allmusic.com/artist/mn0000118503#awards.

The Bottom Line Archive Series: In Their Own Words: With Vin Scelsa, CD, recorded February 1994, released 2017, Bottom Line Record Company.

Bahar Anooshahr, "People Took to Reddit to Reminisce About These 1980s Phoenix Restaurants. What Are They Now?," *Arizona Republic*, August 19, 2022, accessed December 6, 2023, https://www.azcentral.com/story/entertainment/dining/2022/08/19/classic-phoenix-tempe-restaurants-on-reddit/10309351002/.

Kris Kristofferson, quoted in Carrier, "Kris Kristofferson."

Billy Swann, quoted in Kris Kristofferson, *Live at Gilley's—Pasadena, TX: September 15, 1981*, CD, New West Records, liner notes, 2022.

Dayton, *Beaumonster*, 60, 64, 66–67, 72–75, 78–79, 97, 191–192.

John Gerome, "Kris Kristofferson to Receive CMT Award," *Washington Post*, March 12, 2007, accessed December 6, 2023, https://www.washingtonpost.com/wp-dyn/content/article/2007/03/12/AR2007031200851.html.

Alison Bonaguro, "Offstage: Taylor Swift on Emulating Effervescence," CMT, January 18, 2012, accessed December 6, 2023, https://www.cmt.com/news/xizmza/offstage-taylor-swift-on-emulating-effervescence.

John Preston, "Taylor Swift: The 19-Year-Old Country Music Star Conquering America—and Now Britain," *Telegraph*, April 26, 2009, accessed November 13, 2023.

Sarah Sadowski Pfoor, personal communication, July 10, 2022.

Baron Lane, "Kris Kristofferson Receives the Grammy for Lifetime Achievement," YouTube Video, January 25, 2014, accessed December 6, 2023, https://www.youtube.com/watch?v=JJPwZa971RY.

Leydon, "Kris Kristofferson."

Margo Price, personal interview, November 30, 2022.

Nelson with Pipkin, *The Tao of Willie*, xiii, 12–13, 36, 53, 69, 85, 151, 159. 175–176, 179, 189.

Casey Young, "I Could Listen to Morgan Wade Cover Kris Kristofferson's 'Help Me Make It Through the Night' All Damn Day," Whiskey Riff, November 28, 2021, accessed December 6, 2023, https://www.whiskeyriff.com/2021/11/28/i-could-listen-to-morgan-wade-cover-kris-kristoffersons-help-me-make-it-through-the-night-all-damn-day/.

Spong, "That '70s."

Kennedi Johnson, "Lifelong Activist Kris Kristofferson to Receive Woody Guthrie Prize," Music for Good, July 12, 2016, accessed January 8, 2022, https://musicforgood.tv/2016/07/lifelong-activist-kris-kristofferson-to-receive-woody-guthrie-prize/.

Patoski, *Willie Nelson*, 386, 406, 417.

Nelson with Ritz, *It's a Long Story*, 304, 343.

Nelson with McMurtry, *The Facts of Life*, 61–62, 103, 118.

Doyle, "All Roads."

Nelson with Shrake, *Willie*, 138, 202, 238.

Spong, "Willie Nelson's."

Andrew Leahey, "'Band of Brothers' Shoots Shotgun Willie to Top of the Charts," *Rolling Stone*, June 25, 2014, dead link.

Jody Rosen, "Willie Nelson's Long Encore," *New York Times Magazine*, August 17, 2022, 26, https://www.nytimes.com/2022/08/17/magazine/willie-nelson.html.

Nelson and Nelson with Ritz, *Me and Sister Bobbie*, 249–250, 257.

Jennings with Kaye, *Waylon*, 233, 257, 314–315, 324–325, 360, 362, 372–373.

Wes Langeler, "Tyler Childers Delivers Gritty Cover of Willie Nelson's 'Time of the Preacher,'" Whiskey Riff, January 6, 2022, accessed December 6, 2023, https://www.whiskeyriff.com/2022/01/06/tyler-childers-delivers-gritty-cover-of-willie-nelsons-time-of-the-preacher/.

Patoski, *Willie Nelson*, 446, 464, 470.

Anastasia Tsioulcas, "Bobbie Nelson, a Country Music Pioneer and Willie Nelson's Sister, Dies at Age 91," NPR.org, March 11, 2022, accessed December 6, 2023, https://www.npr.org/2022/03/11/1086000679/bobbie-nelson-a-country-music-pioneer-and-willie-nelsons-sister-dies-at-age-91.

Spong and Hall, "Sister Bobbie."

Amanda Shires, email newsletter, April 26, 2023.

Amanda Shires, interview with Earle, July 30, 2022.

Casey Young, "Lukas Nelson on How His Dad, Willie Nelson, Has Managed to Stay So Grounded Throughout His Legendary Career: 'He's a Normal Person,'" Whiskey Riff, April 27, 2023, accessed December 6, 2023, https://www whiskeyriff.com/2023/04/27/lukas-nelson-on-how-his-dad-willie-nelson-has-managed-to-stay-so-grounded-throughout-his-legendary-career-hes-a-normal-person/.

Cunniff, *Waylon Jennings*, 129.

Will Hodge, "Toil and Trouble: Uncle Tupelo's 'No Depression' Turns 30," *No Depression*, June 19, 2020, accessed December 6, 2023, https://www.nodepression.com/toil-and-trouble-uncle-tupelos-no-depression-turns-30/.

Shooter Jennings, Electric Rodeo, Outlaw Country / Sirius/XM radio, March 23, 2002, 10:00pm.

Calvin Gilbert, "Shooter Jennings Amused by Response to 'Outlaw You,'" CMT, September 1, 2011, accessed December 6, 2023, https://www.cmt.com/news/u7ztst/shooter-jennings-amused-by-response-to-outlaw-you.

"Shooter Jennings Fires Big Shot with 'Outlaw You,'" SavingCountryMusic.com, August 17, 2011, accessed December 6, 2023, https://www.savingcountrymusic.com/shooter-jennings-fires-big-shot-with-outlaw-you/.

Country Rebel, "Johnny Cash and Waylon Jennings' Grandsons Perform 'Highwayman' (Whey Jennings & Thomas Gabriel)," YouTube Video, November 24, 2021, accessed December 6, 2023, https://www.youtube.com/watch?v=ieIc5nv8vbE.

Giller, "Johnny Cash."

Johnny Cash, quoted in Guralnick, *Johnny Cash*, xii, 79–81, 109–110.

David "Fergie" Ferguson, phone interview, September 23, 2022.

Cash with Carr, *Cash*, 27, 247, 253–254, 259–260.

Carter Cash, *The House of Cash*, 76, 104, 109, 111, 114, 118, 129, 132, 136, 233.

"The Observatory," Eventective.com, undated, accessed December 6, 2023, https://www.eventective.com/santa-ana-ca/the-observatory-448870.html.

3.Cameras.and.a.Microphone, "Uncle Tupelo—Rhythm Cafe, Santa Ana Ca 2/27/93 Acoustic set DAT Master opening for Johnny Cash," YouTube Video, May 13, 2021, accessed October 31, 2022, https://www.youtube.com/watch?v=l4cCQrt1f-E.

"Rick Rubin Admits He Doesn't Know How to Use a Mixing Desk: 'I Have No Technical Ability, and I Know Nothing About Music,'" Music Radar,

January 18, 2023, accessed December 6, 2023, https://www.musicradar.com/news/rick-rubin-technical-ability.

Carlile, *Broken Horses*, 266–267.

Light, *Johnny Cash*, 97, 135, 165–166, 183, 190, 192–193.

Hilburn, *Johnny Cash*, 161, 441, 493–494, 550, 557, 563, 594, 599–600, 603, 606, 610, 616, 626, 631.

Nick Cave, *The Red Hand Files* 224, February 2023, accessed December 6, 2023, https://www.theredhandfiles.com/ive-recently-been-listening-to-your-duet-of-im-so-lonesome-i-could-cry-with-johnny-cash-on-repeat-whilst-its-melancholy-the-harmonising-thats-happening-just-makes-me-feel-so-comforted/.

Ryan Gilbey, "A Renaissance Man for Our Times," *The Guardian*, March 12, 2006, accessed November 20, 2022, https://www.theguardian.com/music/2006/mar/12/popandrock.

Johnny Cash, Irving Plaza, New York: July 9, 1996, unauthorized recording.

Grant with Zar, *I Was There*, 112, 253, 335, 337.

Earl Poole Ball, phone interview, August 4, 2022.

Chris DeCubellis, personal communication, July 14, 2022.

R. Cash, *Composed*, 29.

"Stars Gather for Johnny Cash Funeral," *Irish Times*, September 15, 2003, accessed December 6, 2023, https://www.irishtimes.com/news/stars-gather-for-johnny-cash-funeral-1.499002.

Streissguth, *Johnny Cash*, xi.

Kerry Marx, personal communication, April 15, 2022.

Joseph Hudak, "Jesse Dayton Played with Waylon and Cash. He Writes About That and More in New Memoir," Yahoo News, December 21, 2021, dead link, https://www.yahoo.com/entertainment/jesse-dayton-played-waylon-cash-170316427.html; see alt: *Rolling Stone*, December 21, 2021, accessed December 6, 2023, https://www.rollingstone.com/music/music-country/jesse-dayton-beaumonster-book-1274606/.

Weatherby, "The Outlaw."

"Jeff Bridges," ABC News.

Gilmore, *The Highwaymen—Live.*

Hurd, *Kris Kristofferson*, 83.

Colter with Ritz, *An Outlaw and a Lady*, 242–245, 251, 264–270.

"Waylon Jennings Called Keith Whitley the Greatest Country Singer Ever on the Day That He Died," Whiskey Riff, January 5, 2022, accessed January 10, 2022, dead link, https://www.whiskeyriff.com/2022/01/05/waylon-jennings-called-keith-whitley-the-greatest-country-singer-ever-on-the-day-that-he-died/.

"Country Throwback: Waylon Jennings Walks Out of the Tom Snyder Show in 1998," *Outsider*, January 19, 2021, accessed December 6, 2023, https://outsider.com/news/country-music/country-throwback-waylon-jennings-walks-out-tom-snyder-show-1998/.

"10 Badass," SavingCountryMusic.com.

Steven Allan Jones, "Waylon Jennings Walks Out on Tom Snyder," YouTube Video, September 23, 2014, accessed December 22, 2021, https://www.youtube.com/watch?v=UgxUfdEcfgM.

"Jennings Suffering Effects of Too Much Guitar Picking," *Buffalo News*, June 20, 1994, accessed December 6, 2023, https://buffalonews.com/news/jennings-suffering-effects-of-too-much-guitar-picking/article_36cf4d45-9839-5757-b63d-5abdfc7c8d9c.html.

T. Jennings, *Waylon*, 25, 198.

"Danny Dawson—Full Bio," Jango, undated, dead link, https://webcache.googleusercontent.com/search?q=cache:XeBRKgH62P8J:https://www.jango.com/music/Danny%2BDawson/_full_bio&hl=en&gl=us and https://www.jango.com/music/Danny+Dawson/_full_bio.

On'ry Waymore, "Big Boss Man by Waylon Jennings, Travis Tritt, Lee Roy Parnell and Danny Dawson," YouTube Video, January 14, 2017, accessed December 6, 2023, https://www.youtube.com/watch?v=IUrl0V4xlj4.

Jeremy Roberts, "Never Givin' Up with Foremost Country Troubadour Danny Dawson," *Medium*, October 25, 2019, accessed December 6, 2023, https://medium.com/@jeremylr/never-givin-up-with-foremost-country-troubadour-danny-dawson-6a274e21cc3c.

Dixele, YouTube comment screenshot, Hal Wright, Facebook.com, December 25, 2022, accessed December 6, 2023, https://www.facebook.com/photo/?fbid=6438156479544533&set=gm.1391360378069487&idorvanity=136666776872193.

"Waylon Jennings Has Foot Amputated," KCBD 11, January 4, 2002, accessed December 6, 2023, https://www.kcbd.com/story/609502/waylon-jennings-has-foot-amputated/.

Sterling Whitaker, "Remember When Waylon Jennings Gave His Final Performance?," February 13, 2020, accessed December 5, 2021, https://tasteofcountry.com/waylon-jennings-final-performance/.

"Waylon Jennings Setlist at Ryman Auditorium, Nashville, TN, USA," Setlist.fm, January 6, 2000, accessed December 6, 2023, https://www.setlist.fm/setlist waylon-jennings/2000/ryman-auditorium-nashville-tn-7b8512dc.html.

"1953 Fender Telecaster Owned by Waylon Jennings," Denmark Street Guitars, undated, accessed December 6, 2023, http://hanksguitarshop.com/product-details/1953-Fender-Telecaster-owned-by-Waylon-Jennings.

Waylon Jennings, "Waylon Jennings, The Waymore Blues Band—Can't You See (Never Say Die Film)," YouTube Video, May 16, 2019, accessed December 5, 2021, https://www.youtube.com/watch?v=u68fT-99tfY.

Matthew Leimkuehler, "'Why Would He Die and Not Me?' Waylon Jennings' Life-Changing Choice on 'The Day the Music Died,'" *Nashville Tennessean*, February 3, 2020, accessed December 6, 2023, https://www.tennessean.com/story/entertainment/music/2020/02/03/buddy-holly-death-plane-crash-the-day-the-music-died-waylon-jennings-surf-ballroom/2858976001/.

Bob Weir, quoted in Michael Broerman, "Bob Weir Talks Jerry's Death, Pigpen & Janis Joplin, More with Andy Cohen [Watch]," Live for Music, October 5, 2022, accessed December 6, 2023, https://liveforlivemusic.com/news/bob-weir-watch-what-happens-andy-cohen/.

Steve Leggett, "The Crickets & Their Buddies," AllMusic.com, undated, accessed December 6, 2023, https://www.allmusic.com/album/the-crickets-their-buddies-mw0000207352.

AManOfManyFaces, "CMT Waylon's Dead This One's for Waylon Pt 1," YouTube Video, March 30, 2018, accessed December 6, 2023, https://www.youtube.com/watch?v=kJrq4LlaG3w.

"Waylon Jennings Laid to Rest at Private Ceremony," *Arizona Daily Sun*/Associated Press, February 15, 2002, A-4, accessed May 4, 2021, https://www.newspapers.com/clip/77033356/arizona-daily-sun/.

Chet Flippo, "Waylon Jennings Gets a Rousing Nashville Send-Off," CMT, March 25, 2002.

Chapman, *They Came to Nashville*, 240.

James Jennings, personal interview, July 5, 2022.

David Byrne, email newsletter, August 1, 2022.

Tricia Despres, "Colby Acuff's Debut Single Inspired by Intense Waylon Jennings Dream [Exclusive Premiere]," February 17, 2022, accessed December 6, 2023, https://tasteofcountry.com/colby-acuff-once-in-a-lifetime/.

Brady Cox, "Colby Acuff Drops Live Acoustic Performance of New Single, 'Once in a Lifetime,'" Whiskey Riff, February 23, 2022, accessed December 6, 2023, https://www.whiskeyriff.com/2022/02/23/colby-acuff-drops-live-acoustic-performance-of-new-single-once-in-a-lifetime/.

Shannon McNally, quoted in *Lyric Magazine*, dead link.

Martin Johnson, "Interview: Shannon McNally on Why Waylon's Legacy Needed a Refresh," Americana UK, June 7, 2021, accessed December 6, 2023, https://americana-uk.com/interview-shannon-mcnally-on-why-waylons-legacy-needed-a-refresh.

Shannon McNally, *The Waylon Sessions*, CD, liner notes, Compass Records, 2021.

Tommy Townsend, personal communication, July 5, 2022.

Spring Sault, "Waylon Jennings Was Forever Haunted by His Last Words to Buddy Holly," *Texas Hill Country*, April 11, 2019, accessed December 6, 2023, https://texashillcountry.com/waylon-jennings-last-words-buddy-holly/.

"Jennings Returns to Surf Ballroom," *Post-Bulletin*, October 12, 1995, accessed December 6, 2023, https://www.postbulletin.com/jennings-returns-to-surf-ballroom.

"Weather History for Clear Lake, IA," Almanac.com, undated, accessed December 6, 2023, https://www.almanac.com/weather/history/IA/Clear%20Lake/1995-10-06.

"Jennings Returns to Surf," *Sun-Sentinel*, October 8, 1995, accessed December 6, 2023, https://www.sun-sentinel.com/1995/10/08/jennings-returns-to-surf/.

INDEX